CANON/ARCHIVE

P.S. 1 Symposium: A Practical Avant-Garde

What We Should Have Known: Two Discussions

What Was the Hipster?: A Sociological Investigation

The Trouble is the Banks: Letters to Wall Street

No Regrets: Three Discussions

Buzz: A Play

Other Russias

CANON/ARCHIVE

Studies in Quantitative Formalism
From the Stanford Literary Lab

Mark Algee-Hewitt, Sarah Allison,
Marissa Gemma, Ryan Heuser, Matthew Jockers,
Holst Katsma, Long Le-Khac, Franco Moretti,
Dominique Pestre, Erik Steiner, Amir Tevel,
Hannah Walser, Michael Witmore, Irena Yamboliev

FRANCO MORETTI, EDITOR

---

n+1 BOOKS

n+1 FOUNDATION   NEW YORK

Published 2017 by n+1 Foundation

68 Jay Street, Ste. 405

Brooklyn, New York

www.nplusonemag.com

The chapters in this book were originally published as pamphlets by the
Stanford Literary Lab. They can be read in their original form at https://litlab.
stanford.edu/pamphlets/. "Quantitative Formalism" and "Style at the Scale of
the Sentence" also appeared in Issues 13 (Winter 2012) and 17 (Fall 2013) of *n+1*.
"'Operationalizing,'" "Bankspeak," and "Mapping London's Emotions" also
appeared in Issues 84 (November–December 2013), 92 (March–April 2015),
and 101 (September–October 2016) of the *New Left Review*.

n+1 thanks Jake Coolidge, Laura Cremer, and Dan O. Williams.

ISBN 978-0-9970318-7-4

Printed by the Sheridan Press
Manufactured in the United States of America

Design by Rachel Ossip

First Printing

CONTENTS

Literature, Measured

Franco Moretti

PAMPHLET ONE. In 2010, none of the five authors of "Quantitative Formalism," the first chapter of this book, had any idea they were writing a "pamphlet." A well-known scholarly journal had been asking for an article on new critical approaches, and that's where we sent the piece once it was finished. But it came back with so many requests for corrections that it felt like a straightforward rejection. It was dismaying; a few years ago, computational criticism was still shunned by the academic world, and we couldn't help thinking that what was being turned down was not just an article, but a whole critical perspective. And since we also thought that the essay was perfectly fine as it was, we decided that—instead of trying our fortune with another journal (or, god forbid, making the required alterations)—we would publish it on our own, as a document of the Literary Lab. I cannot remember how the term "pamphlet" came up; and, frankly, it wasn't even the right one: pamphlets have a public vocation that our work, with its heavily technical aspects, couldn't possibly have. But the word captured the euphoria of being on our own; the freedom to publish what we wanted, when and how we wanted: short, long, even *very* long, our pamphlets never come out a minute earlier than they're ready, nor a minute later, either; and without going through the grinder of editing "styles." And all this, because "Quantitative Formalism" was rejected by—Never mind. They did us a favor.

MEANDERING. "Nothing is as rare as a plan," Napoleon is supposed to have said, and we have certainly proved him right. We never know where the next pamphlet will come from: they have ranged from the individual research of undergraduate theses ("Loudness in the Novel") and PhD dissertations, to the elective affinity of a pair of like-minded researchers ("From Keywords to Cohorts: Tracing Language Change in the Novel, 1785–1900"; "Bankspeak: the Language of World Bank Reports"), and the complex polyphony of larger groups ("Quantitative Formalism"; "Style at the Scale of the Sentence"; "On Paragraphs: Scale, Themes, and Narrative Form"; "Canon/Archive: Large-Scale Dynamics in the Literary Field"; plus several ongoing projects). With time, however, a team of five or six researchers has emerged as the most frequent formation, and the one that best embodies the novelty of laboratory work. Take "Style at the Scale of the Sentence." It began with the six of us dividing the initial tasks among ourselves; we promptly disagreed on the path to follow; research options were opened, then abandoned; there were two or three collective presentations at the Lab in the first year; in between, bursts of solitary work, small-group discussions, and rivers of emails; later, a long coda of drafts, discussions, and reformulations. The last few months were crucial for the final section of the pamphlet, which condensed two years of empirical findings, bringing them to bear on the theory of style. "Without the concepts of the second half," we wrote, "the results of the first would have remained blind; and without the empirical content of the first part, the categories of the second would have remained empty. Only from their encounter did critical knowledge arise." At the time we didn't know it, but we had just put into words the back-and-forth between the empirical and the conceptual that would characterize all our future research.

WORK. Laboratorium, laborare, labor. That's what a lab is: a place to do work. Group work, mostly; and now that I have experienced it in a variety of forms (in small and large groups; with students and with faculty, from the same discipline and university and from different ones), I would say that almost every project goes through two very different stages. In the initial phase, the group functions like a single organism, where every individual attends to a specific task. The first of such tasks is clearly that of programming: something Matthew Jockers laid the foundations for even before the Lab was officially opened, and Ryan Heuser sustained over the years with his unique imaginative talent, and whose mathematical implications have eventually been made clear to us all by Mark Algee-Hewitt. On the basis of programming, much more becomes possible: from the refinement of the corpus to the analysis of initial results; from the review of the critical literature to the design of follow-up experiments. This functional division of labor, whose results no individual scholar could ever achieve in isolation, is clearly indispensable to modern research. But the second stage of group work is, if possible, even better. Now, the team sits together around a table—the lab table, as essential a tool as the really expensive ones—and discusses how to make sense of the results. Here, the efficient integration of the first stage gives way to a swirl of disparate associations: C reflects on the language of a specific excerpt, and A on the historical categories that could explain it; F recalls something D had said a few months earlier (and then forgotten); E recognizes a grammatical pattern, for which B suggests an evolutionary explanation . . . All researchers bring to this phase their interests, and even fixations. At times, there is a lot of noise. But in a few magic moments, the group becomes truly more than the sum of its parts; it "sees" things that no single pair of eyes could have. If, in the pamphlets that follow, there are some genuine discoveries, that's where they have always begun.

ADAGIETTO. A scientific essay, composed like a Mahler symphony: discordant registers that barely manage to coexist; a forward movement endlessly diverted; the easiest of melodies, followed by leaps into the unknown. I have often tried to write like this, and always failed. Then, with the pamphlets, the form has suddenly emerged. It unfolds along four distinct, nearly equivalent levels: images, captions, text, and footnotes. Images, first of all: time plots, histograms, trees, networks, diagrams, scatterplots . . . Images come first, in our pamphlets, because—by visualizing empirical findings—they constitute *the specific object of study of computational criticism*; they are our "text"; the counterpart to what a well-defined excerpt is to close reading. Next to them, and equally new, captions: almost absent from the early pamphlets, captions have since become as essential for our work as descriptions are in art history, or observations in scientific reports; writing them has taught us to observe more attentively, and to declare what we "see" in any given image, thus announcing what the first steps of the analysis will be. After images and captions, comes the main body of the text. Challenged and compressed by the two newcomers, the text is forced to become tighter, sharper: it must weave the four registers into a single argument without robbing them of their newfound autonomy;

it must be narrative *and* theoretical; take a sequence of discrete events, and transform them into a conceptual grid; and all of this, in fewer pages than most academic articles! It's hard; but it's also good for the clarity of the argument. And if one really needs more space, there are always the footnotes: the space where we put our bibliographical cards on the table, examine theoretical alternatives, and fantasize on future studies; a mix of homework, polemics, and speculation that adds its own subterranean twist to the complexity of the whole. It's strange, and wonderful, and a little unsettling, seeing your thinking mirrored so closely in the shape of the page. At times, more than Mahler, it feels like *Tristram Shandy*.

PAST AND PRESENT. In the early 1990s, as I was trying to put together a collective *Atlas of World Literature*, Fredric Jameson suggested that keeping a logbook of the whole enterprise would be a valuable document in its own right. As funding agencies turned down the *Atlas*, that original logbook never materialized; but Jameson's idea resurfaced, twenty years later, in the detailed reporting that is typical of our pamphlets. Reporting is the right form for the "exploratory" aspect of digital humanities work: it keeps track of our forays into the immensity of the new digital archive, anchoring them to solid facts. Such and such data *have* been found, and here they are, black on white. And then, recording the doubts and the decisions of the research process makes you fully understand what you have done. It's not by accident that many of our pages are initially drafted in the past tense, and then revised into the present: it's never quite clear whether the main point lies in relating a specific moment in the unfolding of past research, or presenting a thesis for present discussion. And it's not clear, because most of the time it's both. A section of "Style at the Scale of the Sentence" begins by explaining how we came to correlate verb forms and novelistic genres, and in the space of four or five paragraphs has turned into a discussion of how the bildungsroman shaped the idea of modern youth. Empirical findings, and conceptual work, again. But, as we will see next, the process is not always so adroit.

"TILL A MAN IS SURE HE IS INFALLIBLE . . ." In the shift from report to reflection, a very special role is played by—failures. In the early days of experimental science, write Steven Shapin and Simon Schaffer, Robert Boyle considered it "necessary . . . to offer readers circumstantial accounts of failed experiments," because they showed that he "was not willfully suppressing inconvenient evidence," thus assuring his readers "that he was such a man as should be believed."[1] Now, there is no doubt that the reporting of failures has something to do with persuasion; missteps make for an entertaining narrative, and self-criticism is always a good way to preempt the criticism of others. Yet, the main reason to report failures has nothing to do with capturing the benevolence of readers; it's that failures *throw a unique light on the research process.* Failures take us all the way back to our starting points: to those unspoken assumptions that go "without saying," and thus easily escape critical scrutiny. Looking for the semantic center of tragic form in moments of maximum conflict, for instance—a "failure" discussed at length in "Operationalizing"—rested on the assumption that, in drama, words and deeds are in synchrony with each other; discovering that this was not the case showed that the theory of tragedy needed a fundamental rethinking. Looking for style at the scale of the paragraph—and, again, not finding it—convinced us that a single top-to-bottom theory of the literary text (like that of stylistics) couldn't possibly be right, and opened the way to the hypotheses on textual scale described in the following section. "What may produce a decisive advance," wrote Popper in *The Logic of Scientific Discovery*, is more often than not "the modification of what we are inclined to regard [because of its complete agreement with our normal habits of thought] as obviously innocuous."[2] Exactly. By frustrating our expectations, failed experiments "estrange" our natural habits of thought, offering a chance to transcend them. Or as Boyle had memorably put it four centuries ago: "till a man is sure he is infallible, it is not fit for him to be unalterable."[3]

SO WHAT? There comes a moment, in digital humanities talks, when someone raises a hand and says: "OK. Interesting. But is it really *new*?" Good question . . . And let's leave aside the obvious defensive maneuvers, such as "but the field is still only at its beginning!" or "traditional literary

---

1 Steven Shapin and Simon Schaffer, *Leviathan and the Air-Pump: Hobbes, Boyle, and the Experimental Life* (Princeton, NJ: Princeton University Press, 1985), 64–5.

2 Karl Popper, *The Logic of Scientific Discovery* (New York: Harper & Row, 1965), 76.

3 Robert Boyle, "A Proemial Essay, wherein, with some Considerations touching Experimental Essays in general, Is interwoven such an Introduction to all those written by the Author, as is necessary to be perused for the better understanding of them," in *The Works of the Honourable Robert Boyle*, ed. Thomas Birch, 2nd ed. (London: J. and F. Rivington, 1772), 299–318.

criticism, is *that* always new?" All true, and all irrelevant; because the digital humanities have presented themselves as a radical break with the past, and must therefore produce evidence of such a break. The evidence, let's be frank, is not strong. What is there, moreover, comes in a variety of forms, beginning with the slightly paradoxical fact that, in a new approach, not everything has to be new. When the pamphlet "Network Theory, Plot Analysis"[4] pointed out, in passing, that a network of *Hamlet* had Hamlet at its center, the *New York Times* mentioned the passage as an unmistakable sign of stupidity. Maybe; but the point, of course, was not to present Hamlet's centrality as a surprise; had the new approach *not* found Hamlet at the center of the play, its plausibility would have disintegrated. Before *using* network theory for dramatic analysis, I had to *test* it, and prove that it corroborated the main results of previous research. Corroboration, alas, is often boring to humanities scholars (and clever journalists); but it *has* long played a role in scientific research, and having introduced it into our field is an achievement, not a weakness of the digital humanities. Besides, seldom is corroboration *just* corroboration. By and large, "On Paragraphs" validates a thematic approach to literature; but it adds that themes have an elective affinity with the scale of the paragraph; that the typical paragraph has, not one, but between two and four distinct themes; that the connection between thematics and narratology rests precisely on this plural-yet-limited number; and so on, from specification to specification. Thematics has not been revolutionized; but it has certainly been changed, and—why not?—improved. It's the "encounter between concepts and measurements" of "Style at the Scale of the Sentence"; a few months later, in "Operationalizing," the encounter had become a "radicalization of our relationship to concepts"; radicalization, in the sense that—when you have to turn a concept into a series of operations—you look at it in an analytical fashion that opens the way to its critique. I am thinking of how the concept of "scale" changed across three of our pamphlets, for instance: still largely a metaphor in the "mortar, bricks, and architecture" of "Quantitative Formalism," "scale" found a solid textual anchor in the sentence of "Style at the Scale of the Sentence," and was then generalized in the refrain of "different scales, different features" that concluded "On Paragraphs." It's fascinating, how a series of quantitative measurements enters into a dialogue with concepts

---

4 Reprinted in Franco Moretti, *Distant Reading* (New York: Verso, 2013).

and slowly transforms them. *Slowly*. Forget the hype about computation
making everything faster. Yes, data are gathered and analyzed with amazing speed; but the *explanation* of those results—unless you're happy with
the first commonplace that crosses your mind—is a different story; here,
only patience will do. For rapidity, nothing beats traditional interpretation:
Verne's Nautilus means—childhood; Count Dracula—monopoly capital.
One second, and everything changes. In the lab, it takes months of work.

BEYOND CONCEPTS? After corroboration and conceptual revision, a few
results that seem to be genuinely new. First of all, the "loudness" of Holst
Katsma's pamphlet, "Loudness in the Novel": a notion that, despite all the
interest in "voices" and "polyphony," had never become part of the theory
of the novel. Katsma found a way of operationalizing his intuition, and of
articulating it into a semantics and a grammar of loudness; he supported
it with readings of *Pride and Prejudice* and *The Idiot*, and concluded with
the discovery of the "quieting down of the English novel," which he followed in its decade-by-decade unfolding. "Bankspeak" also focused on
a gradual historical process—the transformation of the language of the
World Bank's yearly reports—and in fact took precisely *the slowness* of this
evolution as the most distinctive feature of how an "institutional style,"
with its complex of rules and constraints, eventually crystallizes. (And
now, it's impossible not to dream of a follow-up study in which slowness
becomes the key tempo of all that is "institutional" in literary life—genres,
styles, movements, canons . . .—thus also transforming our idea of literary
history as a whole.) And finally, after loudness and slowness, a novelty that
is not a concept, but—a script: Correlator. Developed by Ryan Heuser and
Long Le-Khac in order to find "the words that most closely correlate with
a given 'seed' word" in terms of historical frequency, Correlator generated
large "word cohorts," allowing Heuser and Le-Khac to discover unexpected
long-term trends. We have here a typical product of what could be called
"the programming imagination"; a form of thinking *that fuses together the
formulation and the operationalization of concepts*, leaving them often half-
implicit *as concepts*, while liberating their full force *as algorithms*. People
of an older generation may miss the clarity of categorical distinction; but
in the years to come, the main contribution of computational criticism to
literary study may well come from these centaur-like creatures, half script,
and half theory. Correlator is the harbinger of a new species.

TRIANGULATIONS. As concepts moved increasingly to the foreground of our work, so did our engagement with existing theories. Three distinct intellectual areas have been particularly significant in this respect. The first is the great formalist tradition, from the Russian Formalists to Leo Spitzer's and Erich Auerbach's stylistics, some aspects of structuralism, and recent work in corpus linguistics. This lineage is the one we are closest to in terms of objects and categories ("morphology," "genre," "register," "system," "style"); and, since form is the repeatable element of literature, this is also where we turn to in order to set the process of quantification in motion. In "Canon/Archive," for instance, we operationalized the difference between canon and archive, not via their respective semantic content, but in terms of formal features like redundancy and lexical variety. After this first lineage, so clearly hyper-literary, one that is not literary at all: the epistemology of the natural sciences, taken in a rather broad sense. Here, we have found our inspiration a little haphazardly, borrowing principal component analysis from genetics, for instance, and network theory from mathematics and physics, and entropy from information theory; not to mention specific concepts like "measurement" (Thomas Kuhn), "instrument" (Alexandre Koyré), or "normal/pathological" (Georges Canguilhem), all of which have played a role in this or that pamphlet. That it all required a double work of translation—from natural to literary objects, and from concepts to algorithms—became itself part of the point: it defined our view of the digital humanities as *the form taken by a scientific-explanatory approach in the digital age*: triangulating Canguilhem with charts of type-token ratio and forgotten Victorian novels, or Koyré with network statistics and minor characters in plays—*this* is how we understand the new approach. Finally, the third major presence, Pierre Bourdieu. Evoked, for one reason or another, in "Quantitative Formalism," and "Style," and engaged at length in "Canon/Archive," "Bourdieu" stands for a literary study that is empirical and sociological at once. Which, of course, is obvious. But he also may stand for something less obvious, and rather perplexing: the near-absence from the digital humanities, and from our own work as well, of that other sociological approach: that is, Marxist criticism (Raymond Williams, in "From Keywords to Cohorts," being the lone exception). This disjunction—perfectly mutual, as the indifference of Marxist criticism is only shaken by the occasional salvo against the digital humanities as an accessory to the corporate attack on the university—is puzzling, considering the vast social horizon that digital archives could open to historical materialism and the critical depth that the latter could inject into the "programming imagination." It's a strange state of affairs; and it's not clear what, if anything, may eventually change it. For now, let's just acknowledge that this is how things stand; and that—for the present writer—something needs to be done. It would be nice if, one day, big data could lead us back to the big questions.

2016

PART

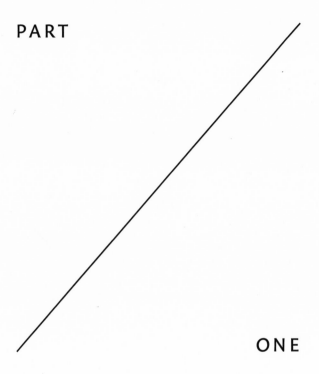

ONE

Quantitative Formalism

AN EXPERIMENT

Sarah Allison, Ryan Heuser, Matthew Jockers, Franco Moretti, Michael Witmore

This chapter is the report of a study conducted by five people—four at Stanford and one at the University of Wisconsin—that tried to establish whether computer-generated algorithms could "recognize" literary genres. You take *David Copperfield*, run it through a program without any human input—"unsupervised," as the expression goes—and . . . can the program figure out whether it's a gothic novel or a bildungsroman? The answer is, fundamentally, yes: but a yes with so many complications that it is necessary to look at the entire process of our study. These are new methods we are using, and with new methods the process is almost as important as the results.

PROLOGUE: DOCUSCOPE READS SHAKESPEARE

During the fall of 2008, Franco Moretti was visiting Madison, where Michael Witmore introduced him to work he and Jonathan Hope had been doing on Shakespeare's dramatic genres, using a text-tagging device known as Docuscope, a hand-curated corpus of several million English words (and strings of words) that had been sorted into grammatical, semantic, and rhetorical categories.[1]

---

[1] See Jonathan Hope and Michael Witmore, "The Very Large Textual Object: A Prosthetic Reading of Shakespeare," special issue, *Early Modern Literary Studies* 9, no. 3 (January 2004): 1–36; Hope and Witmore, "Shakespeare by the Numbers: On the Linguistic Texture of the Late Plays," in *Early Modern Tragicomedy*, ed. Subha Mukherji and Raphael Lyne (London: Boydell and Brewer, 2007), 133–53; Hope and Witmore,

Docuscope is essentially a smart dictionary: it consists of a list of more than two hundred million possible strings of English, each assigned to one of 101 functional linguistic categories called Language Action Types (LATs).[2] When Docuscope "reads" a text, it does so by looking for words, and strings of words, that it can "recognize"—that is to say, that it can match to one of its 101 LATs. When this happens, the associated LAT is credited with one appearance. For example, since Docuscope assigns *I* and *me* to the LAT "FirstPerson," their occurrence in a text is recorded as an appearance of the LAT FirstPerson.[3]

Based on these counts, Hope and Witmore used unsupervised factor analysis—a factor, here, being a pattern that includes some categories, in variable proportions, and excludes others—to create portraits of received genre distinctions such as those made by the editors of the First Folio (Heminges and Condell), and of the genre of "late romances" that was first identified in the 19th century. Multivariate analyses and clustering techniques made groupings of the plays that not only corresponded to conventional genre groupings but also picked out texts that critics had identified as outliers.[4] Thus, in clustering Shakespeare's Folio plays—as shown in

---

"The Hundredth Psalm to the Tune of 'Greensleeves': Digital Approaches to Shakespeare's Language of Genre," in "New Media Approaches to Shakespeare," ed. Katherine Rowe, special issue, *Shakespeare Quarterly* 61, no. 3 (Fall 2010): 357–90; and Witmore's blog, http://www.winedarksea.org.

2 For Docuscope, see David Kaufer, Suguru Ishizaki, Brian Butler, and Jeff Collins, *The Power of Words: Unveiling the Speaker and Writer's Hidden Craft* (Mahwah, NJ: Lawrence Erlbaum Associates, 2004). A fascinating discussion of how the program came to be designed and an early précis of its categories can be found at http://archive.li/R8cZO.

3 Because of the way they are used in the program, LATs must be given names without spaces. Obviously the characterization of the words that are contained in each of these categories is a matter of interpretation, as is the choice of those words themselves, which took place over the course of almost a decade of hand-coding. In general, Witmore and Hope use the categories or LATs to identify statistical patterns, then move from the categories to concrete textual instances in order to see how particular words are functioning in context.

4 They discovered, for instance, that Shakespeare's "late romances" were distinguished, linguistically, from those that went before them by word patterns that allowed speakers to narrate past action while highlighting their own emotional stance with respect to those actions (a process they called focalized retrospection). Specific linguistic features of these plays were responsible for this effect, for example 1) certain types of subordinated conjunction (a comma, followed by the word *which*) and 2) past-tense verb forms introduced by a past-tense auxiliary form of the verb *to be*. Comedies and histories were also shown to be significantly distinct from one another, with comedy possessing a high degree of first- and second-person pronouns (classed under the LATs FirstPerson and DirectAddress); a high degree of language expressing uncertainty (the LAT Uncertainty); an absence of nouns and verbs used to re-

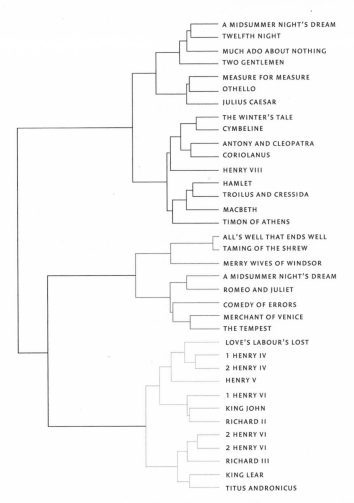

FIGURE 1.1 **Dendrogram illustrating clustering of Shakespeare plays rated on Docuscope's Language Action Types (LATs) produced in 2003.** Clustering method: complete linkage, Euclidean distances. Notice the presence of comedies in the first and third clusters, late plays and tragedies in the second, and histories in the fourth and fifth. "Incorrect classifications" such as *Othello* and *Love's Labour's Lost* are discussed on Witmore's blog.

Figure 1.1—the program managed to take *Henry VIII* out of the history plays cluster and place it near other "late plays," a readjustment from the initial Folio designations that later critics have advocated as well. One can

---

fer to motion, the properties of sensed objects, and sensed changes in objects (LATs labeled Motions, SenseProperty, SenseObject); an absence of first-person plural pronouns (the LAT Inclusive); and an absence of words indicating social entities or expectations that must be shared or mutually acknowledged (the LAT CommonAuthority).

see this grouping pattern in **Figure 1.1**, taken from an early complete linkage clustering of the plays.

After seeing these results, Moretti asked Witmore whether he would consider clustering novelistic genres. Witmore agreed, and a meeting was planned for February 2009 at Stanford.

1. DOCUSCOPE RECOGNIZES NOVELISTIC GENRES

The starting point of the study was a corpus of 250 19th-century British novels from the Chadwyck-Healey collection.[5] Working with existing genre bibliographies, Moretti put together a sample of thirty-six texts loosely comparable to the Shakespeare corpus of the first Docuscope experiment, which comprised twelve genre sets, divided into two groups of six. The first group (sets 1 through 6) included four gothic novels, four historical novels, four national tales, four industrial novels, four silver-fork novels, and four bildungsromane. Of the six sets in the second group, three were also present in the first (sets 8, 9, and 12: two texts each from industrial novels, gothic novels, and bildungsromane), whereas the other three were not (sets 7, 10, and 1: two texts each from anti-Jacobin, evangelical, and Newgate novels).[6] Docuscope's task was to find and match the three sets from the second group that were also present in the first.[7]

---

5 We limited ourselves to this database because most other texts available on the web in 2006–08 appeared too unreliable for our purposes. Today, our assessment would be different, and a new initial pool would probably modify important aspects of our research.

6 Silver-fork novels focused on the fashionable lives of the British aristocracy and detailed their manners and possessions for nouveaux riches audiences after the Regency, from the 1820s to the 1840s. (The name derives from Hazlitt's criticism of the sort of writer who "gives you the address of his heroine's milliner . . . and also informs you that the quality eat fish with silver forks.") In the same period, Newgate novels provided gleeful accounts of London's underworld, often inspired by biographies of criminals anthologized in collections such as *The Newgate Calendar*. The genre is often said to be a precursor to later Victorian detective fiction.

7 This is the complete list of the texts: set 1 (gothic novels): *A Sicilian Romance, The Old Manor House, The Monk*, and *Melmoth the Wanderer*; set 2 (historical novels): *Waverley, Ivanhoe, The Entail*, and *Valperga*; set 3 (national tales): *Castle Rackrent, The Wild Irish Girl, The Absentee*, and *Marriage*; set 4 (industrial novels): *Shirley, Alton Locke, Hard Times*, and *North and South*; set 5 (silver-fork novels): *Glenarvon, Vivian Grey, Pelham*, and *Mrs. Armytage, or Female Domination*; set 6 (bildungsromane): *Jane Eyre, The History of Pendennis, David Copperfield*, and *Daniel Deronda*; set 7 (anti-Jacobin novels): *Mordaunt* and *Adeline Mowbray*; set 8 (industrial novels): *The Life and Adventures of Michael Armstrong, the Factory Boy*, and *Mary Barton*; set 9 (gothic novels): *The Mysteries of*

To be sure he wouldn't unconsciously "tilt" his work on Docuscope's results in a predetermined direction, Witmore asked to be told nothing about the texts he was receiving; title pages were removed from the files ("They often provide giveaway clues that are less interesting than the micro-linguistic moves that get made in the text"), and he literally walked into the meeting without knowing how Docuscope had performed. He was "hoping that Docuscope would fail at this test," he emailed us a few days before the meeting, "since I have a stake in arguing that it is material constraints on performance (in plays) that allows Docuscope to make intelligible genre discriminations when it comes to Shakespeare. If Docuscope turns out to be good at picking genres of novels as well, I am going to have to expand my notion of 'material constraint' in its relationship to language practices." (Later, though, he seemed pleased at how well Docuscope had done.)

Witmore used a variety of measures to match the genres from the two groups. For example, he assessed the degree to which multivariate statistical analysis could produce "factors" that would pry apart pairs from one another—a factor being a pattern of having certain LATs and lacking certain others.[8] He also compared each pairing against a collection of texts called the Frown Corpus (early 1990s American English) to see when they both exhibited identical elevated and depressed scores on LATs in comparison with the average score from Frown. By combining these techniques, Witmore came up with the following matches: 2:9 (with 1:9

Udolpho and *Zofloya; or, The Moor*; set 10 (evangelical novels): *Coelebs in Search of a Wife* and *Self-Control*; set 11 (Newgate novels): *Eugene Aram* and *Jack Sheppard*; set 12 (bildungsromane): *Great Expectations* and *Middlemarch*. Retrospectively, this list is odd—and flawed—in two opposite ways. First, the thirty-six texts were chosen so as to maximize variation within each given genre. Although quite wrong as a way to select a sample from a population, this choice was meant to increase the severity of the test: Docuscope had to prove it could "recognize" a genre even when given a quite disparate bundle of specimens. If this increased the difficulty of the enterprise, a second decision did the exact opposite: instead of giving Witmore thirty-six texts to be assigned to various generic classes, Moretti gave him discrete groups that were already subdivided into genres. This, clearly, made matters much easier, as the internal variation within any given genre could be averaged out by looking at the group as a whole. These odd, anti-thetical decisions show how unprepared we were as a group—or should we say: as a discipline?—for this type of research. The idea of a random sample, for instance, never really crossed our minds . . .

8 One can think of a factor as a recipe for describing recurring patterns of variation in a larger collection of items. If each novel is a stack of cards, Docuscope examines all of the decks and counts what is in them. Then factor analysis goes through all of the contents of each stack and says, "Whenever I see lots of red sixes, I see very few fours and fives of any kind." These recipes of "presences and absences" can then be tested against imposed groups of those stacks (genres) to see if the factors reliably distinguish from each other.

a close second), 4:8, and 6:12. When the curtain was lifted, it turned out that Docuscope's only mistake consisted in mismatching group 9 (gothic novels) with group 2 (historical) rather than 1 (gothic): a mix-up most literary historians would consider venial, or maybe even inevitable, given the porous borders between these two genres. (And then, as Witmore wrote in his presentation, the correct 1:9 pairing was indeed "a close second.")

As the meeting was nearing its end, John Bender asked the hard question that was hanging in the air: Striking as these results were, did we think they had produced new knowledge? The answer, of course, was no: Docuscope had corroborated what literary scholars already knew—or at least were convinced of—that certain texts belonged to the same class. No new knowledge there. But that human judgment and unsupervised statistical analysis would agree on genre classification—this *was* a novelty that had emerged from the test. Just as Docuscope had corroborated existing scholarship, the latter had proved Docuscope's reliability. We wanted to know whether it could replicate its Shakespeare results in unfamiliar territory, and it could; that first experiment had not been a fluke. A computer could classify literary texts. And when Witmore—in passing, and almost as an afterthought—showed an old, unpublished chart from his Shakespeare study, the possibility seemed even richer in implications.

2. MOST FREQUENT WORDS RECOGNIZE NOVELISTIC GENRES

Docuscope had passed the test. Was it the only program that could do so? Matthew Jockers, who had been working on authorship studies for a while, wanted to see whether the methods he had been developing could be applied to genre recognition as well. In many ways, genre classification is akin to authorship attribution. But there is one important difference. With authorship problems, one attempts to extract a feature set that excludes context-sensitive features from the analysis, the consensus being that a set made up primarily of frequent, or closed-class, word features yields the most accurate results. For genre classification, however, one would intuitively assume that context words—say, "castle" in gothic novels—would be critical. Yet, Jockers's preliminary results suggested that an equally distinct genre "signal" may be detected from a small set of high-frequency features.

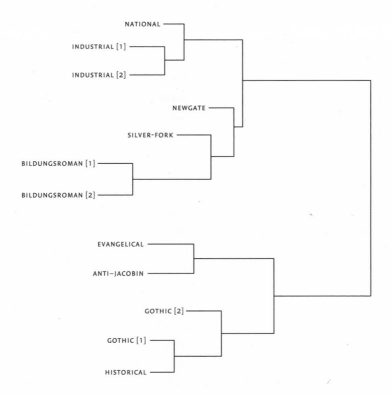

NATIONAL

INDUSTRIAL [1]

INDUSTRIAL [2]

NEWGATE

SILVER-FORK

BILDUNGSROMAN [1]

BILDUNGSROMAN [2]

EVANGELICAL

ANTI−JACOBIN

GOTHIC [2]

GOTHIC [1]

HISTORICAL

FIGURE 1.2 **Cluster dendrogram of novel genres using Most Frequent Words (MFW)**

Using just forty-four word and punctuation features—which we eventually ended up calling Most Frequent Words, or MFW—Jockers was able to classify the novels in the corpus as well as Witmore had done with Docuscope (and its far more complex feature set).[9] Using the "dist" and "hclust" functions in the open-source "R" statistics application,[10] Jockers clustered the texts in the dendrogram of **Figure 1.2**.

After Jockers shared his results with Witmore, Witmore suggested testing this methodology on the Shakespeare corpus. Once again, MFW

---

9 To derive his feature set, Jockers lowercased the texts, counted and converted to relative frequencies the various feature types, and then winnowed the feature set by choosing only those features that have a mean relative frequency of 0.03 percent or greater. This resulted in a matrix consisting of the following forty-four features (the prefix p_ indicates a punctuation token type instead of a word token): *a, all, and, as, at, be, but, by, for, from, had, have, he, her, him, his, i, in, is, it, me, my, not, of, on, p_apos, p_comma, p_exclam, p_hyphen, p_period, p_ques, p_quote, p_semi, said, she, so, that, the, this, to, was, which, with, you.*

10 http://www.r-project.org/.

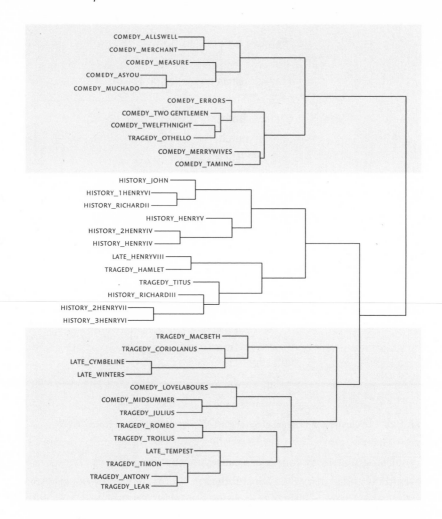

FIGURE 1.3 **Dendrogram of Shakespeare First Folio plays using Most Frequent Words with major clusters highlighted.** Here Jockers used the thirty-seven features from the Shakespeare plays that had a mean relative frequency of greater than or equal to 0.03 percent. Note the similarity between this tree and Docuscope's diagram in Figure 1.1, with the close pairings of *Winter's Tale* and *Cymbeline* and *2 Henry VI* and *3 Henry VI*, and the proximity of *Coriolanus* to the *Cymbeline–Winter's Tale* pair.

accurately clustered the majority of Shakespeare's plays into the "tragedies," "comedies," "histories," and "late plays" of **Figure 1.3**.

"Quantitative Formalism," reads the title of this article. Formalism, because all of us, in one way or another, were interested in the formal conventions of genre; and quantitative, because we were looking for more precise—ideally, measurable—ways to establish generic differences. So we really wanted Docuscope and MFW to do well. But so well, no one had thought possible: not only were genre signals quite strong—they were *equally strong at wholly different textual levels*: just as recognizable by Docuscope's mix of grammar and semantics, as by the handful of function words of MFW. The convergence was so clear, it was almost spooky: it suggested that the logic of genre reached a depth that no one had imagined and no one really knew how to explain. The frequency of articles and conjunctions that allowed the identification of Newgate novels or bildungsromane in text after text—could this really be essential to the functioning of a genre? Why?

As soon as school was over, we met again.

3. FORKING PATHS

Our next meeting, at Stanford, began with Witmore showing a page that Docuscope had isolated as the most "gothic" of the entire corpus—that is to say, the one that presented an extremely high number of typically gothic features (**Figure 1.4**).

It was an interesting moment; not just because the idea of a genre's "typical" page was unusual and intriguing, but because, as Sarah Allison immediately pointed out, the gothic of Docuscope appeared to be quite different from that of "Humanscope" (as she called it): it was not the same gothic we saw. For us, that page was gothic because of the subdued terror and the archway, the ruin and apprehension and the limbs that trembled—not because of the *he, him, his, had, was, struck the*, and *heard the* that caught Docuscope's attention. Between the two approaches, there seemed to be nothing in common. Or perhaps, more precisely: nothing in common *in terms of their units of analysis*; but everything in common *in terms of results*: whether via banditti and blood, or *uttered the* and *covered him*, Humanscope and Docuscope agreed that this page belonged to the gothic, and to no other genre. And at this point, the idea that had first confusedly crossed our minds a few months earlier crystallized once and for all: genres, like buildings, possess distinctive features at every possible scale of analysis: mortar, bricks, and architecture, as Ryan Heuser put it: the mortar, the grains of sand, of Most Frequent Words, the bricks of Docuscope's lexico-grammatical categories, and the architecture of themes and episodes that readers recognize. The three layers were not even overlapping; their signals were largely distinct

FIGURE 1.4 **Representation of Docuscope tokens differentiating the gothic from several other genres, drawn from Ann Radcliffe's *A Sicilian Romance* (1790).** These differentiating bundles of LATs were identified through factor analysis and ANOVA, with factors winnowed through the Tukey test.

a moment deserted him. An invincible curiosity, however, **subdued** his TERROR, and <u>he</u> determined to *pursue*, if possible, the way the figure <u>had</u> taken. <u>He</u> passed over loose stones through a sort of court, **till he** came to the arch-way; here <u>he</u> stopped, FOR FEAR *returned* UPON HIM. **Resuming** <u>his</u> courage, however, <u>he</u> **went on**, still endeavouring to follow the way the figure <u>had</u> passed, and SUDDENLY found himself in an enclosed part of the ruin, <u>whose</u> appearance <u>was</u> more wild and desolate than any <u>he had</u> yet seen. Seized with unconquerable APPREHENSION, <u>he</u> <u>was</u> *retiring*, when the low voice of a distressed person **struck his** ear. <u>His</u> heart *sunk* at the sound, <u>his</u> limbs trembled, and <u>he was</u> utterly unable to move. The sound which appeared to be the last groan of a dying person, <u>was</u> repeated. Hippolitus *made* a strong effort, and sprang forward, when a light burst upon <u>him</u> from a shattered casement of the building, and AT THE SAME INSTANT <u>he</u> **heard the** voices of men! <u>He</u> *advanced* softly to the window, and beheld in a small room, which <u>was</u> less decayed than the rest of the edifice, a group of men, who from the savageness of their looks, and from <u>their</u> dress, appeared to be banditti. They surrounded a man who lay on the ground wounded, and bathed in blood, and who it <u>was</u> very evident <u>had</u> **uttered the** groans heard by the count. The obscurity of the place prevented Hippolitus from distinguishing the features of the dying man. From the blood which **covered him**

bold = Narrative Verbs, Time Shifts, Time Intervals
italics = Reporting Events
<u>dotted underline</u> = Projecting Back
<u>solid underline</u> = Person Pronoun
SMALL CAPS = Fear, Sadness

from one another. Different as the three layers were among themselves, though, they were also different from the corresponding layers of other genres: the gothic "mortar" totally unlike the "mortar" of the national tale, or the anti-Jacobin novel; the gothic "bricks" unlike the "bricks" used by other genres, and the same for the more visible architectural shapes.

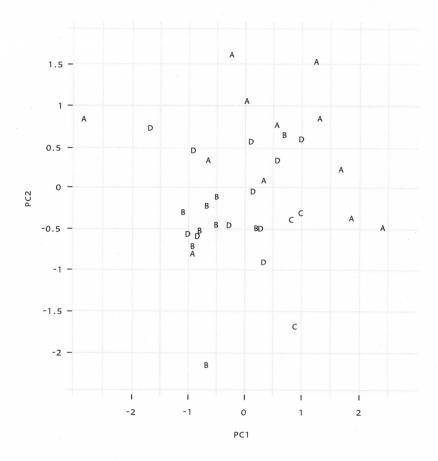

FIGURE 1.5 **Scatterplot matrix in which Shakespeare's plays are rated on their first two principal components after having been counted by Docuscope and analyzed in terms of aggregates of LATs.** PCA performed on the covariance matrix, unscaled data. Item key: A = Comedy, B = History, C = Late Plays, D = Tragedies. Note how the two components place comedies in the upper right quadrant, histories in the lower left, and several late plays in the lower right (whereas tragedies, for some reason, are dispersed all over the field).

We will return to the conceptual questions posed by these observations toward the end of this article. On that day in June, though, something else seemed even more inspiring: the chart we briefly mentioned at the end of section two, which displayed all of Shakespeare's plays along two orthogonal axes (**Figure 1.5**).

Witmore and Hope had abandoned the idea of publishing this diagram in a scholarly book of traditional literary criticism: they felt it would be more effective to make their point entirely with words. But the group saw in the chart the promise of an intuitive, synthetic view of the literary field, with each genre placed in relation to all the others. Moretti, in particular, was struck by the similarity between the chart and the principal components charts that Cavalli-Sforza et al., in *The History and Geography of Human Genes*, had used to trace relationships among human populations.[11] Could narrative genres similarly be reduced to two basic variables? And would the ensuing distribution correlate with, say, Bourdieu's sociological (but highly subjective) map of the French literary field? Could we actually map morphology over social distinction?

Witmore's chart seemed perfect for all this. Even the fact that it wasn't perfect—with those tragedies fudging the more orderly patterns of the other genres—seemed a sign of reliability, as history is itself never perfect. So we decided to repeat the attempt with novelistic genres. If the results were good, two further developments would become imaginable. First, the system of genres might turn from a hodgepodge of unrelated categories[12] to a single matrix of interconnected formal variables.

And, second, it might become possible to chart the Great Unread—the vast, unexplored archive that lies underneath the narrow canon of literary history. One could give Docuscope and MFW thousands of texts of unknown generic affiliation, and see where they would fall in the gravitational field of better-known genres. One could envisage generation-by-generation maps of the literary universe, with galaxies, supernovae, black holes . . .

With these questions running through our heads, we redeployed the February and March 2009 data along the lines of **Figure 1.5**. The first visualization, produced by MFW—**Figure 1.6**—turned out to be perfectly

11 See L. Luca Cavalli-Sforza, Paolo Menozzi, and Alberto Piazza, *The History and Geography of Human Genes* (Princeton, NJ: Princeton University Press, 1994), especially 39–41. Principal component analysis is a procedure, similar to factor analysis, that reduces the variance existing within a group of objects—in our case, the linguistic-stylistic difference among literary texts—to two orthogonal axes, called Principal Component 1 and 2 (PC1 and PC2). Principal Component 1 is the combination of features that expresses the maximum amount of variance available to a single component; Principal Component 2 displays a further increase of variance orthogonally with respect to PC1. Taken together, PC1 and PC2 are a very economical way of representing as much variance as is possible on two dimensions; however, they never express the total amount of variance within a system, but, rather, a trade-off between high intuitive visibility and a (limited) loss of precision.

12 Right now, the very names of novelistic genres are a telling—even maddening—sign of categorical confusion highlighting now the novel's medium (the epistolary novel), now its content (historical, industrial), style (naturalist), protagonist (picaresque, pastoral), all the way to more or less fanciful metaphors (gothic, silver-fork).

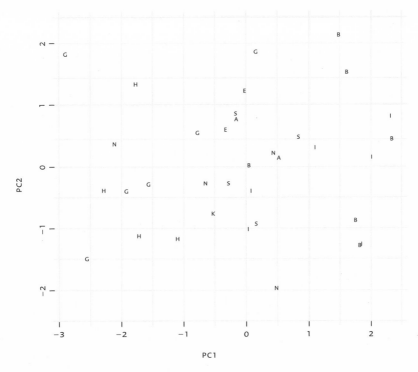

FIGURE 1.6 **A graphical representation of the first two principal components in a PCA analysis of the Most Frequent Words.** Each letter represents a single text (A = Anti-Jacobin novels, B = Bildungsromane, E = Evangelical novels, G = Gothic novels, I = Industrial novels, K = Newgate novels, N = National tales, S = Silver-fork novels).

ambiguous: promising and perplexing in equal measure. There was certainly less clarity than in the Shakespeare case; but we were charting twice as many genres, and over a much longer period. And then, some patterns were visible: with a few exceptions, gothic and historical novels lay on the negative side of Principal Component 1 (the left side of the horizontal axis), while the bildungsromane and industrial novels were clearly on its positive side. For us, this was both good and bad news. Good, because a pattern is what one always looks for in exploratory work. But bad, because the pattern was *chronological*, more than formal: one generation, then a second, more confused one, and then a third. Was Principal Component 1 capturing genre signals, then—or historical ones? The latter seemed more likely, especially given how poorly those genres that flourished in the same years (gothic/historical; silver-fork/Newgate; industrial/bildungsroman) were separated. History seemed definitely stronger than form.

But there were also some data that contradicted the historical alignment: in the crowded central section, which contained genres from two different generations, the vertical axis of PC2—which separated anti-Jacobin and evangelical novels from Newgate stories—might be capturing genre signals after all.[13] Would it be possible to isolate such signals, and magnify them?

4. DEAD END

From June to September 2009, Witmore and Jockers kept looking for ways to improve the early results of PC analysis. First, they segmented the texts to see whether smaller units would improve differentiation. All texts were divided into ten equal parts—but the results did not change much. Then, noticing that the segments' distribution was often very uneven—as in **Figure 1.7**, where about one third of them fudge an otherwise good separation between gothic and historical novels—we decided to label all the segments. "Historical.8.1" would indicate the first segment of W. H. Ainsworth's *Windsor Castle* (which happened to be the eighth historical novel in our corpus); "Gothic.1.10" the tenth segment of William Beckford's *Vathek* (which was the first gothic text), and so on. The overlap among different genres might turn out to be limited to specific portions of the texts (beginnings, or endings); if that were so, and genres became more distinctive—more "themselves," as it were—at specific moments in the plot, then one could focus on those moments and magnify their separation. It was a plausible, perhaps even an ingenious hypothesis. But—no. Some novels were most distinctive early on; others, late in the plot; or in the middle; or nowhere in particular.

Next, we turned to the composition of our corpus: the initial collection of 36 texts tended to exaggerate variation within each genre, making life unnecessarily hard for Docuscope and MFW. We returned to the Chadwyck-Healey database and added to the initial corpus all those texts that existing bibliographies had assigned to specific genres; included two new genres (Jacobin and sensation novels); and repeated all the calculations on the new corpus of 106 texts.[14]

---

13 Then again, with only two texts each for these genres, this could easily be the result of chance. Or not.

14 This second corpus also included a few texts, mostly from "minor" genres, scanned for us by the Stanford libraries. But since the Chadwyck-Healey database remained the major source, canonical texts

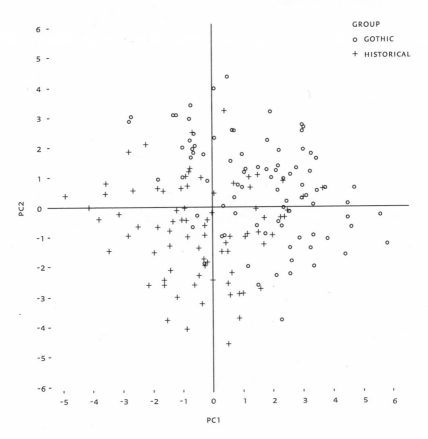

FIGURE 1.7 **Eight-thousand-word segments of the first two groups of thirty-six novels, rated by Docuscope on first two principal components.** In all PCA analyses below, data are scaled (that is, PCA is performed on the correlation matrix of percentage scores).

Nothing.

Maybe trying to chart eight decades at once was too much. We divided the corpus into three generations;[15] though of course less crowded, the new charts were just as indecisive. By the end of summer, it was clear that the results were no longer changing.

o   o   o

still predominated: of twenty-eight historical novels, for instance, fourteen were by Walter Scott.

15 The first generation (ca. 1790–1820) included gothic, Jacobin, anti-Jacobin, national tales, and evangelical novels; the second (ca. 1815–50) historical, silver-fork, and Newgate novels; the third (ca. 1845–75) industrial, bildungsroman, and sensation novels.

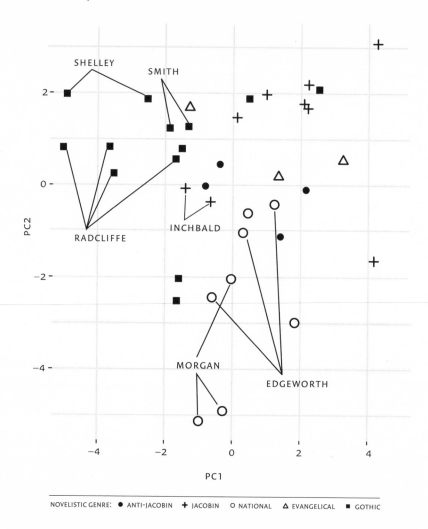

NOVELISTIC GENRE: ● ANTI-JACOBIN ✛ JACOBIN ○ NATIONAL △ EVANGELICAL ■ GOTHIC

FIGURE 1.8 **Figures 1.8–1.10: Generational analysis of original thirty-six novels as rated by Docuscope on first two principal components.** Notice the proximity among the texts by Elizabeth Inchbald, Charlotte Smith, Ann Radcliffe, Percy Shelley, Lady Morgan (Sydney Owenson), and Maria Edgeworth in **1.8**; by W. H. Ainsworth, Jane Porter, Edward Bulwer-Lytton, John Galt, and of course Walter Scott, in **1.9**; by Elizabeth Gaskell, Charles Dickens, Charlotte Brontë, Wilkie Collins, and George Eliot in **1.10**.

5. AUTHORS VERSUS GENRES

In November 2009, in the course of a teleconference that included the five authors and a few Stanford grad students, we looked again at the three generational maps, which now included all individual texts (**Figures 1.8–1.10**),

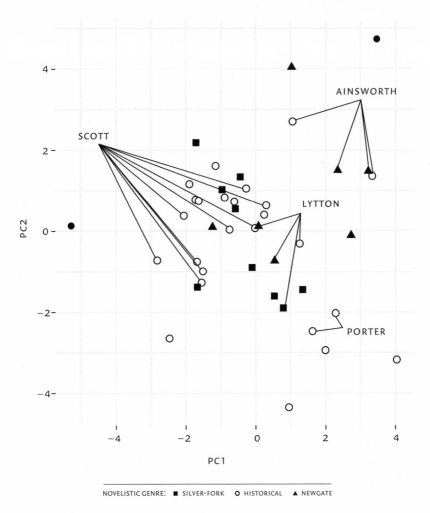

NOVELISTIC GENRE: ■ SILVER-FORK ○ HISTORICAL ▲ NEWGATE

FIGURE 1.9 **Docuscope generational analysis**

and all of a sudden realized how strong the "author" signal was. Remember, we didn't want authors; we wanted genres. But it was impossible not to notice that Docuscope and MFW clustered the former much better than the latter. With Charles Dickens, Anne Brontë, and George Eliot for instance—who had all written both industrial novels and bildungsromane—the "pull" of the author in **Figure 1.10** was clearly much stronger than that of the genre; and the same was true for Edward Bulwer-Lytton's *Last Days of Pompeii, Eugene Aram,* and *Pelham,* closely clustered together in **Figure 1.9**, despite the fact that they belong to the rather different genres of historical, Newgate, and silver-fork fiction.

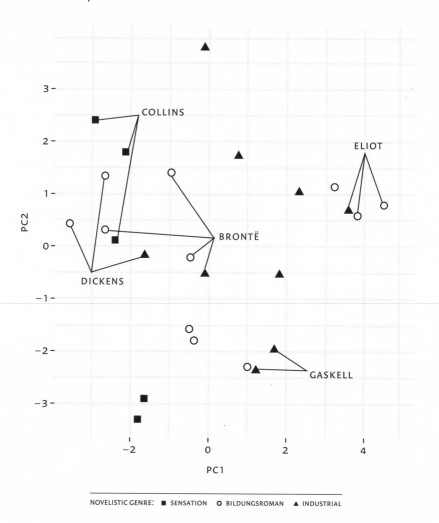

NOVELISTIC GENRE: ■ SENSATION   O BILDUNGSROMAN   ▲ INDUSTRIAL

FIGURE 1.10 **Docuscope generational analysis**

Why should authors be so much more recognizable than genres? Probably because Docuscope and MFW are very good at capturing something all writers do, whether they know it or not: using imperceptible linguistic patterns that provide an unmistakable stylistic "signature." Genres also have such stylistic signatures, of course; but genres have a narrative signature, too—their plot—which is at least as important. The episodes that so powerfully identify the bildungsroman for instance—discussions with old mentors and young friends, false starts, disappointments, the discovery of one's vocation—all this has no equivalent in a sensation novel; just as a sensation novel's mysteries and murders would make no sense in an industrial novel, and so on. So, what happens when the same writer moves from one genre to another—when, say, Dickens moves from the industrial novel *Hard Times* to the urban multiplot of *Little Dorrit*, the historical *Tale of Two Cities*, or the bildungsroman of *Great Expectations*—what happens is that his plots change, but his style doesn't. Or not as much. The stories of Coketown, London, or Paris are much more different than the words Dickens uses to narrate them. His language remains basically the same.

Why did Docuscope and MFW recognize authors so well, then—and genres less well? Because they had been designed to recognize language, but not plot.[16] They were probably doing the best that could be done in separating genres on the sole basis of their language and style; but language and style are just not enough to delimit one genre from another. And after all, why should they be? In addressing their readers, genres use both style and plot (in the 19th century, probably, more plot than style): our programs were missing half of the structure, and it made sense that they should be only half successful. Half successful does not mean unsuccessful. But it does suggest that an analytical tool capable of quantifying plot is still missing.[17] And as long as that is the case, the generic distribution effected by Docuscope and MFW was too random to support a good literary taxonomy, let alone an exploration of the archive. The Great Unread would, for the time being, remain unread.

6. 220 CHARTS

In December 2009, Allison, Heuser, and Moretti turned to a new set of visualizations: two series of charts that included all possible pairings

---

16 They can certainly see how actions are described: with simple or complex sentences, stressing subjective mood or objective results, surprise or retrospection. But they can hardly see what actions consist in: a story's chronological (and semantic) chain largely eludes them.

17 This finding cheered Witmore, since it suggests that in novelistic representation, plot provides an avenue of generic differentiation that has to be less visible to Docuscope because it does not have to be tied to the physical limits of the medium, whereas Renaissance drama—constantly grappling with the difficulty of telling stories with real bodies in a few hours—might have this extrastylistic avenue foreclosed, leading to more legible (because materially constrained) generic styles at the level of the sentence.

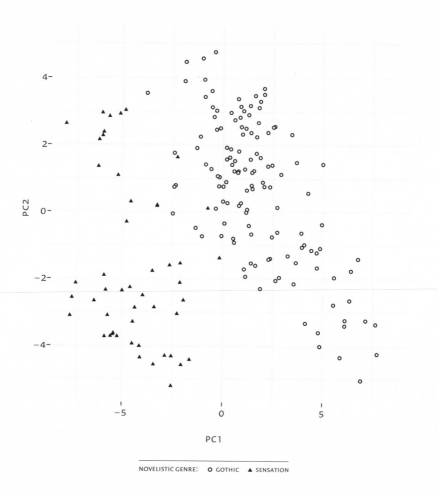

NOVELISTIC GENRE: O GOTHIC   ▲ SENSATION

FIGURE 1.11 **Most Frequent Word scatterplot.** Here, and in all other PCA charts, each point (circle or triangle) on the plot stands for one segment (one tenth) of a text.

among the eleven genres of the enlarged corpus (gothic/Jacobin, gothic/anti-Jacobin, gothic/national tale, and so on, all the way to the other end of the chronological spectrum). These charts came in two forms; the first showed the distribution of two genres based on MFW (**Figure 1.11**) and Docuscope (**Figure 1.12**). These were our basic tools, allowing us to intuitively grasp whether two specific genres separated well—as gothic and sensation novels in **Figures 1.11–12**—or not. (MFW and Docuscope, incidentally, turned out to be equally able—or unable, as the case may be—to separate genres from each other.)

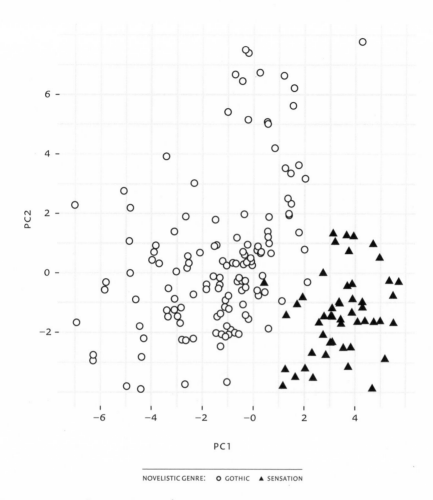

NOVELISTIC GENRE: ○ GOTHIC ▲ SENSATION

FIGURE 1.12 **Docuscope scatterplot**

The second type of chart redeployed the circles and triangles of **Figures 1.11–12**, adding two further features. First, it tagged each segment, making explicit which (part of which) text it came from: the circles in the lower right corner of **Figure 1.11**, for instance, turned out in **Figure 1.13** to belong to *Vathek*, thus bringing to light the "centrality"—or "eccentricity," as the case may be—of each text within its genre (an issue that may have profound consequences for our knowledge of genre, and which we plan to investigate in the future). And then, **Figures 1.13–14** also indicated which traits of the two principal components contributed to the specific shape of

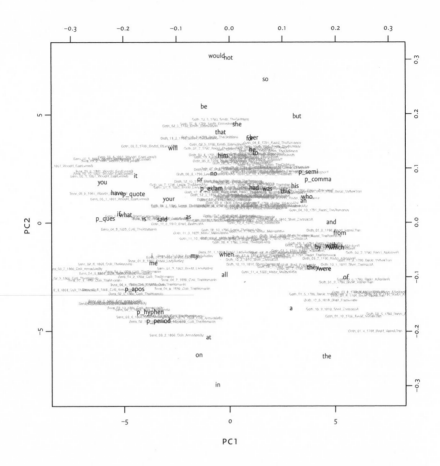

FIGURE 1.13 **Most Frequent Word scatterplot (gray titles) and component loadings (black)**

a genre's distribution: which words or Docuscope Dimensions exerted a stronger pull in separating gothic from sensation novels. So, for instance, the lower right quadrant of **Figure 1.13** highlights the definite article as an important differential feature of the gothic in MFW analysis (compare with **Figure 1.11**); in **Figure 1.14**, a similar role is played, in the lower left quadrant, by "Narrative VP," "Pronouns," and "Reporting Events" (compare with **Figure 1.12**).[18]

18 As each of the fifty-five genre pairings appeared in this double form, we examined 110 charts produced by Docuscope, and 110 produced by MFW. The mapping technique used in **Figures 1.13–14**, in which differential traits become visible within the distribution of the data themselves, is described in chapter 4 of Mick Alt, *Exploring Hyperspace: A Non-Mathematical Explanation of Multivariate Analysis* (New York: McGraw-Hill, 1990).

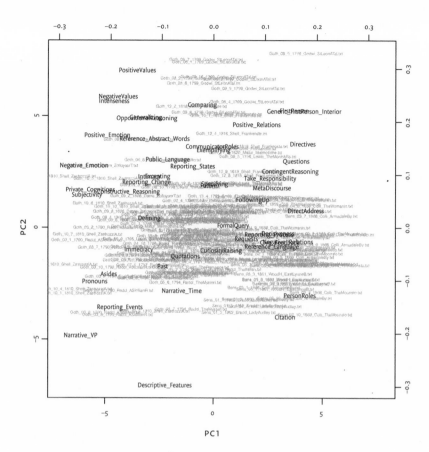

FIGURE 1.14 **Docuscope scatterplot (gray titles) and component loadings (black)**

As we studied our charts, it became clear that they rested on two premises that were quite different from those of current genre theory: they never looked at a genre per se, in isolation, but always and only in relation to another genre; and they were not interested in those features that could add up to a synthetic ideal-type, but only in those that could *differentiate* one genre from another. This relational-differential emphasis made for a very "realistic" approach, reminiscent of Bourdieu's "position-taking": just like authors or schools, genres engage in a struggle for recognition: one could almost feel not just the difference, but the *conflict* of forms in those traits that pulled them in one direction or the other. And yet this image of genre was clearly also incomplete, because differential features may tell us all we need to know in order to demarcate one form from another, and yet

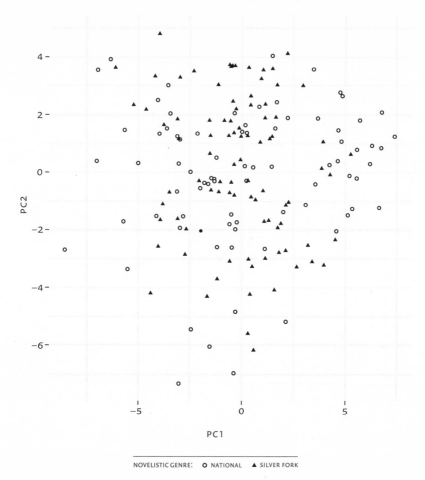

NOVELISTIC GENRE: ○ NATIONAL   ▲ SILVER FORK

FIGURE 1.15 **Most Frequent Word scatterplot of two genres rated on first two principal components**

very little about that form's inner structure. If all men in an audience wore pink, and all women blue, the colors would differentiate them *perfectly*, and tell us *nothing* about them. We'll return to this point at the end of the article.

Now, one thing that the charts made clear was the *variability* of genre signals: quite strong in **Figures 1.11–12**, for instance, but rather weak in about one-fourth of the cases—like **Figures 1.15–16**, where neither MFW nor Docuscope managed to extricate national tales from silver-fork novels. Why some genres should be so hard to separate—especially in a case like this, where the difference, intuitively, ought to be quite vivid—was an intriguing question; but we decided to leave it for another study, and

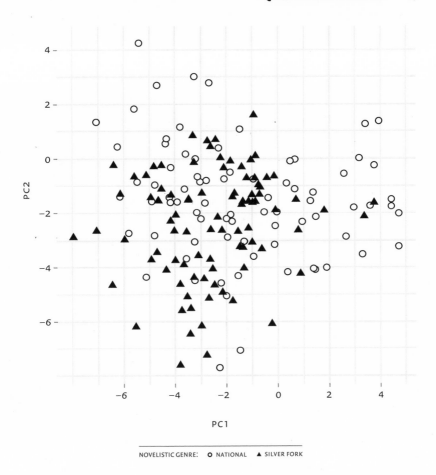

NOVELISTIC GENRE: O NATIONAL ▲ SILVER FORK

FIGURE 1.16 **Docuscope scatterplot of two genres rated on first two principal components**

focus instead on a group of charts for which the separation was rather good, and dependent on a recurring set of traits: the pairings of gothic novels with the three "ideological" genres—Jacobin, anti-Jacobin, and evangelical novels—that were their short-lived contemporaries.[19] Since the charts were all similar, we reproduce here only the gothic/Jacobin pairings:

19 One of our problems was that we had automated our comparisons, using only the first two (and therefore, most powerful) principal components to pull apart the genres. Of course, PCA generates multiple components and there are ways of establishing (for example, the Tukey test) whether any given component sorts two groups. But we wanted some raw measure of "sortability" among pairs, which is what led us to simply profile all the pairs on their first two components and leave other—potentially quite powerful—components aside.

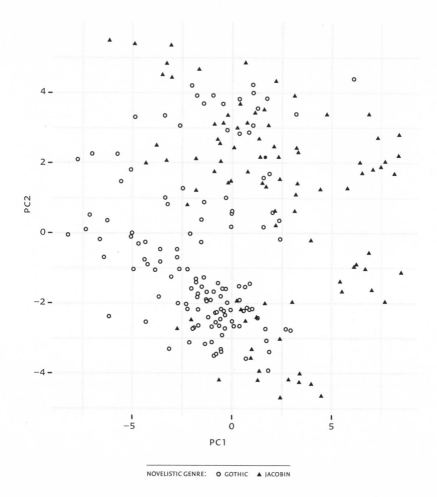

NOVELISTIC GENRE: O GOTHIC   ▲ JACOBIN

FIGURE 1.17 **Most Frequent Word scatterplot of two genres rated on first two principal components**

Figures 1.17–18, based on MFW, and **Figures 1.19–20**, based on Docuscope and its Dimensions.

To better understand the relationship between the two genres—and to begin to put the figures into language—we looked closely at the features that were particularly effective at separating gothic from Jacobin along the first principal component (PC1: the x-axis in **Figures 1.17–20**). A principal component ranks the likelihood of certain features occurring, so texts are sorted according to the features they lack, as well as by the features they have.

Roughly speaking, we found that the gothic novel averages less talk and more action than the Jacobin. Words and phrases that characterize

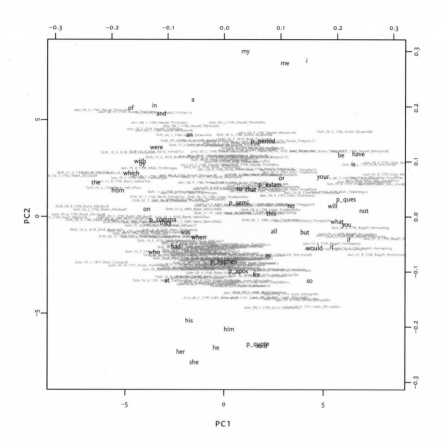

FIGURE 1.18 **Most Frequent Word scatterplot with titles (light gray) and component loadings (black)**

gothic texts show a marked "narrative" inclination: past tense and pronouns; spatial prepositions; and words marked by Docuscope as "Narrative Time" (for example, *whilst, when he, as he*). See in MFW, on the left side of **Figure 1.18**: *was, had, who, she, he, her, his, they*, the ubiquitous *the*, and the large group of locative prepositions *from, on, in, at*; in Docuscope, on the left side of **Figure 1.20**, see Narrative VP (for example, *heard the, reached the, commanded the*) and Pronouns. Markers associated with oral discourse, on the other hand, tend not to occur in gothic novels: a foregrounding of the addressee (*you, your*), questions, polemical markers (*but, no*), and verbs inflected in the present, future, and conditional. In MFW,

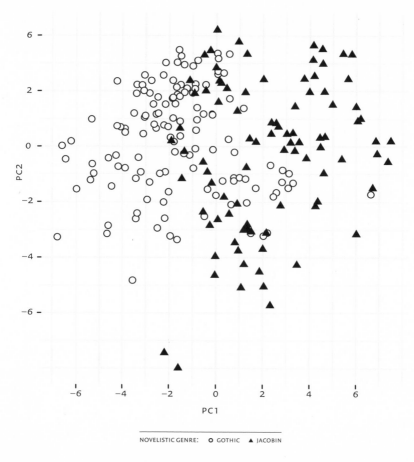

NOVELISTIC GENRE: O GOTHIC   ▲ JACOBIN

FIGURE 1.19 **Docuscope scatterplot of two genres rated on first two principal components**

note on the right-hand side of **Figure 1.18** the cluster of *you, p_ques, but, if, not, is, will,* and *would*; in Docuscope, on the right of **Figure 1.20**, see Questions, Oppositional Reasoning (*not, but, however*), and, just below it, Directives (*should, must, you will soon*). Though Jacobin texts generally tack in this direction, they are more scattered than the gothic ones. What separates the genres here seems to be not so much the absence of narrative in Jacobin texts, but the presence of talk, something like an argumentative style.

Such, then, were the raw data that our analytic techniques had placed in front of us. Could they become good interpretive questions? We tried. Noticing, for instance, the high frequency of the conditional in the

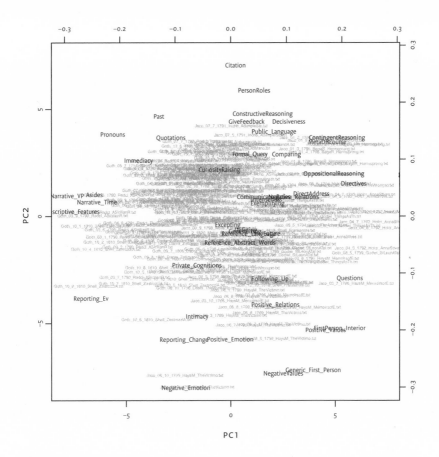

FIGURE 1.20 **Most Frequent Word scatterplot with titles (light gray) and component loadings (black)**

ideological genres—where, indeed, possibility is important—Jockers and Moretti compiled a list of the (more or less) thirteen thousand sentences that included "would"; looked at the associated pronouns, adjectives, and adverbs; at the types of verbs involved; at the negative forms, the past tense, and so on. A few results stood out: *would+never* occurred twice as often in the gloomy evangelical novels as elsewhere, for instance; and the impersonal pronoun *it* was 50 percent more frequent in Jacobin and anti-Jacobin novels—full of abstract discussions of principle—than anywhere else. Both findings made perfect sense. But were they also surprising? They certainly corroborated and enriched existing knowledge of the genres in question. Did they also *change* it?

7. EXPERIMENTS, EXPLORATIONS, HYPOTHESES

In March 2010, we met for one last retrospective glance at a year of work. Why had we turned to Docuscope and MFW in the first place? Because we were looking for an explicit, quantifiable way to assign texts to this or that genre. It was, in part at least, a matter of attribution. Attribution . . . "To trace every piece to its real creator," writes Carlo Ginzburg,

> we should not depend . . . on the most conspicuous characteristics of a painting, which are the easiest to imitate: eyes raised towards the heavens in the figures of Perugino, Leonardo's smiles, and so on. We should examine, instead, the most trivial details that would have been influenced least by the mannerisms of the artist's school: earlobes, fingernails, shapes of fingers and of toes.

Earlobes, fingernails . . . It is in these "involuntary signs," Ginzburg continues,

> in the "material trifles"—a calligrapher might call them "flourishes"— comparable to "favorite words and phrases" which "most people introduce into their speaking and writing unintentionally, often without realizing it," that Morelli recognized the surest clue to an artist's identity.[20]

Involuntary signs: this is certainly what MFW and LATs are. But are they *just* that? Clearly, there is a problem with earlobes and fingernails: good as they might be at identifying the author of a painting, they are worthless at explaining its meaning. In fact, they are good at the one *because* they are bad at the other: it's only because "trifles" have no structural function that authors let go and "write unintentionally, without realizing it"—thus betraying themselves. If those words were important, they would be more careful.

There is something paradoxical in these traits that classify so well, and explain so little. Especially so in our case: after all, MFW and LATs were in at least one respect the very opposite of earlobes and fingernails: instead of being rare and peripheral details, they were so frequent as to be almost

---

20 Carlo Ginzburg, *Clues, Myths, and the Historical Method*, trans. John and Anne C. Tedeschi (Baltimore: Johns Hopkins University Press, 1989), 88, 107.

ubiquitous. How could such pervasive traits tell us nothing about the structure of genre? It was possible, of course, that it was all our fault; that, although we had managed to isolate the data, and were probably the first to "see" them, we just didn't know how to make sense of them. Possible; and we are ready to place our data at the disposal of others, who may obtain better results.

But there is also a simpler explanation: namely, that these features, which are so effective at differentiating genres, and so entwined with their overall texture—these features cannot offer new insights into structure, *because they aren't independent traits, but mere consequences of higher-order choices*. Do you want to write a story where each and every room may be full of surprises? Then locative prepositions, articles, and verbs in the past tense are bound to follow. They are the *effects* of the chosen narrative structure. And, yes, once Docuscope and MFW foreground them, making us fully aware of their presence, our knowledge is analytically enriched: we "see" the space of the gothic, or the link between action verbs and objects (highlighted by the frequency of articles), with much greater clarity. But, for the time being, the gain seems to be comparative more than qualitative: greater clarity, rather than clarity of a different type.

We started with an experiment: testing the classifying power of Docuscope in a new and controlled setting. The experiment then turned into an exploration: Docuscope and MFW, charting the field of novelistic genres, and their inner composition. "Exploratory Data Analysis," as John Tukey has called it: detective work, focusing on clues that lead to new questions, and a broader understanding of the data. Statistical findings, said Heuser, made us realize that genres are icebergs: with a visible portion floating above the water, and a much larger part hidden below, and extending to unknown depths. Realizing that these depths exist; that they can be systematically explored; and that they may lead to a multidimensional reconceptualization of genre: such, we think, are solid findings of our research. Now more explorations are on the horizon: the switch from unsupervised to supervised techniques, for instance; or the explicit inclusion of semantic data, which we have so far mostly avoided so as to focus more strictly on the formal properties of genres. And then, at the end of it all, the great challenge of experimental work: the construction of hypotheses and models capable of explaining the data. This study is a step in that direction.

CHAPTER 2

Style at the Scale of the Sentence

Sarah Allison, Marissa Gemma, Ryan Heuser, Franco Moretti, Amir Tevel, Irena Yamboliev

In April 2011, the Literary Lab held a broad retrospective discussion of its first year's work. Among other things, we talked about "Quantitative Formalism" and wondered whether its object had been style, as we had rather casually claimed at some points in the pamphlet, or whether the method followed had been too reductionist to capture that elusive object. Could the different frequencies of *she* and *you* and *the* really be called "style"? On this, we disagreed. Some of us claimed that, though all styles do entail linguistic choices, not all linguistic choices create style; others countered this argument by stating that style follows necessarily from this fundamental level and that all we need to analyze it is the set of linguistic choices made by an author or a genre. This was the genuinely reductionist position—style as *nothing but* its components—and the more logically consistent one; the other position admitted that it couldn't specify the exact difference or the precise moment when a "linguistic choice" turned into a "style," but it insisted nonetheless that reducing style to a strictly functional dimension missed the very point of the concept, which lay in its capacity to hint, however hazily, at something that went *beyond* functionality. Our job should consist of removing the haze, not disregarding the hint.

We will return at the end to the "not merely functional" nature of style. For now, let's just say that since the antireductionist position was the more common one, we used it as the basis for developing the next stage of the argument. We considered a series of linguistic structures of increasing complexity to try and capture the moment at which style became visible. The series went something like this: gothic novels have many locative prepositions; but a thousand occurrences of *from, on, in*, and *at* are not style in any conceivable sense of the word. Jacobin novels have a lot of conditionals; a little better, perhaps, but not much. Then came the formula Franco Moretti had noticed in gothic titles and analyzed a few years earlier in "Style, Inc.: Reflections on 7,000 Titles": "The X of Y."[1] *The Castle of Otranto*, or *The Rock of Glotzden*: the formula was a perfect expression of the gothic obsession with space. But, once more, functionality was not really style. The next layer was a formula that Gemma had identified in Poe and discussed in her dissertation: "The X of Y of Z," she had called it—as in *The Fall of the House of Usher*, or "the gray stones of the home of his forefathers." This authorial exaggeration of a generic trait, with its defiance of any mere functionality, offered a first glimpse of what we were looking for; maybe it was style, maybe it wasn't, but we were finally getting close. And with the next instance, the opening words of *Middlemarch*—"Miss Brooke had that kind of beauty which seems to be thrown into relief by poor dress"—we all agreed we had entered the territory of style proper. As Sarah Allison had shown in her dissertation's analysis of this type of sentence, a whole series of connections and transformations coalesce around the relative pronoun "which." As the past tense of the main clause becomes the present of the dependent one, narrative distance turns into engaged comment, and character description ("Miss Brooke had beauty") into a nuanced qualification of the type and meaning of that beauty.[2] One reads the sentence and immediately gets the sense of a work capable of modulating from novel into essay, and from the relative simplicity of the story to the subtlety of reflection. The sentence is certainly perfectly functional to the opening of a novel—but it also possesses many other layers of meaning, all closely interconnected. Now, *this* was style.

We had found a starting point. We would study not style as such, but style *at the scale of the sentence*—the lowest level, it seemed, at which style as a distinct phenomenon became visible. Implicitly, we were defining style as a combination of smaller linguistic units, which made it, in consequence, particularly sensitive to changes in scale—from words to clauses to whole sentences. Yet we also hesitated, because the sentence

---

1 Reprinted in Moretti, *Distant Reading.*

2 A version of this argument appears in Sarah Allison, "Discerning Syntax: George Eliot's Relative Clauses," *ELH* 81, no. 4 (Winter 2014): 1275–97.

wasn't at all an obvious choice for stylistic analysis; Auerbach in *Mimesis* and Ian Watt in his essay on *The Ambassadors* had, for instance, operated at the quite different scale of the *paragraph*: ten, twenty, thirty lines that included a much greater variety of linguistic traits and could thus be seen (most clearly in *Mimesis*) as a model and miniature of the work as a whole.[3] Sentences seemed much too short to play the same role. Perhaps they could play a different one? Did something happen at the scale of the sentence *that could not happen at any other scale*?

2. SENTENCE TYPES: THE INITIAL CHOICE

We would be studying sentences, then. And, given that a long tradition of narrative theory—from Émile Benveniste's *Problems in General Linguistics* to Roland Barthes's *Writing Degree Zero* and Harald Weinrich's *Tempus*—had recognized a categorical difference between story and discourse, we began by separating the sentences that belonged to the dialogue among characters from those that belonged to the narrative system.[4] We needed texts where speech was marked with enough clarity and consistency for our tagger to recognize it, so we turned to the Chadwyck-Healey 19th-century database and separated the sentences into three types: those containing dialogue, those containing a mixture of narrative and dialogue, and those containing only narrative. Allison and Moretti concentrated on the "mixed sentences," where the intersection of dialogue and narrative—which had not been much studied by narrative theory—seemed to promise interesting stylistic effects; but this line of inquiry quickly became so specific that we decided it would require a study of its own. Meanwhile, Gemma, Heuser, Tevel, and Yamboliev chose to focus exclusively on narrative sentences and on a few well-defined combinations of clauses. **Figure 2.1** shows the one- and two-clause sentences that quickly emerged as the most prevalent in the corpus.

---

3 Erich Auerbach, *Mimesis*, trans. Willard R. Trask (Princeton, NJ: Princeton University Press, 1974); Ian Watt, "The First Paragraph of *The Ambassadors*: An Explication," in *Twentieth Century Interpretations of The Ambassadors*, ed. A. E. Stone, Jr. (Englewood Cliffs, NJ: Prentice-Hall, 1969), 75–87.

4 Émile Benveniste, *Problems in General Linguistics*, trans. Mary Elizabeth Meek (Coral Gables, FL: University of Miami Press, 1971); Roland Barthes, *Writing Degree Zero*, trans. Annette Lavers and Colin Smith (New York: Hill and Wang, 1967); Harald Weinrich, *Tempus* (Stuttgart: W. Kohlhammer, 1964).

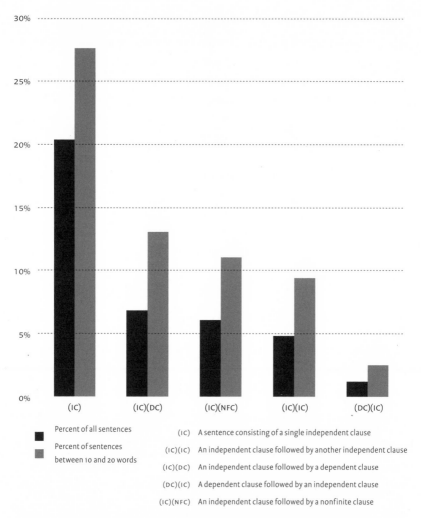

FIGURE 2.1 **Distribution of sentence types by clause combination in the 19th-century novel corpus.** As the chart shows, these five sentence types account for 40 percent of all narrative sentences and about 65 percent of sentences between ten and twenty words.

Initially, the group concentrated on three types above all others: IC-IC sentences, which consisted of two independent clauses; IC-DC, where an independent clause was followed by a dependent one; and DC-IC, where the dependent clause preceded the independent one. Two-clause sequences established a relationship between propositions that—in line with our initial plan—might allow us to see style emerging from their combination, while remaining small enough to capture the narrative or semantic logic contained therein. Here, the turning point of the entire project occurred. Allison suggested that we start with conjunctions, as they provided a grammatical condensation of a logico-semantic relationship—adversative, causal, coordinating, correlative, defining, predicative, etc.[5]—and were thus the perfect place to begin our investigation. By and large, we expected that the *distribution* of the logico-semantic relationship would be extremely variable—with texts inclining toward the causal register, or the predicative, or the coordinating one—while the *order* of the clauses would often be completely unrelated to logical function; so that, for example, a text with a preference for "narrative sequencing"[6] would be equally likely to express such relations in IC-DC sentences as in DC-IC ones.[7] But the results of our inquiry—summarized in **Figure 2.2**—surprised us.

For us, the most striking aspect of this figure was the radical asymmetry between two logico-semantic relationships and two sentence types: the "sequencing" relation, which appeared in 51 percent of the DC-IC sentences but only 13 percent of the IC-DC ones, and the "defining" relation, which appeared in 41 percent of IC-DC and a mere 5 percent of DC-IC. The asymmetry was so marked that, at the meeting when it was first presented,

---

5 Needless to say, grammatical nomenclature nowadays is highly variable: in the main, we have followed the categories of Rodney Huddleston and George K. Pullum's *Cambridge Grammar of the English Language* (Cambridge, UK: Cambridge University Press, 2002).

6 Our notion of a "sequencing" relation between clauses is based on the *Cambridge Grammar*'s discussion of "temporal sequence," where the ordering of events is indicated by the coordinating conjunction "and": "his companion smiled; and he left the room" (Brontë). As we aimed to capture the full spectrum of temporal ordering conveyed by conjunctions, we found it necessary to expand the category of "sequencing" to include both coordination and subordination. "Sequencing" relations are for us those in which the conjunction creates any temporal order—linear, nonlinear, or simultaneous. As a result, sentences like "Before the shades of evening had closed around us, I had a dozen awakening letters for my aunt, instead of a dozen awakening books" (Collins) and "While I was anticipating the terrors of a heroine, he introduced me to his Cardinal" (Disraeli) are tagged as "sequencing" sentences.

7 One case in which we did not expect the order of clauses to be unrelated to function was that of the "defining" relation. Like the category of "sequencing," we based our category of "defining" relations on grammatical terminology: a defining sentence is one in which the relative clause—that is, a dependent clause using "which," "who," or "that"—defines or characterizes the other clause: "This was Mrs Finn, the wife of Phineas Finn, who had been one of the Duke's colleagues when in office" (Trollope). Since it is nearly impossible to place a dependent defining clause before the clause that it elaborates, it makes grammatical sense that we would find more defining sentences in IC-DCs (like the Trollope example here). And indeed, our findings for the order of clauses among "defining" sentences conformed neatly to the demands of grammatical correctness—and thus proved rather unproductive for our literary analysis.

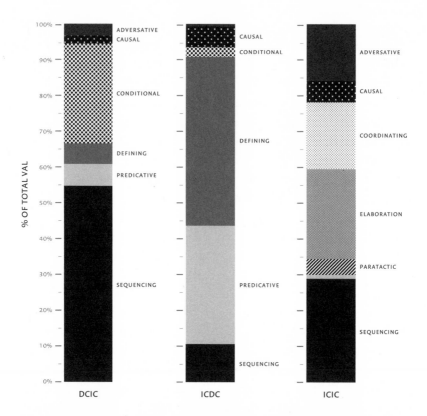

FIGURE 2.2 **Distribution of the prominent clause relations across sentence type.** Notice the almost perfectly inverse relationship between the DC-IC, dominated by a "sequencing" and "conditional" relationship, and the IC-DC, almost entirely taken by "predicative" and "defining" ones. (We used "defining" to categorize both restrictive and nonrestrictive relative clauses, since we found that distinguishing between them did not substantively add to our analysis. For the fine-grained distinctions between these types of clauses, see Huddleston and Pullum.) The IC-IC, for its part, resembles neither of the two other sentence types, and specializes in coordination and, to a lesser extent, parataxis.

it was received with a lot of ambivalence: though the IC-DC findings could be explained by grammatical necessity, what about the DC-ICs? We had been looking for the emergence of style ("Miss Brooke had that kind of beauty . . .")—but the structure of DC-IC sentences seemed to alert the reader to *narrative* developments instead. From the very first word, its inner form implied a preparation, then a pause—"When the day came round for my return to the scene of the deed of violence,"—and then, after the comma, the rapid completion of the mini-sequence ("my terrors reached their height" [Dickens]). When, as in **Figure 2.3**, we noticed that 86 percent of Radcliffe's

SENTENCE TYPE

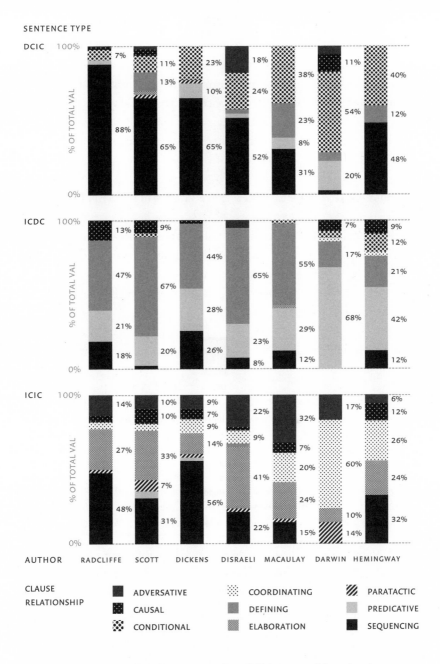

FIGURE 2.3 **Sentence types: the spectrum of possibilities.** Some of the authors in our corpus (like Dickens and Radcliffe) overwhelmingly favored sequencing over other possible relations, while others (Scott and Disraeli) were more moderate. Most strikingly, Darwin used almost no sequencing (2 percent) compared with Radcliffe's stunning 86 percent.

DC-IC sentences had a "sequencing" function, we felt we had found a very significant metric of narrativity—especially when we compared these results with our nonnarrative control text, Charles Darwin's *On the Origin of Species*, in which such sentences were nearly absent (2 percent). But this metric seemed to have little to do with the concept of style. And when, a few weeks later, Tevel found some unexpected narrative traits in IC-DC sentences, the switch in focus from style to narrative seemed even more inevitable.

3. TOWARD A TYPOLOGY OF NARRATIVE SENTENCES

While working on the structure of IC-DC sentences—which, as we have noted, generally have much more to do with predication and definition than with sequencing—Tevel noticed among predicative and defining sentences an embedded narrative configuration that seemed typical of them. Here are a few examples:

> **2.a** Her extreme beauty softened the inquisitor who had spoken last. (Percy Shelley)
>
> But no matter; I will be the friend, the brother, the protector of the girl who has thrown herself into my arms. (Charlotte Dacre)
>
> It was then offered to the Palmer, who, after a low obeisance, tasted a few drops. (Walter Scott)
>
> He uttered an involuntary exclamation, and called to the driver, who brought the horses to a stop with all speed. (Charles Dickens)
>
> Fanny called the post-boy to the window of the chaise, and gave him directions, at which he a little stared, but said nothing. (Mary Shelley)

In looking at these sentences, Tevel noticed that the dependent clause did two things at once: it introduced *a different character* from the subject of the main clause—the post-boy, the driver, the inquisitor, the Palmer, the girl who had thrown herself—while also allowing these newcomers *a very limited role* in the text: the post-boy stares but says nothing, the driver stops the horses, the Palmer tastes a few drops. It's an opening of the story to the Many, to use Alex Woloch's term for minor characters, but these Many get to do only a little. A little, in the sense that they complete an already initiated sequence rather than inaugurate an independent action. The syntax itself nudges writers in this direction: since it's hard to imagine a dependent clause that does something independent from the main clause, these (half) sentences slide almost "naturally" into a form of *narrative attenuation*. They narrate—but minor episodes only. Arthur Conan Doyle used the unconscious expectations arising from this grammatical fact to perfection when he placed clues in dependent clauses, thus making them visible while suggesting to readers that nothing important was being said.[8] In the following example, for instance, the smell of the cigar, which is the decisive piece of information, appears only as the third link of a tight chain of subordinates, and is further deflected in a nonnarrative direction by the relative clause that follows:

> That fatal night Dr Roylott had gone to his room early, though we knew that he had not retired to rest, for my sister was troubled by the smell of the strong Indian cigars which it was his custom to smoke. ("The Adventure of the Speckled Band")

This, then, was the characteristic narrative function of these IC-DC sentences. And when we turned to DC-IC sentences, the mirror-image configuration emerged: here, the dependent clause—which of course in this case *preceded* the main clause rather than following it—tended to report a muted preparatory event, while the main clause included the more surprising one:

2.b   While she looked on him, his features changed and seemed convulsed in the agonies of death. (Ann Radcliffe)

When it was once fairly put before her, the effect was appalling. (Benjamin Disraeli)

When she awoke, it was to the sound of guns. (George Eliot)

---

8 As always, Viktor Shklovsky understood it all a century ago: "[In the Holmes stories] instructions are given not directly but in passing (i.e., in subordinate clauses, on which the storyteller does not dwell, but which are nonetheless of major importance). . . . This clue is intentionally placed in the oblique form of a subordinate clause." (Viktor Shklovsky, *Theory of Prose*, trans. Benjamin Sher (Elmwood Park, IL: Dalkey Archive Press, 1990), 106).

In all these examples, the shift in grammatical subject—she/his features, it/the effect, she/guns—coincided with an increase in narrative intensity: a semantic crescendo—agonies, appalling, explosions—that mirrored the diminuendo we had found in IC-DC. It was as if these two types of sentences embodied the systole and diastole of the narrative system: contraction-attenuation in IC-DC, and expansion-intensification in DC-IC. As both functions are indispensable to storytelling, we decided to try and find out whether expansion and contraction alternated as regularly in novels as they do in living organisms, and we began by looking for the diastolic-systolic patterns of the other three most frequent types of narrative sentences (IC, IC-IC, IC-NFC—non-finite clause). Here, the most interesting result was Yamboliev's discovery that, in a (relatively small) group of IC-IC sentences, the relationship between the two clauses was one of slight elaboration, or reiteration, or restatement. In other words, fundamentally, of *stasis*:

2.c   Perseverance alone was requisite, and I could persevere. (Thomas Holcroft)

She raised her head; she lifted her hand and pointed steadily to the envelopes. (Wilkie Collins)

Oh she looked very pretty, she looked very, very pretty! (Charles Dickens)

Will Ladislaw, meanwhile, was mortified, and knew the reason of it clearly enough. (George Eliot)

He showed no sign of displeasure; he hardly noticed. (William Francis Barry)

As stories have to intensify, attenuate, and remain in some way static, Yamboliev's finding seemed intuitively right; and when a large group of IC-NFC, with gerunds in the dependent clause, added the nuance of actions moving parallel to each other and overlapping in the process, a genuine typology of narrative sentences seemed within reach—and with it, the possibility of "sequencing" entire novels, charting the distribution of narrative intensity throughout their length.

But there were two obstacles on the road to the narrative genomics we were beginning to envision. First, in order to identify the signs of narrative intensity in the thousands of sentences contained in a single novel, or the millions of a broader corpus, we had to find a way to machine-gather the evidence. Our parser was, however, far from perfect even at recognizing the five main sentence types; anything needing a finer grain—like expansion, contraction, inertia, and so on—would make it completely unreliable. And then, the two-clause sentences with a "sequencing" function that we had singled out were a small minority of a novel's narrative sentences[9]—even smaller if dialogue and "mixed" sentences were restored to the mix. If we wanted to chart narrative rhythm *at the scale of the novel as a whole*, we had to find a way of systematically integrating our small subset of sentences into the rest of the novelistic system.

We realized that ambition required patience. A general typology of narrative sentences, so clearly defined as to be recognizable by a computer program, needed its own ad hoc project.

4. SEMANTIC VECTORS

What we had found so far were striking correlations between particular syntactic forms and two seemingly unrelated domains—logical relations like "causal" or "sequencing," and effects of narrative rhythm like "attenuation" or "stasis." How far might these links extend? Could sentence structures be so powerful as to make certain words more likely to appear, thus establishing a link between syntax and semantics? This additional correlation seemed unlikely but worth exploring: in contrast to higher-order domains like logic and narrative rhythm (which require human annotation), the likelihood of a word's occurrence can be quantified automatically by a computer. We took all the words in all the sentences of our corpus and calculated their average, or "expected," frequency; then we calculated the actual—or "observed"—occurrence in each sentence type; finally, we focused on those instances that revealed a significant observed-over-expected ratio. We had developed this procedure, called Most Distinctive Words, in a study of drama. Some results leapt immediately leapt to the

---

9 If only taking into account two-clause sentences, the total of these "sequencing" sentences would be about 9 percent of all narrative sentences; if including also single-clause ICs (those that "sequence" a shift between states or events in a single clause) the total would rise to 28 percent.

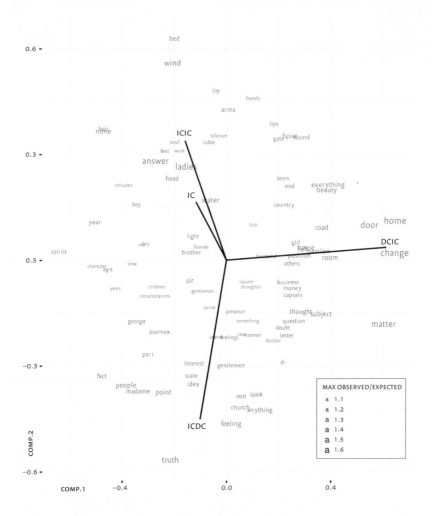

FIGURE 2.4 **Sentence types and their semantic space (all words)**

eye,[10] but the approach remained fundamentally atomistic: analysis could only proceed one word at a time. By contrast, principal component analysis offered a synthetic view of the entire semantic distribution of four sentence types with a single image (**Figures 2.4** and **2.5**).

Looking at the semantic differentiation of **Figures 2.4** and **2.5**, the differences between the four sentence types—or three, considering that

---

10 Two figures included in the original pamphlet but omitted here may be found at http://litlab. stanford.edu/LiteraryLabPamphlet5.pdf.

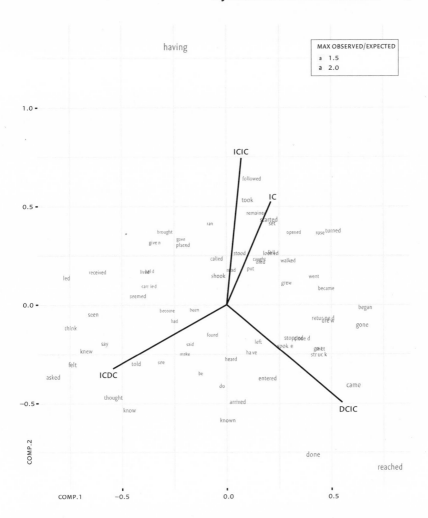

FIGURE 2.5 **Sentence types and their semantic space (verbs).** These charts (**Figure 2.4** and **Figure 2.5**) express several variables at once. Font size indicates the "distinctiveness," that is to say, the observed-over-expected ratio of a word: the rather large *having*, at the top of **Figure 2.5**, occurs 2.4 times more frequently than one would expect, whereas the slightly smaller *came*, on the lower right, only 1.6 times. In addition to font size indicating relative frequency, what most matters here is the spatial position of the various words: *came*, on the right side, and having, at the top, are where they are because they are correlated with the black lines (the "vectors") that represent, respectively, DC-IC and IC-IC; while *knew*, *felt*, and *thought* are on the right side because they are correlated with IC-DC. What emerges clearly is that although there are four sentence types involved, there are only three semantic "positions": IC and IC-IC tend to share the same semantic traits, and hence the same space in the diagram. This suggests, somewhat surprisingly, that while the introduction of a dependent clause produces a distinct semantic space, the introduction of a second independent clause is characterized mostly by redundancy and repetition.

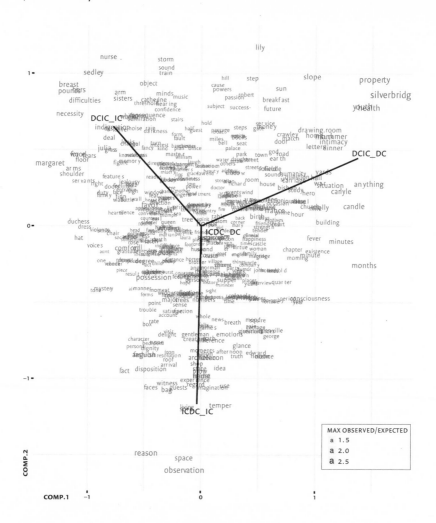

FIGURE 2.6 **Two-clause sentences and their semantic spaces**

IC and IC-IC occupied the same semantic space—were acquiring more definite contours. In several cases, though, the results were somewhat puzzling: finding *home*, *door*, and *change* as very typical of DC-IC on the right side of the chart, for instance, one couldn't help but wonder what on earth the first two terms had to do with the third. Then we realized that we could push the analysis a step further: eliminate IC and IC-IC, for instance, and use principal component analysis to differentiate not only between the various *sentence* types but between their *clauses* as well. If semantic differences emerged among sentences, perhaps they would also emerge within them: between the dependent and independent clause of DC-IC, for instance, or between the independent clause of DC-IC and that of IC-DC. And indeed, as **Figure 2.6** shows, a semantic separation occurred at this lower scale as well.

The odd trio of *home, door,* and *change,* for instance—whose coexistence near the DC-IC vector of **Figure 2.4** had so puzzled us—disaggregated into two very different semantic fields: *home* and *door* (plus *drawing-room, hall, church, gate, carriage, road,* and other spatial terms) turned out to be typical of the dependent clause in the upper-right quadrant of the chart, whereas *change* (plus *matter, feelings, indignation, despair, admiration, tears*) all clustered around the independent one, in the upper-left quadrant. And the more one looked, the clearer the semantic distance between the dependent and independent clause of DC-IC became.[11]

A correlation between grammar and semantics was thus beginning to emerge. Not a *necessary* correlation: rather a "line of least resistance," as Roman Jakobson had put it, in linking metaphors to poetry and metonymies to prose; a "preference," more than anything else, that attracted space to the dependent clause of DC-IC and strong emotions to the independent one. It was to this strange elective affinity emerging from the most "narrative" of our sentence types that we now turned our attention.

5. "WHEN THE PROCESSION CAME TO THE GRAVE"

2.d When the procession **came to the grave** the music ceased. (Ann Radcliffe)

As they landed, a low growl of thunder was heard at a distance. (Walter Scott)

As she **came out of church**, she was joined by Mr Bellingham. (Elizabeth Gaskell)

---

11 IC-DC sentences behaved somewhat differently: the independent clause possessed its own specific semantic pole (*idea, reason, observation, imagination, hate*), but the vector of the dependent clause was far less specified than the other three, as shown by its greater proximity to the center of the diagram. Given that these dependent clauses are often relative ones, which must be free to move in multiple semantic directions, their not being committed to any specific semantic domain intuitively seemed appropriate.

> As I **passed the steps of the portico**, I encountered, at the corner, a woman's face. (Charles Dickens)

> When they **were in the streets** Esther hardly spoke. (George Eliot)

Five different DC-IC sentences, from a large random sample that included very different authors, and always the same pattern: a spatial movement (bolded) occurs, *and then something else happens*: thunder growls, Mr. Bellingham joins the heroine, a woman's face appears. If DC-IC sentences are in charge of narrative expansion, as we wrote a few pages back, these examples add the further specification that *a spatial movement in the dependent clause is often the springboard of narrativity*: first Ruth has to leave the church, and only then does the man who will ultimately seduce her approach. In the 19th century the milieu enters European narrative and space becomes a more tangible presence; but as the example of Auerbach's *Mimesis* makes clear, the obvious place for space and the milieu is within novelistic *descriptions*. Instead, we had found them at the very source—at the *microscopic* source, one could almost say—of narrative developments. It was strange.

And when we turned to the independent clause of DC-IC sentences, a comparable surprise was awaiting us. As the DC-IC is the sentence of narrative intensification, and perhaps even acceleration, we expected its main clause—which is where intensity increases—to resemble the Radcliffe sentence quoted in **2.b** ("While she looked on him, *his features changed and seemed convulsed in the agonies of death*") or this one from Dickens: "As I watched him in silence, he put his hand into the corner at his side, *and took up a gun*." Instead, this is what we found:

2.e   When the ceremony was over he blessed and embraced them all with tears of fatherly affection. (Radcliffe)

As he recovered from a sort of half swoon, he cast his eyes eagerly around. (Scott)

While he listened, she ended her grateful prayers. (Gaskell)

When Miss Dartle spoke again, it was through her set teeth, and with a stamp upon the ground. (Dickens)

When Esther looked at him she relented, and <u>felt ashamed of her gratuitous impatience</u>. (Eliot)

In case after case, the semantic center of gravity of the independent clause had much more to do with *emotions* (sorrow, gratitude, shame, anger) than with guns or throes of death. When a narrative intensification occurred, in other words, feelings mattered much more than actions or events. Or perhaps, more precisely, emotional intensity was the event. It was a second surprise, and a third quickly followed when we shifted our attention from the two clauses taken separately to their combination. Since the semantic centers of gravity of the two clauses were so completely different—spatial movement in the dependent clause and the expression of emotions in the independent one—it made sense that, in general, one of them should occur while the other did not. But there were also quite a few cases in which the two semantic clusters were simultaneously activated:

2.f   When Peter **perceived the village**, he burst <u>into a shout of joy</u>. (Radcliffe)

When he **came up to Butler again**, he found him with his eyes fixed on the entrance of the Tolbooth, and <u>apparently in deep thought</u>. (Scott)

When she had got **behind the curtain**, she <u>jumped on her father's neck, and burst into tears</u>. (Disraeli)

When the day came round **for my return to the scene of the deed of violence**, <u>my terrors reached their height</u>. (Dickens)

When she **had once got to the seat** she <u>broke out with suppressed passion of grief</u>. (Gaskell)

When she **reached home** she found Mrs Pettifer there, <u>anxious for her return</u>. (Eliot)

We read these sentences with a mix of perplexity and disappointment: they were so—clumsy. Perhaps inevitably so: space and emotions—which express, respectively, the power of the "milieu" and the melodramatic undercurrent of the age—are such heterogeneous entities that combining them in the same short sentence may be simply impossible. And yet, every now and then, something seemed to happen:

2.g When Deronda **met Gwendolen and Grandcourt** on the staircase, his mind was seriously preoccupied. (Eliot)

But when he **came in**, she started up. (Gaskell)

Yet when he **arrived at Stone Court** he could not see the change in Raffles without a shock. (Eliot)

When **their hands fell again**, their eyes were bright with tears. (Eliot)

These are much more evocative sentences. Instead of being activated in a mechanically uninspired way, the relationship between space and emotions becomes sharp and dynamic: the "realism" of setting and the "melodrama" of feeling animate each other with an almost Balzacian energy. It was an interesting find, this meeting place between the two main axes of the 19th-century imagination. But once again, it wasn't really what we had been looking for. The strength and elegance of these sentences seemed to exceed the semantic peculiarities we had meant to study. Would we have to change direction one more time?

6. VERBS AND GENRES

Slightly. Now that we had quantified so many sentence-level features—number and types of clauses, sentence length, logical relations—we decided to make an explicit connection with the research conducted two years earlier in "Quantitative Formalism," where we had shown that the usage of the most frequent words (MFW) in English (like *the* and *of*) can accurately distinguish genres. Could sentence-level choices also distinguish genres? In other words, do genres have sentence styles? To answer this question, we tested which of our quantified sentence features (such as length, clause use and number, verb tense, and mood) could be used to meaningfully separate texts by genre. Among these features, it turned out that verb tense and mood were the most successful at creating generic distinctions. **Figures 2.7** and **2.8** show a couple of PCA charts from this

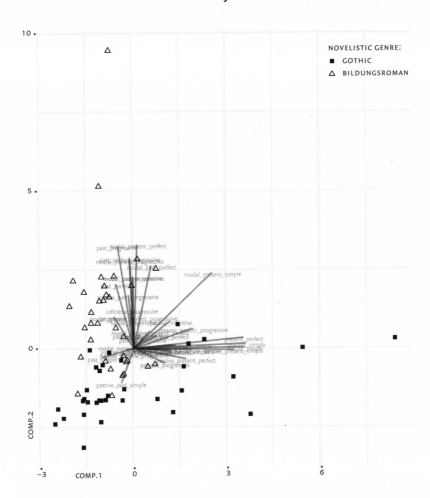

FIGURE 2.7 Verb forms as distinctive traits: gothic novels and bildungsromane. Figure 2.7 shows gothic novels (squares) clustering in the lower left quadrant, and the bildungsromane (triangles) in the quadrant above; **Figure 2.8** shows Jacobin novels (squares) spread along the horizontal axis left to right, and the bildungsromane in the same location as **2.7**. The units in the chart (Goth_03_0_1790_Radcl_ASicilianR in the bottom left corner of **2.8**, and Bild_06_1_1874_Eliot_ Middlemarc in the upper left one) are sections of the novels in our database, each containing 200 narrative sentences. The separation between the genres is equally clear in the two images, but the verb forms responsible for it are different: in the case of gothic they are the perfect and the passive past simple, whereas for the Jacobin novel the key tenses are the present and the future. (For the bildungsroman, on the other hand, modals and progressives remain constant as the key traits in both charts.)

Initially, we were taken aback by the fact that the past simple, or preterit, which a long theoretical tradition—from Benveniste to Barthes and Weinrich—had described as the fundamental tense of narration, played a negligible role in many of our charts. Placed slightly to the left of the point of origin of the vectors, along an axis where variance is seldom very strong, this tense contributes almost nothing to the separation between bildungsromane and gothic novels, which tends to be at its

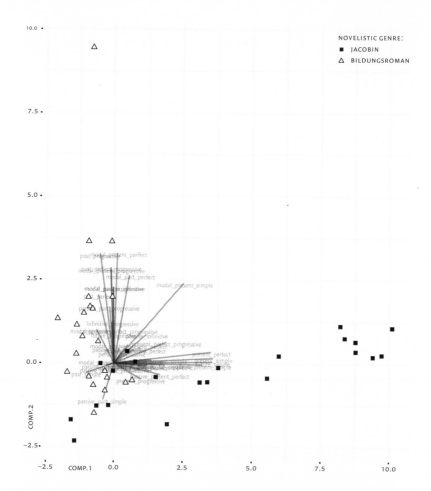

FIGURE 2.8 **Verb forms as distinctive traits: Jacobin novels and bildungsromane**

most dramatic along the vertical axis. On second thought, however, this lack of distinctiveness made sense: *precisely* because the simple past is the fundamental tense of narration, all novels use it quite often, and the increase in general frequency makes a strong variation from genre to genre unlikely. Perfect for telling apart novels from essays or scientific texts, the past simple is thus often useless in separating one novelistic genre from another. (Notice, however, that it *does* play a significant role in the case of Jacobin novels, with their strong orientation toward dialogue and away from narration.)

phase of our research, involving the bildungsroman, the gothic, and the Jacobin novel.

As chart followed chart, the results began to resemble those of "Quantitative Formalism": in most cases the separation was good, in others less so—but none of the charts was truly surprising. Except, that is, for one detail that kept sticking out in chart after chart (including a mega-diagram in which we plotted eleven genres at once, mostly out of curiosity to see what would happen): segment 1 of *Middlemarch* was a total, almost ridiculous outlier. So we took the 200 sentences contained in that segment and read them carefully.[12] The PCA charts had already told us that we would find a large number of modals and progressive forms.[13] Now the question was: Would this computer-generated series modify our understanding of the style of *Middlemarch*, or that of the bildungsroman as a genre? And if not, what was the point of the whole enterprise?

Let's begin with some instances of the progressive:

2.h   Mary was in her usual corner, **laughing** over Mrs Piozzi's recollections of Johnson, and looked up with the fun still in her face. It gradually faded as she saw Fred approach her without **speaking**, and stand before her with his elbow on the mantelpiece, **looking** ill. . . . She looked straight before her and took no notice of Fred, all the consequences at home **becoming** present to her. . . . Fred followed her with his eyes, **hoping** that they would meet hers, and in that way find access for his **imploring** penitence. . . . And when, **looking** up, her eyes met his dull **despairing** glance, her pity for him surmounted her anger and all her other anxieties.[14]

---

12 Very carefully, in fact. Were we therefore doing a "close reading" of *Middlemarch*? Almost certainly not, for the simple reason that we were not reading *Middlemarch* but rather a series that did not exist as such in the text; it was entirely an artifact of our own methodology, an "artificial" object that "no one had ever seen and no one could ever see," to quote Krzysztof Pomian's *L'Ordre du temps* (Paris: Gallimard, 1984). Although we try to be as attentive as any close reader to the details and formal properties of our sentences, the difference in the objects of analysis—a text versus an artificial series—makes the use of the same term for the two practices quite misleading: "quantitative formalism" remains a much better description of our methodology.

13 As will become clear in the examples below, the forms in *-ing* are not always progressives in the strict sense, but often gerunds or present participles. Though all these forms imply an event in progress, thus justifying a single, synthetic analysis, speaking simply of "progressives" is a misnomer, which we have had recourse to for lack of a more descriptive general category.

14 The beginning of chapter 25 of *Middlemarch*, where these sentences appear, contains an extremely large number of forms in *-ing*:

> Fred Vincy wanted to arrive at Stone Court when Mary could not expect him, and when his uncle was not down-stairs in that case she might be **sitting** alone in the wainscoted parlor. He left his horse in the yard to avoid **making** a noise on the gravel in front, and entered the parlor without other notice than the noise of the door-handle. Mary was in her usual corner, **laughing** over Mrs Piozzi's recollections of Johnson, and looked up with the fun still in her face. It gradually faded as she saw Fred

2.i   Lydgate, naturally, never thought of **staying** long with her, yet it seemed that the brief impersonal conversations they had together were **creating** that peculiar intimacy which consists in shyness. They were obliged to look at each other in **speaking**, and somehow the **looking** could not be carried through as the matter of course which it really was.

2.j   And by a sad contradiction Dorothea's ideas and resolves seemed like **melting** ice **floating** and lost in the warm flood of which they had been but another form.

The sentences in **2.h** come from the passage when Fred Vincy is about to confess to Mary Garth that he has lost a lot of money, thus creating serious financial problems for her family; **2.i**, from the moment when Rosamond and Lydgate become aware that they may be falling in love with each other; **2.j**, from the page when Dorothea's certainties about Casaubon begin to crumble. Very different situations, but with one trait in common: something important is about to happen—but hasn't yet fully crystallized. That's what the progressive (and the gerund) are for: presenting events as in progress, overlapping with others, not yet locked into a linear narrative; these are processes, more than results. Perfect for the novel of youth, a season of life whose point lies in developing, changing, *becoming*.

And now, modals:

2.k   If a man <u>could not love and be wise</u>, surely he could flirt and be wise at the same time? . . . Now Lydgate <u>might have called</u> at the warehouse, or <u>might have written</u> a message on a leaf of his pocket-book and left it at the door. . . . A man <u>may</u>, from various motives, <u>decline</u> to give his company, but perhaps not even a sage <u>would be gratified</u> that nobody missed him.

---

approach her without speaking, and stand before her with his elbow on the mantel-piece, **looking** ill. She too was silent, only **raising** her eyes to him inquiringly.

"Mary," he began, "I am a good-for-nothing blackguard."

"I should think one of those epithets would do at a time," said Mary, **trying** to smile, but **feeling** alarmed. . . .

"Oh, poor mother, poor father!" said Mary, her eyes **filling** with tears, and a little sob **rising** which she tried to repress. She looked straight before her and took no notice of Fred, all the consequences at home **becoming** present to her. He too remained silent for some moments, **feeling** more miserable than ever.

2.l   In this solemnly-pledged union of her life, duty <u>would present</u> itself
in some new form of inspiration and <u>give</u> a new meaning to wifely
love. . . . She felt a new companionship with it, as if it had an ear for
her and <u>could see</u> how she was looking at it. . . . She felt as if all her
morning's gloom <u>would vanish</u> if she <u>could see</u> her husband glad
because of her presence.

Here we are no longer in a fluid world of processes and transformations,
but in one of uncertainty, politeness, and subdued emotions. In **2.k**, for
instance, the modals express Lydgate's erotic desire for Rosamond under
the guise of impersonal and slightly ironic maxims: in part, a sign that
Lydgate is not taking his own eros too seriously; in part, that he's ready to
follow the Middlemarch notions of sexual decorum. By contrast, Dorothea's thoughts about her marriage in **2.l** offer a version of youthful desire
in which hopes too large to be expressed in the indicative ("duty would
present itself . . .") morph sorrowfully into a "morning gloom" and are
reborn only as a humble, hypothetical consolation ("would vanish if she
could see . . ."). In both cases, however, modals operate in a similar fashion: they take the open potentiality of the protagonists—youth, becoming—and overdetermine it with hermeneutic hesitation or the codes of
social conformity.

Did the study of our series modify our understanding of *Middlemarch*,
then, or of the style of the bildungsroman? The first impulse was to answer
both questions in the negative. That processes would be more important
than punctual events, and possibility would mix uneasily with conventions—these were well-known features of the bildungsroman, and it makes
sense to find them visible in the novel's very diction. But a comparison
with the analogous findings in "Quantitative Formalism" threw a different
light on the matter. The spatial prepositions in the gothic, we had written,
were clearly "consequences of higher-order choices": "*effects* of the chosen
narrative structure"—of the desire to have a story where "every room may
be full of surprises." No one would ever say that spatial prepositions *make*
a gothic novel. But can progressives and modals make a bildungsroman?
Maybe, maybe not, but the question is a real one: these sentence-level
choices don't just *descend* from the larger imperatives of the genre; they
can plausibly play a *causal* role in creating its overall atmosphere, shaping
the linguistic sensibility that makes readers intuitively grasp the "sense"

of the form as a whole. Progressives were "perfect" for the bildungsroman, as we wrote a few paragraphs above; perfect, yes, but not obvious. In theory, youth could have been defined just as well by a strong use of the future, for instance, rather than by the progressive. Once a writer starts using the latter, however, her decision has higher-order consequences: it emphasizes the (present) instability of youth over its (future) aims clearly enough; it shifts the narrative center of gravity from the novel's ending (which would be emphasized by a frequent recourse to the future) to its "middle," which is where transformations occur. The scale of the sentence has a much more *constructive* role than anything we had encountered in "Quantitative Formalism."

Then there was something else. Modals and progressives, though they both distinguish the bildungsroman from other genres, do so in very different ways. Progressives represent processes that are slow and perhaps inconclusive, but are definitely part of the reality of the plot: in **2.h**, Fred is perplexingly silent, the cause for his "looking ill" is unknown, and the consequences of his act are incalculable, but there is no question that all these indeterminate events are actually *happening*. Modals, on the other hand, represent what is being *merely imagined* by the characters and often protected from public scrutiny. The two verb forms embody that great polarity of "world" and "soul" that is essential to the bildungsroman: not just different but *antithetical* dimensions. And yet there are moments when the two suddenly converge:

2.m His obligations to Mr Casaubon were not known to his hearer, but Will himself was **thinking** of them, and **wishing** that he <u>could discharge</u> them all by a cheque. . . . The allusion to Mr Casaubon <u>would have spoiled</u> all if anything at that moment <u>could have spoiled</u> the **subduing** power, the sweet dignity, of her noble unsuspicious inexperience. . . . If he never said a cutting word about Mr Casaubon again and left off **receiving** favors from him, it <u>would clearly be permissible</u> to hate him the more.

2.n Moreover, Lydgate did not like the consciousness that in **voting** for Tyke he <u>should be</u> **voting** on the side obviously convenient for himself. . . . Other people <u>would say</u> so, and would allege that he was **currying** favor with Bulstrode for the sake of **making** himself important and **getting** on in the world.

The sentences in **2.m** refer to Will Ladislaw's attempt to balance his new desire for Dorothea with his old obligations toward her husband; those in **2.n**, to the vote for the hospital chaplaincy, when Lydgate feels torn between the assertion of his own autonomy and the incipient realization of the force of circumstances. In both episodes, the friction between reality, desires, and social norms is particularly harsh, and further strengthened by Eliot's virtuoso use of free indirect style, which makes it hard to separate the character's voice, social *doxa*, and the narrator's judgment.[15] Insofar as the bildungsroman presents a growing entanglement—a "web," in Eliot's famous trope—of factual processes, subjective hopes, and symbolic norms, these sentences offered a true distillation of *Middlemarch* as a whole. The novel in one sentence, one was tempted to say.

7. STYLE AT THE SCALE OF THE SENTENCE

It was time for some final reflections. We had begun by imagining a study of style. Then, our initial findings had made us switch our focus to narrative, and later to semantics. Finally, the space-emotions continuum of DC-IC and the orchestration of progressives and modals in *Middlemarch*—different as the two cases were—had created yet another scenario: elements that could exist perfectly well independently of each other (the delineation of space and the expression of emotions, the slow processes unfolding through progressives and the hypothetical worlds conjured up by modals) showed a tendency to become amalgamated into powerful composite sentences. And then we realized that the scenario wasn't new after all, since the sentence that had triggered our entire research—"Miss Brooke had that kind of beauty which

---

15 The Lydgate passage goes on endlessly oscillating between one register and the other, into the famous formulation: "For the first time Lydgate **was feeling** the **hampering** threadlike pressure of small social conditions, and their **frustrating** complexity. At the end of his inward debate, when he set out for the hospital, his hope was really in the chance that discussion might somehow give a new aspect to the question, and make the scale dip so as to exclude the necessity for voting. I think he trusted a little also to the energy which is begotten by circumstances—some feeling **rushing** warmly and **making** resolve easy, while debate in cool blood had only made it more difficult. However it was, he did not distinctly say to himself on which side he would vote; and all the while he **was inwardly resenting** the subjection which had been forced upon him. It would have seemed beforehand like a ridiculous piece of bad logic that he, with his unmixed resolutions of independence and his select purposes, would find himself at the very outset in the grasp of petty alternatives, each of which was repugnant to him."

seems to be thrown into relief by poor dress" (in the terms of this pamphlet, an IC-DC "defining" sentence)—was itself a product of the same mechanism: the narrative statement (Miss Brooke had a peculiar kind of beauty) and the essayistic specification (there is a kind of beauty that is emphasized by poor dress) could have perfectly well existed side by side without interacting; once linked, however, their convergence into a single short statement made the opening of *Middlemarch* impossible to forget.

A completely unrelated project (Moretti's book *The Bourgeois*) provided one more instance of the same phenomenon. This time, the process came in three stages. While working on *Robinson Crusoe*, Moretti had noticed an unusual frequency of final clauses (IC-NFC), interpreting them as the stamp of "instrumental reason" over Robinson's activity ("I did this, *in order to* do that"). Later, he noticed an even higher frequency of the mirror configuration (NFC-IC), in which the grammatical "aspect" of the past gerund suggested the mastery over the flow of time typical of Daniel Defoe's novel ("*having done* this, I then did that"). Finally, he had found several instances in which past gerund, main clause, and final clause (NFC-IC-NFC: "and *having stowed* my boat very safe, I *went* on shore *to look* about me") were so tightly interwoven that the sentence's very grammar, in its uninterrupted movement from past to present to future, seemed to embody that "forever renewed" activity that Max Weber had singled out as the psychological basis of capitalist accumulation. If there was a style of bourgeois laboriousness, Moretti had concluded, this was certainly it.[16]

If there was a style . . . After having been abandoned, the concept had returned to the center of our research. Defoe's interconnected clause chains, the modals and progressives of *Middlemarch*, the essayistic relative clause attached to a narrative statement, the space and emotions in DC-IC: in every instance, a specific style had "emerged"[17] from a pro-

---

16 Franco Moretti, *The Bourgeois: Between History and Literature* (2013).

17 Retrospectively, the concept of "emergence" explained the initial disagreement about reductionism. For reductionism, what happens at the most elementary levels of organization is really *all* that happens, and higher levels are simply a magnification of the basic processes. For the concept of emergence, by contrast, larger structures acquire properties that were not present in their separate components and that therefore cannot be explained on their basis. This said, there is a significant difference between our use of the concept of emergence and the one current in the natural and social sciences: in the latter, emergence indicates a process in which the agents involved (ants, passersby, competitors on the market, etc.), though continuously interacting, exist *independently* of one another in ways that are unimaginable for clauses and sentences belonging to the same text.

cess of syntactico-semantic condensation that was both *unexpected* and *reiterated*.[18] Style *was* this condensation. That was why the frame of the sentence—and of *two-clause* sentences in particular—had become so important for us: it was the smallest linguistic construct whose parts could freely coalesce into new, emergent complexes, *making the genesis of style empirically observable*. Two-clause sentences were the laboratories of literary style.

Style as a "condensation" of discrete elements within a sentence, then. We had encountered so many instances of this process, and so varied, that we had no doubts as to its existence. But why had the condensation occurred in the first place? Why had modals and progressives, or gerunds and final clauses, become so deeply associated within a single sentence? The best answer seemed to be: because they could. The semantic fields of space and emotions, or the verb forms of *Middlemarch* and *Robinson Crusoe*, were present in hundreds of clauses, which interacted in a variety of ways in the course of the novel. Their encounter was thus firmly in the realm of the possible—of the "*adjacent* possible," as Steven Johnson has called it, following Stuart Kauffman: good solutions that come into being not as inventions ex nihilo, but as lucky discoveries of a fertile relationship between already given and often widely circulating ideas.[19]

The "adjacent possible" was a great formula to capture both the nature and the emergence of style. As something that was merely *possible*, style did not have to be there for a given text to exist more or less in its current form. Eliot didn't *need* the "Miss Brooke" type of sentence in the same sense that she needed to resolve the various marriage plots of *Middlemarch*. At the same time, that sentence belonged not just to the realm of the possible but to the realm of the *adjacent* possible: given Eliot's passion for both storytelling and essayistic reflection, it was definitely likely to occur. Neither inevitable nor truly exceptional, style occupied a middle position between logical extremes, where borderline cases were necessarily frequent—as in the case of the "Is this style, or not?" of our initial discussion,

---

18 That style needs both deviation and repetition had been clearly formulated by Marissa Gemma in her dissertation: "I define style as a deviance from patterns that becomes a recurrent pattern itself; style emerges at the moment that it is both divergent enough from some norm to be noticeable and frequent enough to constitute a pattern of its own" ("Exceedingly Correct: Stylistic Polemics in Nineteenth-Century American Literature"[PhD diss., Stanford University, 2012]).

19 Steven Johnson, *Where Good Ideas Come From: The Natural History of Innovation* (New York: Riverhead, 2010).

or of the elusive border between success and failure in the space-emotions combinations at the end of section 5. This was why a slightly indeterminate definition such as "emerging from the condensation of independent elements" was so appropriate: there are concepts—like "blue," "bald," or "tadpole"—that signify *through* a certain amount of vagueness, rather than despite it,[20] and style is probably one of them. The uncertain boundaries of terms such as "condensation" and "elements" allowed us to see the peculiarity of the phenomenon of style, and its process of formation: trying to cleanse them of all fuzziness, and all borderline cases, would not make our understanding more precise, but destroy its possibility altogether.

Neither inevitable nor exceptional, style appeared as an eminently *comparative* fact: something that was not *necessary* to accomplish a given aim (which would amount to a functional definition of style) but that allowed that aim to be accomplished *better*. Subject to all sorts of unpredictable contingencies, style never really *had* to emerge. When it did so, however, it immediately became typical and recognizable: it distinguished an author, a genre, or a literary movement in the most direct and unambiguous way. Here, the decisive category seemed to remain that of the author: a fact that had already become evident in "Quantitative Formalism" and that returned in this study with the growing role played by Defoe and Eliot in the final sections. Here, however, the relationship between author and genre revealed something that we had completely missed in the earlier pamphlet. What Eliot did with her modals and progressives, or the mix of narration and comment, did not *contradict* the logic of the bildungsroman (the author *versus* the genre, as we had written in "Quantitative Formalism") but rather expressed its central point with particular cogency (the author as *the highest embodiment* of the genre). If every bildungsroman told the story of a young person and explicated it, on a distinct textual level, with the voice of a reflective adult narrator, *Middlemarch* showed the spark that arose from the direct encounter of the two planes. In Eliot's sentence, two separate generic "traits" had turned into a structure.

Style as a process of condensation that transcended what was strictly functional and necessary. The adjacent possible as the source of the condensation, and the author-genre dialectic as its historical horizon. And the sentence? Had anything happened at the scale of the sentence *that could*

---

20 See Rosanna Keefe and Peter Smith's *Vagueness: A Reader* (Cambridge, MA: MIT Press, 1997).

not have happened at any other scale? Compared to other units analyzed by stylistics, the sentence's brevity made it the perfect vehicle of textual *concentration*: taking the central meaning of a text and compressing it in such a way as to make it unforgettable. And it's not just a matter of brevity. When the "wisdom" of Eliot's comments is conveyed by a relative clause seamlessly blended into a narrative statement, her values seem to emerge "naturally" from the story that is unfolding rather than externally reflect on it. When Robinson's "forever renewed" activity is expressed by Defoe's NFC-IC-NFC—*"Having mastered* this difficulty, and *employed* a world of time about it, I *bestirred* myself *to see*, if possible, how to supply two wants"—bourgeois work ethic becomes inscribed in the novel's very grammar and hence enormously strengthened. The message becomes twice as effective, because it manifests itself not just as a specific statement but as a repeatable *linguistic practice*. Bourdieu:

> Structured structures predisposed to function as structuring structures, that is, as principles of the generation and structuring of practices and representations which can be objectively "regulated" and "regular" without in any way being the product of obedience to rules, objectively adapted to their goals without presupposing a conscious aiming at ends or an express mastery of the operations necessary to attain them.[21]

"Structured structures" that come into being by the slow accretion of distinct yet compatible elements; and that, without "consciously aiming" to do so, "regulate" the reader's "practice and representation" of temporality, or of possibility, or of ethical behavior. This is what style at the scale of the sentence can do: spacious enough to include a whole structure, it is also small enough to be easily grasped and absorbed, thus indeed "regulating" expression, as Bourdieu puts it. Style as habitus, in other words: as something that could spill over from grammar and literature into psychic structures and social interactions.

This broader, "social" notion of style, we concluded, deserved its own study. As for this pamphlet, its central contribution was simpler: a notion of style as combination and condensation, derived from the study of how

---

21 Pierre Bourdieu, *Outline of a Theory of Practice*, trans. Richard Nice (Cambridge, UK: Cambridge University Press, 1977), 72.

clauses combine. That style resulted from the combination of originally discrete elements, Gemma and Heuser observed during our final exchanges,
also meant that these elements could be independently formalized, and
that a computer program could gather and measure them. Our "definition"
of style also entailed, in other words, *a method of looking for it*: it was the
beginning of a possible "operationalizing" of the concept. It was precisely
as a result of our successful (though partial) operationalizing that we had
so often found ourselves in front of striking patterns—in particular, correlations between syntax and narrative, and syntax and semantics—that
our critical categories were incapable of explaining. The instructions we
had given our programs—that is, finding which elements of the sentence
vary according to syntactic choices, like beginning the sentence with a
dependent clause—had worked only too well, placing us in front of solid,
clear, and intuitively significant data, which we didn't quite know what to
do with. This seemed to be one of the most revolutionary aspects of the
digital humanities: one in which the "digital" challenged the "humanities"
with an entirely new type of problem.

But it was just as relevant, Gemma and Heuser added, that our programs *could neither detect nor explain the combinations that led to the
emergence of style*. Able to identify the separate parts of the process, the
programs were however blind to the significance of their interactions,
because the latter rested on conjectural connections between syntactical
choices and broader cultural phenomena, like the sudden convergence of
novel and essay, space and emotions, or past, present, and future. Here,
the "digital" clearly needed the "humanities" to make sense of its findings.
The two sides of the enterprise revealed their profound complementarity.
This was mirrored in the composition of the present chapter, in which
sections 2–4 had been devoted to the quantification and correlation of
discrete elements and sections 5–6 to the growing awareness that the patterns we had found required interpretations on a different plane. Without
the concepts of the second half of the chapter, the results of the first would
have remained blind, and without the empirical content of the first part,
the categories of the second would have remained empty. Only from their
encounter did critical knowledge arise.

An encounter between concepts and measurements, then. And, as
our iterative research shows, this encounter is a feedback loop wherein
concepts inform measurements and further measurements bring into

play further concepts. Though there was something rigid—as well as partial—about our initial mandate to look for style at the level of the sentence and to tie its occurrence to quantifiable phenomena, the interaction of concept and measurement had triggered a dynamic process in the course of which we had found not only a new definition of style, but a definition that sharply differentiated our work from the great stylistic tradition of Spitzer and Auerbach. In their classic works—much richer, let us be clear, than anything we have done—the different components of style tend to add up, or to reiterate with minor differences the same general point, but they don't *interact*, let alone acquire emergent properties as a result of the process. Though far from incompatible, the two approaches study style at two different scales: that of the paragraph, or of the text as a whole, with its often near-invisible touches, and that of the sentence, with its intuitively recognizable effects. Unifying these two scales of the phenomenon (and of the concept)—here, a whole new pamphlet could definitely begin. And this one could, finally, come to an end.

2013

CHAPTER 3

On Paragraphs

SCALE, THEMES, AND NARRATIVE FORM

Mark Algee-Hewitt, Ryan Heuser, Franco Moretti

1. MICROMÉGAS

Figure 3.1 is the final image, and book cover, of Matthew Jockers's book *Macroanalysis*: a network of over 3,000 nodes, each standing for a 19th-century novel, and of 165,000 edges among them, based on the similarity of 104 distinct features.[1] The novels are mere dots, but there are so many of them, and with so many inter-connections, that the result is a big, complicated cloud.

Though the amount of information in this image is unusual, the conjunction of very small units and a very large outcome is typical of the digital humanities. Look at Mark Algee-Hewitt's use of bigrams to investigate 19th-century fiction in **Figure 3.2**: millions of minuscule two-word combinations, and a secret divide emerges from a century of novels. Or take the diagram of "metricality" in **Figure 3.3**: two sets of very simple variables—rising-or-falling rhythm, and binary-or-ternary feet—and centuries of English poetry are mapped onto a single chart.

By now, this mix of micro and macro has become the signature of the digital humanities, and of their dramatic impact on the scale at which literature is studied. Dramatic, because what we encounter in these images are the extremes of the literary scale, whereas criticism has traditionally worked with *the middle* of the scale: a text, a scene, a stanza, an episode, an excerpt . . . An *anthropocentric* scale, where readers are truly "the measure

---

1 Matthew Jockers, *Macroanalysis: Digital Methods and Literary History* (Urbana, IL: University of Illinois Press, 2013).

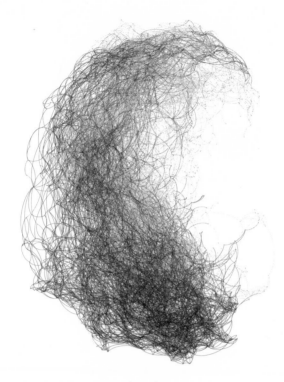

FIGURE 3.1 **A network of three thousand novels**

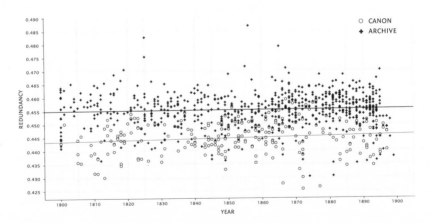

FIGURE 3.2 *Canon* and *archive* **in 19th-century Britain.** This image charts the frequency with which combinations of any two consecutive words repeat themselves in a sample of 19th-century novels: the greater the repetition, the less informative the given text. As can be seen, this very simple measure of linguistic redundancy reveals a striking difference between canonical texts and non-canonical ones.

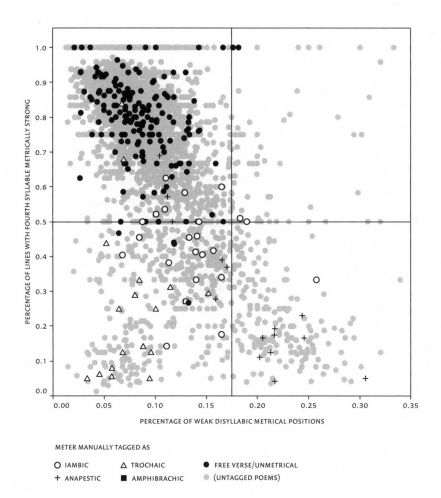

FIGURE 3.3 **Mapping English Poetry.** A plot of 6,400 poems, sampled evenly, period by period, from the 16th through the 20th century. The subsample of poems whose meter was manually annotated is indicated by the cross, triangle, square, and white dot. Gray dots indicate poems whose meter is not directly known; their position within a specific quadrant indicates what our program considers their most likely meter (iambic, trochaic, anapestic, or dactylic). Black dots indicate poems in free verse, or with no discernible meter.

of things." But the digital humanities, Alan Liu has written, have changed these coordinates, by "[focusing] on microlevel linguistic features . . . that map directly over macrolevel phenomena."[2] Exactly. And how does one study literature, in this new situation?

One option would be to focus exclusively on the very small and the very large. This is very much what happened with Leo Spitzer's *Stilkritik*—one of the great theoretical precedents of computational criticism. For Spitzer, all that mattered were the "detail" and the "whole"; no middle scale, but only a long series of "back-and-forth movements (first the detail, then the whole, then another detail, etc.) . . . until the characteristic 'click' occurs, which is the indication that detail and whole have found a common denominator." From a certain type of conjunctions, to French symbolist poetry; from neologisms, to Rabelais's oeuvre in its entirety; from the detail of noun deformation, to the worldview of Don Quixote. Detail and whole—very small and very large: Micromégas—and *only* detail and whole:

> At its most perfect, the solution attained by means of the circular operation is a negation of steps: once attained, it tends to obliterate the steps leading up to it (one may remember the lion of medieval bestiaries—concludes the critic named Leo—who, at every step forward, wiped out his footprints with his tail, in order to elude his pursuers!)[3]

The present project is the opposite of Spitzer's lovely simile: instead of "obliterating" intermediate steps, we want to make them totally explicit, by proposing a new middle scale for the study of literature. This scale is that of the paragraph.

o   o   o

---

2 Alan Liu, "Where Is Cultural Criticism in the Digital Humanities?," in *Debates in the Digital Humanities*, ed. Matthew K. Gold (Minneapolis: University of Minnesota Press, 2012). Also available at http://dhdebates. gc.cuny.edu/debates/text/20.

3 Leo Spitzer, "Linguistics and Literary History," in *Representative Essays* (Stanford: Stanford University Press, 1988), 36, 38, 37.

2. AUERBACH, WATT, AND THE PARAGRAPH

Unlike sentences and (to a lesser extent) chapters, paragraphs remain an understudied scale of prose writing.[4] We all know they exist—we all *write* paragraphs all the time—but we don't really know how they work.[5] So, as a first step, we turned back to "Style at the Scale of the Sentence" with the idea of studying how style changes when one shifts from the scale of the sentence to that of the paragraph. After all, wasn't the most programmatic essay of American stylistics entitled "The First Paragraph of *The Ambassadors*"? And think of the opening words of the pilot essay for Auerbach's *Mimesis*: "Dieser Absatz steht im neunten Kapitel des ersten Teils . . ."[6] Dieser Absatz: this paragraph. *Mimesis* is beginning to take shape—the title of the 1937 essay is the first occurrence of that "serious imitation of the everyday" that will provide the *Leitmotiv* of the book—and "paragraph" is the first word that crosses Auerbach's mind.

Style at the scale of the paragraph. But there was something odd about the status of the paragraph in Watt and in Auerbach. They both

---

4 The first systematic study of the paragraph in English appears to have been Edwin Herbert Lewis's excellent PhD dissertation *The History of the English Paragraph* (Chicago: University of Chicago Press, 1894). For more recent studies, see Paul C. Rodgers, Jr., "Alexander Bain and the Rise of the Organic Paragraph," *Quarterly Journal of Speech* 51, no. 4 (December 1965): 399–408 and "A Discourse-Centered Rhetoric of the Paragraph," *College Composition and Communication* 17, no. 1 (February 1966): 2–11; Francis Christensen, "A Generative Rhetoric of the Paragraph," *College Composition and Communication* 16, no. 3 (October 1965): 144–56; and R. E. Longacre, "The Paragraph as a Grammatical Unit," in *Discourse and Syntax*, ed. Talmy Givón, *Syntax and Semantics* 12 (New York: Academic Press, 1979), 115–134.

Most of these scholars consider the structure and function of the paragraph to be fundamentally the same as that of the sentence, and they usually mention Alexander Bain's *English Composition and Rhetoric: A Manual* (London: Longmans, Green, and Co., 1866) as the basis for this type of approach. "[Bain's] paragraph," writes Rodgers, for instance, "is simply a sentence writ large . . . sentence and paragraph alike display an organic structure and employ the same means to secure it"; and then, summarizing the developments of paragraph theory in the late 19th century: "the paragraph now is an expanded sentence not only structurally but logically and semantically as well . . . devoted to the amplification and enforcement of the single idea announced in its topic sentence" (406, 408). An even more radical continuity between distinct textual scales is asserted by Longacre, for whom "a paragraph resembles a long sentence on the one hand and a short discourse on the other hand."

5 Or at least: how they work *within narrative fiction*. Most studies of the paragraph have focused on non-literary discourse, and composition courses—where American students encounter the paragraph as form—are also structured around critical exposition, not narrative form.

6 See Erich Auerbach, "Über die ernste Nachahmung des Alltäglichen," in *Travaux du séminaire de philologie romane* (Istanbul: Devlet Basimevi, 1937).

analyzed style, and drew their evidence from paragraphs that were explicitly reproduced as such; the *form* of the paragraph, though, never entered
their analysis. Paragraphs contained style, but they did not *shape* it. Tell-
ingly, Watt referred to the opening of *The Ambassadors* three times as a
"paragraph," and thirteen times as a "passage": although he was analyzing
a paragraph, he didn't see it as one. Something similar happened in Auerbach's chapters on French realism: he referred to paragraphs obliquely, by
turning to cognitive metaphors of a pictorial (the paragraph as "a 'scene,'"
"a portrait," "a picture," "the coarse realism [of] Dutch painting") or musical ("a leading motif, which is several times repeated," "the first words of
the paragraph state the theme, and all that follows is but a development
of it . . . a resumption, a variation") nature.[7] Scene, portrait, picture, motif,
theme. . . . For Auerbach, paragraphs were clearly not stylistic units, but
thematic ones. And in the world of the digital humanities, *thematic* study
means: topic modeling.[8]

3. THEMATIC FOCUS

Though thematic concepts may no longer be the "chaos" evoked by
Vladimir Propp in the opening pages of the *Morphology,*[9] most theorists
agree that they remain disturbingly opaque, especially when it comes to
the articulation of "theme" and "motif."[10] Here, we will follow the widely
shared assumption that themes tend to be large, abstract, synthetic,[11] and

---

7 Auerbach, *Mimesis*, 455, 470, 483, 509, 510, 470, 484.

8 In what follows, we assume the existence of a relationship between thematics and topic modeling—so much so that we will use the adjectives "thematic" and "topical" almost interchangeably—though we are aware that our observations on this point have hardly a systematic character.

9 "If a division into categories is unsuccessful, the division according to theme leads to total chaos.
We shall not even speak about the fact that such a complex, indefinite concept as 'theme' is either left
completely undefined or is defined by every author in his own way." Vladimir Propp, *Morphology of the
Folktale*, trans. Laurence Scott (Austin, TX: University of the Texas Press, 1968), 7.

10 "The various distinctions that have been drawn between *theme* and motif remain vaguer still, so
much so that their definitions are often interchangeable." Cesare Segre, "From Motif to Function and
Back Again," in *Thematics: New Approaches*, ed. Claude Bremond, Joshua Landy, and Thomas Pavel (Albany,
NY: State University of New York Press, 1995), 22.

11 "The theme (what is being said in a work) unites the separate elements of a work. . . . The idea
expressed by the theme is the idea that *summarizes* and unifies the verbal material in the work." Boris

are usually not stated openly in the text, but produced by an act of inter-pretation;[12] whereas motifs tend to be explicit, delimited,[13] and concrete.[14]

Our initial hypothesis was simple: if paragraphs were indeed thematic units, then they would have a higher "thematic focus" than the abstract textual segments that were routinely used by topic modeling researchers.[15] Testing this hypothesis required however a series of preliminary steps, the first of which consisted in establishing the length of the paragraphs in our corpus. Initially, we measured all paragraphs, mixing narrative instances, like those analyzed by Auerbach and Watt, with exchanges of dialogue among characters (**Figure 3.4**). Though typographically marked in the same way, however, the two types of paragraphs played quite different roles in the architecture of the novel—especially in the mid-Victorian corpus we had selected—and we decided to disaggregate them, obtaining the results that are presented in **Figure 3.5**.

Tomashevsky, "Thematics," in *Russian Formalist Criticism: Four Essays*, trans. Lee T. Lemon and Marion J. Reis (Lincoln, NE: University of Nebraska Press, 1965), 63, 67.

12 "A theme . . . is not a component: there is no element in a literary work that can be called its theme . . . A theme is not an expression: although the theme is sometimes formulated explicitly, more usually it emerges implicitly, without corresponding to any specific expression in the text. . . . A theme is not a segment within the text-continuum but a construct put together from discontinuous elements in the text. . . . Theme is a construct (a conceptual construct, to be precise), put together from discon-tinuous elements in the text." Shlomith Rimmon-Kenan, "What is Theme and How Do We Get at It?," in *Thematics: New Approaches*, 10-11, 14.

13 "After reducing a work to its thematic elements, we come to parts that are irreducible, the small-est particles of thematic material: 'evening comes,' 'Raskolnikov kills the old woman,' 'the hero dies,' 'the letter is received,' and so on. The theme of an irreducible part of a work is called the motif: each sentence, in fact, has its own motif." Boris Tomashevsky, "Thematics," 67.

14 "Undoubtedly motif is more concrete, theme more abstract," concludes Bremond; while Segre, taking his cue from musicology, points out that "according to [various musicological] definitions, *theme* and *motif* are in a relationship of complex to simple, composite to unitary. . . . Themes are elements that span an entire text or a considerable part thereof, while motifs—of which there may be many—are more localized elements." See Claude Bremond, "Concept and Theme," in *The Return of Thematic Criticism*, ed. Werner Sollors (Cambridge, MA: Harvard University Press, 1993), 49–50n; and Cesare Segre, "From Motif to Function and Back Again," 24, 25.

15 "Abstract," in the sense that most researchers select as their units segments of equal length (usually one thousand words), regardless of the actual subdivisions of the text; "mechanical" would be another way to describe the relationship between segment and text. In principle we have nothing against ab-stract and mechanical approaches to literature; it's just that—in this specific case—we think that a different choice might produce better results.

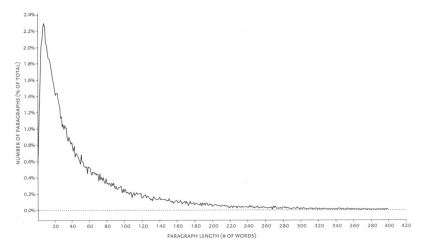

FIGURE 3.4 **Paragraph length (in words).** About 15 percent of the paragraphs in our corpus were between one and ten words long, and 18 percent between eleven and twenty; then the frequency began to decline: 13 percent between twenty-one and thirty, 9.3 between thirty-one and forty, and so on, until—at about one hundred words, and 2 percent frequency—a very long tail began. Paragraphs one hundred words or longer amounted to only about 15 percent of paragraphs—but comprised 49 percent of the words of the corpus. Since, initially, we were thinking of studying style, we had prepared an unusually small corpus consisting only of nineteen mid-Victorian bildungsromane, whose paragraphs had all been individually hand-tagged. This choice of genre and period may of course have biased results in ways that later research will correct.

From this point onwards, we restricted our investigation to narrative paragraphs, along the lines of Auerbach and Watt, proceeding to a three-way comparison between paragraphs, textual segments eighty-two words in length (eighty-two being the mean length of narrative paragraphs), and a second group of segments two hundred words in length (to approximate the 1,000-word size usual in topic modeling). In order to measure these three groups' thematic focus we borrowed from economics two statistical indicators—Gini's index of wealth inequality, and Herfindahl's measure of market concentration—that aim at establishing how finite resources (in our case, the number of words in a given paragraph) are distributed among different actors (in our case, the different topics present in the corpus). Combining the two measures, we determined how much of a paragraph's semantic space was concentrated into the "hands" of a single (or a few) topics. And, as **Figure 3.6** shows, thematic concentration turned out to be indeed significantly higher in paragraphs than in segments of equivalent length, and *much* higher than in 200-words segments.

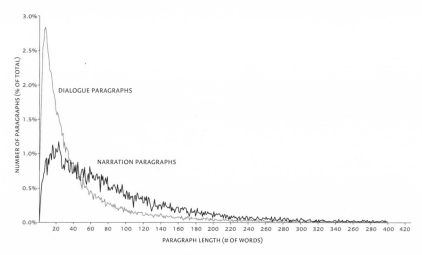

FIGURE 3.5 **Paragraph length (in words): dialogue and narration.** Separating dialogue and narration produced two very different curves, supporting the idea that they formed two distinct (though obviously interacting) systems. Paragraphs of dialogue peaked right away, at a length of about 6 to 8 words—well below the average length of 19th-century novelistic sentences, let alone paragraphs. Their frequency declined rather quickly. Narrative paragraphs peaked at 20 to 25 words, had a mean length of 82 words (the *Madame Bovary* paragraph examined by Auerbach is 89 words long), and declined very slowly, reaching the 1 percent mark at around 215 words (the opening paragraph of *The Ambassadors* is 250 words long). The chart suggested that 19th-century novels required readers to shift between long (and even very long) narrative stretches, and pointed dialogue among characters: a counterpoint of "written" and "oral" that seems to have crystallized in mid-century, and was later radicalized in the novels of Henry James. Flaubert offered his own striking version of the short/long alternation: the shock of his most legendary paragraph—"Il voyagea," near the end of *Sentimental Education*—lies in seeing a paragraph reduced to the simplest of sentences (pronoun + intransitive verb). Implicitly, this radical compression reveals how different the functions of paragraphs and sentences usually are.

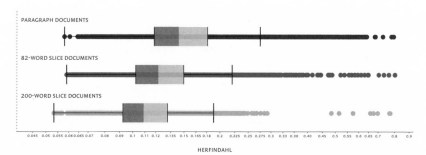

FIGURE 3.6 **Thematic Focus.** In this image, the line bisecting the three "boxes" indicates the median value for the group; the dark gray and light gray sections indicate the two central quartiles; and the "whiskers" represent the upper and lower quartile, with outliers indicated by individual dots.

We topic modeled the three groups separately, on the basis of fifty topics, with hyperparameters on; for each segment, the model would consider at least ten "Mallet" words, excluding names and very frequent words, and overlay the topics to the given segment.

Let us be clear about the meaning of these findings. First of all, we did *not* "discover" that paragraphs were thematic units; scholars who had studied the paragraph had long established this "fact," which we had all learned in elementary school, and had "known" ever since. But we proved that this "well-known fact" was actually true, and could be "recognized" by a topic modeling program, thus proving its reliability; two instances of corroboration which, though hardly exciting in themselves, have their modest role to play in the process of research. More significantly, our results suggest that—if one wants to use topic modeling to analyze literature—then *paragraphs are a better unit than "mechanical" segments*, and should replace them in future research. And the same for thematics: if, as we have seen, no one really knows "where" to look for themes in a text, our findings suggest that paragraphs are probably the best starting point: by concentrating thematic material within their limited space, they act *as the textual habitat of themes*. What this concretely means, is the object of the next two sections.

4. MONO-TOPICAL PARAGRAPHS

Paragraphs specialize in the "concentration" of themes. But how, exactly? **Figures 3.7**, **3.8**, and **3.9** offer the beginning of an answer, exemplifying what we ended up calling "mono-topical" paragraphs: that is to say, paragraphs in which a single topic occupies at least half of the available semantic space.[16] On the basis of their top fifty words, such dominant topics could be described as "marriage and expectations" (*Middlemarch*), "entering a house" (*Villette*), and "direct, emotional communication" (*Adam Bede*).

---

16 All the paragraphs we discuss from now on consist of thirty "Mallet" words: a length that correlates with the highest combined Gini/Herfindahl scores, and is therefore ideal to investigate thematic focus. Since Mallet does not consider proper names, function words, and other very frequent entities, a paragraph with thirty Mallet words has on average about one hundred actual words. "Mallet Topic Score" indicates the amount of paragraph space that Mallet considers occupied by a given topic. As most words participate in several topics (though, usually, with a different "rank" within them), all fifty topics have a non-zero Mallet score in every paragraph in the corpus. "Assigned Topic Score" indicates for its part how many of the thirty Mallet words in the given paragraph are being "assigned" by the program to a specific topic. In this case, the only topics with non-zero values are those that have been assigned at least one of the thirty Mallet words.

FIGURE 3.7 **Mono-topical paragraph (*Middlemarch*, George Eliot, 1872)**

"Then, why **DON'T** you *extend* your *liberality* to others?" said Will, still **NETTLED**. "My *personal independence* is as *important* to me as yours is to you. You have no more *reason* to *imagine* that I have *personal expectations* from Brooke, than I have to IMAGINE that you have personal expectations from Bulstrode. *Motives* are *points* of HONOR, I *suppose*—nobody can **prove** them. But as to *money* and PLACE in the WORLD," Will **ended**, *tossing* back his *head*, "I think it is **pretty clear** that I am not *determined* by *considerations* of that *sort*."

TOPIC # & STYLE	TOPIC SCORE (MALLET)	#. OF MODELED WORDS IN TOPIC	TOP 50 WORDS FOR TOPIC
0 *bold* *italic*	60.47%	21 / 30 [70.0%]	mind, marriage, husband, fact, present, wife, time, subject, question, kind, opinion, family, wished, felt, sort, give, feeling, knew, point, making, position, interest, grandcourt, idea, expected, reason, case, regard, uncle, means, determined, aware, sense, giving, side, circumstances, reasons, person, affair, held, occasion, future, general, object, opportunity, view, personal, find, speak
22 SMALL CAPS BOLD	2.57%	4 / 30 [13.3%]	n't, dear, sir, suppose, give, hear, mind, things, wo, care, woman, father, call, remember, speak, ah, talk, married, friend, poor, feel, glad, continued, wife, bad, fellow, tone, boy, mine, understand, husband, people, leave, word, live, aunt, girl, stay, trouble, papa, place, bear, sort, head, pretty, exclaimed, kind, matter, fool
39 SMALL CAPS	6.3%	2 / 30 [6.7%]	things, people, world, men, find, time, knew, life, feel, women, matter, set, wrong, times, end, sort, deal, hard, bad, person, work, suppose, kind, poor, mind, worse, half, lose, felt, fancy, wanted, making, friends, true, ways, doubt, care, show, story, easy, clever, thoughts, reason, give, fault, stupid, place, began, spite
42 *italic*	6.21%	2 / 30 [6.7%]	hand, head, looked, chair, round, hands, side, turned, hat, eyes, table, face, sat, forward, arm, sit, seated, standing, room, stood, seat, sitting, turning, window, feet, walk, end, corner, distance, rising, held, began, leaning, close, book, laid, holding, threw, suddenly, time, fingers, walked, open, ground, turn, fire, entered, ring, sofa
27 **bold**	2.99%	1 / 30 [3.3%]	dress, white, hair, black, wear, bonnet, silk, pink, wore, gold, dressed, round, small, red, gown, blue, lace, handkerchief, diamonds, necklace, shawl, cap, large, silver, clothes, frock, plain, pretty, curls, ring, short, green, jewels, tied, brown, bright, satin, suit, handsome, neck, mama, gray, muslin, yellow, robe, gloves, fingers, bracelet, colored

FIGURE 3.8 **Mono-topical paragraph** (*Villette*, Charlotte Brontë, 1853)

"All at once, **quick** *rang* the bell—**quick**, but not *loud*—a *cautious tinkle*—a **sort** of *WARNING*, *metal* **whisper**. Rosine **darted** from her *cabinet* and ran to *open*. The *person* she *admitted stood* with her two *minutes* in *parley*: there seemed a **demur**, a **delay**. Rosine came to the *garden door*, *lamp in hand*; she *stood* on the *steps*, l̲i̲f̲t̲i̲n̲g̲ her *lamp*, looking *round* **vaguely**."

TOPIC # & STYLE	TOPIC SCORE (MALLET)	#. OF MODELED WORDS IN TOPIC	TOP 50 WORDS FOR TOPIC
14 *italic*	56.9%	20 / 30 [66.7%]	door, room, opened, open, house, stood, entered, window, heard, hall, looked, stairs, fire, light, table, round, closed, shut, passed, side, doors, place, step, led, parlor, small, dark, chamber, staircase, front, steps, bed, floor, corner, furniture, glass, library, end, key, large, servant, hand, candle, servants, chair, sat, rooms, brought, empty
19 **bold** <u>underline</u>	12.21%	4 / 30 [13.3%]	looked, eyes, voice, turned, tone, face, spoke, felt, heard, speak, smile, answer, speaking, glance, manner, time, eye, silent, silence, began, gave, met, pause, question, stranger, word, round, surprise, hand, expression, strange, turning, room, sat, knew, passed, usual, low, reply, feeling, quick, quickly, smiled, quiet, conversation, slight, countenance, speech, questions
43 **bold**	12.05%	4 / 30 [13.3%]	hand, eyes, face, head, hands, tears, looked, lips, arms, heart, voice, turned, arm, shook, father, held, round, kissed, mother, pale, stood, pressed, kiss, felt, spoke, fell, laid, cheek, child, cry, touch, bent, gave, neck, touched, door, speak, sat, answer, whispered, trembling, burst, smiled, lifted, whisper, silence, paused, shoulder, suddenly
25 SMALL CAPS ITALIC	3.57%	1 / 30 [3.3%]	felt, mind, feeling, sense, life, strong, consciousness, mother, presence, husband, brought, painful, feel, dread, effect, state, conscious, future, sort, nature, reason, present, longer, power, feelings, pain, effort, experience, trouble, thoughts, fear, turned, speech, creature, moments, change, wanted, stronger, brother, began, strength, pride, care, pity, turn, ready, imagination, hard, shock
33 <u>dotted</u> <u>underline</u>	3.12%	1 / 30 [3.3%]	eyes, face, hair, looked, eye, head, beauty, figure, woman, features, dark, light, white, black, mouth, large, smile, brow, tall, fine, expression, girl, full, blue, delicate, pale, nose, handsome, glance, color, soft, red, dress, fair, countenance, brown, thin, air, bright, pretty, sort, lips, appearance, set, forehead, shape, contrast, fire, age

FIGURE 3.9 **Mono-topical paragraphs** (*Adam Bede*, George Eliot, 1859)

"Slowly, while Dinah was speaking, Hetty rose, took a step forward, and was CLASPED in Dinah's ***arms***. They stood so a long while, for neither of them felt the IMPULSE to move apart again. Hetty, without any distinct thought of it, hung on this something that was come to ***clasp*** her now, while she was SINKING HELPLESS in a dark GULF; and Dinah FELT a deep joy in the first sign that her love was *welcomed* by the WRETCHED **lost** one. The light got FAINTER as they stood, and when at last they sat down on the **straw** pallet together, their faces had become indistinct."

TOPIC # & STYLE	TOPIC SCORE (MALLET)	#. OF MODELED WORDS IN TOPIC	TOP 40 WORDS FOR TOPIC
48 dotted underline	45.68%	16 / 30 [53.3%]	looked, eyes, face, turned, hand, voice, sat, stood, spoke, round, heard, silence, tone, time, speak, felt, room, smile, door, silent, minutes, speaking, low, glance, word, eye, turning, began, passed, paused, suddenly, head, expression, manner, quick, answer, met, half, slowly
25 SMALL CAPS ITALIC	23.3%	8 / 30 [26.7%]	heart, poor, tears, face, death, dead, cry, felt, eyes, fear, pain, die, soul, child, knew, fell, bear, time, woman, voice, cold, hard, broken, strange, grief, life, bitter, weak, burst, hands, body, terror, deep, strength, hand, lips, sight, pale, cruel
21 ***bold italic***	68.94%	3 / 30 [10%]	mother, father, child, horn, poor, children, daughter, girl, looked, baby, wc, mamma, years, boy, dear, woman, wife, darling, husband, sister, knew, world, brother, time, brought, face, beautiful, sweet, nurse, mid, dead, house, heart, happy, boys, papa, pretty, loved, arms
31 **bold**	3.06%	1 / 30 [3.3%]	white, black, dress, hair, looked, bonnet, round, wear, clothes, wore, large, coat, dressed, gold, silk, hat, cap, gray, gown, blue, pretty, red, small, gloves, shawl, hands, lace, waistcoat, pink, pair, shoes, head, clean, yellow, green, tied, boots, box, neck
28 underline	3.13%	1 / 30 [3.3%]	door, room, house, opened, open, window, table, stood, looked, entered, hall, large, light, small, chair, side, place, stairs, dark, windows, parlor, rooms, floor, staircase, closed, key, corner, furniture, round, walls, shut, glass, fire, hand, led, passage, chamber, locked, end
5 *italic* underline	3.45%	1 / 30 [3.3%]	family, gentleman, person, knew, acquaintance, called, fact, society, conversation, friends, present, pleasure, manner, talk, time, house, gentlemen, kind, friend, held, appeared, character, ladies, subject, general, fine, air, business, visit, appearance, pleased, interest, received, place, company, observed, excellent, agreeable, daughter,

Let us say right away that the semantic consistency of these topics is often questionable,[17] and that, whereas the paragraph from *Adam Bede* is semantically very close to the core of its dominant topic—many of whose fifty top words appear in the paragraph itself—the opposite is true of the *Middlemarch* case, where it's hard not to feel a strong disconnect between the meaning of the paragraph and that of its supposedly dominant topic. A possible way out is offered by Claude Bremond, with his distinction between concept and theme:

> There is in Rousseau's work a concept of the social contract, but a theme of reverie. . . . One . . . takes off from the varied concrete and goes towards abstract unity. The other tends to exemplify a supposedly defined notion by immersing it in the context of various situations; it takes an abstract entity and makes it a point of departure for a series of concrete variations. . . . Theme overflows and incessantly calls into question the concepts forged in order to apprehend it. This is the consequence of *exemplification*: to the characteristics judged as pertinent for the definition of concept, theme adds a network of associated ideas. . . . Thematization therefore consists of an indefinite series of variations on a theme whose conceptualization . . . still remains to be completed.[18]

"Variations" that generate "networks of associated ideas": this is the key. The *Middlemarch* paragraph exemplifies the theme of "Personal Independence" by placing it in the context of comparable choices (Lydgate, to whom the words are addressed, faces very similar problems to Will's), thus providing a variation that "calls into question" the initial idea. Furthermore,

---

17 In the *Middlemarch* passage, for instance, the terms *liberality, personal independence,* and *expectations* suggest the idea of "personal identity," whereas *reason, imagine, suppose,* and *prove* point towards some kind of interpretive activity. The same in *Villette*—where *garden, door, cabinet, steps,* and *round* refer to space, and *loud, cautious, tinkle,* and *parley* to sound—and in *Adam Bede,* where *felt, deep,* and *sign* indicate emotions, and *stood* and *move* location. These contradictions are ubiquitous in topic modeling, and clearly weaken its analytical power; in "Words Alone: Dismantling Topic Models in the Humanities," *Journal of Digital Humanities* 2, no. 1 (Winter 2012), Benjamin M. Schmidt has convincingly explained this Janus-faced behavior with the excessively long historical arcs of the corpora from which topics are extracted. It's a very plausible hypothesis, which however doesn't apply to our corpus, which is entirely drawn from a single, rather homogenous generation.

18 Claude Bremond, "Concept and Theme," 47, 48, 49.

the idea of themes as an "indefinite series of variations" explains why the internal contradictions of topics exist in the first place: they arise from that open-ended activity of association that—far from being an unfortunate accident—is for Bremond *the very point* of thematization.

Bremond's thesis accounted for the semantic contradictions of topics; *removing* those contradictions was however a different story—and, finding ourselves unable to do so, we concluded that topics remained too slippery for an in-depth semantic analysis of our corpus. So, we turned once again to "Style at the Scale of the Sentence," but this time to completely reverse its approach: instead of taking the scale of the sentence as the means to investigate the literary phenomenon of style, the other way around: we would take the literary phenomenon of themes, and use it to study the scale of the paragraph. This reversal of ends and means had a memorable precedent in Tomashevsky's 1925 essay, where the distinction between "bound" and "free" motifs—which was supposed to throw light on their thematic content—ended up having nothing to do with thematics, and everything to do with the theory of plot.[19] Something similar here: mono-topical paragraphs interested us less for what their central topic "meant," than for what it "did" in the narrative structure: defining a major character (*Middlemarch*), introducing an enigma (*Villette*), or announcing a major turning point in the plot (*Adam Bede*). All functions, we realized, that made mono-topical paragraphs quite similar to Tomashevsky's bound motifs, thus opening an unexpected and promising path from thematics to narratology.

But there was a problem. Unlike fairy tales, modern novels are known to have very few bound motives; and indeed, once we calculated how many mono-topical paragraphs were to be found in our corpus, the total oscillated between 1 and 4 percent (**Figure 3.10**). And the other paragraphs?

---

19 "Mutually related motifs form the thematic bonds of the work. From this point of view, the story is the aggregate of motifs in their logical, causal-chronological order. . . . The motifs which cannot be omitted are *bound motifs*; those which may be omitted without disturbing the whole causal-chronological course of events are *free motifs*." Boris Tomashevsky, "Thematics," 68. Notice the silent slippage from "thematic bonds" to "causal-chronological order."

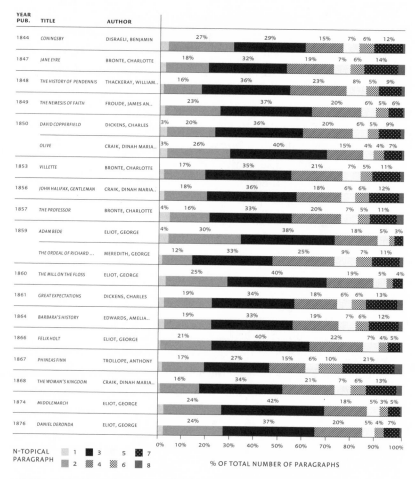

FIGURE 3.10 **Thematic concentration in mid-Victorian bildungsromane.** We will return again to the contents of this chart. For now, let's simply point out that the highest frequency of mono-topical paragraphs is a mere 4 percent—one paragraph every twenty-five—and in just two of our nineteen texts: *The Professor* and *Adam Bede*.

5. PHYSIOLOGY OF THE PARAGRAPH

Faced with the evidence of **Figure 3.10**, our first impulse was to run to the opposite end of the spectrum, turning our attention to those "poly-topical" passages where five or more topics were needed to occupy 50 percent of the available thematic space (**Figures 3.11** and **3.12**).[20] In lieu of the

---

20 The paragraph in **Figure 3.11** occurs in the middle of an agitated episode in Richard Feverel's childhood, in which his mind oscillates between several courses of action. The *Middlemarch* passage

intensity of turning points and central characters, the rapid crisscrossing of themes produced the light-hearted "surprise" of Meredith's paragraph (**Figure 3.10**), and opened the door to the inflow of the *Middlemarch* minor characters; or more exactly, squeezing so many characters in such a small space—nine in a hundred words, in Eliot's case—made them all appear "minor," enlarging by contrast the space for the narrator's ironical comments (**Figure 3.12**).

These paragraphs offered a neat counterpoint to mono-topical paragraphs, and were also more frequent than them: between 9 and 40 percent as opposed to 1–4 percent. But, once again, they were relatively atypical of the corpus as a whole: in **Figure 3.10**, a single group of paragraphs ("three-topical" ones, in which three topics occupy 50 percent of semantic space) had a larger presence than the mono- and poly-topical cases combined. **Figures 3.13** and **3.14** offer two typical instances of these "middle" paragraphs, which make up over one third (on average, 37 percent) of our corpus.[21]

Here, finally, we were looking at the "typical" paragraph in our corpus, and at the thematic configuration that characterized it. In the case of *David Copperfield*, one of the three topics appeared to be centered around feelings and expectations (influence, feel, uneasiness, doubts, fears, hopeful); a second one around house and furniture (house, knocked, room, staircase); while the third, more uncertain, had something to do with the passing of time (began, softening, past: not much, but among the fifty top words of the topic the temporal dimension was more visible). *John Halifax* presented a similar tripartition: a topic clustering around rational decisions (wisest, safest, expected, consent, kindness); one around family relations (mother, boy, petted, boy); and a third, more opaque, related to a general idea of human nature (instinct, accustomed, children; in this case, too, a look at the entire topic strengthened these otherwise tenuous hints). In both novels, the first two topics recalled the polarity of "soul" and "world"

---

in **Figure 3.12** is part of a larger scene that originates in anonymous gossip, and acquires momentum thanks to the intervention of Sir James Chettam and Mrs. Cadwallader; it is one of the many moments when Eliot's minor characters occupy the center of the stage.

21 The two paragraphs describe the immediate aftermath of an important (though not decisive) episode: in *David Copperfield*, David is back from his first day in a new school, and is worried about his future there; while the paragraph from *John Halifax* presents the consequences of a fight between John's two sons, Guy and Edwin.

FIGURE 3.11 **Poly-topical Paragraph** (*The Ordeal of Richard Feverel. A History of Father and Son*, George Meredith, 1859).

"Richard **faced** about to make a querulous *retort*. The **injured** and **hapless** *visage* that *met* his **eye** *disarmed* him. The LAD'S UNHAPPY *nose*, though not exactly of the DREADED hue, was really becoming discolored. To **upbraid** him would be CRUEL. Richard lifted his HEAD, **surveyed** the *position*, and **exclaiming**, "Here!" *dropped* down on a WITHERED BANK, LEAVING Ripton to CONTEMPLATE him as a **puzzle** whose every new **move** was a WORSE *perplexity*."

TOPIC # & STYLE	TOPIC SCORE (MALLET)	#. OF MODELED WORDS IN TOPIC	TOP 40 WORDS FOR TOPIC
19 **bold** **underline**	12.21%	4/30 [13.3%]	looked, eyes, voice, turned, tone, face, spoke, felt, heard, speak, smile, answer, speaking, glance, manner, time, eye, silent, silence, began, gave, met, pause, question, stranger, word, round, surprise, hand, expression, strange, turning, room, sat, knew, passed, usual, low, reply
5 *italic* *underline*	11.76%	4/30 [13.3%]	character, time, circumstances, life, friends, degree, spirit, grandfather, present, influence, mind, friend, means, feelings, society, considerable, received, position, purpose, intelligence, scarcely, period, interest, deeply, returned, respect, impossible, visit, knowledge, days, family, youth, devoted, conduct, secret, result, met, existence, quitted
25 SMALL CAPS ITALIC	9.23%	3/30 [10%]	felt, mind, feeling, sense, life, strong, consciousness, mother, presence, husband, brought, painful, feel, dread, effect, state, conscious, future, sort, nature, reason, present, longer, power, feelings, pain, effort, experience, trouble, thoughts, fear, turned, speech, creature, moments, change, wanted, stronger, brother
22 SMALL CAPS BOLD	9.75%	3/30 [10%]	n't, dear, sir, suppose, give, hear, mind, things, wo, care, woman, father, call, remember, speak, ah, talk, married, friend, poor, feel, glad, continued, wife, bad, fellow, tone, boy, mine, understand, husband, people, leave, word, live, aunt, girl, stay, trouble
43 **bold**	29.22%	3/30 [10.0%]	hand, eyes, face, head, hands, tears, looked, lips, arms, heart, voice, turned, arm, shook, father, held, round, kissed, mother, pale, stood, pressed, kiss, felt, spoke, fell, laid, cheek, child, cry, touch, bent, gave, neck, touched, door, speak, sat, answer

39 SMALL CAPS	6.3%	2 / 30 [6.7%]	things, people, world, men, find, time, knew, life, feel, women, matter, set, wrong, times, end, sort, deal, hard, bad, person, work, suppose, kind, poor, mind, worse, half, lose, felt, fancy, wanted, making, friends, true, ways, doubt, care, show, story
15 **bold** **dotted** **underline**	6.3%	2 / 30 [6.7%]	heart, life, soul, death, poor, woman, word, die, give, feel, knew, bear, true, speak, leave, world, lost, strength, time, loved, live, fear, pain, spirit, human, mine, dead, pity, misery, suffering, deep, comfort, truth, child, miserable, living, duty, earth, evil
28 underline	6.2%	2 / 30 [6.7%]	night, bed, light, time, sleep, lay, cold, strange, sat, fell, day, heard, hour, felt, morning, fire, dark, half, knew, evening, sound, silence, silent, heart, hours, room, stood, passed, past, darkness, dream, wind, slept, hear, asleep, dead, grew, lie, warm
42 *italic*	6.21%	2 / 30 [6.7%]	hand, head, looked, chair, round, hands, side, turned, hat, eyes, table, face, sat, forward, arm, sit, seated, standing, room, stood, seat, sitting, turning, window, feet, walk, end, corner, distance, rising, held, began, leaning, close, book, laid, holding, threw, suddenly
24 SMALL CAPS UNDERLINE	2.99%	1 / 30 [3.3%]	men, world, race, religion, people, find, jew, spiritual, reason, human, mankind, fathers, children, system, history, strange, earth, jewish, true, blood, spirit, ages, religious, experience, nature, minds, called, ignorance, souls, form, intellect, knowledge, age, doctrine, christians, ignorant, pure, divine, law
33 dotted underline	3.12%	1 / 30 [3.3%]	eyes, face, hair, looked, eye, head, beauty, figure, woman, features, dark, light, white, black, mouth, large, smile, brow, tall, fine, expression, girl, full, blue, delicate, pale, nose, handsome, glance, color, soft, red, dress, fair, countenance, brown, thin, air, bright
34 SMALL CAPS DOTTED UNDERLINE	2.89%	1 / 30 [3.3%]	boat, sea, water, river, land, signora, board, tide, ship, vessel, signore, island, waves, deck, carried, steamer, oar, sail, row, yacht, current, waters, sailor, flood, cabin, rowing, foreign, stream, ships, boating, boats, number, harbor, drowned, banks, pilot, voyage, rocks, oars
0 **bold** *italic*	3.91%	1 / 30 [3.3%]	mind, marriage, husband, fact, present, wife, time, subject, question, kind, opinion, family, wished, felt, sort, give, feeling, knew, point, making, position, interest, grandcourt, idea, expected, reason, case, regard, uncle, means, determined, aware, sense, giving, side, circumstances, reasons, person, affair
8 *italic* *dotted* *underline*	3.25%	1 / 30 [3.3%]	case, question, men, people, present, true, law, duty, character, matter, point, truth, fact, call, doubt, opinion, answer, find, state, justice, judgment, power, clear, believed, view, difficulties, nature, natural, action, reason, position, moral, conduct, understand, ground, conscience, circumstances, admit, follow

FIGURE 3.12 **Poly-topical Paragraph** (*Middlemarch*, George Eliot, 1872)

"It came very *lightly* indeed. When Dorothea **quitted** Caleb and *turned* to **meet** them, it *appeared* that Mrs Cadwallader had *stepped* across the **park** by the MEREST chance in the *world*, just to *chat* with Celia in a **matronly** way about the **baby**. And so Mr Brooke was *coming* back? *Delightful!*—COMING back, it was to be *hoped*, quite cured of **Parliamentary** fever and **pioneering**. Apropos of the 'Pioneer'—somebody had *prophesied* that it would soon be like a dying **dolphin**, and *turn* all **colors** for want of knowing how to help itself, because Mr Brooke's PROTÉGÉ, the *brilliant* young Ladislaw, was gone or going. Had Sir James heard that?"

TOPIC # & STYLE	TOPIC SCORE (MALLET)	#. OF MODELED WORDS IN TOPIC	TOP 50 WORDS FOR TOPIC
42 *italic*	14.7%	5/30 [16.7%]	hand, head, looked, chair, round, hands, side, turned, hat, eyes, table, face, sat, forward, arm, sit, seated, standing, room, stood, seat, sitting, turning, window, feet, walk, end, corner, distance, rising, held, began, leaning, close, book, laid, holding, threw, suddenly, time, fingers, walked, open, ground, turn, fire, entered, ring, sofa
35 **bold**	14.48%	5/30 [16.7%]	mother, horn, child, daughter, wc, woman, father, heart, wife, girl, dear, loved, friend, poor, mid, beautiful, sister, happy, looked, world, nurse, years, mc, care, sweet, face, quiet, mamma, talk, husband, grave, creature, papa, scarcely, darling, loving, strange, baby, tender, times, pride, learned, thinking, memory, beloved, true, kiss, tenderness, meet
2 *italic* underline	11.67%	4/30 [13.1%]	ladies, gentlemen, fine, air, pretty, society, gentleman, party, guests, pleasure, company, dinner, french, conversation, dance, agreeable, gave, women, charming, style, handsome, taste, beautiful, pleasant, perfect, evening, fair, admiration, called, fashion, talked, ball, english, amusement, general, full, high, grand, delightful, beauty, appeared, visitors, distinguished, girl, country, lively, girls, present, world
28 underline	11.86%	4/30 [13.1%]	night, bed, light, time, sleep, lay, cold, strange, sat, fell, day, heard, hour, felt, morning, fire, dark, half, knew, evening, sound, silence, silent, heart, hours, room, stood, passed, past, darkness, dream, wind, slept, hear, asleep, dead, grew, lie, warm, rest, remembered, fast, thoughts, face, weary, voice, breath, rain, broke

18	8.92%	3 / 30	life, heart, world, happy, sweet, happiness, beautiful, day, loved, youth,
italic		[10.0%]	beauty, years, nature, live, delight, felt, pure, full, dream, soul, real, days,
dotted			affection, thoughts, kind, secret, eyes, read, friendship, light, calm, future,
underline			fair, lived, fancy, sad, hearts, bright, strange, tenderness, earth, peace, fresh,
			spirit, presence, lives, passion, charm, passed

20	6.69%	2 / 30	day, time, morning, house, evening, hour, place, days, night, week, return,
SMALL		[6.7%]	leave, coming, late, hours, usual, stay, brought, half, called, visit, walk,
CAPS			passed, longer, early, afternoon, change, dinner, work, returned, room,
			knew, order, o'clock, sit, glad, wished, met, heard, happy, aunt, town, began,
			breakfast, quiet, journey, pleased, talk, minutes

21	5.78%	2 / 30	political, public, country, party, men, government, conservative, principles,
bold		[6.7%]	opinion, power, high, principle, position, nation, present, parliamentary,
italic			influence, member, vote, national, candidate, inevitable, town, election,
			leader, parties, politics, members, state, called, office, county, class,
			authority, reform, times, aristocracy, constitution, age, borough, body,
			opinions, people, individual, established, popular, social, institutions, estate

37	5.73%	2 / 30	medical, doctor, practice, profession, work, town, patients, general,
dotted		[6.7%]	physician, patient, disease, treatment, fever, hospital, deal, called, cure, case,
underline			medicine, professional, doctors, drugs, illness, skill, constitution, lydgate,
			fellow, practitioner, gentlemen, opium, attack, symptoms, particulars,
			system, public, dose, scientific, headache, attendance, instance, tyke,
			poison, health, knowledge, country, large, vote, reform, physicians

19	3.73%	1 / 30	looked, eyes, voice, turned, tone, face, spoke, felt, heard, speak, smile,
bold		[3.3%]	answer, speaking, glance, manner, time, eye, silent, silence, began, gave, met,
underline			pause, question, stranger, word, round, surprise, hand, expression, strange,
			turning, room, sat, knew, passed, usual, low, reply, feeling, quick, quickly,
			smiled, quiet, conversation, slight, countenance, speech, questions

29	3.2%	1 / 30	trees, sky, green, air, round, dark, white, lay, road, garden, side, high, light,
bold		[3.3%]	day, river, walk, morning, blue, stood, leaves, walked, windows, spot, house,
dotted			wide, fields, city, distance, gray, park, path, grass, window, scene, shadow,
underline			stone, wood, ground, wind, flowers, rest, country, tree, wall, place, broad,
			hill, clouds, wild

41	3.19%	1 / 30	men, nature, life, woman, character, power, women, mind, human, high,
BOLD		[3.3%]	fine, strong, mere, form, sense, moral, fact, manners, common, apt, natural,
SMALL			society, manner, social, held, pride, generally, easily, rank, understood, kind,
CAPS			order, age, hold, appeared, mental, disposition, principle, force, gentleman,
			small, powers, ambition, influence, qualities, knowledge, general, naturally,
			tastes

FIGURE 3.13 **Mid-topical paragraph (*David Copperfield*, Charles Dickens, 1850).**

"But there was such an *influence* in Mr. Wickfield's old house, that when I knocked at it, with my new *school-books* under my ARM, I **began** to *feel* my *uneasiness* **softening** away. As I went up to my **airy** old room, the **grave** *shadow* of the staircase seemed to FALL upon my *doubts* and *fears*, and to make the **past** more indistinct. I SAT there, STURDILY *conning* my books, until **dinner** *time* (we were out of **school** for good at three); and went down, *hopeful* of becoming a **passable** SORT of BOY yet."

TOPIC # & STYLE	TOPIC SCORE	MODELED WORDS	TOP 20 WORDS FOR TOPIC
8 *italic dotted underline*	26.13%	9 / 30 [30.0%]	felt, mind, feeling, life, sense, strong, dread, presence, consciousness, thoughts, feel, change, painful, pain, husband, future, state, nature, feelings, anxiety
11 **bold underline**	17.45%	6 / 30 [20.0%]	life, years, time, day, days, ago, year, remember, lived, knew, place, happy, past, things, world, strange, heart, mind, change, passed
28 underline	14.5%	5 / 30 [16.7%]	door, room, house, opened, open, window, table, stood, looked, entered, hall, large, light, small, chair, side, place, stairs, dark, windows
13 SMALL CAPS ITALIC	9.1%	3 / 30 [10%]	hand, head, hands, eyes, arm, round, looked, face, shook, chair, sat, arms, turned, laid, side, shoulder, held, table, stood
9 SMALL CAPS	9.55%	3 / 30 [10.0%]	n't, fellow, suppose, sir, things, mind, give, wo, dear, people, poor, bad, care, pretty, sort, boy, deal, woman, hear, call
48 dotted underline	4.06%	1 / 30 [3.3%]	looked, eyes, face, turned, hand, voice, sat, stood, spoke, round, heard, silence, tone, time, speak, felt, room, smile, door, silent
42 *italic*	3.19%	1 / 30 [3.3%]	night, bed, sleep, day, lay, light, hour, sat, fire, room, morning, time, heard, dark, asleep, fell, door, wind, hours, house
29 **bold dotted underline**	3.03%	1 / 30 [3.3%]	ladies, dance, play, grand, gentlemen, beautiful, gave, party, stage, beauty, pleasure, french, pretty, scene, fine, dancing, time, ball, music, charming
43 **bold**	3.96%	1 / 30 [3.3%]	knew, question, mind, time, give, subject, matter, friend, speak, doubt, word, truth, answer, idea, present, point, felt, case, understand, place,

FIGURE 3.14 **Mid-topical Paragraph** (*John Halifax, Gentleman*, Dinah Maria Craik , 1856)

"Guy's INSTINCT of *flight* was, his ***mother*** *felt*, **wisest**, **safest**, best. "My ***boy***, you shall have your desire; you shall go." I had not **expected** it of her—at least, not so **immediately**. I had thought, **bound** up in him as she was, *accustomed* to his **daily sight**, his **daily** fondness—for he was more with her, and "***petted***" her more than any other of the CHILDREN—I had thought to have seen some *reluctance*, some GRIEVED entreaty—but no! Not even when, **gaining** her **consent**, the ***boy looked*** up as if her *allowing* him to **quit** her was the GREATEST **kindness** she had ever in his LIFE bestowed."

TOPIC # & STYLE	TOPIC SCORE	MODELED WORDS	TOP 20 WORDS FOR TOPIC
43 **bold**	26.69%	9 / 30 [30.0%]	knew, question, mind, time, give, subject, matter, friend, speak, doubt, word, truth, answer, idea, present, point, felt, case, understand, place
21 ***bold italic***	14.62%	5 / 30 [16.7%]	mother, father, child, horn, poor, children, daughter, girl, looked, baby, wc, mamma, years, boy, dear, woman, wife, darling, husband, sister
20 SMALL CAPS	11.72%	4 / 30 [13.3%]	men, people, women, things, life, world, work, sort, true, children, woman, hard, find, learn, set, wrong, care, poor, end, live
8 *italic dotted* *underline*	11.93%	4 / 30 [13.3%]	felt, mind, feeling, life, sense, strong, dread, presence, consciousness, thoughts, feel, change, painful, pain, husband, future, state, nature, feelings, anxiety
11 **bold underline**	8.93%	3 / 30 [10.0%]	life, years, time, day, days, ago, year, remember, lived, knew, place, happy, past, things, world, strange, heart, mind, change, passed
33 dotted underline	9.06%	1 / 30 [3.3%]	heart, life, woman, loved, happy, world, happiness, sweet, felt, affection, nature, knew, loving, beautiful, soul, passion, feeling, true, tender, care
22 SMALL CAPS BOLD	3.43%	1 / 30 [3.3%]	dear, aunt, sir, n't, father, friend, speak, papa, leave, happy, glad, returned, give, hear, word, remember, pardon, child, beg, kind
5 *italic underline*	3.45%	1 / 30 [3.3%]	family, gentleman, person, knew, acquaintance, called, fact, society, conversation, friends, present, pleasure, manner, talk, time, house, gentlemen, kind, friend, held

Lukács's *Theory of the Novel*: one was concerned with the inner sphere (emotional or rational), and the other with a part of the external context (house, family); while the third topic, less clearly defined, was more open to the narrator's comments, and narrative framing in general.

Paragraphs are the textual *habitat* of themes, we wrote earlier; and within this *habitat*, the most typical combination is this mix of three topics (or thereabouts). "Three" is here a strictly empirical result, without any Hegelian grandeur; two topics, or four, wouldn't change anything (and in fact, given the different ways of measuring thematic focus, a topic's "score" may easily vary). All that matters is the clear prevalence of these "middle" paragraphs: taken together, two-, three-, and four-topical paragraphs add up to 75 percent of **Figure 3.10**, suggesting that, most of the time, novelistic thematics will avoid both the intensity of mono-topical paragraphs, and the ironic orchestration of poly-topical ones, settling for a simpler, slightly unremarkable modulation between a small group of elements; a quiet, solid "fit" between the soul, the world—and the narrator.

If the initial comparison between paragraphs and "mechanical" segments had established the greater thematic focus of paragraphs, then, these later findings specify that focus as a kind of *thematic combination*: neither the large notions routinely associated with the idea of the "theme" (War; Nature; Travel), nor those "indivisible units" often labeled as "motifs" ("a bomb explodes"; "falling leaves"; "the train leaves the station"), but *the interaction of a few topics within the frame of an everyday event*. Event; because, let's not forget it, these are paragraphs in a story; paragraphs that *make* the story. David's state of mind changes after returning to Mr. Wickfield's house; Guy's mother accepts the fact that it's best for him to go away. An action has occurred; the initial situation has been transformed ("I had not expected it of her") into a different one. And it has been transformed, by *the encounter of distinct topics*: David's feelings don't simply change straightforwardly from "fears" to "hopefulness": they do so, by taking a detour through "house" and "room" and "staircase" ("there was such influence in Mr. Wickfield's old house"). The paragraph is not a pawn that makes its orderly one-way move towards the end of the story; it's a knight that advances by combining two axes in a single move. For now, it's just a metaphor for how paragraphs contribute to the plot. But more can be expected, in the future, from the encounter of thematics and narratology.

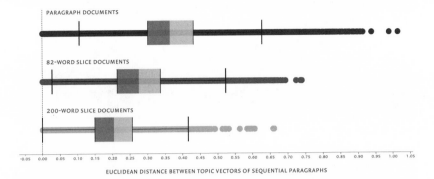

FIGURE 3.15 **Thematic Discontinuity.** While there are several possible reasons for two paragraphs to be discontinuous with each other, meaningful discontinuities tend to fall into three main categories: shifts in narrative perspective (from one character or setting to a different one), movement from cause to effect (or vice versa), and a sort of thematic "unfolding" in which a highly focused paragraph is followed by one which introduces associated notions, or places the primary topic in the wider world of the novel.

Though the present chapter is an attempt at a quantitative morphology of the paragraph, and not a historical study, that discontinuity *between* paragraphs should be stronger than focus within paragraphs is bound to be the result of evolution: of the fact that a "paragraph" originally indicated "a symbol placed in the margin to indicate a noteworthy break in the flow of discourse," and only later did it "come to signify the stretch of language between breaks" (Rodgers, "A Discourse-Centered Rhetoric," 4). Or in other words: first came the impulse to segment the flow of discourse, and only later did writers strengthen the internal consistency of each segment. First came discontinuity, and then focus.

In this chart, discontinuity is measured by comparing the posterior probabilities for all topics in two sequential paragraphs. By measuring the Euclidean distance between the probability vectors, we are able to compare the similarity of paragraphs based upon which topics they share and with what probability each of them is present in the paragraph.

6. LATERAL EXPLORATIONS

So far, we have been focusing on the internal structure of paragraphs. But what about their "external" borders? Was the typographical break between one paragraph and the next also the sign of a *thematic* discontinuity? Since we had already established which topics were present in any given paragraph (and in the 82- and 200-word segments as well), measuring their discontinuity was relatively simple, and revealed an even greater difference among the three groups than had been the case for thematic focus (**Figure 3.15**; for thematic focus, see **Figure 3.6**).

Since discontinuity is based on pairs of consecutive paragraphs, it was inevitable that, at some point, we would wonder: Why not examine longer

THE MILL ON THE FLOSS

PHINEAS FINN

NUMBER OF TOPICS

■ 1   ■ 2   ■ 3   ■ 4   5   6

FIGURE 3.16 **Paragraph sequences in** *The Mill on the Floss* **and** *Phineas Finn*. The density of dark and light gray in these images conveys an immediate sense of the thematic "temperature" of the two novels, contrasting Eliot's intense concentration with Trollope's sardonic tone. The affinity between poly-topical paragraphs and irony in *Phineas Finn* is the same we have briefly discussed in connection with **Figure 3.12**.

paragraph series—in principle, as long as the text itself? Did thematic discontinuity follow a hidden rhythm that would allow us to "sequence" the novels we were studying? **Figure 3.16** attempts to do exactly that: each bar represents a paragraph in *The Mill on the Floss* and *Phineas Finn*, assigned varying depths of gray for thematic focus, from the dark gray of monotopical paragraphs, to the light gray of six or more topics.

Suggestive as these first findings were, no clear pattern emerged from the way paragraphs followed each other; the only constant seemed to be the frequent shift between different types, none of which novels would pause too long on. In a follow-up study, we plan to examine paragraph sequences within chapters, to see if "local" patterns—here dwarfed by the text as a whole—become discernible at that intermediate scale. Meanwhile, our final exploration took us (half) outside of literature, as we decided to compare the thematic organization of our novelistic corpus with two different forms of discourse: a corpus of biographical texts (nonfictional, but with a strong

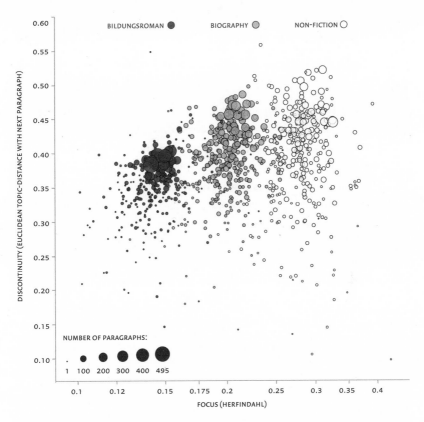

FIGURE 3.17 **Focus and Discontinuity in three Different Registers.** In this chart, the x-axis measures the focus of paragraphs, and the y-axis their discontinuity. The separation between the three discourses—and especially between fiction and non-narrative nonfiction—is unmistakable, and persists even if we topic model each text separately: that is to say, the greater focus of nonfictional texts is not due to the fact that the topics of two books dealing with Kansas and pessimism tend to be more unlike each other than those of two novels (although this is also true); rather, non-fictional paragraphs are both more focused and more discontinuous *even within each individual text.*

narrative component), and a miscellaneous sample of non-narrative non-fiction, ranging from *Kansas; its interior and exterior life* to *Pessimism: A History and a Criticism.* (Both corpora were drawn from the same period as the *bildungsroman,* and had the same total number of words.) We wanted to know whether the affinity between topics and paragraphs was specific to novels, or appeared in other forms of writing as well. And the results were perfectly clear: both discontinuity and—more dramatically—focus scores were much higher in biography, and especially in nonfiction, than in the novelistic corpus. **Figure 3.17,** which combines the two measurements, makes the difference between the three groups impossible to miss.

FIGURE 3.18 Thematic focus in a nonfictional paragraph (*Description of the Skeleton of an Extinct Gigantic Sloth, Mylodon robustus, Owen, with Observations on the Osteology, Natural Affinities, and Probable Habits of the Megatherioid Quadrupeds in General*, Richard Owen, 1842)

"The **bones forming** the **body** of the **sternum** may be **divided** into two **parts**, a **broad** and **flat posterior plate** of a **quadrate form**, and an **anterior rhomb** or **cube projecting** from the **middle** of the **plate**; and they each **present** not **fewer** than ten **articular surfaces**, two for the **contiguous sternal bones**, and the **remaining** eight for **portions** of two **pairs** of **sternal ribs**."

TOPIC # & STYLE	TOPIC SCORE (MALLET)	#. OF MODELED WORDS IN TOPIC	TOP 50 WORDS FOR TOPIC
36 **bold**	92.77%	30 / 30 [100.0%]	surface, bone, anterior, articular, side, posterior, bones, outer, process, form, upper, convex, middle, lower, base, metacarpal, concave, size, ridge, end, vertebrae, distal, slightly, large, rough, species, margin, length, proximal, transverse, fig, articulation, teeth, small, half, broad, presents, phalanx, surfaces, dorsal, skull, vertical, breadth, cavity, processes, skeleton, plate, extinct, diameter

Why such a dramatic gap? The paragraph in **Figure 3.18**, from the appropriately named *Description of the Skeleton of an Extinct Gigantic Sloth*, is a good instance of the thematic focus that can be achieved by a nonfictional text: all thirty Mallet words in the paragraph, no one excluded, belong to the same "skeletal" topic. In a novel, such single-mindedness is unimaginable: not only are the most frequent paragraphs dominated by two-three distinct topics, but, even in the most intense of mono-topical paragraphs, ten, twelve, fifteen of the thirty Mallet words fall routinely outside of the dominant topic. It's not that themes are less relevant, in fiction; rather, they become relevant—they contribute to the advancement of plot—*by associating with other themes*, rather than by fully unfolding in isolation. If their "focus score" is lower than that of nonfiction, then, that is not a flaw, but the very condition of their presence in narrative texts.

o   o   o

7. LITERARY SCALE

"Quantitative Formalism" had been mostly concerned with the frequency of individual words: units that proved to be surprisingly effective at distinguishing literary genres, but not complex enough for an analysis of their internal mechanisms. Two years later, in "Style at the Scale of the Sentence," the shift in scale from words to sentences allowed us to investigate a literary phenomenon—the emergence of style—which had remained inaccessible at the level of individual words. After two more years, another change of scale—this time, from sentences to paragraphs—has brought to light thematic structures which had not been visible at the level of sentences. And the first glimpses of the scale of the chapter suggest the possibility of a further shift, from themes to the narrative unit of the "episode." It's impossible not to venture a general hypothesis: *in literature, different scales activate different structural features.*

Different scales, different features. It's the main difference between the thesis we have presented here, and the one that has so far dominated the study of the paragraph. By defining it as "a sentence writ large," or, symmetrically, as "a short discourse,"[22] previous research was implicitly asserting the irrelevance of scale: sentence, paragraph, and discourse were all equally involved in the "development of one topic." We have found the exact opposite: *scale is directly correlated to the differentiation of textual functions.* By this, we don't simply mean that the scale of sentences or paragraphs allows us to "see" style or themes more clearly. This is true, but secondary. Paragraphs allows us to "see" themes, because *themes fully "exist" only at the scale of the paragraph.* Ours is not just an epistemological claim, but an ontological one: if style and themes and episodes exist in the form they do, it's *because writers work at different scales—and do different things according to the level at which they are operating.*[23]

---

22 Here is a typical passage, from Lewis's *History of the English Paragraph*, 22: "Devoted, like the sentence, to the development of one topic, a good paragraph is also, like a good essay, a complete treatment in itself."

23 In fairness to previous work on the paragraph, the role of scale in multiplying textual functions may be greater in literature than in other types of discourse. The researchers mentioned in footnote 4 have frequently pointed out that Bain's foundational thinking had a strong "logical" component, and much of their own work has been conducted on a type of text—philosophical, legal, and in general nonfic-

Different scales, different features. But if style "emerges" at the scale of the sentences, and themes at that of the paragraph, this does not mean that they "disappear" at a different scale: since chapters are made of paragraphs, and paragraphs of sentences, the larger unit cannot but retain (some of) the features that had emerged at the lower scale. So, for instance, although we had abandoned the idea of studying style at the scale of the paragraph, we couldn't help noticing that we *had* encountered style in the course of our research—most clearly in the "irony" evoked in relation to the poly-topical paragraphs of **Figures 3.12** and **3.16**.[24] At the opposite end of the spectrum, mono-topical paragraphs with a strong dominant topic (**Figures 3.7–3.9**) had a narrative force that could easily "carry over" into the higher scale of the chapter, influencing in depth its narrative composition.[25]

Different scales, different features; and with each new scale, a significant increase in textual complexity. This is not because "higher" scales are *in themselves* more complex: themes are not "more complex" than style, nor episodes more complex than either; they are just completely different—incommensurable, really—in the task they perform. Complexity does not reside "in" any feature or scale of the text: it arises from the fact that multiple scales are embedded into each other, and interact in multiple ways. In the paragraph, we have uncovered the specific "play" of a mid-level structure, which both builds upon smaller components, and acts as a building block of a much larger object. In this looking both "below" and "above" itself, paragraphs enjoy a uniquely central position in the economy of texts.

2015

---

tional—in which a continuity of scale, linking sentences and paragraphs (and perhaps the text in its entirety) is more plausible than in literary discourse.

24 Significantly, this persistence of style was mostly associated with those cases in which *the paragraph's internal unity was weakest, and the autonomy of sentences correspondingly strongest*; in other words, style was more visible when its elective scale—the sentence—retained a certain independence vis-à-vis higher forms of integration.

25 The narrative potential of paragraphs is clear in Watt's essay on *The Ambassadors*, with its frequent evocation of James's "progress towards the foreordained illumination," "progressive and yet artfully delayed clarification," and so on. By contrast, narrativity is silently downplayed in Auerbach's pages on *Madame Bovary*: "nothing particular happens in the scene, nothing particular has happened just before it. It is a random moment from the regularly recurring hours . . ." (*Mimesis*, 488).

PART

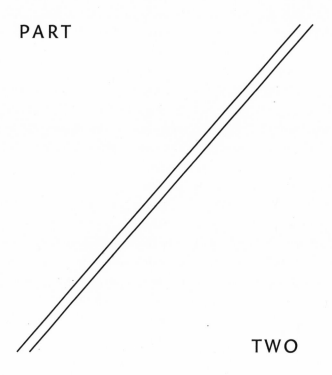

TWO

CHAPTER 4

"Operationalizing"

OR, THE FUNCTION OF MEASUREMENT IN LITERARY THEORY

Franco Moretti

"Operationalizing" must be the ugliest word I've ever used, but it is never-theless the hero of the pages that follow, because it refers to a process that is absolutely central to the new field of computational criticism, or, as it has come to be called, of the digital humanities. Though the word is often used merely as a complicated synonym for "realizing" or "implementing"—the Merriam-Webster online, for instance, mentions "operationalizing a program" and adds a quote on "operationalizing the artistic vision of the organization"—the original root of the term was different, and much more precise; and for once origin is right, this is one of those rare cases when a term has an actual birth date: 1927, when P. W. Bridgman devoted the opening of his *Logic of Modern Physics* to "the operational point of view." Here are the key passages:

> We may illustrate [the meaning of the term] by considering the concept of length: what do we mean by the length of an object? . . . To find the length of an object we have to perform certain physical operations. The concept of length is therefore fixed when the operations by which length is fixed are fixed: that is, the concept of length involves as much and nothing more than the set of operations by which length is determined. In general, we mean by any concept nothing more than a set of operations; *the concept is synonymous with the corresponding set of operations* . . . the proper definition of a concept is not in terms of its properties but in terms of actual operations.[1]

---

1 P. W. Bridgman, *The Logic of Modern Physics*, (New York: Macmillan, 1927), 5–6.

The concept of length, the concept is synonymous, the concept is nothing more than, the proper definition of a concept . . . Forget programs and visions; the operational approach refers specifically to *concepts*, and in a very particular way: it describes the process whereby concepts are transformed into a series of operations—which, in their turn, allow us to measure all sorts of objects. Operationalizing means building a bridge from concepts to measurement, and then to the world. In our case: from the concepts of literary theory, through some form of quantification, to literary texts.

1. OPERATIONALIZING CHARACTER-SPACE

Taking a concept, and transforming it into a series of operations. Concretely, how does one do that? My first example concerns one of the most important contributions to literary theory of the past twenty or thirty years: the concept of "character-space," coined by Alex Woloch in *The One vs. the Many*. Here is the initial cluster of definitions:

> the amount of narrative space allocated to a particular character . . . the space of the character within the narrative structure . . . the space that he or she occupies within the narrative totality . . . the narrative's continual apportioning of attention to different characters who jostle for limited space within the narrative totality.[2]

So, what are the "operations we have to perform," to find out the amount of narrative space allotted to Molly Bloom, or Iago, or any other character? Graham Sack has answered by taking the path of so-called "instrumental variables": features that we use as proxies for the variables we are interested in, when the latter are—for whatever reason—impossible to measure. Working on 19th-century novels, Sack calculated how often they mentioned the names of the various characters; though name frequency is not the same as character-space, they are clearly correlated—and Sack's proxy worked quite well for Austen, Dickens and many other writers.[3]

---

2 Alex Woloch, *The One vs. the Many: Minor Characters and the Space of the Protagonist in the Novel*, (Princeton, NJ: Princeton University Press, 2003), 13–14.

3 Graham Alexander Sack, "Simulating Plot: Towards a Generative Model of Narrative Structure," Papers from the AAAI Fall Symposium, 2011.

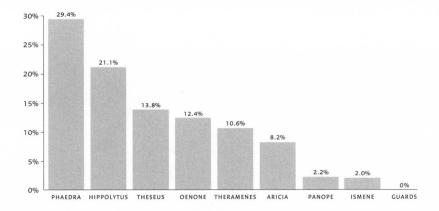

FIGURE 4.1 *Phèdre*, characters' percentage of word-space

I took a different approach, which assumed that character-space could actually be measured directly. Texts are made of words, lines, pages, and one can definitely measure those. But there are complications. Take this sentence from the first chapter of *Pride and Prejudice*: "Mr Bennet was so odd a mixture of quick parts, sarcastic humour, reserve and caprice, that the experience of three-and-twenty years had been insufficient to make his wife understand his character."

Where does Mr. Bennet's "space" end and Mrs. Bennet's begin, in this sentence? Sack's proxy would score one for Mr. Bennet and zero for his wife, and it's reasonable, in so far as naming a character is always a way of foregrounding it; on the other hand, a larger portion of the sentence refers to Mrs. Bennet's perception, and all that is completely lost. Plays are easier in this respect: as there are no ambiguities in how words are distributed among the various speakers, character-space turns smoothly into "word-space"—"the number of words allocated to a particular character"—and, by counting the words each character utters, we can determine how much textual space it occupies. In Jean Racine's *Phèdre*, for instance, Phaedra utters 29 percent of words, Hippolytus 21, Theseus 14, and so on all the way to the 0 percent of the guards who silently obey Theseus's orders in the final act of the play (**Figure 4.1**).

It is a simple, plausible way of measuring character-space. But it's not the only way. Network theory, for instance, has taught us to measure the links a character has with the rest of the "character-system" (another of Woloch's concepts), and the "weight" of those links—the number of

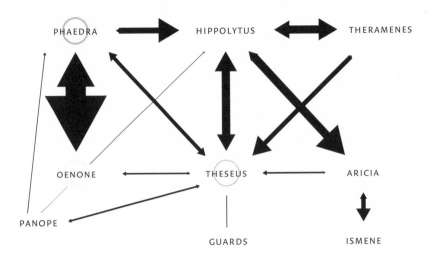

FIGURE 4.2 *Phèdre*: nodes, links, weight, direction

words exchanged between any two characters—as well as their "direction"—who is speaking to whom; and, with each new measurement, new aspects of *Phèdre* become visible (**Figure 4.2**). If the bar graph has already shown that Phaedra speaks more than the other characters in the play, the network tells us that the largest part of her word-space is taken, not by exchanges with her husband Theseus or would-be lover Hippolytus, but with her "confidante" Oenone: a result that is not inevitable, and is in fact quite revealing of neo-classical poetics. The network also shows how uneven—"an-isotropic"—word-spaces tend to be: in most cases, language doesn't flow equally in every direction. Phaedra speaks to Oenone much more than the other way around; same between Phaedra and Hippolytus, Hippolytus and Aricia, Aricia and Ismene. Or again; if one thinks of *Phèdre*'s most famous narrative passage—the *récit* of Theramenes—the network makes immediately visible how *decentered* that speech act is from much of the play, and especially from Phaedra herself; and I could continue to use this diagram to analyze other aspects of the play. But I'd rather take a step back and ask: so, what has operationalizing actually *done*? Let's assume that deriving quantitative data from Woloch's concept has added something to our knowledge of *Phèdre*: what exactly is that "something"?

o   o   o

2. CONCEPT AGAINST CONCEPT

Fifty years ago, Thomas Kuhn wrote an essay that presents measurement—that is to say, the act of "producing actual numbers": like those that are behind **Figures 4.1** and **4.2**—as something which, far from being obvious, is in fact badly in need of theoretical and practical justification. Though many believe that measurement is useful because "numerical data are likely to be productive of new generalizations," for Kuhn this hope is completely groundless: "numbers gathered without some knowledge of the regularity to be expected," he observes, in a before-the-fact critique of what today would be called "data-driven" research, "almost certainly remain just numbers"; no new "laws of nature" will ever be "discovered simply by inspecting the results of measurements." Measurement does not lead from the world, via quantification, to the constructions of theories; if anything, it leads *back* from theories, through data, to the empirical world. "The new order provided by a new theory is always overwhelmingly a *potential* order," writes Kuhn; potential, because the "laws" of the theory "have so few quantitative points of contact with nature" that they are, as it were, floating above the world of empirical facts. Measurement rectifies this weakness; it provides "an investigation of those contact points," thus strengthening the connections between laws and reality, and transforming that "overwhelmingly *potential* order" into an "*actual*" one. Measurement anchors theories to the world they describe.[4]

Now, I don't know whether scientific theories really have so few points of contact with nature; for literary theories, though, this is certainly the case, and it is also why measurement matters so much: it makes some concepts "actual" in the strong sense of the word; it takes character-space, and proves that there is something in the real world (the real world of fictions) that corresponds to it. Not all concepts are born equal, some are better than others, and operationalization, though not the only test of a theory, is an important one. It shows that, by following a series of steps, you can turn abstractions into a clear and, hopefully, unexpected elaboration of reality. Like the diagram in **Figure 4.2**: a pair of concepts, a few simple rules, and a new image of *Phèdre* emerges. But, again: new, how?

---

4 Thomas Kuhn, "The Function of Measurement in Modern Physical Science" (1961), in *The Essential Tension: Selected Studies in Scientific Tradition and Change* (Chicago: University of Chicago Press, 1977), 180, 183, 197–8, 188 (italics in the original).

First of all, it's new because it's precise. Phaedra is allocated 29 percent of the word-space, not 25, or 39. Historical novels have recently become more frequent in high literature, observed Perry Anderson a few years ago; and, in a workshop at the Literary Lab, James English showed how that "more frequent" can be translated into "between 40 and 50 per cent of novels nominated for literary prizes"; and "recently" into: "beginning in the 1980s."

Precision is always good. Or is it? "It is ridiculous to attempt a precise measurement of the dimensions of a natural being," wrote Alexandre Koyré, in an essay with the wonderful title "From the World of the 'More-or-Less' to the Universe of Precision":

> Reality, the reality of everyday life, within which we exist and live, is not mathematical . . . there is everywhere a margin of imprecision, of "play," of "more or less," of "just about" . . . A little more, a little less . . . what importance can that have? In most cases, undoubtedly, none whatsoever.[5]

Establishing that Phaedra speaks 29 per cent of the words in the play instead of 25 or 39—what importance does this have? We knew she spoke "more" than the other characters; does the "actual number" produced by measurement modify that? No. It adds detail, but it doesn't change what we already knew. And if this is all measurement can do, then its role within literary study will only be a limited and ancillary one; making existing knowledge somewhat better, but not really different.

Disappointing. In another region of literary theory, however, measurement has rather different consequences. When one looks at the word-space chart of **Figure 4.1**, that Phaedra is the protagonist of the play seems to go without saying. When we measure the number of links in the play's network, though, Theseus is clearly more central than her. Two conflicting criteria for protagonism emerge from the two types of measurement: the volume of words, and the number of interactions. And it's not that one criterion is right and the other is wrong; rather, they capture different features of dramatic networks, and of the conflict that is latent at their

---

5 Alexandre Koyré, "Du monde de l'"à-peu-près' à l'univers de la précision" (1948), in *Études d'histoire de la pensée philosophique* (Paris: Armand Colin, 1961), 340, 348.

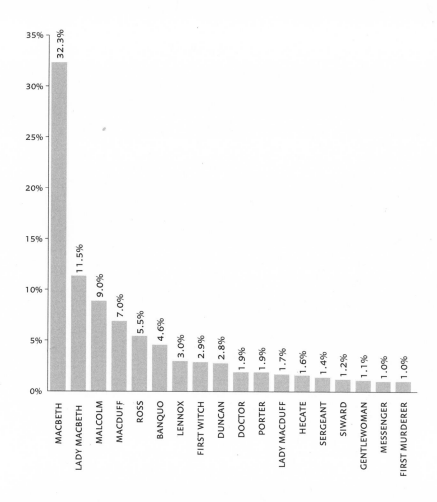

FIGURE 4.3 *Macbeth*, **characters' percentage of word-space.** The twenty-plus characters with percentages below 1 percent have been omitted from this chart.

center: the number of links tells us how connected a character is (and is often correlated with proximity to power, as with Theseus); the number of words tells us how much meaning the character brings into the play (and is often correlated with a discord with power, as with Phaedra here).

There are cases in which the two criteria of centrality coincide, most spectacularly in *Macbeth* (**Figure 4.3**), where Macbeth dominates both the word-space and the network of the play; but disagreement between them, or a difference too slight to be meaningful, are actually much more frequent, as illustrated in the figures that follow. In *Othello*, for instance,

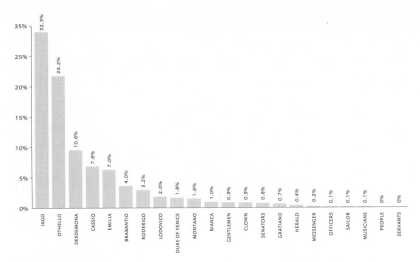

FIGURE 4.4 *Othello*

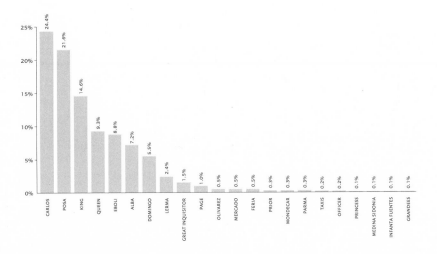

FIGURE 4.5 *Don Carlos*

Iago has a larger word-space than Othello, but not by much (**Figure 4.4**); same with Carlos and Posa in *Don Carlos* (**Figure 4.5**), or several characters in *Ghosts* (**Figure 4.6**); or, most striking of all, in *Antigone*; the paradigm of tragic conflict for Hegel and so many others, yet one in which the heroine speaks far fewer words, and has significantly fewer connections to the rest of the character-system than either Creon or the Chorus (**Figures 4.7** and **4.8**).

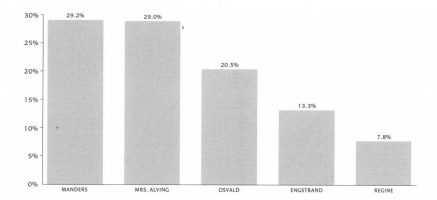

FIGURE 4.6 *Ghosts*

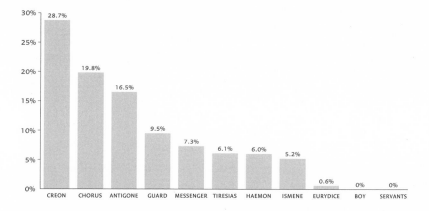

FIGURE 4.7 *Antigone*

What can measurement do for literary study? In this case, it shows that the "protagonist," far from being a fundamental reality of dramatic construction, *is only a special instance of the more general category of "centrality."* Centrality exists always; Macbeth is a limit case. Concept against concept: the measurement of character-space undermines the older notion, replacing it with the idea of a conflict arising near the center of the network. And something very similar happens at the opposite end of

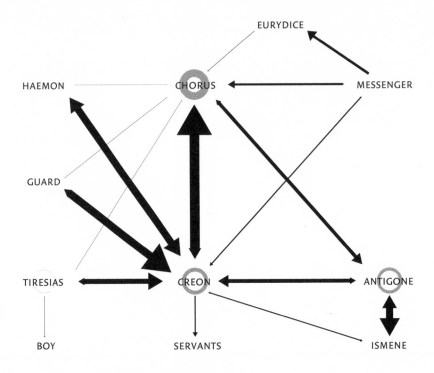

FIGURE 4.8 *Antigone*: nodes, links, weight, direction

the spectrum, among the "minor characters" that populate the periphery of dramatic systems. In this network of *Hamlet*, for instance (**Figure 4.9**), reproduced from my earlier *New Left Review* article on "Network Theory, Plot Analysis," we find Reynaldo, the Priest, the second gravedigger, all the attendants and messengers who hang to the plot by a single thread—and who, in Shakespeare, add up to about half of the character-system: are they all "minor characters" in the same sense as Gertrude, Polonius, or even Rosencrantz?[6] In *The One vs. the Many*, Woloch evokes the idea of "minor minor characters," and **Figure 4.9** radicalizes his insight: to be connected to a network by a single link, or by four or five, is not a matter of emphasis ("minor," and "minor minor"), but of function: "obedience"—or, much more rarely, disobedience—for single-link characters;

---

6 Franco Moretti, "Network Theory, Plot Analysis," *New Left Review* 68 (March–April 2011), 80–102.

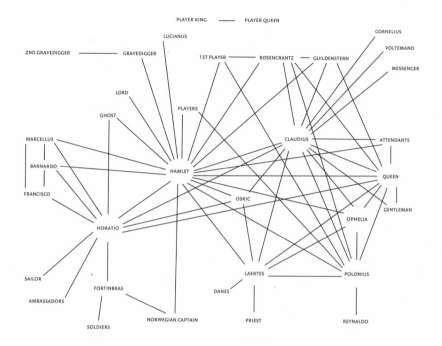

FIGURE 4.9 *Hamlet*: **nodes and links**

and "mediation" for those who, because of their various connections, are almost always linked to more than one network region.[7]

Needless to say, the trio of "conflict," "mediation," and "obedience" is a hypothesis, as is the older pair of protagonist and minor character. But the new categories have the advantage of referring to specific aspects of the plot, and of the social world that is being represented; plus, they agree much better with quantitative evidence. Koyré again:

> A utensil . . . amplifies and strengthens the action of our body, of our sense organs: it is something that belongs to the world of common sense—and that will never allow us to go beyond that world. Such, by contrast, is precisely the function of the instrument: which is not

---

7 Almost always: so-called "cliques" possess several local connections, while remaining substantially disconnected from the body of the play (more or less like the group formed by Bernardo, Francisco and Marcellus in **Figure 4.9**). In the relatively small character-systems of drama, cliques tend to be rare; in novels, they are much more significant.

an amplification of our senses but, in the strongest and most literal sense of the term, is an incarnation of the spirit, a materialization of thought . . . the conscious realization of a theory. . . . It is for purely theoretical reasons, in order to reach what does not fall under the domain of our senses, to see what no one had ever seen before, that Galileo constructed his instruments, the telescope and then the microscope.[8]

The protagonist is a utensil; character-space is an instrument. The protagonist is a utensil because it belongs to the world of readerly common sense, and doesn't go beyond it. Character-space is an instrument, because it's the realization of a theory that wants to understand something "that does not fall under the domain of our senses": instead of individual characters, the *relations* among characters. That's why, in the end, its operationalization produced more than the refinement of already-existing knowledge: not the protagonist, improved, but an altogether new set of categories. Measurement as a challenge to literary theory, one could say, echoing a famous essay by Hans Robert Jauss. This is not what I expected from the encounter of computation and criticism; I assumed, like so many others, that the new approach would change the history, rather than the theory of literature; and, ultimately, that may still be the case. But since the logic of research has brought us face to face with conceptual issues, they should openly become the task of the day, countering the pervasive clichés on the simple-minded positivism of the digital humanities. Computation has theoretical consequences—possibly, more far-reaching than any other field of literary study. The time has come to make them explicit.

3. OPERATIONALIZING TRAGIC COLLISION

I have spent so much time on character-space because the concept is clear, fruitful—and easy to operationalize; not that Woloch had this in mind as he was writing his book, but he was writing from within a paradigm—broadly speaking, structuralism—where quantification, though seldom activated, was in principle a perfectly acceptable option. The trouble is, most literary

---

8 Koyré, "Du monde de l'"à-peu-près' à l'univers de la precision," 352, 357.

concepts are emphatically *not* designed to be quantified; and the question arises of what to do with them.

Bridgman, in his book, had sketched out an answer of sorts. In the light of the operational point of view, he had written, "thinking becomes simpler": "old generalizations . . . become incapable of use," and "many of the speculations of the early natural philosophers become simply unreadable."[9] I disagree with this nonchalant dismissal, and, in the second part of this article, will do exactly the opposite of what Bridgman recommends: I will take one of the peaks of speculative aesthetics—Hegel's conception of tragic conflict—and try to chart a path from this "old generalization" to the world of empirical data.[10]

To begin with, a few definitions:

> What is properly dramatic is the speech of individuals in the conflict of their interests and the discord of their characters and passions.

> The completely dramatic form is the *dialogue*. For in it alone can the individual agents express face to face their character and aim, both their personal character and the substance of their animating "pathos"; in it alone can they come into conflict and so actually move the action forwards.

> What drives them to act is precisely an ethically justified "pathos" that they assert against one another with the eloquence of their "pathos" not in sentimental and personal rhetoric or in the sophistries of passion, but in solid and cultivated objective language.[11]

---

9 Bridgman, *Logic of Modern Physics*, 31–2.

10 As will become clear, I assume that Hegel's theory *can* be operationalized. This leaves open two further questions. First: and if it couldn't? Would the theory lose all its value, and deserve to be forgotten? The second question is almost opposite in nature: if applied too loosely and widely, wouldn't operationalizing lose the strict falsifying potential that had made it so valuable in the first place? In principle (though a full motivation will have to wait for another occasion), my answers would be, No to the first question, and Yes to the second. On how uncritical operationalizations have ended up "legitimating . . . 'metaphysical' concepts instead of replacing them" in the fields of both economics and psychology, see D. Wade Hands, "On Operationalisms and Economics," *Journal of Economic Issues* 38, no. 4 (December 2004), 953–968.

11 G. W. F. Hegel, *Aesthetics: Lectures on Fine Art*, vol. 1, trans. T. M. Knox (Oxford: Clarendon Press, 1975), 1171, 1172–3, 1214–5.

There are some differences among these passages, but they all converge on the same two main points. The first is conflict: *Kampf,* "battle," "fight." But for Hegel, tragic *Kampf* is not (just) destruction; it is also a *productive* process that gives rise to "speech," "dialogue," "ethically justified 'pathos'," "cultivated objective language." With them, a new element enters the discussion. Character-space could be directly translated into other spatial configurations, such as bar charts, or networks; "ethically justified 'pathos'" and "cultivated objective language," however, entail *meaning*—and, in order to operationalize that, additional steps become necessary. In this case, I took ten Greek tragedies in which a central collision was particularly clear,[12] and proceeded to establish the meanings—or at least, the words—most distinctive of their main antagonists. As the results were similar throughout the corpus, I focused on Hegel's master example of *Antigone*: where the "chief conflict," reads the famous formulation of the *Aesthetics,* occurs "between the state, i.e. ethical life in its *spiritual* universality, and the family, i.e. *natural* ethical life."[13] And here are the nouns that emerged as most distinctive of, respectively, Antigone and Creon:

> ANTIGONE: *brother, mother, marriage, home, friend, love, honour, tomb, Hades, misery, law*
>
> CREON: *ruin, evil, fear, woman, men, god, money*

Antigone's terms clearly incline toward family and mourning; Creon's are more abstract and threatening. But they are, more or less, what one would have expected. Then, verbs:

> ANTIGONE: *die, leave, go, share, rest*
>
> CREON: *let, take, stand, shall, find, tell, make, may, know, be*

Here, Creon's peremptory tone produced a modestly interesting finding vis-à-vis Hegel: if Antigone's results again evoked the "natural ethical life" of family piety, Creon's language was not that of the state as "spiritual universality"—it was the state as *mere power to coerce*: let take stand find tell

---

12 Five tragedies by Aeschylus, and five by Sophocles: *Agamemnon, Libation Bearers, Eumenides, Suppliant Maidens, Prometheus; Antigone, Philoctetes, Oedipus at Colonus, Ajax, Electra.*

13 Hegel, *Aesthetics,* 1213.

make . . . Imperative, often callous: "Take yourself away"; "If you do not find the author . . ."; "Tell me, did you know of the proclamation"; "Tell me, do you admit being a party to the burial"; "Let there be no delay, take her"; "Let her keep invoking the Zeus of kindred"; "Let him act so, let him go." Still, the finding was indeed modest; many had already observed that Hegel had exaggerated the spiritual significance of Creon; our evidence corroborated this critique, and corroboration is not nothing, but is also not much. Antigone and Creon, *the* tragic conflict; I was hoping for more than this.

4. TRAGIC COLLISION, SECOND ATTEMPT

Then I realized that the words I was looking at were indeed distinctive of Antigone and Creon, but they were so at the scale of the play as a whole; they included what each of them said to the Chorus, to Ismene, the guard, Haemon, Tiresias . . . The words were distinctive, yes, but not *of their conflict*. And instead, on this point, Hegel had been extremely clear:

> in [dialogue] alone can the individual agents express face to face their character and aim . . . come into conflict and so actually move the action forwards.

> An ethically justified "pathos" which they assert against one another with the eloquence of their "pathos" . . . in solid and cultivated objective language.[14]

"Express face to face," "assert against one another"; in both cases, the German is the same: *gegeneinander*, an adverb that inscribes conflict (*gegen*, against) in the very body of the word. In establishing Antigone's and Creon's most distinctive words, I had completely overlooked this conjunction of self-expression with the *gegeneinander*; that's why the results had been so predictable. On my second attempt, I extracted only the passages when Antigone and Creon speak to each other, generated a new list of most distinctive words, and—

---

14 Hegel, *Aesthetics*, 1172–3, 1214–5.

ANTIGONE: *gods, son, power, corpse*

CREON: *death, woman, evil*

Possibly the opposition was sharper than before; certainly it was much more limited. In part this was so because the new pool of words was smaller than the old one; but the truth is that, when Antigone and Creon are face to face, their language becomes, not more substantial and objective, as Hegel would have it, but less so:

CREON: You alone among the Cadmeans see this.

ANTIGONE: They see it too; but they curb their tongues to please you.

CREON: Are you not ashamed of thinking differently from them?

ANTIGONE: There is no shame in showing regard for those of one's own stock.

CREON: Was not he who died on the other side also your brother?

ANTIGONE: My brother with the same mother and the same father.[15]

Tragedy is "a real murder via words," wrote Hölderlin in his annotations to *Antigone*, and this line-by-line attack and defense—known as stichomythia, or verse-speech—is probably what he had in mind; a rhetoric that makes tragic opposition at once extremely clear, and extremely narrow. Clear: You alone see this / They see it too. Are you not ashamed / There is no shame. But narrow: because the conflict between the speakers is expressed by *reiterating–negating the same terms* (see, shame, brother), rather than evoking the large value systems (brother–home– love–tomb–law; let–take–stand–find–tell) that had been plainly visible at the scale of the play as a whole. There, the conflict between Antigone and Creon had found expression in their very different "objective languages"; in stichomythia, it has been drastically contracted to the opposite sides of a lowest common denominator. The dramatic effect is heightened—but at the expense of semantics. It is not in these lines that we can find the meaning of *Antigone*.

It is not in these lines . . . Yet, the operationalization of Hegel's theory of tragic collision has led us precisely to these lines. Another mistake? No; this time, god forgive me, the mistake was Hegel's—it lay in the connection he posited between face-to-face confrontations and the *"gebildete*

---

15 All quotes from *Antigone* are from the Loeb edition (Cambridge, MA: Harvard University Press, 1995).

Objectivität" of tragic language. Separately, both notions are true; it is their conjunction that isn't. Face-to-face confrontations *do* occur in tragedy, and find a memorable expression in the rhetoric of stichomythia; but stichomythia does not convey the "ethically justified pathos" that Hegel had in mind. This pathos also exists, of course, and constitutes the very core of Greek tragedy; but it is not dependent on the *gegeneinander* of face-to-face encounters; it emerges much more clearly in Antigone's exchanges with her sister Ismene, or in her long speech to the Chorus (and, through the Chorus, to the audience: "Look at me, citizens of my fatherland . . ."), than in her confrontation with Creon. The moment of crisis is not a moment of truth: it exerts too much pressure on the acting subjects for Hegel's "cultivated objectivity" to shine through. And a whole new relationship between conflict and values becomes necessary as a result.[16]

Did we need operationalizing to reach this conclusion? This is not for me to say. What I will say is that the leap from measurement to reconceptualization that has characterized both parts of this essay (though in Hegel's case the new categories have yet to emerge), demonstrates how the unprecedented empirical power of digital tools and archives offers a unique chance to rethink the categories of literary study. The digital humanities may not yet have changed the territory of the literary historian, or the reading of individual texts; but operationalizing has certainly changed, and radicalized, our relationship to concepts: it has raised our expectations, by turning concepts into magic spells that can call into being a whole world of empirical data; and it has sharpened our skepticism, because, if the data revolt against their creator, then the concept is really in trouble.

---

16 A parallel line of argument would stress the unique role played in stichomythia by Greek particles. Half conjunctions, half sentence adverbs for mood and attitude—*men, ge, kai, de, gar, alla, oun, te, kai ge, kai men*: surely, yes but, at least, in fact, truly, on the other hand, indeed, of course, even . . . —particles are very frequent in stichomythia (though they are often lost in translation), because they are great at expressing conflict. But they express it in their own unique way: *Färbung*, "coloring," is the favorite cognitive metaphor of the critical literature. Particles bring about "a loss of definiteness (compensated) by increased subtlety," states their classic study: "less body, and more bouquet." It's hard to imagine a less Hegelian statement—and that's precisely the problem: the style of face-to-face confrontations, by making a large use of particles and of their peculiar rhetoric, results in the *opposite* of the "cultivated objective language" that Hegel had identified with tragic collision. See Adolf Gross, *Die Stichomythie in der griechischen Tragödie und Komödie, ihre Anwendung und ihr Ursprung* (Berlin: Weidmann, 1905); John Leonard Hancock, *Studies in Stichomythia* (Chicago: University of Chicago Press, 1917); J. D. Denniston, *The Greek Particles*, 2nd ed. revised by K. J. Dover (Oxford, UK: Oxford University Press, 1950), xxxvii.

A theory-driven, data-rich research program has become imaginable, bent on testing, and, when needed, falsifying the received knowledge of literary study. Of this enterprise, operationalizing will be the central ingredient.

2013

CHAPTER 5

Loudness in the Novel

Holst Katsma

"In the novel, we can always hear voices (even while reading silently
to ourselves)."

—*Mikhail Bakhtin*

The novel is composed entirely of voices: the most prominent among them
is typically that of the narrator, which is regularly intermixed with those of
the various characters. In reading through a novel, the reader "hears" these
heterogeneous voices as they occur in the text. When the novel is read out
loud, the voices are audibly heard. They are also heard, however, when the
novel is read silently: in this latter case, the voices are not verbalized for
others to hear, but acoustically created and perceived in the mind of the
reader. Simply put: sound, in the context of the novel, is fundamentally a
product of the novel's voices. This conception of sound mechanics may
at first seem unintuitive—sound seems to be the product of oral reading—but it is only by starting with the voice that one can fully appreciate sound's function in the novel. Moreover, such a conception of sound
mechanics finds affirmation in the works of both Mikhail Bakhtin and
Elaine Scarry: "In the novel," writes Bakhtin, "we can always hear voices
(even while reading silently to ourselves)."[1]

---

1 Mikhail Bakhtin, "Forms of Time and of the Chronotope in the Novel," in *The Dialogic Imagination*, trans.
Caryl Emerson and Michael Holquist (Austin, TX: University of Texas Press, 1981), 252. Elaine Scarry
confirms this description of sound mechanics: "When we read [a] passage aloud or almost aloud, the
sound of the words is sensorially present. . . . When we read silently, the spoken words are acoustically
imaged rather than actually heard." Elaine Scarry, *Dreaming by the Book* (Princeton: Princeton University
Press, 2001), 132.

Now, the voices of the novel, heard by the reader, are particularly interesting and diverse. Each voice sounds unique. Each voice has its own unique semantic content. And, in the case of dialogue, the manner of speaking is often described, meaning that to each instance of a voice a particular quality and sound can be ascribed. So, sound is a continuous aspect of the novel—we can always hear voices—that directly affects the reader regardless of whether he reads orally or in silence, and the novel is one of the few genres to experiment with the diversity and distribution of multiple voices. Yet despite these facts, little has come of the study of sound in the novel: in part due to the absence of categories by which to distinguish between different types of sound; in part due to a general skepticism regarding the novel's degree of control over how its voices are heard. At the highest level, this paper proposes loudness—a concept that is in fact explicitly associated in the novel with certain voices—as a means to break down, analyze, and make sense of sound's functions in the novel.[2]

o   o   o

LOUDNESS CAN BE broken down into three basic levels: quiet, neutral, and loud. These three levels provide a simple schema for grouping and analyzing all voices in the novel.[3] While each reader hears the voices of the novel with slight variation, it is my belief that these differences do not typically transgress into our broader three levels of volume. *However, in order to locate loudness in the novel as objectively as possible, this paper will take as its starting point and as its central object of study a select set of voices—what*

---

2 The type of sound studied in this paper may be contrasted with a second type of novelistic sound: not only does the reader hear the voices of the novel as he comes across them, but on certain occasions these novelistic voices ask the reader to imagine secondary sounds (sometimes referred to as "soundscapes"). For instance, as Elaine Scarry acutely discerns, when the reader is reading *Madame Bovary* and comes across the phrase "drops of water could be heard falling one by one on the taut moiré," he not only hears these words being spoken by the narrator, but further, "lightly piggybacking on top" of the sound of the narrator's voice is "the imagined scrims of the sound of raindrops." (*Dreaming by the Book*, 116, 132). So, two types of sound: the sound of the narrator speaking the phrase "drops of water could be heard . . ." and the less intense and more fleeting sound of rain falling on a parasol. I will leave these fleeting and rather infrequent descriptions of sound for a different study, and instead focus on the continuous and sonorous sounds of novelistic voices.

3 Loudness's classificatory nature makes it a particularly productive concept for making sense of the many dynamic voices of the novel. The same cannot be said of concepts like tone, timbre, and pitch, which emphasize subtle and minute aspects of sound and as a result tend to differentiate between sounds rather than group sounds together.

I term the voices of tagged dialogue; that is, voices that are described as being
spoken in a certain manner; voices that are shouted, whispered, exclaimed.
Take, for example, the following sentence: "'Off with their heads!' shouted
the Queen." In this case, the Queen's manner of speaking is made explicit
by the verb "shouted" located just outside the dialogue in the external narration. I will call such verbs—verbs that describe how a section of dialogue
is spoken—speaking verbs. Dialogue with a speaking verb will be called
tagged dialogue; dialogue without a speaking verb, *suspended dialogue.*[4]
Within tagged dialogue, tonal subjectivity is reduced to a minimum,
because the sound of the voice is explicitly described.

Speaking verbs are the first step toward quantifying textual loudness.
In fact, all tagged dialogue can be objectively parsed into one of three levels
of loudness based on the respective speaking verb. For example:

> LOUD: "Off with their heads!" **shouted** the Queen.
> NEUTRAL: "I suppose so," **said** Alice.
> QUIET: He **whispered**, "She's under sentence of execution."

Speaking verbs indicate that loudness is an unequivocal part of the novel:
certain voices in the novel are explicitly loud, and as such their loudness
is undeniably based within the novel (not the result of a subjective whim
on the part of the reader). The fact that these voices are explicitly loud in
no way entails that they are the only loud voices in the novel; however,
their clearly stated loudness suggests that these voices are significantly
loud—most likely, the loudest ones.

This, then, is the background and topic of the present study. The study
itself will be divided into three parts, each of which develops the concept of
loudness (as found in tagged dialogue) in a different direction.

Part 1 examines the words that occur within loud dialogue that is
cried, exclaimed, shouted, roared, and screamed. When, for instance, the
reader reads the sentence, "'Off with their heads!' shouted the Queen," it
is the words and punctuation inside the quotations ("Off," "with," "their,"
"heads," and the exclamation mark) that are typical of what I will call the
semantics of loudness. I have relied on speaking verbs to define dialogue

---

4 I took the term "suspended dialogue" from Mark Lambert, *Dickens and the Suspended Quotation* (New Haven, CT: Yale University Press, 1981).

that is explicitly loud; however, speaking verbs are not responsible for *making* loud dialogue loud. In my example, the dialogue is not transubstantiated into loud dialogue once the word "shouted" is read. Rather, it is the semantic content of the Queen's voice that suggests and elicits within the reader's imagination a speaker who is speaking loudly. As such, a semantic study of loud dialogue is a natural first step toward understanding the roles and functions of loudness in the novel.

Part 2 examines the structural potential of loudness and loud dialogue. Oscillating between two tiers of structure—the organization of loud dialogue amongst the voices that make up a novel and the organization of the reader's aural experience while reading—this section will explore how the loudest and quietest sections of the novel affect both the plot and the psychology of the reader.

Part 3 uses loudness as a means of measuring historical change. There is no requirement regarding how many voices in the novel are loud, quiet, and neutral. Part III describes a quieting down of the British novel over the course of the 19th century by measuring the change in the percentage of loud speaking verbs per decade.[5]

The primary goal in the following pages is to open up new conceptual possibilities. As such, each section is only a beginning. The three parts do not pretend to any completeness.

1. THE SEMANTICS OF LOUD DIALOGUE

The following semantic analysis takes the form of a most-distinctive-word test. In this MDW, loud dialogue was compared with neutral dialogue, the most common form of dialogue in the novel. Speaking verbs made possible the compilation of two large samples: one of 500 instances of explicitly neutral dialogue, framed by *said, replied, observed, rejoined,* or *asked*; and another composed of 500 instances of explicitly loud dialogue, framed by *cried, exclaimed, shouted, roared,* or *screamed*.[6] Both samples were ran-

---

5 At the start, I intended to include a fourth part on the role of loudness in free indirect discourse. The complexity of the subject, however, requires a study of its own.

6 The two samples are based on the five most common speaking verbs for each category. A more extensive list of speaking verbs might include the following: (Loud) *cried, exclaimed, shouted, roared, screamed, shrieked, vociferated, bawled, called, ejaculated, retorted, proclaimed, announced, protested, accosted, de-*

domly selected from a corpus of 19th-century novels written in English. The computer returned the words that occurred both frequently in loud dialogue and infrequently in neutral dialogue. These "loud words" are displayed in **Figure 5.1**.

The initial expectation was that loud words would cluster around specific topics, perhaps defined by nouns like *scoundrel, murderer, fool,* and *guilt,* or adjectives like *wretched, despicable,* and *miserable.* Instead, *loudness showed an affinity, not to topics, but to grammatical structures.* This emerged first at the most basic grammatical level—part of speech. Loud dialogue exhibits a preference for verbs, pronouns, and questions, and simultaneously a disinclination for adjectives, nouns, and prepositions. Among the twenty-seven loud words there are no adjectives, one preposition (till), and two nouns (life, fellow). **Figure 5.2** arranges these loud words into broad grammatical categories with the addition of a third column similarly categorizing the words distinctive of neutral dialogue. I have classified *God* and *heaven* as interjections, despite technically being nouns, because they almost always function in loud dialogue as interjections: "My God!" "O, God!" "Heaven in mercy!" etc.

Moving from part of speech to the next level of grammatical complexity, many loud words tend to occur in loud dialogue *with the same grammatical function.* For example: based on our sample, "tell" functions within loud dialogue as a command 40 percent of the time, while in neutral dialogue it does so only 15 percent of the time. This imperative tendency is shared by all six loud verbs (*tell, let, stop, hold, save, bless*) and is completely absent in the seven neutral verbs: only two of them—*suppose* and *find*—can function as imperatives, and in neutral dialogue they rarely do. Thus, the correlation is not only between loudness and certain words, but between loudness and a grammatical mood.

The grammar of loudness finds its clearest articulation in three structures described below. These structures in turn offer an explanation for how to recognize loud voices in the absence of speaking verbs. In fact, grammar is possibly a better designator of loudness than the speaking verb itself, given that the latter is sometimes incorrectly paired with dialogue.

---

clared; (Neutral) *said, replied, observed, rejoined, asked, answered, returned, repeated, remarked, enquired, responded, suggested, explained, uttered, mentioned;* (Quiet) *whispered, murmured, sighed, grumbled, mumbled, muttered, whimpered, hushed, faltered, stammered, trembled, gasped, shuddered.*

WORD	OBSERVED TOTAL	EXPECTED VALUE	OBSERVED: LOUD DIALOGUE	OBSERVED: NEUTRAL DIALOGUE	OBSERVED: (LOUD)/ EXP	P-VALUE
exclamation mark	675	337.5	566	109	1.68	0.000
mark	675	337.5	566	109	1.68	0.000
oh	75	37.5	60	15	1.60	0.000
em dash	288	144	179	109	1.24	0.000
what	157	78.5	103	54	1.31	0.000
God	46	23	35	11	1.52	0.000
heaven	12	6	11	1	1.83	0.003
yet	25	12.5	19	6	1.52	0.007
tell	40	20	28	12	1.40	0.008
comma	1885	942.5	993	892	1.05	0.011
how	49	24.5	33	16	1.35	0.011
down	21	10.5	16	5	1.52	0.013
me	241	120.5	138	103	1.15	0.014
o	43	21.5	29	14	1.35	0.016
ye	33	16.5	23	10	1.39	0.018
your	155	77.5	91	64	1.17	0.018
hold	12	6	10	2	1.67	0.019
bless	9	4.5	8	1	1.78	0.020
fellow	20	10	15	5	1.50	0.020
never	69	34.5	43	26	1.25	0.027
let	62	31	39	23	1.26	0.028
save	8	4	7	1	1.75	0.035
question mark	296	148	164	132	1.11	0.036
life	21	10.5	15	6	1.43	0.039
why	40	20	26	14	1.30	0.040
stop	13	6.5	10	3	1.54	0.046
till	13	6.5	10	3	1.54	0.046
thee	30	15	20	10	1.33	0.049

FIGURE 5.1 **Words statistically distinctive of loud dialogue (loud words).** The relevant statistical values are as follows. The first column displays the word's observed total (obs_total), that is to say, how often the word occurred in both samples combined. The "expected" value signals how often we would expect the word to occur in each sample if it was equally likely to occur in either one. The two specific observed values that follow—observed: loud dialogue and observed: neutral dialogue—indicate how often the given word actually occurred in the loud sample and in the neutral one. The penultimate column—observed(loud)/exp—displays the ratio between the word's observed value in loud dialogue and the expected value: this ratio, in its turn, expresses the word's deviation from the average, and hence its "distinctiveness." Finally, the p-value is a measure of statistical significance: when its value is less than or equal to 0.05, the result is "significant" in the sense that it is not likely to be a consequence of chance (only words with a p-value of 0.05 or less were

included in our figure). As an example, the word "what" occurred a total of 157 times in the two samples combined, and we would therefore expect it to occur 78.5 times in the loud sample and 78.5 times in the neutral sample. In actuality, however, it occurred 103 times in the loud sample and 54 times in the neutral sample. With an observed/expected that is greater than one and a p-value under 0.05, "what" is thus distinctive of loud dialogue.

PART OF SPEECH	LOUD WORDS	NEUTRAL WORDS
Verbs	tell, let, stop, hold, save, bless	was, has, should, may, said, find, suppose
Nouns	life, fellow	night, friend, place
Pronouns	me, your, ye, thee	we, whom
Adjectives		any, good, long, enough, young, which, the
Adverbs	never, down	well, just, when
Prepositions	till	to, in, for, before, as
Conjunctions	yet	and, since
Interjections	oh, o, God, heaven	
Questions	what, why, how, question mark	
Punctuation	exclamation mark, em dash, comma	period, semicolon

FIGURE 5.2 **Loud and neutral words organized by part of speech.**

Take the following sentence from Henry William Herbert's *Marmaduke Wyvil*: "Never!" he said—"Never! So help me He, who looks on all things—no, never!" The utterance is packed full of loud grammar—exclamation marks, em dashes, an imperative, the word *me*, three repetitions of the word *never*, a reference to God—yet it is framed by a neutral speaking verb. This is a particularly extreme example, but the point remains: speaking verbs in the novel are not always reliable. Much like the construction of a Roman arch, the speaking verbs are a scaffolding, an easily discernible unit, which, after a semantic study is complete, can be pulled away leaving grammar as a more accurate sign of loudness. The study of these three grammatical structures, then, gives us the clearest picture of novelistic loudness. It is from them that we can begin formulating what it means for the novel to raise its voice (with the lingering question of why it might want to).

5.a   "O, speak to me!" she cried, kneeling to him—"tell me, O, Randolph, art thou the author of those letters?—anonymous, too! I am thunderstruck." (John Neal)

"I tell you you have!" she exclaimed, in high temper. "I insist upon undoing it. Now, allow me!" (Thomas Hardy)

She nodded her head again reluctantly; then cried out,—"Let me go! I'll have the police on you two." (Robert Herrick)

Effie exclaimed, in a tone which went through the heart of all who heard her—"O Jeanie, Jeanie, save me, save me!" (Walter Scott)

"Don't defy me, sir! Don't defy me!" he cried. "You forget that I am your mother's brother!" (John Cooke)

Five loud utterances, and each time the same grammatical structure—an imperative verb followed by the word *me*: Tell me; Allow me; Let me; Save me; Don't defy me. Because *me* is always the object of a verb, it signifies a unique displacement of the speaker from subject to object. What results in loud dialogue is a particularly codified structure in which the other (subject of the verb) and the speaker (object of the verb) are overwhelmingly compressed together, often to the point of conflict: (*You*) let *me* go. Loud commands are not made by the all-powerful—then God said, "Let there be light"—nor are they masked in polite etiquette—"Please pass the butter." Instead, loud commands are vehement, often angry cries to another to be freed from a state of ignorance (tell me), restriction (allow me, let me go), danger (save me), rage (don't defy me), or, more generally, misfortune. In loud dialogue, a conflictual or unbalanced state of affairs is typical, and it finds a particularly elegant manifestation in this first structure.

This description of novelistic loudness can be compared with other types of non-novelistic loudness, such as the united loudness of national anthems or the choral unity of Gustav Mahler's *Symphony for a Thousand*, where loudness is hopeful, triumphant, and powerful. Franco Moretti observes that the word "we" sits at the center of most European anthems—in fact, it is their most frequent word.[7] This loudness of the "we" is, linguistically, the

---

7 "Of twenty-eight European anthems I have been able to check, twenty-two establish a significant semantic field around the first person plural, beginning of course with the very first word *Allons*—of the greatest of them all. Nothing seems as essential to national anthems as this grammatical sign of collective identity; even the name of the country receives fewer mentions (20)." Franco Moretti, *Graphs, Maps, Trees* (New York: Verso, 2005), 52.

very opposite—plural subject / singular object—of what one might call the loudness of the "me." Add to this the fact that "we" is statistically distinctive of neutral dialogue (see **Figure 5.2**), almost never occurring within novelistic passages of loud dialogue, and it becomes clear that novelistic loudness is of a particular type. Loudness in the 19th-century English-language novel is distinctively singular: it is the voice of the individual, not the group, that is crying and exclaiming at the loudest moments.

5.b "What, you've heard their lies too, have ye!" she exclaimed fiercely. (Caroline Kirkland)

"What!" he cried, "to draw breath day by day, and not to pay for it by striking daily at the rock iniquity? Are you for that, Beauchamp?" (George Meredith)

"What is it, Wilbur? What have they done to you? What has happened?" Selma cried, looking from one to the other, though she had discerned the truth in a flash. (Robert Grant)

"Good God!" she exclaimed, "What an opinion must you have of me! Can you possibly suppose that I was aware of her unhappiness?" (Jane Austen)

"Vjera!" he cried. "Have you cut off your beautiful hair? What have you done, child? How could you do it?" (Francis Crawford)

Questions constitute a second grammatical structure characteristic of loudness—interrogative terms like *what*, *why*, and *how* being in fact as distinctive of loud dialogue as question marks. To be sure, not all questions are loud; when they are, it's owing to the generating force of *surprise*; usually, an unpleasant or frightened surprise. Loud questions are not thoughtfully formulated ("I suppose," said the doctor, upon Israel's concluding, "that you desire to return to your friends across the sea?"); they are spontaneous reactions to the unexpected. Whence the half interrogatory, half exclamatory "What!" found in the first two examples and the agonistic quality audible throughout.

Loud questions often map out externally the speaker's attempt to come to terms with an unpleasant revelation. As a result, they are often rhetorical—rarely does the speaker actually need or want an informative answer: "What has happened?" Selma cried . . . *though she had discerned the truth in a flash.* It is the emotional process of acquiescence—moving from disbelief to acknowledgement—that is central to loud questions, not the request for information. This process typically begins with a "What!"—"What have you done, child?"—and then, after a disbelieving acceptance of the event, turns to motive—"How could you do it?" Notably absent from these questions are the words "when," "where," and "who." (In fact, "when" and "whom" are statistically significant of *neutral* dialogue). Loud voices seldom ask specific contextually-based questions, because the speakers have yet to fully accept the event itself; they are still coming to terms with *what* happened, and with the motives behind the event (why and how); details of time (when), place (where), and person (who) are irrelevant.

5.c   "Ah! Tell me—tell me, whose and what am I?" exclaimed the agitated girl, seizing the hand of her instructress. (Epes Sargent)

"I receive it," cried he, "as the pledge of <u>my</u> happiness;—yet—yet let <u>your</u> voice ratify the gift." (Ann Radcliffe)

"Do not—do not leave me," she exclaimed passionately, as she beheld his departure, while with hands clasped in something like a mortal agony of fear, she approached me. "He will soon return—he is terrible in <u>his</u> anger—he will do some **dreadful** act." (William Simms)

"And now, father, <u>your</u> blessing—<u>your</u> consent!" cried Thames. (W. H. Ainsworth)

"Sarah! Sarah!" cried Frances, in terror; "<u>my</u> sister—<u>my</u> **only** sister—oh! do not smile so horridly, know me or you will break <u>my</u> heart." (James Cooper)

Two final structures: one that is present and one whose absence is itself significant. The manifest structure, that of repetition, frequently centers around the em dash: "Tell me—tell me," "yet—yet," "Do not—do not," "your blessing—your consent," "my sister—my only sister." Loud dialogue is full of em dashes accompanied by frantic stammering repetition. The result: the reader's extended experience of a cry or exclamation along with a focused intensity on an object (your blessing, my sister) or an action (tell me, do not). Incomplete or fragmentary as these loud cries may be, they manage to concentrate the attention on what is most important. This loud use of the em dash is very different from the essayistic use, in which an appositive thought is inserted in between two independent sentences.[8]

The absent structure, which would act as a counterpoint to the structure of repetition, is that of description. Notice the nearly complete lack of adjectives in all of the above loud utterances. I have bolded the two lone adjectives—"dreadful" and "only"—and underlined the possessive adjectives, which are more common, but which are of course not descriptive but relational. The absence of adjectives was already visible in **Figure 5.2**, where loud dialogue has none of them among its most distinctive words, whereas neutral dialogue has multiple: *any, good, long, enough, young, which*. In short, loudness in the novel is anti-descriptive. The absence suggests a certain rigidity present in loud language. There is a certain primal bleakness.

The loudest points in the novel are not effective at conveying information. Loud dialogue is repetitive, and therefore inefficient. It inclines towards rigid, non-descriptive structures: the (You)-[imperative]-me construction is a stark frame, with little room for embellishment; the absence of "when-" and "where-" questions reveals a lack of interest in details and subtlety. If we think of reading as a purely mental act—as something we do because it is interesting and makes us think—then there seems to be no reason for the presence of loud dialogue. However, the fact is that nearly all 19th-century English-language novels incorporate these loud structures. The reason must be partially due to the fact that these loud structures affect the reader in a way that details, no matter how interesting, cannot. I would go so far as to say that a lack of loudness can emotionally alienate the reader from a character. Take the following passage from *Robinson Crusoe*:

> The third day in the morning, the wind having abated over night, the sea was calm, and I ventur'd; but I am a warning piece again, to all rash and ignorant pilots; for no sooner was I come to the point, when even I was

---

8 Mere repetition, without the em dash, is often loud as well: "'O, stop, stop!' she cried out. 'There's my father! O, father, father!'" (George Eliot, *The Mill on the Floss*)

> not my boat's length from the shore, but I found myself in a great depth
> of water, and a current like the sluice of a mill: It carry'd my boat along
> with it with such violence, that all I could do, could not keep her so much
> as on the edge of it; but I found it hurry'd me farther and farther out
> from the eddy, which was on my left hand. There was no wind stirring to
> help me, and all I could do with my paddlers signify'd nothing, and now
> I began to give myself over for lost; for as the current was on both sides
> the island, I knew in a few leagues distance they must joyn again, and
> then I was irrecoverably gone; nor did I see any possibility of avoiding it.

Robinson finds himself in a near death situation and yet the passage is
completely void of any feeling of panic. But imagine *if Robinson were to cry
out, and his speech were to assume a grammatically loud structure.* Then his
emotional intensity would be dramatized aurally and psychologically for
the reader, and the act of reading itself would become louder, more intense.
Through the "loud" grammatical structures I have described, *we come to
experience the character's emotion as an event, in all its importance.* Loudness brings us into the novel, and near its characters, like no other device.

2. LOUDNESS AS A STRUCTURAL ASPECT OF NOVELS AND NOVEL READING

Leaving our grammar of loudness where it is, I want to pick up a new strand
of thought—loudness as a structural device. Given that loudness is heard
by the reader, one would expect it to contribute to the arrangement of the
novel's parts, occurring neither always nor in random fashion, but according to meaningful and analyzable tendencies. Loudness has, after all, been
a structural aspect of music and music notation since at least the 17th
century.[9] Now, at the level of textual mechanics, a novel's aural trajectory,
heard by the reader, is created via the novel's string of consecutive voices.
Accordingly, the loudness of a chapter can be approximated by measuring
the proportion of loud dialogue within it; plotting these data points for
each chapter will more or less capture a novel's overall loudness contour.

---

9 "Dynamic changes were almost certainly a part of performance earlier, but, like tempos, only came
to be notated with any regularity in the 17th century. Until the late 18th century, however, such nota-
tions were far from extensive." Don Randel, *The Harvard Concise Dictionary of Music and Musicians* (Cambridge,
MA: Harvard University Press, 1999), 506.

The structural characteristics of loudness formulated here are based almost entirely on Book I of Dostoevsky's *The Idiot* and will take form through three successive graphs.[10] First, a graph of the general contour of loudness in Book I; second, a closer look at its organization within a smaller three-chapter segment; third, an illustration of loudness as it is allocated between the voices of different characters. Though loudness is not a structural aspect of *all* novels, I believe that the structure derived from *The Idiot* will find recapitulation elsewhere, and I will offer a hint of possibilities to come in the final pages of this section, devoted to the third volume of *Pride and Prejudice*.

In the study of the novel, the concept of structure has, for the most part, been associated—via Roland Barthes and his "Introduction to the Structural Analysis of Narratives"—with the nature of narrative events and episodes, their functions ("nuclei" or "catalyzer"), their duration, sequence, and so on.[11] However, loudness provides a means for thinking about novelistic order while maintaining an interesting distance from plot. Its study is dependent on *the way* that events are told rather than the events themselves (the same plot can theoretically be communicated either loudly or neutrally). These differences should not, however, discourage an investigation of the interplay between loudness and plot—in fact, I will often try to show precisely how loudness exerts an influence on a plot's twists and turns. As Viktor Shklovsky wrote, "The methods and devices of plot construction are similar, and in principle identical with the devices of, for instance, musical orchestration. Works of literature represent a warp of sounds, of articulatory movements and thoughts."[12] While Shklovsky may not have had such a literal interpretation in mind, the study of loudness as a structural device is one way of analyzing a novel's "articulatory movements."

o   o   o

---

10 It was while reading *The Idiot* that the structural significance of loudness first occurred to me: the text retains a particularly oral quality, perhaps because Dostoevsky composed much of *The Idiot* by reading it out loud to a stenographer.

11 Roland Barthes, "Introduction to the Structural Analysis of Narratives," in *Image-Music-Text*, trans. Stephen Heath (New York: Hill and Wang, 1977).

12 Viktor Shklovsky, "The Relationship between Devices of Plot Construction and General Devices of Style," in *Theory of Prose*, 45.

FIGURE 5.3 GRAPHS loudness over time in Book I of *The Idiot*. For each chapter the loudness level is plotted based on the average loudness of the chapter's speaking verbs. Speaking verbs are assigned a value from 0 to 4 according to the following rubric: neutral or "empty" speaking verbs like *said* and *replied*, which offer no account of tone, take a value of 0; speaking verbs like *picked up* and *warmly approved*, which have a trace of resonance, take a value of 1; medium-loud speaking verbs like *retorted*, *interrupted*, and *said sternly* take a value of 2; loud speaking verbs like *said loudly* and *interrupted hotly* take a value of 3; very loud speaking verbs like *shouted*, *screamed*, and *exclaimed* take a value of 4.

A graph and also a striking pattern. Three crescendos: a tentative crescendo broken by chapters of narration (chapters 2–7), a second more extreme crescendo (chapters 8–10), then two chapters of relaxation (11–12), and a final crescendo (13–16). The first crescendo significantly quieter than the latter two; the latter two about equal at their extremities. The concept of the crescendo offers one way of describing organized loudness: it is a simple pattern—loud, louder, louder—but versatile. In the current graph, a crescendo describes an increase in the overall loudness of successive chapters. However, one can think of crescendos more generally (a propensity for the novel as a whole to begin quietly and end loudly), or more specifically (a series of utterances that become progressively louder).

At the bottom of **Figure 5.3** are brackets describing the narrative space of each chapter: chapter 1 is set on a train; chapters 2–7 in the various rooms of the Epanchins' house; etc. Interestingly, the three main spaces of Book I—the Epanchins', Ganya's, and Nastasya's—and the three crescendos align with remarkable precision. More particularly, each major space begins with a relatively neutral conversation that becomes progressively louder until an outburst of loud dialogue precipitates a crisis: a scene of departure is then followed by a new chapter that is both quieter and set in a different location.[13] What I initially described as the broad interplay

---

13 The second crescendo provides a particularly elegant example of the pattern. In this case, the dialogue of chapter 8 becomes progressively louder until the loud dialogue of chapter 10 gives rise to a clamorous dispersal—Rogozhin shouts to the Prince: "Prince, my dear soul, drop them all, spit on them, and let's go! You'll learn how Rogozhin loves!"; Nastasya calls to Ganya: "Don't see me off! . . . Good-bye, till this evening! Without fail, you hear!"; and the narrator tells us that Ganya was "so oblivious that he barely noticed how the whole Rogozhin crowd poured past him and even jostled him in the doorway quickly making their way out of the apartment after Rogozhin." The next chapter begins in a new space, quietly—"The prince left the drawing room and shut himself up in his room." Fyodor

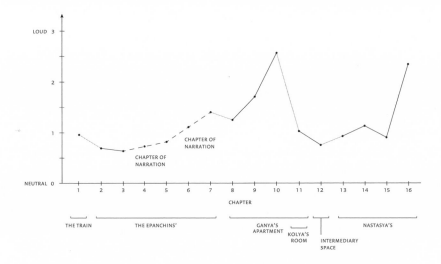

FIGURE 5.3 **Loudness at the scale of the chapter:** *The Idiot*, **Book I.** This figure does not take into account quiet speaking verbs, which make up less than 2 percent of the total speaking verbs in Book I. It should be noted, however, that quiet speaking verbs tend to increase in tandem with loud speaking verbs—both register a movement away from the neutral, normal methods of speaking. Accordingly, quiet speaking verbs do not produce quietness, as we might have thought; rather they produce a type of intensification. This, at least, is the tendency.

between loudness and plot might therefore be more clearly articulated in this specific case as the synchronization of loudness, narrative space, and chapter division.

So, **Figure 5.3**: the aural experience of reading is condensed into an image with a recognizable pattern; this pattern in turn suggests that loudness is organized; and this organization offers a new perspective for thinking about novelistic structure—one that foregrounds the voices that make up the novel (that is, the way the events are told) rather than the events themselves. At the same time, this organized loudness, important to the aural and psychological experience of the reader, is also integrated with plot via narrative space and chapter divisions. Thus, in a conversation-dominated novel, loudness offers both a formal climax within the story-world (the dialogic argument rather than the description of physical combat) and an affective climax uniquely felt by the reader during novel reading.

Dostoevsky, *The Idiot*, trans. Richard Pevear and Larissa Volokhonsky (New York: Vintage Classics, 2003), 117–118.

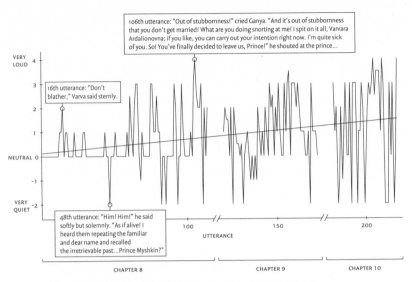

FIGURE 5.4 **Loudness at the scale of the utterance:** *The Idiot,* **chapters 8–10**

Given the general trajectory of loudness in Book I, it is only natural to wonder what specifically is happening within these chapters. Thus, **Figure 5.4**, with a smaller time span—only three chapters (chapters 8–10)—but in which every dialogic speech act is given a loudness ranking, this time from -2 to 4: -2 being quiet, 0 being neutral, 4 being loud. Quiet dialogue is aligned with -2 (rather than -4, the opposite of loud dialogue at 4), so that the scale will reflect simultaneously the wide dynamic range between loud and neutral dialogue and the much smaller dynamic range between neutral and quiet dialogue. As in **Figure 5.3**, numbers are based on speaking verbs, if present: quiet speaking verbs like *observed timidly* and *repeated in a half-whisper* take a value of -1; very quiet speaking verbs like *whispered, murmured,* and *said softly* take a value of -2. In the absence of speaking verbs, I have tagged suspended quotations according to the loudness of surrounding utterances and readerly intuition.

Figure 5.4 provides a closer look at the mechanics and distribution of loudness within the chapter as well as a second opportunity to analyze the effects of patterned voices on plot. First, mechanics. The general crescendo of chapters 8–10 (indicated here by the trend line) becomes, in **Figure 5.4**, much more complicated. Clearly observable is a movement away from neutral dialogue: 62 percent of dialogue is neutral in chapter 8, 27 percent is neutral in chapter 9, and 12 percent is neutral in chapter 10. The graph looks, in fact, much like a seismograph registering a high-intensity tremor. In chapter 8, the brief fluctuations in loudness keep returning to neutral dialogue, and the line remains fixed at 0 for eight separate intervals. There is constancy here: these are relatively stable conversations. In chapter 9, the oscillations become more frequent, the peak-to-peak amplitudes increase, and the conversations become more volatile. In chapter 10, the conversations reach the height of instability: dialogue keeps swinging between the two extremes (-2 and 3), rarely stopping for a neutral utterance.

Because each point in **Figure 5.4** represents a unique dialogic utterance, the graph closely follows both the dynamic trajectory felt by the reader and the dynamic organization of the novel's voices. We have zoomed in on the streamline three-point crescendo of **Figure 5.3** and can now see the twists and turns of the novel's dynamic organism. And twists and turns they truly are. Take, for instance, the loudest moment of chapter 8 (labeled in **Figure 5.4** as the 106th utterance: "'Out of stubbornness!' cried Ganya. 'And it's out of stubbornness that you don't get married! . . .'"). This very loud utterance, on par with subsequent peaks in chapter 10, must be quickly restrained in order that the loud climax and dispersal can be held off for another two chapters and the gradual, three-chapter crescendo can be maintained. Here is the restraining passage as it appears in the text, beginning with Ganya's shout and ending with the first words of chapter 9:

> "Out of stubbornness!" cried Ganya. "And it's out of stubbornness that you don't get married! What are you doing snorting at me! I spit on it all, Varvara Ardalionovna; if you like, you can carry out your intention right now. I'm quite sick of you. So! You've finally decided to leave us, Prince!" he shouted at the prince, seeing him get up from his place.
>
> In Ganya's voice that degree of irritation could be heard in which a man almost enjoys his irritation, gives himself over to it without restraint and almost with increasing pleasure, whatever may come of it. The prince turned around at the door in order to make some reply, but, seeing from the pained expression on his offender's face that with one more drop the vessel would overflow, he turned again and silently went out. A few minutes later he heard, by the noises coming from the drawing room, that in his absence the conversation had become more noisy and frank.
>
> He went through the large room to the front hall, in order to get to the corridor and from there to his room. Passing by the door to the stairs,

he heard and saw that someone outside the door was trying very hard to ring the bell; but something must have been wrong with the bell: it only jiggled slightly but made no sound. The prince lifted the bar, opened the door, and—stepped back in amazement, even shuddered all over: before him stood Nastasya Filippovna.

[Medium-loud dialogue between Nastasya and the prince.]

"They're quarreling," the prince replied and went to the drawing room.

He came in at a rather decisive moment: Nina Alexandrovna was ready to forget entirely that she was "resigned to everything"; she was, however, defending Varya. Ptitsyn, too, was standing beside Varya, having abandoned his scribbled-over paper. Varya herself was not intimidated, nor was she the timid sort; but her brother's rudeness was becoming more and more impolite and insufferable. On such occasions she usually stopped talking and merely looked at her brother silently, mockingly, not taking her eyes off him. This maneuver, as she knew, was apt to drive him to the utmost limits. At that very moment the prince stepped into the room and said loudly:

"Nastasya Filippovna!"

Chapter IX

A general hush fell . . .[14]

The passage captures a scene on the verge of explosion, and yet Dostoevsky is able, by a series of restraining maneuvers, to quickly subdue the clamor for the reader. First, a spatial transformation. Simultaneous with the loudest utterance in chapter 8 is the prince "get[ting] up from his place" in order to leave. There are still two chapters to come, each progressively louder—now is not the time for a fracas. So the prince leaves—"he went through the large room to the front hall, in order to get to the corridor and from there to his room"—and the loudness that the reader was experiencing firsthand is now reported in the neutral tone of narration: "the conversation had become more noisy and frank." The authorial decision to assume the narrative voice tempers the previous loudness, pacifying it. Then a new character is introduced and a brief conversation of *mezzo forte* follows. The reader returns,

---

14 Dostoevsky, *The Idiot*, 100–102.

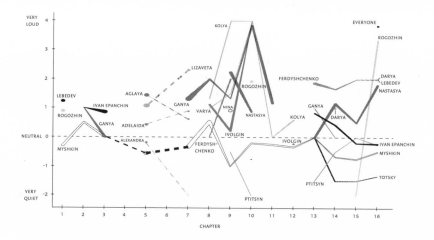

FIGURE 5.5 Loudness allocated between characters: *The Idiot*, Book I

with the prince, at a decisive moment in the conversation just abandoned. Again, the reader does not hear the loudness of the conversation, because it is being communicated in the neutral voice of the narrator. The prince announces Nastasya. Chapter break. And a general hush.

Thus, a three-part sequence: spatial change; loudness resets; and, acknowledging the aural break for the reader, the chapter ends. These micro-level interrelationships between loudness, space, and chapter division are everywhere in Book I. The narrator follows Prince Myshkin, and Dostoevsky moves Myshkin like a knight in a game of chess: the many small-scale maneuvers creating the three large-scale progression in **Figure 5.3**. And the large scale cannot be emphasized enough. The three escalations are particularly impressive given the time span over which they occur: 200 pages, approximately four hours of reading. These movements from neutrality to loudness (and, to a lesser degree, from loudness to neutrality) seem to capture a deep structural component of *The Idiot*, Book I—a structural component so fundamental that its gradual progressions span hourly periods in real time.

A final visualization from *The Idiot*: **Figure 5.5**, the most experimental by far. In this case, each character is given a specific texture. Next, the overall loudness of a character's speech is plotted per chapter (based solely on speaking verbs). Here, the dashed horizontal line represents a character whose average speech was neutral in every chapter. Any point above the horizontal line indicates a character who speaks loudly in the specified chapter. Any point below the horizontal line indicates a character who speaks quietly in the specified chapter. Finally, the diameter of each point represents how often the character speaks: the thicker the point, the more speaking verbs attributed to that character during the stipulated chapter. I have added lines connecting points of the same texture to make it easier to distinguish the individual characters.

If **Figure 5.3** illustrates a dynamic progression, **Figure 5.5** reveals the individual characters who create it. It is as if each line is a voice or a singer. Though the loudness is created by many discrete individuals, **Figure 5.5** is not a graph of cacophony. Emerging from the many vocal lines, one can see the three climaxes of **Figure 5.3**: first, a slight peak in chapter 7; second, the dramatic peak in chapter 10; third, a bifurcation of dialogue into the extremes: Rogozhin, Lebedev, Ferdyshchenko, Darya, Nastasya, and Everyone filling the room with loudness; Myshkin, Ivan Epanchin, Ptitsyn, and Totsky creating an undercurrent of whispers. **Figure 5.5** is truly a graph of polyphony, of voices "artistically organized."[15]

At the same time, one voice—that of Myshkin—stands out from the rest as the only voice to hover in the neutral range, averse to extremes and particularly averse to loudness. Myshkin is noticeably unrelated to the dynamic progressions of Book I. He therefore plays no part in the aural reading experience that I have been stressing throughout this section. In fact, the vocal organization of Book I prefigures the central difficulty of the novel: to portray the "perfectly beautiful man" within a novel that is expected to fulfill certain expectations of plot. As Reinhold Niebuhr remarks in *The Nature and Destiny of Man*, "It is impossible to symbolize the divine goodness in history in any other way than by complete powerlessness."[16] But how can a powerless, *quiet* character like Prince Myshkin generate an engaging plot requiring conflict, and thus moments of loudness? In the end, he cannot, leading Joseph Frank to write, "It is not hard to point out the flaws [of *The Idiot*] if we take the nineteenth-century conception of the well-made novel as a standard; more difficult is to explain why it triumphs so effortlessly over all the inconsistencies and awkwardnesses

---

15 "The novel can be defined as a diversity of social speech types (sometimes even diversity of languages) and a diversity of individual voices, artistically organized." Bakhtin, "Discourse in the Novel," in *The Dialogic Imagination*, 262.

16 From the epigraph to chapter 17 of Joseph Frank, *Dostoevsky, The Miraculous Years, 1865–1871* (Princeton, NJ: Princeton University Press, 1995), 316.

of its structure and motivation."[17] Yet importantly, Frank brackets Book I from this harsh criticism. He brackets it precisely because it feels structurally organized.

Beyond the confines of *The Idiot*, Myshkin also exemplifies a unique type of protagonist—the quiet or neutral-speaking protagonist thrown into a loud environment. It is a type that I conjecture begins to occur for the first time with frequency in the 19th century, and a type that has not yet received a clear formulation. Franco Moretti locates a second example of this character-type in *The Bourgeois*:

> As the hero of *Mastro-Don Gesualdo* (1889) mixes for the first time with the
> town's old elite, at a party early in the novel, he truly seems to belong
> to a new human species: envious and malevolent, the local notables
> surround him, inquiring with hypocritical concern about his first big loan;
> and he answers, "tranquillamente"—"quietly," "evenly" . . . The notables
> scream, act out, threaten, curse; Gesualdo remains seated, silent, polite,
> "quietly continuing to cast up his accounts in his pocketbook, that
> lay open on his knee. Then he raised his hand, and retorted in a calm
> voice . . ."[18]

The structural consequences of a quiet or neutral-speaking protagonist have yet to be clearly articulated. Like other moments in this paper, loose ends are an inevitable (and exciting) aspect of research in the digital humanities.

o   o   o

THE STRUCTURAL ANALYSIS of loudness in Book I of *The Idiot*, which I have presented above, is intended as a prototype, opening the broader question of whether the concepts outlined in this section also apply to other novels. On this point, the jury is still out. However, the results of a first test on *Pride and Prejudice* strengthen my confidence for the future.

There are different ways to measure textual loudness. With *The Idiot*, I could not use the loud lexicon defined in Part I, because that lexicon was unique to the English language; as a consequence, I had to measure

---

17 Frank, *Dostoevsky*, 340.

18 Moretti, *The Bourgeois*, 150.

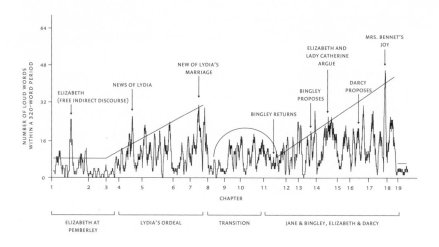

FIGURE 5.6 **Loudness in** *Pride and Prejudice*, **Volume 3**

loudness by counting speaking verbs—a choice that worked quite nicely, as Dostoevsky was particularly careful and prolific with his use of these special verbs. With *Pride and Prejudice*, however, I chose to return to the grammar of loudness, partly out of curiosity, partly because it required less manual work. **Figure 5.6** attempts to measure the density of loud words as one reads through *Pride and Prejudice*. More specifically, the calculation relies on the concept of a "moving average"—first measuring the number of loud words occurring within a 320-word period, then shifting this period through the novel—the higher the line, the higher the density of loud words clustered within the corresponding point. Needless to say, as "loud words" are not actually *always* loud (only *frequently* so), the graph is based on a significant amount of estimations and averages. Add to this the fact that all loud words were weighted equally, and it becomes clear that I am pushing the loud lexicon to its limit, if not beyond. The conclusions, while interesting, must thus remain speculative.

Nevertheless, loudness appears to be acutely organized in the third volume of *Pride and Prejudice*, as illustrated in **Figure 5.6**, where I have labeled certain moments in the plot for ease of orientation. Loudness divides the third volume into four parts: a quiet beginning at Pemberley (chapters 1–3); the first crescendo centering on Lydia and Wickham (chapters 4–7); a transitional regrouping (chapters 8–10); and finally the second crescendo focused first on Bingley and Jane's courtship, then on Darcy and

Elizabeth's. To these four parts, one might add a fifth: the final chapter tacked on to the end—so much quieter than the rest, and so much more conducive to the "happy" ending. If we were to smooth out the progressions in each part, the graph of loudness would look something like the overlaid line. The graph calls to mind what Nicholas Dames has described as a "wave-theory of novelistic affect: a picture of novelistic rhythm as a continual oscillation between 'relaxing' subplots, or purely discursive passages, and the more rigidly hermeneutic drives of suspense and revelation that create a particularly rapt, if necessarily short-lived, form of attentiveness."[19] It is an interesting theory, and a theory that a study of loudness might be able to substantiate and adjust.

The graph of *Pride and Prejudice* does indeed exhibit these "waves," but with the added benefit of turning the abstract concept into a concrete image—not only a wave, but a wave with a specific length and degree.

3. THE QUIETING DOWN OF THE BRITISH NOVEL

The previous section was premised on the fact that a novel's loudness is constantly in flux, each voice in turn appropriating a degree in the step-like spectrum from quiet to loud. But the variability of loudness—this idea that some text is louder or quieter than other text—can be dilated to apply in broader senses. The overall loudness of a single novel—say, *Pamela*—might be louder than the overall loudness of another novel, say *The Old Man and the Sea*. The novels of one author might typically be louder than the novels of a second author. Some genres might be particularly quiet, while other genres might be particularly loud. The British novel might be quieter than the Russian novel, just as the British grammar of loudness might be different from the Russian grammar. Finally, the novels of a single culture may become more or less loud over time. It is on this final variation—variation over time in the British novel over the course of the 19th century—that I will focus here.

There are different ways to measure the change in the average loudness of the aggregate "British novel." I will begin with the most basic—plotting

---

19 Nicholas Dames, "Wave-Theories and Affective Physiologies," *Victorian Studies* 46, no. 2 (Winter 2004), 214.

the percentage of loud speaking verbs, decade by decade. The resulting graph (**Figure 5.7**) shows a striking drop in the percentage of loud speaking verbs: from 19 percent in the first decade of the 19th century, to 6 percent in the last decade. Conversely, the trend could also be described as a growing monopoly of the speaking verb "said"—the most neutral of all speaking verbs—in the context of dialogic utterances. Note how the space of "said" increases from about 50 percent to about 85 percent of all utterances, while all other neutral speaking verbs decline.

As a result of this quieting progression, novels like *Adeline Mowbray* (1804) and *Jack Sheppard* (1839), in which nearly half of the speaking verbs are loud, become progressively less and less common and acceptable. In their place, one finds novels like *Middlemarch* (1874), in which less than 1 percent of speaking verbs are loud. (*Middlemarch* incorporates a mere twenty-one loud speaking verbs, while relying heavily on approximately 1,840 occurrences of the speaking verb "said.") The triumph of the "said": this is one way to describe *Middlemarch*. A triumph that allows subtle variation in tone—"said falteringly," "said easily," "said in her easy staccato"—but significantly diminishes the dynamic range (there is no "said loudly" in *Middlemarch*). Oftentimes, the neutrality of the "said" is even explicitly emphasized: "Mrs Waule . . . happened to say this very morning (not at all with a defiant air, but in a low, muffled, neutral tone, as of a voice heard through cotton wool) that she did not wish 'to enjoy their good opinion.'" Or, more simply: "'What are you laughing at so profanely?' said Rosamond, with bland neutrality."

The general muting of the novel over the course of the 19th century aligns closely with what Philip Fisher describes as a terminological shift in English philosophy and psychology from *passions* to *emotions* and *moods*.

> We can see in mid-eighteenth-century English philosophy and rhetoric the banishing of the term "passion" and its replacement by the new term "emotion" . . . What remained unchanged, when the passions came to be called the emotions, were the words for the specific passions or emotions. We still speak of the emotion of fear, or the emotion of anger, or of angry feelings and jealous feelings. If the full specificity of fear and anger and jealousy is preserved, what difference can it make to have gone from speaking of fear as a passion to regarding fear as an emotion or feeling? The answer lies, in part, in what would count as salient or

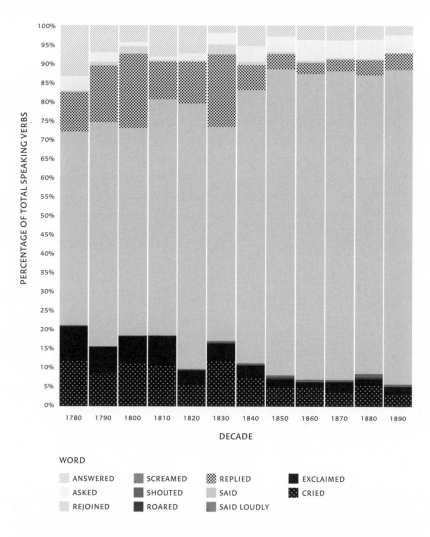

FIGURE 5.7 **Distribution of speaking verb types by decade in British 19th-century fiction.** Of course, the words themselves—*cried, exclaimed, said,* etc.—do not always function as speaking verbs. The challenge was thus to computationally eliminate instances like "She cried but no one noticed" in which cried does not frame dialogue and does not function as a speaking verb. This was accomplished by counting the number of occurrences of *cried, exclaimed, said,* etc., in the narrative portion of "mixed sentences"—sentences containing a mixture of dialogue and narration—a process made possible by the fact that "mixed sentences" are a labeled category in the Chadwyck-Healey corpus. Loud speaking verbs are indicated by darker shades of gray and black; neutral speaking verbs by lighter shades of gray. Although not visible in this graph, which represents percentages, it is interesting to note that the total number of speaking verbs remains relatively constant throughout the century.

typical examples of fear when one is speaking of a feeling of fear or an emotion of fear or of fear as a passion. A fear of mice or a phobia about sticky tactile surfaces (to use a Freudian example) might seem useful as instances of emotions. Such modern, quirky, therapeutic instances often govern twentieth-century discussions of inner states. But when describing the passions, Aristotle went at once to the single greatest, universal fear: the fear of imminent death, as a soldier might experience it on a battlefield, or as a trembling passenger might on a ship that seems about to sink. The inflection given to our tacit understanding of fear by what seem to be natural or colorless examples is often the most revealing snapshot of the shift from a vocabulary of passions to one of feelings, emotions, or moods.

The passions transformed into "colorless" (or "noiseless") emotions and moods—this is the idea. Fisher continues:

> What does it mean to speak, as we often do in the twentieth century, as though moods were our preferred version of inner states? Passions, moods, emotions, and feelings are profoundly different configurations of the underlying notion of a temporary state of a person. Each term makes plausible a very distinct template. Boredom, depression, nostalgia, and anxiety might be natural first instances of what we mean by mood, but such states could never have been plausible examples of passions. Rage and wonder, central to any idea of what the passions are, seem out of place with the low-energy conditions generally meant by the term "mood."[20]

The progression from passions to emotions to moods outlines a broad diminutive trend in the conception of feeling—a trend in which the common feelings become less poignant and more subtle. Moreover, the trend centers on the 19th century (Fisher catalogues it as beginning in the mid-18th century and continuing into the 20th), such that the muting of the passions is concurrent with the muting of the novel seen in **Figure 5.7**.[21]

---

20 Philip Fisher, *The Vehement Passions* (Princeton, NJ: Princeton University Press, 2002), 6, 6–7.

21 It should be noted that loud speaking verbs, when isolated from dialogue, are the inarticulate utterances typical of the passionate experience: crying, exclaiming, shouting, roaring, screaming.

It is not coincidental that Fisher pulls his example of a shift from passions to emotions from *"English* philosophy and rhetoric." The century long diminuendo has a particularly British facet; it appears that British culture was maximally receptive to this tempering of the loud voice. Richard Wagner similarly notes a British preference for the neutral voice, commenting at length in his *Über das Dirigieren [On Conducting]* (1869) on the tendency of British orchestras to play at a level volume: "The orchestra generally played *mezzoforte*; no real *forte*, no real *piano* was attained."[22] But while the British may have taken the muting farther and more seriously than other Western nationalities, I do not think the quieting of the novel will prove solely endemic to British culture. There are other, more general phenomena that likely contributed to the quieting of the novel so visible in the British variant. For example, Georg Simmel claims in "The Metropolis and Mental Life" that the "violent stimuli [of the] metropolis" led to changes in the mental life of persons and, more importantly, to the proliferation of two particular attitudes—the "blasé attitude" and the slightly more formal attitude of "reserve"—both of which correspond with the reduction of passionate, loud utterances: the blasé being too unaffected to speak loudly; the reserved choosing seldom to reveal any internal loud utterances throbbing within.[23] Similarly broad, the quieting of the British novel is consonant with and likely a result of the general process of socialization and rationalization within the novel. As Franco Moretti argues in "The Serious Century," the 19th century witnessed an attempt to "rationalize the novelistic universe: turning it into a world of few surprises, fewer adventures, and no miracles."[24] It was a century of *rational softening* both in terms of novelistic content and novelistic voice.[25] The world of the novel became

---

Given the similarity between passionate utterances and loud dialogue, it would be interesting to use the preceding linguistic study of loud dialogue as a means for studying 19th-century passions.

22 Quoted in Nicholas Dames, *Physiology of the Novel: Reading, Neural Science, and the Form of Victorian Fiction* (Oxford: Oxford University Press, 2007), 145.

23 Georg Simmel, "The Metropolis and Mental Life," in *On Individual and Social Forms: Selected Writings* (Chicago: University of Chicago Press, 1971), 329–331.

24 Franco Moretti, "The Serious Century," in *The Novel: History, Geography, Culture* (Princeton, NJ: Princeton University Press, 2006), 381.

25 I have taken the phrase "rational softening" from the narrator of *Pride and Prejudice*, who says of Charlotte's letter to Elizabeth: "It was Mr. Collins's picture of Hunsford and Rosings rationally softened." The musical word *pianissimo* provides an explicit link between softening and quieting.

socialized, less dramatic, focused on quotidian life, and concurrently its voices became less dramatic, more moderate—the speaking verb "said" displacing loud speaking verbs like "cried" and "exclaimed."

As Part I clearly demonstrated, novelistic loudness can be registered not only by speaking verbs, but also by grammar. It is to this second grammatical method that I now turn. What was happening to loud grammar during the 19th century while the percentage of loud speaking verbs was reduced by over half? Among the many possible trajectories, one can imagine two extremes: on the one hand, a world in which loud grammar diminished concurrently with the neutralization of the speaking verbs—a complete quieting; on the other hand, a world in which the speaking verbs were neutralized but the loud grammar stayed constant—a superficial quieting. As should be apparent, the speaking verb/grammar distinction plays an important role in the overall understanding of novelistic loudness. It should be noted, however, that readers most likely come to recognize and learn loud grammar through recurrent instances of dialogue framed by loud speaking verbs. As a result, the decline in loud speaking verbs implies a muddying or obfuscation of the grammar itself.

Unfortunately, little can presently be said regarding the amplification or diminution of loud grammar—I am still developing the tools necessary to accurately measure such changes. Calculating the frequency of loud words within each decade of the corpus is too inaccurate: the overall frequency of the loud word "tell," for example, might increase over the course of the 19th century because it occurs repeatedly in non-loud narrative sentences like "she couldn't tell if . . ." while simultaneously occurring less and less often in the loud command+me form "tell me!" At the same time, the density calculation used in the graph of *Pride and Prejudice* is not easily applied to a corpus of novels. To reiterate, this calculation relies on the concept of a "moving average"—first measuring the number of loud words occurring within a 320-word period, then shifting this period through the novel—the higher the density of loud words, the louder that period in the novel. As can be imagined, the 320-word density calculation, iterated over an entire corpus, cannot be converted into a single number that ranks the loudness of a decade without some controversy. Such a conversion would require making decisions regarding questions like whether or not a novel with a significant number of really loud passages is louder than a novel that is constantly at *mezzo forte*—questions that we are still thinking about and working through. And so, after looking at a variety of graphs, each of which attempted to measure the overall frequency of grammatical loudness over time, the only thing I can confidently say is that our loud grammar certainly does not disappear.

What, then, to make of this wish-wash? Here is one possibility:

On the one hand, a first form of pressure (probably social in origin) urges the novel to mute itself. In response to this stimulus, the British novel abandons its one explicit reference to vocal loudness—the loud speaking verb. The characters of the late 19th century are seldom crying and exclaiming, and this, in its turn, obscures the reader's perception of loud grammar. At the same time, a second pressure (which probably has its source in the needs of narrative construction) compels the novel to retain some degree of loudness. Seemingly indispensable, loud grammar does not disappear. What results is the creation of a few, peculiar compromise formations. I have mentioned a first compromise formation earlier—the oxymoronic creation of loud grammatical dialogue framed by a neutral speaking verb, as seen in the passage from *Marmaduke Wyvil*: "'Never!' he said—'Never! So help me He, who looks on all things—no, never!'" More interesting, however, is the emergence of loud grammar in new, *less dense*, configurations—the paramount example of this second compromise formation being free indirect discourse. Take, for example, this passage from *Emma* (where I have bolded the loud grammar):

> **How** could she have been so deceived!—He protested that he had
> **never** thought seriously of Harriet—**never!** She looked back as well
> as she could; but it was all confusion.

The passage relies on our loud lexicon: a semantic reliance on "how," "never," and the exclamation point as well as a grammatical reliance on repetition (via the em dash) and an exclamatory question ("How could she have been so deceived!"). However, the loud grammar is less dense and the passage is less intense than a loud dialogic utterance—"'**How** could you deceive **me!**' cried Emma"—would have been. What we have, then, is an instance of our loud grammar trying to peek out from under a neutral narrative sentence yet remaining somewhat muffled. In a different instance of free indirect discourse, this time from the end of *Pride and Prejudice*, the content of the passage itself describes the concept of muting: "**How** earnestly did she then wish that her former opinions had been more reasonable, her expressions more moderate!" Upon further investigation, the appropriation of a diluted loud grammar can be found in many, if not most, passages of free indirect discourse:

> She was feeling, thinking, trembling, about everything;—agitated, happy, miserable, infinitely obliged, absolutely angry. It was all beyond belief! He was inexcusable, incomprehensible!—But such were his habits, that he could do nothing without a mixture of evil. He had previously made her the happiest of human beings, and now he had insulted—she knew not **what** to say—**how** to class or **how** to regard it. She would not have him serious, and **yet what** could excuse the use of such words and offers, if they meant but to trifle? (Jane Austen)

> But if there had been somewhere a strong and handsome individual, a gallant nature, . . . **why**, by chance, should she not find him? **Oh, what** an impossibility! Nothing, moreover, was worth the effort of a search, all was false! (Gustave Flaubert)

> Something had happened—he forgot **what**—in the smoking room. He had insulted her—kissed her? Incredible! Nobody believed a word against Hugh, of course. Who could? Kissing Sally in the smoking-room! (Virginia Woolf)

> Was there blood on his face? Was hot blood flowing? Or was it dry blood congealing **down** his cheek? It took him hours even to ask the question: time being no more than an agony in darkness, without measurement. A long time after he opened his eyes he realized he was seeing something—something, something, but the effort to recall was too great. No, no; no recall! (D. H. Lawrence)

> She had always **let** herself be dominated by her elder sister. Now, though somewhere inside herself she was weeping, she was free of the dominion of other women. **Ah!** That in itself was a relief, like being given another **life**: to be free of the strange dominion and obsession of other women. **How** awful they were, women! (D. H. Lawrence)[26]

---

26 These passages of free indirect discourse are taken from two classic studies: Ann Banfield, *Unspeakable Sentences* (Boston: Routledge & Kegan Paul, 1982); Roy Pascal, *The Dual Voice: Free Indirect Speech and Its*

Yet again, I find myself on the verge of a new subject, in this case on the function of loudness in free indirect discourse. And yet, again, it is necessary to leave off *in medias res*.

CONCLUSION

Three parts with the ghost of a fourth part to come. Each part pushing loudness into a different direction: into grammar, into narrative structure, into culture (and soon into style). What began as a concept fashioned from a semantic study of loud dialogue, literary loudness has become a concept that reaches beyond dialogue into the structural organization of a novel's voices, into a culture's relationship with passions and emotions, and into grammatical systems that appear to emerge even within the narrative passages of free indirect discourse. *Yet the main revelation is the discovery that loudness is perceivable and measurable within the novel. This is the primary achievement. Written language codifies loudness; the word becomes its own type of gramophone record; and the text preserves variations in loudness over time.*

Latent within much of this study is a cultural-historical constraint. The majority of my analysis was based on the 19th century English-language novel, while a third was based solely on the British variant. It remains to be seen how other cultures treat literary loudness. We do not yet know how universal are the grammatical structures of loudness that emerged from the English-language novel, nor whether the quieting down of the British novel is true of the Western novel at large. Yet, despite leaning heavily on a single culture's literature, I hope this study of loudness has led to broader findings, such that they may affect how we interpret novels and even, more basically, how perceptively we read.

Beyond these larger concepts, there is, within this study, an orchidaceous quality. At moments, yes, the sociological component gains predominance. At others, it is the conceptual game itself—the challenge of hearing loudness in text—that takes center stage. This is most apparent, perhaps, in the messy graph of *The Idiot*, but it surfaces at other moments as well. For some reason, these moments are my favorite part. I hope that literary

---

Functioning in the Nineteenth-Century European Novel (Manchester: Manchester University Press, 1977).

criticism continues to leave this orchidaceous space open, for I have found these small moments of finesse—a few passing harmonies in a Schumann sonata, the tiny grotesque turns in an orchid, an iris, a sweet pea—to be a special space of happiness.

2014

CHAPTER 6

From Keywords to Cohorts

TRACING LANGUAGE CHANGE IN THE NOVEL, 1785–1900

Ryan Heuser, Long Le-Khac

The 19th century in Britain witnessed tumultuous changes that reshaped the fabric of society and altered the course of modernization. It also saw the rise of the novel to the height of its cultural power as the most important literary form of the period. This chapter describes a long-term experiment in tracing macroscopic changes in the novel during this crucial period. Specifically, we present findings on two interrelated transformations: a systemic concretization of novelistic language and a fundamental change to the novel's social spaces. We show how these shifts have consequences for setting, characterization, and narration, and suggest the responsiveness of the novel to dramatic changes in British society. The chapter also charts our experiment in developing quantitative and computational methods for tracing changes in literary language. We wanted to see how far quantifiable features such as word usage could be pushed toward complex and nuanced results. We thus braid together the story of the stops and starts to our investigation—including our deliberations and motives—and the record of our results.

1. METHOD: LEARNING TO DEFINE OBJECTS IN THE QUANTITATIVE STUDY OF LITERATURE

Raymond Williams's classic study, *Culture and Society*, evaluated historical semantics in a period of unprecedented change for Britain. We began from that study's premise that changes in discourse reveal broader historical and sociocultural changes. Williams's ambitious attempt to analyze an entire social discourse, astonishing as it was, lacked the tools and corpora now available to digital humanities scholars. We set out to build on Williams's impetus by applying computational methods to a very large corpus of texts.[1]

Quantitative historical semantics was given a boost in visibility from the introduction of Google's Ngram viewer in December 2010, about ten months into our project. The Ngram viewer is an online tool that allows one to trace the historical frequency of any word through the Google Books corpus. The "buzz" around historical semantics increased further with the publication of Jean-Baptiste Michel and Erez Lieberman Aiden's "Culturomics" study in *Science* and Dan Cohen's Ngram-based study of the Victorian period.[2] Faced with Ngrams and the possibility of studying millions of texts at a time . . . what would Raymond Williams do? Would he be tempted to look up that keyword, *culture*? And what would he find if he did?

When we explore word frequency behaviors (something computers can easily do) as a window into cultural trends (something computers can't understand), the results, as in **Figure 6.1**, are both intriguing and frustrating. What does it mean that the use of the word *culture* rose dramatically in the 1770s and once again in the 1790s? What does it tell us about changes in the idea of culture? Is this the idiosyncratic behavior of one word or does it reflect a more general trend? The greatest challenge of developing digital humanities methods may not be how to cull data from humanistic objects, but how to analyze that data in meaningfully, humanly interpretable ways.

We chose in our work to focus on the object of the semantic field. A semantic field can be defined as a group of words that share a specific semantic property. While the words are not synonymous, they are used to talk about the same phenomenon.[3] Given the semantic richness of language and the easy drift and substitution of related words and meanings over time, it's unlikely that cultural trends can be isolated by mechanically tracking the behavior of single words. Tracking the frequency behaviors of semantic

---

1 Raymond Williams, *Culture and Society: 1780–1950* (New York: Columbia University Press, 1958).

2 Jean-Baptiste Michel et al., "Quantitative Analysis of Culture Using Millions of Digitized Books," *Science* 331, no. 6014 (January 14, 2011): 176–82; Dan Cohen, "Searching for the Victorians," *Dan Cohen's Digital Humanities Blog*, October 4, 2010, http://www.dancohen.org/2010/10/04/searching-for-the-victorians/.

3 David Crystal, "Semantics," in *A Dictionary of Linguistics and Phonetics* 5th ed. (Oxford: Wiley-Blackwell, 2003), 410–11.

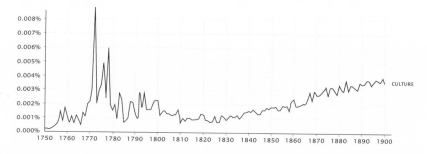

FIGURE 6.1 **Plot of the term frequency behavior of** *culture* **in the Google Books corpus,** **1750–1900**

fields—wider, meaningfully related groups of words—might improve our reach. They hold out the promise of quantitative results that can more accurately reflect changes in big ideas: cultural concepts, values, attitudes.

A. HOW TO BUILD A SEMANTIC FIELD

The practice of building semantic fields revealed serious challenges. We based our initial fields on questions raised by prior literary criticism. But this criticism rarely provided lists of associated keywords. For example, we were interested in the literary history of rural and urban locales, following Williams's *The Country and the City*.[4] After quickly exhausting the rural and urban words mentioned in several different studies, we turned, awkwardly, to thesauruses and free association to add more.

Analyzing the frequency trends of some initial fields and their constituent words, we soon realized there was another problem. The frequency behaviors of individual words often diverged wildly. How could we describe the collective behavior of these groups when their behavior was far from collective? We had included the word *country* in our rural field, for example, but, while having the greatest frequency in the group, it trended differently from every other word (see **Figure 6.2**).

The agricultural words in the field (*land, enclosure, sheep, soil, field*) trended in lock-step with one another. Were we to assemble a field and then look only at the frequency trend of the field as a whole (its aggregate frequency trend), without first confirming the genuine correlation of words

---

4 Raymond Williams, *The Country and the City* (Oxford: Oxford University Press, 1973).

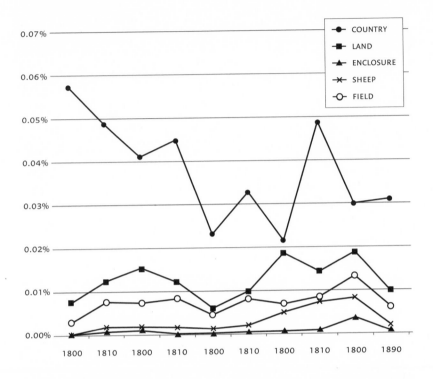

FIGURE 6.2 **The relative frequency of the word** country **and other rural words across decades of the 19th century.** The corpus here is 250 British novels, drawn from Chadwyck-Healey's Nineteenth-Century Fiction Collection.

interior to the proposed cohort, we would be badly misled. In this example, we would have believed the semantic field of rural spaces behaved not like the well-correlated agricultural words, but the unrepresentative but dominatingly high-frequency word country.

Therefore, we formulated an additional requirement our semantic fields must satisfy. Beyond their semantic coherence (to our ears), the included words should correlate with one another in their historical frequency trends. While not conflating semantics and history, this principle required that the semantic link among words reveal itself as a correlation in their historical behaviors. This makes for a conservative definition of semantic fields (some seemingly meaningful semantic fields will not meet this criterion), but such conservatism seemed preferable at this stage. It would guarantee that our blunt instrument picked up only highly reliable signals, focusing us on historically consistent semantic fields whose aggregate frequency trends would be representative and meaningful. The question now became: how could we increase our recall, or the number of words in our fields, so that our trends were not only internally consistent, but large enough to capture real, historical trends in novelistic discourse?

B. CORRELATOR

Our conservative stipulation that all semantic fields must correlate turned out to be helpful in a way we hadn't anticipated. If ultimately words in a semantic field must correlate with each other, we thought, why not find a way to compute, in advance, the degree of correlation of every word in our corpus with every other word? Given certain seed words for a potential field, this computation would reveal correlated words that could also be included.

In March 2010, we built Correlator. We made use of a feature of a novelistic database Matthew Jockers had designed: a data-table of the number of occurrences of each word in our corpus.[5] From this, we selected the words that appeared at least once in each decade of the 19th century, creating a new data-table of the selected words' frequencies of appearance.[6] We used normalized frequencies—the number of occurrences of a given word in a given decade, divided by the total number of word-occurrences in that decade—to correct for the over-representation of late century texts in our corpus. Then, we built a script to loop through each unique word-to-word comparison, calculate the degree of correlation between the two words' decade-by-decade frequencies, and store this information in a new data-table. As a measure of correlation, we used the Pearson product-moment correlation coefficient, a simple and widely-used statistical measure of the covariance of two numerical series, converted into standard deviations so

---

5 Our corpus comprises 2,958 British novels published between 1785 and 1900. The vast majority of these (around 2,500) come from a digital collection of "triple-decker" 19th-century novels that was published online by the University of Illinois at Urbana-Champaign (https://archive.org/details/19thcennov). Another 250 novels come from Chadwyck-Healey's Nineteenth-Century Fiction Collection. The remaining novels were either manually digitized in the Stanford library, or were individually downloaded from either the Project Gutenberg website or from Gale's Eighteenth Century Collections Online. For the full list of novels included in this study, please see Appendix D online: http://litlab.stanford.edu/semanticcohort/.

6 This filtering step ensures reliable correlation calculations; null data points can skew correlation coefficients. It also weeds out words with insignificant frequencies. One casualty of this filter is words adopted or invented in the middle of the 19th century, but we felt this drawback was outweighed by the benefits of filtering.

that differences in relative magnitude were ignored. (This scale-invariance was important, as we hoped to find words that behaved similarly despite differences in their overall frequencies.)[7]

To access this new data, we wrote a script allowing us to query for words that most closely correlate with a given "seed" word. For example: of all the words in our corpus, which have a historical behavior most like the word *tree*? Correlator answered: *elm, beech, shoal, let's, shore, swim, ground, spray, weed, muzzle, branch, bark.*

Which trend, then, most like *country*? *Irreparable, form, inspire, enemy, excel, dupe, species, egregious, visit, pretend, countryman, universal.*

These results seemed to verify our intuition about our earlier *country* problem—that *country* had such an aberrant frequency trend in comparison to other rural words because it was more often being used in its national sense (where it was keeping company with words like *enemy* and *countryman*.)

Beyond this instructive verification of the semantic deviance of *country* from the rural field, the very possibility of this verification surprised us. How did Correlator return such semantically meaningful results? Recall that Correlator knew nothing of "meaning," only the decade-level frequencies of words. Could such coarse historical data really be sensitive to semantics? Querying Correlator for other keywords identified as important in prior literary criticism, we found a word cohort, as we called these groups of words returned by Correlator, that was massive and seemed specific in meaning. While *tree* correlated with 333 other words significantly, and *country*, 523, the word *integrity* correlated with 1,115, many of which shared a clear semantic relation: *conduct, envy, adopt, virtue, accomplishment, acquaint, inclination, suspect, vanity.*

Correlator thus proved to be a method of discovering large word cohorts. Already historically consistent, these word cohorts could potentially be refined into semantic fields if we could ensure their semantic coherence. Correlator raised the possibility of generating semantic fields by pruning semantically-deviant words from an empirically-generated word cohort.

---

7 The Pearson coefficient ranges from +1 (meaning that the two numerical series behaved identically, or that the changes in one could predict exactly the changes in the other), through 0 (meaning that no such prediction was possible), to -1 (meaning that changes in one numerical series could predict the changes in the other, by first reversing the direction of those changes). For a sample size of ten data points (the ten decades of the 19th century), a correlation above 0.632 is considered statistically significant with a p-value below 0.05. A p-value indicates the probability that the result was reached by chance.

C. SEMANTIC TAXONOMIES AND CATEGORIZATION

Having moved through an empirically and historically focused stage of semantic field development, we needed to return to the semantic focus in order to make such purely empirical word cohorts interpretable and meaningful. Our initial approach was to filter through these words for groups that seemed semantically coherent, but this proved too loose and subjective. It had the additional disadvantage of throwing away data in the form of words that correlated historically but seemed not to group semantically with the others. We decided it was irresponsible to decide a priori which words seemed to cohere historically because of a meaningful semantic relation and which words were just statistical noise, coincidences, or accidents.

So we took a different tack. We sought out preexisting semantic taxonomies to help categorize, organize, and make sense of these word cohorts. We turned principally to the *Historical Thesaurus of the Oxford English Dictionary*, an incredible semantic taxonomy of every word sense in the *Oxford English Dictionary*.[8] It is historically exhaustive for our language, its categories are nuanced and specific, and it is truly organized around meaning. We would use this powerful taxonomy to do two things. First, to be more specific in identifying the semantic categories that constituted our word cohorts. Second, to expand these word cohorts with many more words.

Explaining our procedure in using the *OED*'s historical thesaurus requires a brief overview of the thesaurus's structure. The historical thesaurus is a semantic taxonomy of all the word senses in the *OED*. As a taxonomy, it is organized in a tree-like structure starting with three root categories: the external world, the mind, and society. Each of these root categories is divided into smaller and smaller "branches" until it breaks down to individual word senses. For example, the sense of *integrity* that means the lack of moral corruption is categorized as society > morality > virtue > absence of moral flaw. In the structure of the historical thesaurus, word senses that are closely related in meaning cluster together in the same branch or nearby branches. For instance, *rectitude*, in the sense of conforming to standards of morality, lies on the next branch over from *integrity*. Both word senses fall under the overarching category of virtue.

---

8 Christian Kay, Jane Roberts, Michael Samuels, and Irené Wotherspoon, eds., *Historical Thesaurus of the Oxford English Dictionary* (Oxford: Oxford University Press, 2009).

With the addition of the historical thesaurus, we arrived at a dialogic method that drew on both quantitative historical data and qualitative semantic rubrics to construct semantic fields with precision and nuance. We would take the word cohorts generated by Correlator and look up those words in the historical thesaurus, noting their categorizations. These categorizations helped us more precisely identify the semantic content in these proto-semantic fields. To add to the fields, we would then draw words from those categories and from nearby "branches" that shared the same overarching categories. In selecting words, we would filter out ones that would be anachronistic for the period and ones too obscure to have substantial frequencies.

In a final stage, we turned from semantics back to the statistical data, filtering these newly developed semantic fields for two conditions. First, we removed the words in the fields that appeared so infrequently that their trends could not be reliably calculated. We set this minimum threshold at one occurrence per 1 percent slice of the corpus, amounting to once every four million words, or approximately eleven times per decade. Second, we calculated the aggregate trend for the field, and removed any word that correlated negatively with the trend as a whole. While turning to semantic taxonomies ensured the semantic coherence of our fields, this final step ensured their historical consistency. Strictly speaking, the methods developed here do not construct semantic fields, which have semantic coherence but may lack historical relationship, or word cohorts, which have historical consistency but may lack semantic coherence. The real object of study is a specific kind of semantic field that satisfies both requirements, something that we call a *semantic cohort*, a group of words that are semantically related and share a common trajectory through history.

2. PROOF OF CONCEPT: SOME EXAMPLES OF THE GENERATED FIELDS

Following these steps developed our "seed" words into rich, consistent semantic fields that were both semantically and culturally legible.[9] These

---

9 We will use both "field" and "cohort" to refer to the groups of words we studied. Because we understand semantic cohorts to be a special kind of semantic field composed of words whose frequency

were the definitive fields that we investigated in the rest of our research. To allow the reader to follow the method of the research—and have a strong sense of precisely what sorts of semantic cohorts we were dealing with—we here present four examples of the results of our method to demonstrate their legibility, scale, and consistency. The names given to the resulting fields are our own.

The following sample fields developed from a shared, multi-word seed: *integrity, modesty, reason,* and *sensibility*.[10]

Social Restraint Field

EXAMPLE WORDS: *gentle, sensible, vanity, elegant, delicacy, reserve, subdued, mild, restraint*

Largest of the fields, the Social Restraint field includes 136 words relating to social values regarding the moderation of conduct. Words such as *gentle, reserve, mild,* and *restraint* express the positive valuation of this moderation.

Moral Valuation Field

EXAMPLE WORDS: *character, shame, virtue, sin, moral, principle, vice, unworthy*

Like the Social Restraint field, the Moral Valuation field relates to values of behavior, but this set of 118 words concerns the ethical evaluation of such conduct.

Partiality Field

EXAMPLE WORDS: *correct, prejudice, partial, disinterested, partiality, prejudiced, detached, bias*

With only twenty words, the Partiality field is a small but semantically distinct group of words relating to values of disinterestedness.

Sentiment Field

EXAMPLE WORDS: *heart, feeling, passion, bosom, emotion, sentiment, ardent, coldly, callous, pangs*

---

trajectories across time correlate, we will use "field" when emphasizing relations of meaning and "cohort" when emphasizing changes over time.

10 For a full list of the words included in these and our other semantic fields, please see the appendices to this chapter online at http://litlab.stanford.edu/semanticcohort.

The Sentiment field is semantically the most deviant from the other three fields, populated not with values per se but with words relating to emotion and sentiment. The fifty-two words in this field lay out a wide spectrum of emotional expression and implicitly value a range of healthy or proper emotionality.

Beyond their semantic tightness and legibility, the fields' scale and historical correlation were considerable, as the data in **Table 6.1** shows.

FIELD	[A] PERCENT FREQUENCY OF WORDS IN CORPUS	[B] NUMBER OF WORDS AFTER OED	[C] NUMBER OF WORDS AFTER FILTERING	[D] AVERAGE CORRELATION COEFFICIENT	[E] MEDIAN CORRELATION P-VALUE
Social Restraint	0.19%	155	136	.91	.0000231
Moral Valuation	0.24%	124	118	.92	.0000229
Sentiment	0.17%	116	52	.77	.00157
Partiality	0.01%	34	20	.92	.000232
Collectively	**0.61%**	**429**	**326**	**.88**	**.000411**

TABLE 6.1 **Magnitude, number of words, and correlation values in four semantic fields.** Column A indicates the percentage of the word occurrences in our corpus belonging to the respective field. Column B shows the number of words in the field after the initial word cohort was developed with semantic taxonomies. Column C shows the number of words remaining in the field after statistical filtering, which represents the final version of the field and is the basis for all further results. Column D indicates the average correlation coefficient for these words, while Column E indicates their median correlation p-value.

3. RESULTS: MAJOR SHIFTS IN NOVELISTIC LANGUAGE

Developing methods to generate semantic fields of course was only one part of the overarching project of tracking literary and cultural change at large. Now that we've shown that it's possible to isolate linguistic objects large enough to approach the scale of cultural change, we can move to the payoff: examining those changes, the trends these cohorts undergo, and what they might mean for literary history. This was data from close to three thousand novels, a corpus stretching far beyond the canon. In the rest of this paper, we will describe these findings and extract their implications for the literary history of the British novel. This will require some retelling of the story of our research, but with the focus on the results rather than the methods. Continuing in a narrative mode seems the most natural way to present our findings given the process of discovery in the digital humanities, which often feels like taking two steps backward for every wandering step forward.

A. ABSTRACT VALUES FIELDS

As described above, our investigation of semantic fields was rooted in existing literary scholarship. We turned to these sources for words that might be the "seeds" of historically important semantic fields. One attractive possibility was tracing linguistic changes reflecting the shift from rural to urban life, a defining social transformation of this period. We hadn't yet developed our dialogic methods of historical correlation and semantic taxonomy, so filling out these country and city words into large semantic fields was very difficult. Yet, we did produce some data, still loose and messy, but results nonetheless. It was in trying to make sense of the aggregate frequency trends of these proto-semantic fields that the idea behind Correlator was born. With historical correlation as an added criterion for the semantic fields we would track, we were able to be more rigorous in determining the validity of these early aggregate results. More importantly, Correlator gave us a powerful method of filling out semantic fields by empirical means, a big step beyond the imprecise practice of hand-populating these fields.

Working with this tool led us to our first major discovery. Among the groups of potential seed words we had been considering in our early stages of field construction was a group of words related to values and behavior. When inputted into Correlator, these seed words—*integrity, modesty, sensibility*, and *reason*—produced some astonishing results. In our initial trials with Correlator, we had found some relatively large word cohorts, with dozens of words in each, that demonstrated significant, if not strong, correlations in their historical behaviors. The word cohort that emerged from these seed words, however, included almost 900 words with a very high degree of correlation (see **Figure 6.3**).

More importantly, the cohort seemed to have a remarkable degree of semantic coherence. It centered on a semantic field of abstract words

```
forbear 0.9110369440387
[>>>>>>>>>>>>>>>>>>>>>>>>>>>>>>>>>>>>>>>>>>>>>>>>>>>>>>>>>>>>      ]
nobility         0.9111806386093
[>>>>>>>>>>>>>>>>>>>>>>>>>>>>>>>>>>>>>>>>>>>>>>>>>>>>>>>>>>>>      ]
persevere        0.9175002880166
[>>>>>>>>>>>>>>>>>>>>>>>>>>>>>>>>>>>>>>>>>>>>>>>>>>>>>>>>>>>>      ]
proposal         0.91232276674241
[>>>>>>>>>>>>>>>>>>>>>>>>>>>>>>>>>>>>>>>>>>>>>>>>>>>>>>>>>>>>      ]
advantageous     0.91268870937505
[>>>>>>>>>>>>>>>>>>>>>>>>>>>>>>>>>>>>>>>>>>>>>>>>>>>>>>>>>>>>      ]
envy    0.91270718250539
[>>>>>>>>>>>>>>>>>>>>>>>>>>>>>>>>>>>>>>>>>>>>>>>>>>>>>>>>>>>>      ]
bosom   0.91441008658365
[>>>>>>>>>>>>>>>>>>>>>>>>>>>>>>>>>>>>>>>>>>>>>>>>>>>>>>>>>>>>      ]
adopt   0.91462132193945
[>>>>>>>>>>>>>>>>>>>>>>>>>>>>>>>>>>>>>>>>>>>>>>>>>>>>>>>>>>        ]
promote 0.91469292236999
[>>>>>>>>>>>>>>>>>>>>>>>>>>>>>>>>>>>>>>>>>>>>>>>>>>>>>>>>>>        ]
accomplishment  0.91472732597098
[>>>>>>>>>>>>>>>>>>>>>>>>>>>>>>>>>>>>>>>>>>>>>>>>>>>>>>>>>>        ]
renounce         0.91514850386679
[>>>>>>>>>>>>>>>>>>>>>>>>>>>>>>>>>>>>>>>>>>>>>>>>>>>>>>>>>>        ]
inclination      0.91719247748877
[>>>>>>>>>>>>>>>>>>>>>>>>>>>>>>>>>>>>>>>>>>>>>>>>>>>>>>>>>>        ]
ostentation      0.91820350102716
[>>>>>>>>>>>>>>>>>>>>>>>>>>>>>>>>>>>>>>>>>>>>>>>>>>>>>>>>>>>       ]
partiality       0.918696054754
[>>>>>>>>>>>>>>>>>>>>>>>>>>>>>>>>>>>>>>>>>>>>>>>>>>>>>>>>>>>       ]
friendship       0.92017692526863
[>>>>>>>>>>>>>>>>>>>>>>>>>>>>>>>>>>>>>>>>>>>>>>>>>>>>>>>>>>>       ]
adieu   0.92018413859093
[>>>>>>>>>>>>>>>>>>>>>>>>>>>>>>>>>>>>>>>>>>>>>>>>>>>>>>>>>>>       ]
furnish 0.92316122792402
[>>>>>>>>>>>>>>>>>>>>>>>>>>>>>>>>>>>>>>>>>>>>>>>>>>>>>>>>>>>>      ]
elegant 0.92341069408103
[>>>>>>>>>>>>>>>>>>>>>>>>>>>>>>>>>>>>>>>>>>>>>>>>>>>>>>>>>>>>      ]
vanity  0.92359470306079
[>>>>>>>>>>>>>>>>>>>>>>>>>>>>>>>>>>>>>>>>>>>>>>>>>>>>>>>>>>>>      ]
conduct 0.92780418961221
[>>>>>>>>>>>>>>>>>>>>>>>>>>>>>>>>>>>>>>>>>>>>>>>>>>>>>>>>>>>>      ]
1191 options compatible with field (integrity,modesty,reason,sensibility) (0.8122)
```

FIGURE 6.3 **Correlator output from seed words *integrity, modesty, reason,* and *sensibility.***
Words with the highest correlation with the seed words are listed at the bottom. The number to the
right of each word is that word's correlation coefficient with respect to the seed words.

used to talk about values and social behavior. For example, among the
top 20 most correlated results were the words *conduct, vanity, friend-
ship, partiality, ostentation, accomplishment, envy,* and *forbear.* These are
just a few examples; the cohort contained hundreds of words like these.
What we seemed to have discovered was a massive group of words relating to values and social behavior that for some reason followed the same
historical trajectory.

The cohort's trend was as striking as its scale and coherence. Initial
tests showed that this cohort of hundreds of words declined precipitously
in usage across the 19th century. This finding demonstrates some of the
key strengths of Correlator. The tool helped us identify a large-scale
word cohort with high consistency of historical behavior. And because

it compares the usage of words on a decade-by-decade basis, it pointed us to particularly dynamic, century-wide trends. To follow up on these initial findings, we focused on filling out this cohort of social value words to make sure we were catching the full scope of the trend. As mentioned earlier, our first thought was to comb through the cohort, picking out the words that fit within this emerging social values semantic field. That filtering process gave us a rough field of over seventy-five word lemmas:

> integrity, modesty, sensibility, reason, talent, conduct, elegant, ostentation, partiality, friendship, accomplishment, character, persevere, vanity, forbear, benevolence, assiduity, understanding, extravagance, zeal, delicacy, firmness, envy, reluctance, excellence, vexation, esteem, virtue, prejudice, unrelenting, accomplish, sincere, nobility, taste, sedulous, admiration, sentiment, rational, brilliancy, falsehood, prudent, excess, superiority, unworthy, malignant, sensible, genius, reflection, pleasure, dignify, artifice, happiness, indolence, principle, discernment, coldness, self-denial, depravity, indulge, infamy, malice, faultless, adherence, perseverance, profligate, aversion, penetration, solicitous, despise, indulgence, ardent, candour, softness, restraint, impatience, insensibility

As interesting as this group of words was, we had two major reservations with this method. First, the semantic coherence of the group was still loose. It was clear that these words were predominantly abstractions and were related to values of social behavior. To make our conclusions specific and relevant to literary and cultural study, though, we needed to identify and categorize the semantic content of this field more precisely. The second major problem was we didn't know how comprehensive these results were in delineating the entirety of a semantic field; were there many other social values and abstractions we weren't seeing? Thus, while developing ways to categorize and specify the semantic content of these results, we also sought to continue expanding this semantic field with more words.

This led us to semantic taxonomies. We used the *OED*'s historical thesaurus to identify the semantic content of the field, break it down into more specific sub-fields, and fill those out with further words from the *OED*'s semantic categories. As described above, we identified and filled out four sub-fields of abstract values words: words relating to values of social restraint and moderation; words of moral valuation; words relating to sentiment; and words relating to values of objectivity. After using the empirical data to filter out added words that didn't correlate historically, we had four developed semantic cohorts, tighter in their semantic relation and closer to exhaustiveness than before. We finally felt ready to look closely at the aggregate trends of these cohorts.

With these more focused cohorts, the trends we found were dramatic. Tracing their behavior over the 19th century, we found they exhibit parallel downward trends. For instance, the cohort of social restraint and moderation words exhibits a steady downward decline (**Figure 6.4**) from ~0.30 percent of all word tokens[11] (about one in every 325 words) at the beginning of the century to ~0.15 percent of all word tokens (about one in every 700 words) by the end of the century, a decrease of about 55 percent.[12]

The cohort of moral valuation words shows a similar trend (**Figure 6.5**), declining from ~0.43 percent of all word tokens (about one in every 235 words) at the beginning of the century to ~0.15 percent of all word tokens (about one in every 670 words) by the end of the century, a decrease of about 65 percent.

The cohort of sentiment words shows a steady decline (**Figure 6.6**) from ~0.25 percent of all word tokens (about one in every 380 words) at the beginning of the century to ~0.14 percent of all word tokens (about one in every 700 words) by the end of the century, a decrease of almost 45 percent.

The cohort of partiality words exhibited aggregate word frequencies an order of magnitude lower than the other cohorts but nevertheless exhibited a parallel trend (**Figure 6.7**). It declines steadily from ~0.02 percent of all word tokens (about one in every 4,500 words) at the beginning of the century to ~0.006 percent of all word tokens (about one in every 17,500 words) by the end of the century, a decrease of almost 75 percent.

Collectively, the aggregate word frequency for the cohorts of abstract values decreases through the 19th century (**Figure 6.8**), from ~1.0 percent

---

11 A word token is an occurrence of a word. Token is distinguished from type, which stands for the word itself. For example, if a text has a lexicon of 100 unique words but is 800 words long, we say that that text is composed of 100 types but 800 tokens.

12 These percentages are drawn from the linear regression fit of the data. The graph shows the range of frequency values among the novels in any given period while the regression is a useful articulation of the overall trend. We use "century" here as shorthand for the full historical range of our data, extending from 1785 to 1900.

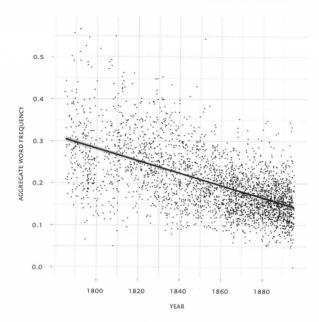

FIGURE 6.4 **Aggregate word frequency of the social restraint cohort in novels, 1785–1900.**
For all the plots in this section, each point represents the frequency of these words in a particular
novel. The x-axis represents the novel's date of publication. The y-axis represents the percentage of
the novel's words that are of the cohort. The trend line over the data represents the best fit from a
linear regression model.

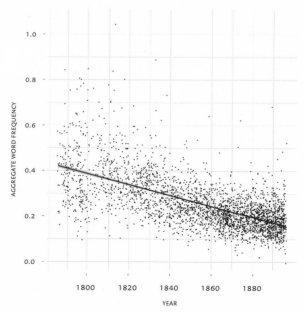

FIGURE 6.5 **Aggregate word frequency of the moral valuation cohort in novels, 1785–1900**

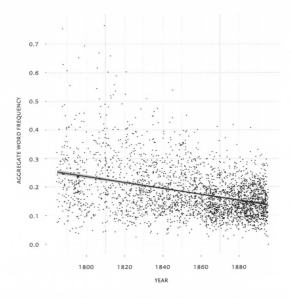

FIGURE 6.6 **Aggregate word frequency of the sentiment cohort in novels, 1785–1900**

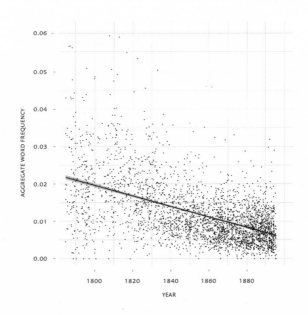

FIGURE 6.7 **Aggregate word frequency of the partiality cohort in novels, 1785–1900**

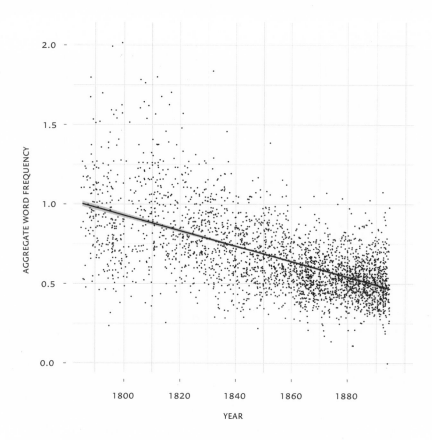

FIGURE 6.8 Aggregate word frequency of the abstract values cohorts combined in novels, 1785–1900

of all word tokens (about one in every 100 words) in the period of 1800–1810, to ~0.44 percent of all word tokens (about one in every 225 words) by the century's end, a decrease of about 55 percent.

Fully interpreting this dramatic declining trend requires looking closely at the shared characteristics of the words in these cohorts and contextualizing them within the literary and cultural history of the period. This gives us a better sense of what sort of linguistic shift is occurring here and opens the investigation into the reasons behind it. Examining the abstract values words, we can isolate several key characteristics. First, the words are largely abstractions: abstract nouns such as *modesty, extravagance,* or *propriety*; and abstract adjectives such as *elegant, indecent,* or *restrained.* More specifically, they form a cluster of abstractions centered on ideas of social normativity and the regulation of behavior. For instance, the Social Restraint field, which includes words like *restraint, moderation, self-control, excess, indulgence,* and *ostentation,* clearly delineates a set of social values prescribing the proper limits of personal behavior, the moderate range of conduct considered socially acceptable. Given this emphasis on social norms, it's no surprise to find that these fields are also rich in highly evaluative, highly polarized language. These are words used to articulate specific social values, judge behavior, and point out lapses and violations. Thus, the fields include many words such as *moral, virtue,* and *decent,* but also their opposites, *immoral, sin,* and *indecent.* It's worth noting as well that the abstract values words are predominantly Latinate, which makes sense given the dominance of abstractions. What we found then was a massive semantic cohort of abstract, socially normative, evaluative, and highly polarized words that underwent a systemic and significant decline in usage over the century.

Our first hunch was to seek a replacement, over the century, of one class of values by another. If what we had isolated in the abstract values fields were late 18th- and early 19th-century British values, perhaps we could find fields of Victorian values that supplanted them. Through many potential seed words though this search proved unfruitful. No major trends in other kinds of values words emerged from the data.

B. "'HARD' SEED" FIELDS

After a long series of fruitless seed words, perhaps on a whim, perhaps on a wild hunch about words completely different from the abstract values, we inputted into Correlator the innocuous little word *hard.* What emerged in the output of Correlator was a massive cohort of over 400 word lemmas that shared an even tighter historical correlation than the abstract values cohort. We named this cohort "'hard' seed." The first thing that struck us about "'hard' seed" was just how different these words were from the abstract values words. Among the top twenty words most correlated with *hard*: *smoke, go, brush, look, rough, liquid, back, come, face, ache, finger.* Even more fascinating though was the aggregate trend of this word cohort. In strict contrast to the behavior of the abstract values cohorts, this cohort showed a dramatic rise over the 19th century. We may not have found the expected shift toward Victorian values, but we found something even more interesting, a massive group of words categorically different from the abstract values cohorts that contextualizes and frames their decline within an even broader movement. It's important to note that finding this other major trend would have been nearly impossible without the quantitative methods at our disposal. When we were searching for semantic cohorts related to the decline in the abstract values fields, it did not and would not have occurred to us to look toward a group of hard seed type words. They are not semantically or culturally related to the abstract values words in any immediately clear way. We might still have discovered the trend for the word *hard*, but without Correlator's ability to aggregate word cohorts around trends, we would have had no sense of its significance. It took a computational method of finding language trends to discover this other group of words that, while not semantically related to the abstract values words, are historically related.

After applying to hard seed the semantic cohort method of identification, correlation, categorization, expansion, and refinement, we found we had isolated quite an interesting creature. Instead of a single semantic field tightly organized around a specific semantic property, this highly correlated word cohort comprised a variety of semantic fields and types of words including:

> ACTION VERBS: come, go, drop, stand, touch, see . . .
>
> BODY PARTS: finger, face, hair, chin, hand, fist . . .
>
> COLORS: red, white, blue, green, brown, scarlet . . .
>
> NUMBERS: three, five, two, seven, eight, four . . .
>
> LOCATIVE AND DIRECTIONAL ADJECTIVES AND PREPOSITIONS: down, out, back, up, over, above
>
> PHYSICAL ADJECTIVES: hard, rough, flat, round, clear, sharp . . .

As seen in **Table 6.2**, these fields were even more massive than the abstract values fields, accounting for almost 4.5 percent of all word occurrences in our corpus.[13]

---

13 Please see **Table 6.1** for an explanation of these columns. See Appendix B online for the full listing of words in these fields: http://litlab.stanford.edu/semanticcohort/.

FIELD	[A] PERCENT FREQUENCY OF WORDS IN CORPUS	[B] NUMBER OF WORDS AFTER OED	[C] NUMBER OF WORDS AFTER FILTERING	[D] AVERAGE CORRELATION COEFFICIENT	[E] MEDIAN CORRELATION P-VALUE
Action Verbs	1.99%	257	248	.73	.00742
Body Parts	0.65%	147	111	.71	.00773
Colors	0.13%	96	46	.57	.0616
Locative Prepositions	1.09%	28	27	.74	.00499
Numbers	0.37%	46	44	.73	.00679
Physical Adjectives	0.20%	32	32	.79	.00227
Collectively	**4.43%**	**606**	**508**	**.71**	**.0151**

TABLE 6.2 **Magnitude, number of words, and correlation values for the hard seed fields.**

Tracing their behavior over the 19th century, we found the hard seed cohorts exhibited parallel *upward* trends. The cohort of action verbs, a field of substantial magnitude, exhibits a steady rise (**Figure 6.9**) from ~0.96 percent of all word tokens (about one in every 100 words) at the beginning of the century to ~2.7 percent of all word tokens (about one in every 40 words) by the end of the century, an increase of over 180 percent.

The body parts cohort also shows a rise (**Figure 6.10**), though of a gentler slope, increasing from ~0.45 percent of all word tokens (about one in every 220 words) at the beginning of the century to ~0.80 percent of all word tokens (about one in every 120 words) by the end of the century, an increase of about 80 percent.

The colors cohort shows an even sharper rise (**Figure 6.11**) from ~0.04 percent of all word tokens (about one in every 2000 words) at the beginning of the century to ~0.19 percent of all word tokens (about one in every 530 words) by the end of the century, an increase of over 290 percent.

The cohort of numbers increases (**Figure 6.12**) from ~0.2 percent of all word tokens (about one in every 470 words) at the beginning of the century to ~0.3 percent of all word tokens (about one in every 300 words) by the end of the century, an increase of about 54 percent.

The cohort of locative and directional adjectives and prepositions shows a rise (**Figure 6.13**) from ~0.59 percent of all word tokens (about one in every 170 words) at the beginning of the century to ~1.43 percent of

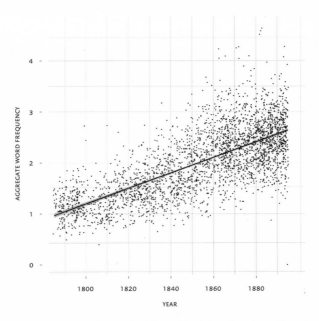

FIGURE 6.9 **Aggregate word frequency of the action verbs cohort in novels, 1785–1900**

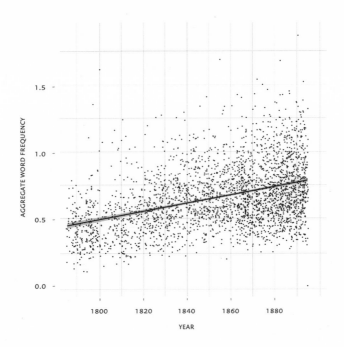

FIGURE 6.10 **Aggregate word frequency of the body parts cohort in novels, 1785–1900**

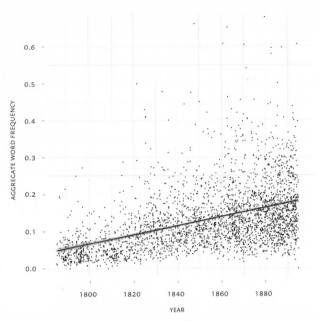

FIGURE 6.11 **Aggregate word frequency of the colors cohort in novels, 1785–1900**

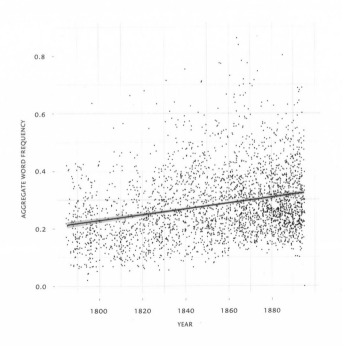

FIGURE 6.12 **Aggregate word frequency of the numbers cohort in novels, 1785–1900**

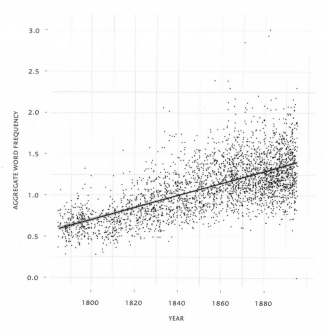

FIGURE 6.13 Aggregate word frequency of the locative prepositions cohort in novels, 1785–1900

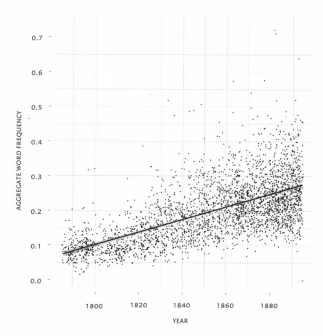

FIGURE 6.14 Aggregate word frequency of the physical adjectives cohort in novels, 1785–1900

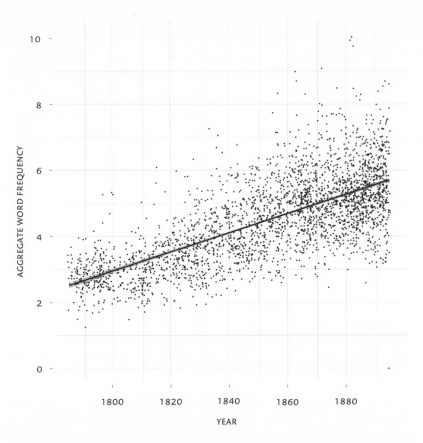

FIGURE 6.15 **Aggregate word frequency of the hard seed cohorts combined in novels, 1785–1900**

all word tokens (about one in every 70 words) by the end of the century, an increase of over 140 percent.

The physical adjectives field rises (**Figure 6.14**) from ~0.07 percent of all word tokens (about one in every 1300 words) at the beginning of the century to ~0.28 percent of all word tokens (about one in every 350 words) by the end of the century, an increase of over 280 percent.

In contrast to the values cohorts, the aggregate word frequency of the hard seed cohorts increases steadily across the 19th century (**Figure 6.15**) from 2.5 percent of all word tokens (~one in every 40 words) to 5.9 percent of all word tokens (~one in every 17 words), an increase in usage of over 130 percent.

As we did with the abstract values fields, we looked closely at the shared characteristics of the hard seed words. The comparison with the abstract values words was particularly revealing. As opposed to abstractions, the hard seed words are concrete and physical—*wet, stiff, crack, knock, jaw, neck,* etc. They are also specific, words used to specify the particular action (*stoop, scratch, tilt, crawl . . .*), physical orientation (*over, under, behind . . .*), physical quality (*heavy, wooden, crooked . . .*), color (*yellow, purple, orange, ruddy . . .*), or quantity (*ten, sixty, hundred, thousand . . .*) of an object or person. Where the abstract values words were evaluative and highly polarized, these words are non-judgmental, too rooted in the physical to refer in any direct way to abstract norms, values, and standards. And where the abstract values words were long and Latinate, these are short, often monosyllabic, and predominantly Anglo-Saxon in origin. In the context of the novel, the hard seed word cohort can be collectively characterized as concrete description words of a direct, everyday kind. It is these kinds of words that are rising significantly in usage over the 19th century.

C. CORROBORATION: TOPIC MODELING DATA

Because these results were so striking, we wanted to make sure what we had found was in fact real. To corroborate these results, these two major trends in novelistic language, we sought another method of gathering large-scale semantic data.

Topic modeling provided this complement to our semantic cohort method. A well-established procedure, topic modeling computationally groups words that tend to appear in the same context within texts; these groups can be thought of as topics or themes.[14] It offers two key differences

---

14 As David M. Blei, one of the developers of the topic modeling algorithm, explains, "a topic model takes a collection of texts as input" and then "find[s] the sets of terms that tend to occur together in the texts. They look like 'topics' because terms that frequently occur together tend to be about the same subject" (David M. Blei, "Topic Modeling and Digital Humanities," *Journal of Digital Humanities* 2, no. 1 (Winter 2012)). Topic modeling is unsupervised because it requires minimal user input: besides a collection of texts, the only user input necessary to the model is the number of topics to discover. This number is a parameter in the model: the higher the number, the more granular the topics. See Blei's "Topic Modeling and Digital Humanities" for an accessible introduction to topic modeling in the digital humanities. For the foundational paper on the algorithm, see David M. Blei, Andrew Y. Ng, and Michael I. Jordan, "Latent Dirichlet Allocation," *Journal of Machine Learning Research* 3 (July 2002–March 2003): 993–1022.

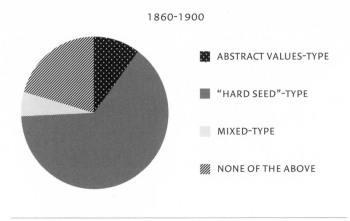

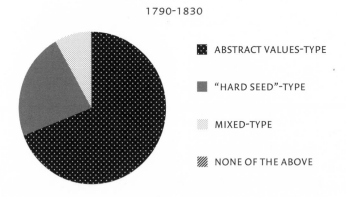

FIGURE 6.16 **Pie charts of abstract values-type and hard seed-type words in topics from** 1790–1830 **and** 1860–1900

from our methods. First, it's an unsupervised method that generates topics without subjective input from users, complementing our methods, which mix supervised and unsupervised procedures. Second, it generates topics based on co-occurrence within texts, rather than on our dual criteria of historical correlation and semantic relatedness. Thus, topic modeling gave us an entirely different lens to look at the semantic patterns in our corpus, a way to test if our results could be replicated when measured by different tools.

After generating 500 topics of nouns, we isolated two sets of topics, those most frequent in novels published toward the beginning of the century, 1790–1830, and those most frequent in novels toward the end of the century, 1860–1900.[15] Comparing these two sets gave us a rough and ready view of historical trends in the topic modeling data. To enable the comparison of these results to our established ones, we categorized each topic into one of four types based on the characteristics of their constituent words: abstract values-type, hard seed-type, mixed type, or none of the above. The results, as shown in **Table 6.3** and **Figure 6.16**, were clear:

PERIOD	ABSTRACT VALUES-TYPE	HARD SEED-TYPE	MIXED-TYPE	NONE OF THE ABOVE
1790-1830	69%	23%	8%	0%
1860-1900	10%	64%	5%	21%

TABLE 6.3 **Comparison of abstract values–type and hard seed–type words in topics from 1790–1830 and 1860–1900 showing the percentage of topics of each type among the most frequent topics of the two periods.** As in the results of our semantic cohort method, the topic modeling data confirmed opposite trends for these two kinds of novelistic language: a decline in abstract values-type words and a rise in concrete, hard seed-type words. What's important here is that these same dramatic trends were found by entirely independent methods, confirming that our results are not an anomalous product of our methods but a real historical transformation in the 19th-century British novel.

As these trends appear real, it's worth pausing here to emphasize their magnitudes. The abstract values cohorts at their height account for about 1 percent of all word usage in 19th-century British novels; the hard seed cohorts, almost 6 percent. These are large-scale, diffuse trends, encompassing the histories of hundreds and hundreds of words. Recognizing the scale of these changes made us all the more eager to probe into the data. What might these changes mean? What might lie behind them?

4. DISCUSSION: THE LANGUAGE AND SOCIAL SPACE OF THE 19TH-CENTURY BRITISH NOVEL

An important first step to cracking open our results was to determine the relationship between the two seemingly opposite trends we had found. So for each of the novels in our corpus we plotted its usage of the abstract

---

15 Please see Appendix E online for a full account of our specific topic modeling procedures: http://litlab.stanford.edu/semanticcohort/.

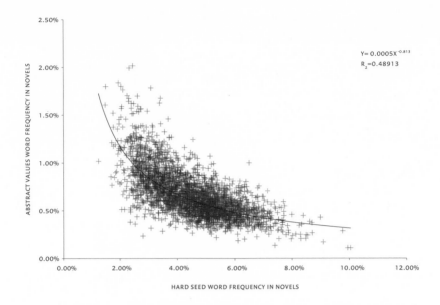

FIGURE 6.17 **Inverse relationship of abstract values and hard seed word frequencies in novels.** An exponential regression is superimposed.

values field against its usage of the hard seed fields. This revealed a strongly inverse relationship between the two (see **Figure 6.17**).

What can be seen from this plot is the tendency for novels with high frequencies of hard seed words to have low frequencies of abstract values words and vice versa. The two fields' mutual exclusivity suggested it would be possible to separate out different groups of novels through their relative usage of the fields. To visualize these groups, we produced two spectra of the novels, ranked by the concentration of abstract values words or hard seed words.

The spectra allowed us to see the trends through units understandable and familiar to us as readers and literary scholars, the actual novels, genres, and authors in our corpus. Instead of trying to make sense of term frequency behaviors of semantic cohorts, a rather abstract object, the spectra let us ask more grounded questions of the data: What kinds of novels correspond to the prevalence of one field over the other? Can we understand these trends in novelistic language more directly as changes in the kinds of novels being written?

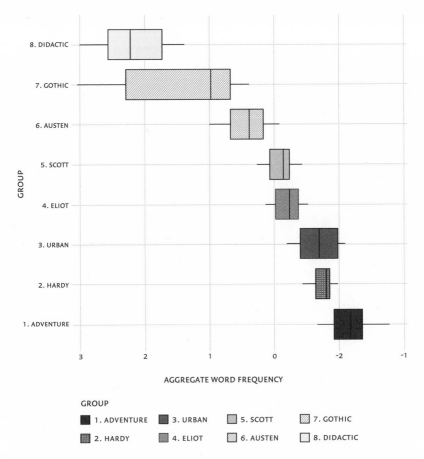

FIGURE 6.18 **Spectrum of novels, authors, and genres as ranked by concentration of the abstract values fields.** The x-axis shows number of standard deviations above the corpus-wide mean concentration of abstract values fields. For example, the median for the evangelical and didactic novels was around 2.25 standard deviations above the mean.

Ranking novels by their usage of the two fields indeed separates out clusters of genres and authors within the spectrum (see **Figure 6.18**).[16] From left to right, this shows novels with highest frequency of abstract values words to lowest (and, conversely, lowest frequency of hard seed words to highest). What we get is a distribution that begins at the extreme left with the didactic and evangelical novel, closely followed by the Gothic novel,

---

16 We will be focusing here on the spectrum produced by the concentrations of abstract values words. The spectrum produced by the hard seed words matched closely, not surprising given their strong inverse relationship.

then Jane Austen, Walter Scott, and George Eliot. Toward the right of the spectrum, we find the urban and industrial novel and Charles Dickens, and at the extreme right, a cluster of genres including adventure novels, fantasy, science fiction, and children's literature.[17] Given that it was generated quantitatively by the concentration of only two features of novelistic language, and that obviously computers have no knowledge of authors or genres, it's amazing just how suggestive the spectrum is.[18] For instance it clusters city novels together and takes Eliot's works out of chronological order and places them back a generation closer to Austen's, bringing out an affinity that many readers and critics have felt. Because of this sensitivity to genres and authors, the spectrum allowed us to see the two historical trends in novelistic language as deeper shifts in narrative mode, changes in the kinds of novels being written.[19]

---

17 We offer here some examples of the texts that make up the spectrum's genre clusters. The Didactic cluster includes novels such as Hannah More's *Coelebs in Search of a Wife*, Mary Brunton's *Self-Control*, William Godwin's *Things as They Are*, and Susan Ferrier's *Marriage*.

The Gothic cluster includes novels such as Matthew Lewis's *The Monk*, Ann Radcliffe's novels, Percy Shelley's *Zastrozzi*, Isabella Kelly's *Madeline, or the Castle of Montgomery*, etc. The Urban cluster includes the novels of Dickens, Gaskell, Gissing, Trollope, and others.

The Adventure tag stands in for a conglomerate of genres: adventure fiction such as Robert Louis Stevenson's novels, H. Rider Haggard's novels, R. M. Ballantyne's *The Coral Island*; science fiction works such as H. G. Wells's *The Time Machine*, and Richard Jefferies's *After London*; children's literature such as Richard Jefferies's *Bevis*; and fantasy works such as Lewis Carroll's novels and George MacDonald's *The Princess and the Goblin*.

18 This spectrum of novels produced purely through quantitative measures suggests the tantalizing possibility of categorizing genre in quantitative terms, a goal pursued to an extent already in "Quantitative Formalism." In our project, the categorization is done not by most frequent words or lexicogrammatical categories but by semantic fields, a different kind of feature that offers certain advantages of interpretability. We have not yet followed up this intriguing possibility, but it seems the nature of this research is the continual opening up of (too) many other directions to pursue.

19 An even more intriguing possibility that emerges from this spectrum was suggested to us by Franco Moretti, who pointed out that the most canonical authors and genres of the 19th-century British novel seem to cluster in a relatively narrow range in the middle of the spectrum while the more minor genres are literally at the fringes. It's as if there were certain features of the novel, in this case, kinds of novelistic language, that can cause an author to drop out of the running for canonization simply from using it too much or too little. In other words, that there might be some kind of acceptable range for these features beyond which you are put beyond the pale. Moretti also pointed out that this seems to contradict the prevalent image of minor works as flawed derivatives of major works. In this spectrum, there seems instead to be whole ranges of form that the canonized works do not even explore, perhaps an argument for the importance of exploring the archive beyond the canon for these underexplored ranges of literary history.

One shift easily seen from the spectrum is the physical spaces of the novel expanding. The distribution moves from the tight, domestic, and village spaces of the moralistic, Gothic, and Austenian rural novel to the cities of Dickens and the exploratory expanses of the adventure, science fiction, and fantasy novels. As an initial observation, this is interesting, but we wanted to move beyond this because it didn't synthesize all the data. Thus, we worked on triangulating the movement revealed by the spectrum with the trend data we'd already found. This might help us see the larger patterns at work.

A. TRACING A DECLINE: THE WANING OF A SOCIAL FORMATION

We began by mapping the abstract values fields onto the spectrum. Recall that those fields comprise highly polarized, explicitly evaluative words related to norms of social regulation. Mapping these characteristics onto the spectrum, we can see that the change shown here goes beyond a change in physical spaces. More fundamentally, it is a change in the *social space* of the novel. By the term social space, we mean to point to the scale, characteristics, and force of the forms of social organization that structure the social worlds depicted in the novels. The change revealed here is an expansion from small, constrained social spaces to wider, freer ones. Think of the rigidity and tightness of social space in the evangelical, Gothic, or village novels where the character systems are limited to families or small communities. In these small social spaces, social behavior, roles, and identity are visible, monitored and tightly constrained. Moving left to right along the spectrum we see an expansion toward wider, less constrained social spaces—rapidly growing cities, London. By the time we reach the cluster of genres at the extreme right, these science-fiction, adventure, and fantasy spaces have expanded outward so far that they move beyond society entirely to exotic islands, fantasy worlds, different eras, etc.[20]

To verify this interpretation of the spectrum as a change in social space, we built on our earlier topic modeling data, this time categorizing

---

20 The case of Thomas Hardy's position on the spectrum was one of these outliers, though not a large one considering his novels account for eleven of our almost three thousand texts. His relatively high usage of the hard seed fields despite predominantly rural settings affirms our suggestion that multiple variables are at work in the hard seed trend. Perhaps most crucial for explaining Hardy's case is the shift from telling to showing that we present in the conclusion of this section.

for types of social space.[21] Again, topic modeling provided an independent, unsupervised method of identifying patterns in language use, a parallel data set in which we could see if social space emerged as the determining variable. Such parallel testing was particularly important in this case given the limitations of interpreting the spectrum. The powerful strategy of translating our data into readily familiar and interpretable forms comes with unavoidable costs: the drastic limitation of the sample size to the relatively canonical texts we are familiar with; and the reliance of the interpretation on our subjective conceptions of the texts. To run this parallel test, we categorized each topic into one of six types of social space:

1. INTIMATE: a private social space of intimate, often romantic, relations;
2. DOMESTIC: a domestic social space of relations between those in the family and household;
3. FAMILIAR: a social space of familiar relations between friends and acquaintances;
4. PUBLIC: the social space of the public sphere and impersonal relations;
5. EXTRA-SOCIETAL: a social space lying outside the boundary of everyday society;
6. UNCATEGORIZED: no indication of a social space of any kind.

This categorization produced the results shown in **Table 6.4**.

SOCIAL SPACE	1790 - 1830	1860 - 1900
Intimate	27%	11%
Domestic	15%	16%
Familiar	15%	14%
Public	12%	35%
Extra-Societal	0%	3%
Uncategorized	31%	22%

TABLE 6.4 **The most frequent topics in 1790–1830 and 1860–1900 characterized by type of social space.** Percentages refer to the percentage of topics in the period characterized as indicating that type of social space.

---

21 For a fuller account and the complete data, please see appendix E online: http://litlab.stanford.edu/semanticcohort/.

While the concentrations of domestic and familiar social spaces in the topics remain essentially unchanged, the major movement here is a shift in the distribution's center of gravity from intimate to public social spaces. This shift in emphasis corroborates what the spectrum suggests: a systemic expansion of social space in the novel across the century.

Thinking in terms of the abstract values, the tight social spaces in the novels at the left of the spectrum are communities where values of conduct and social norms are central. Values like those encompassed by the abstract values fields organize the social structure, influence social position, and set the standards by which individuals are known and their behavior judged. Small, constrained social spaces can be thought of as what Raymond Williams calls "knowable communities," a model of social organization typified in representations of country and village life, which offer readers "people and their relationships in essentially knowable and communicable ways." The knowable community is a sphere of face-to-face contacts "within which we can find and value the real substance of personal relationships."[22] What's important in this social space is the legibility of people, their relationships, and their positions within the community. In these terms, it's easy to see how a unified system of social values and standards could undergird this legibility, providing a major scheme for making sense of people and their relationships, while shaping behavior to keep close interactions harmonious. Indeed, this general point is implicit when Williams characterizes Austen's novels as centered on "a testing and

---

22 Williams, *The Country and the City*, 165. It's important to note that Williams does not see as entirely accurate the characterization of rural communities as knowable communities. He is specifically speaking of the knowable community as a structure represented in novels, and, more broadly, as an idea. He devotes the chapter on knowable communities to complicating this model and interrogating what lies behind the point of view that would be invested in representing rural communities in this way in the 19th century. He points out that while within the novels Austen's communities are wholly knowable, as real communities, they are "precisely selective" (166). What is represented is not the whole social system but a network of propertied families linked by class. "Neighbors in Jane Austen are not the people actually living nearby; they are the people living a little less nearby who, in social recognition, can be visited" (166). The point is well taken and it helps us clarify that we are less interested in whether these novels accurately and comprehensively represent the social realities of community life in 19th-century Britain than in the social worlds as they are constructed within these novels, and the kinds of language used in that construction. Our argument suggests that the novelistic construction of "social recognition," which allows Austen to map a knowable network, may depend on the use of a kind of socially legible language. In fact, the highly polarized character of the abstract values fields would strengthen the systems of social recognition that map a knowable community by creating clear standards by which some may be excluded.

discovery of the standards which govern human behavior," and the relation of these standards to an established social order of property and status; this emphasis on conduct in Austen's work is heightened by the novels' setting within a "close social dimension," in other words, a small social space.[23] Within a small social space, the explicitly evaluative and highly polarized quality of the abstract values fields finds a natural home. Their explicitness and polarization provide clarity, clear-cut standards and categories, even binaries, for legibly representing and perceptually organizing a close community's social life. We can characterize the abstract values words as a kind of language well suited for producing social legibility, efficient engines for producing knowable communities.

If this is how the abstract values fields are linked to a specific kind of social space, then we can make sense of their decline over the century and across the spectrum. The observed movement to wider, less constrained social spaces means opening out to more variability of values and norms. A wider social space, a rapidly growing city for instance, encompasses more competing systems of value. This, combined with the sheer density of people, contributes to the feeling of the city's unordered diversity and randomness. This multiplicity creates a messier, more ambiguous, and more complex landscape of social values, in effect, a less knowable community. Williams articulates this as a rural-urban dichotomy: "In the city kind, experience and community would be essentially opaque; in the country kind, essentially transparent . . . identity and community [in the city] become more problematic, as a matter of perception and as a matter of valuation, as the scale and complexity of the characteristic social organisation increased." Urban population growth, increasing division of labor, changing class relations—these and other factors made it more and more difficult to maintain the idea of a knowable community.[24] In such a social space, the values held by the city's multitudinous classes, communities, and subcultures overlap and conflict as much as the people making up those groups jostle, bump, and cross each other on the crowded streets. The sense of a shared set of values and standards giving cohesion and legibility to this collective dissipates. So we can understand the decline of the abstract values fields—these clear systems of social values organized into

---

23 Williams, *The Country and the City*, 113, 117.

24 Williams, *The Country and the City*, 165.

neat polarizations—as a reflection of their inadequacy and obsolescence in the face of the radically new kind of society that novels were attempting to represent. A transformation of the social space of the novel, even as urbanization, industrialization, and new stages of capitalism were drastically reshaping the actual social spaces of Britain. The decline we see in this kind of language is a trace of the waning of an entire form of social organization, an entire way of life, from the world of the novel.

The change is not a comfortable one. Alienation, disconnection, dissolution—all are common reactions to the new experience of the city. Wordsworth precisely articulates this in his description of London in the seventh book of the 1805 *Prelude*:

> How often, in the overflowing streets,
> Have I gone forwards with the crowd, and said
> Unto myself, 'The face of every one
> That passes by me is a mystery.'
> . . .
> And all the ballast of familiar life—
> The present, and the past, hope, fear, all stays,
> All laws of acting, thinking, speaking man—
> Went from me, neither knowing me, nor known.

Wordsworth brings out the experience of the city, the wide social space, as the experience of close proximity to an anonymous diversity of people, a seemingly endless stream of strangers. What happens to novels as they try to capture this experience? The effect on character would be particularly strong. The protagonist or focalizer within this overwhelming social space is in much the same position as Wordsworth: most everyone in the "overflowing" crowd is a stranger. With the absence of the knowable community's face-to-face relationships ("neither knowing me, nor known") and the dissolution of shared social values ("All laws of acting, thinking, speaking man / Went from me"), this character has neither the knowledge nor the stable schema to place these strangers and in turn make sense of his or her position and relationship to them. The perceptual disorientation of the city corresponds to this breakdown in social legibility. Alongside this is a feeling of loss, the loss of the human connections that ground not only identity but the sense of mutual responsibility at the core of ethics and conduct. Seen another way, the anonymity of wider social spaces dissolves the social accountability and visibility that makes for the regulation of a tightly knit community. In capturing this experience, shifting its language and represented social space, the novel touches deeply on the historical and sociological changes in Britain: the shift from community (*Gemeinschaft*) to society (*Gesellschaft*), to use Ferdinand Tönnies's terms. By the mid-19th century, Britain had become the first place in the history of world to have more people living in cities than in the country.[25] In the context of such transformations, it would be surprising not to see profound changes in the novel.

B. TRACING A RISE: THE HARD SEED COHORTS IN ACTION AND SETTING

Having understood the change manifested in the decline of the abstract values cohorts, a question remains: why is there a correlation between that trend, an expanding social space, and the rise of the hard seed cohort? We present several possibilities. Given the sheer magnitude of the hard seed field, and the fact that it's far more semantically and conceptually diffuse than the abstract values fields, it shouldn't be surprising to find multiple factors at work.

We can begin by considering the experience of setting and character within urban and wider social spaces. To keep this grounded, let's look under the hood of our data at a few sample passages. For example, a passage from *Great Expectations*, which as a whole exhibits the highest concentration of the hard seed fields among the canonical city novels in our corpus.[26] With Pip leaving the marsh country of Kent to pursue his expectations in London, few novels represent the contrast between rural and urban social spaces so memorably. The interface between these two, Pip's first day in London, provides a stark encounter with the city, its spaces and people, in their concrete reality. Words from the hard seed fields are in bold, but note also the preponderance of other concrete words:

---

25 Williams, *The Country and the City*, 217.

26 It's probable that among the close to three thousand novels in our corpus, there are lesser known city novels exhibiting even more extreme concentrations of the hard seed fields, but, as we mentioned in our discussion of the spectra of novels, the usefulness of translating data into familiar forms always comes at this cost of leaving out the less familiar.

Of course I had no experience of a London summer day, and my spirits may have been oppressed by the **hot** exhausted air, and by the dust and grit that **lay thick** on everything. But I **sat** wondering and **waiting** in Mr Jaggers's **close** room, until I really could not bear the **two** casts on the shelf **above** Mr Jaggers's chair, and **got up** and **went out**.

When I told the clerk that I would take a **turn** in the air while I **waited**, he advised me to **go round** the corner and I should **come** into Smithfield. So, I **came** into Smithfield; and the shameful place, being all asmear with filth and fat and **blood** and foam, seemed to stick to me. So, I rubbed it **off** with all possible speed by **turning** into a street where I **saw** the great **black** dome of Saint Paul's bulging at me from **behind** a grim stone building which a bystander said was Newgate Prison. Following the wall of the jail, I found the roadway covered with straw to deaden the noise of passing vehicles; and from this, and from the quantity of people **standing** about, **smelling** strongly of spirits and beer, I inferred that the trials were on.

While I **looked** about me here, an exceedingly dirty and partially drunk minister of justice asked me if I would like to step in and hear a trial . . . As I declined the proposal on the plea of an appointment, he was so good as to take me into a yard and **show** me where the gallows was **kept**, and also where people were publicly whipped, and then he **showed** me the Debtors' Door, **out** of which culprits **came** to be **hanged**: heightening the interest of that dreadful portal by giving me to understand that, "**four** on' em" would **come out** at that door the day after to-morrow at **eight** in the morning, to be killed in a row. This was horrible, and gave me a sickening idea of London: the more so as the Lord Chief Justice's proprietor wore (from his hat **down** to his boots and **up** again to his pocket-handkerchief inclusive) mildewed clothes, which had evidently not belonged to him originally, and which, I took it into my **head**, he had bought cheap of the executioner. **Under** these circumstances I thought myself well rid of him for a shilling.

Of the 399 words in this passage, forty-one are hard seed words. They account for 10.3 percent of the passage, a rate over two times the average in 1860–61 when *Great Expectations* was published. That percentage would be even higher if we included all the other concrete description words in the passage.[27] The hard seed words are truly integral to the linguistic fabric of this passage. So what are they doing?

We see three major uses: constructing setting, narrating actions, and characterization. From "the **hot** exhausted air" and "the dust and grit that **lay thick** on everything" to the "filth and fat and **blood** and foam" and "the Debtors' Door, **out** of which culprits **came** to be **hanged**," this language is instrumental in rendering the physical spaces and settings of this world. They help construct the city's diverse spaces—Jaggers's office, the cattle market at Smithfield, the roadway by Newgate prison, the facilities of the jail—place them in spatial relation, and bring them to life down to the particular ritual, spatial arrangement, and timing of the debtors' executions. Reading Dickens's description, we can almost map out these settings, following Pip's trajectory through the city. The spatial character and concreteness of the hard seed fields make them a language suited for constructing settings that are imaginable as physical spaces.

Within these spaces, of course, there are characters acting. So it's not surprising that another prevalent use of the hard seed words is for narrating actions and movements: "I **sat** wondering and **waiting**," "**got up** and **went out**," etc. Some proportion of the usage of hard seed words, particularly the action verbs and locative prepositions, belongs to this expected baseline of narrative rather than descriptive function. But in light of the construction of setting as imaginable spaces, this function takes on another significance. These action verbs and locative prepositions are more often than not spatial, interdependent with setting as they describe characters' movements within rendered physical spaces. These actions don't merely take place within a setting; their spatial character actively contributes to the sense of the setting as an imaginable space. The integral role of the hard seed words in establishing this kind of setting suggests that part of their rising trend is tied to an increasing spatialization of setting in the 19th-century British novel. This spatialization is a growing treatment of setting as more than a functional backdrop, aspect of mood, or even a historically and socially specific place, but as a material space with physical dimensions, orientation, and constrictions within which characters act. This mode of setting

---

27 Limits we encountered in filling out some of the hard seed fields kept our fields from accounting for all the concrete description language in these passages.

holds that narrative unfolds within spaces. Description, in this mode, draws heavily on hard seed type words and continually makes the reader conscious of space. From the tightness of Jaggers's office to the single view of church and prison to the roadway directed by the walls of the prison, the specific spatial juxtapositions and layout of this part of London (as Dickens imagines it) are decisive elements in the passage; everywhere Pip turns, he deals with the brute materiality of the city as a space.

We may seem to have drifted a long way from our discussion of changing social spaces, but actually the two are closely related. That the rise in the hard seed cohorts comes in part from an increasing spatialization of setting is just one part of the story. The other part of the story is profoundly social. To see it, we have to consider that *how* setting is rendered may be related to *what* settings are being rendered. We observed earlier an expansion of physical spaces across the spectrum. This is another factor in the rise of the hard seed cohorts. As the physical spaces depicted within novels widen and become more varied, it makes sense that more concrete description language would be needed to render those worlds. The novelty, variety, and specialization of physical spaces being represented demands this language. But when we look at why and how this works, we can see that this change in physical spaces stems from the same transformations in social organization we've been tracing. These changes generated new, unfamiliar spaces calling for description, a drastically expanded London for instance. While the space of the city isn't new, urbanization reshaped the city physically and made it predominant imaginatively. The consequent division of labor and differentiation of society led to more and more specialized spaces that needed to be rendered with particularity: factories, urban slums, railroad stations, police stations, professional offices, etc. But as Pip's walk through four distinct spaces in the span of three paragraphs reveals, it wasn't just the proliferation of spaces that mattered but their dense concentration and heterogeneous juxtaposition. The jarring contrasts created by urban density bring forward the particularity of each space, adding to this need for specific description. Another factor explaining the rise of hard seed words, then, is the tangible effect on setting of an expanding and diversifying social space.

o   o   o

C. TRACING A RISE: A SOCIAL TRANSFORMATION IN CHARACTER

The final piece that has been missing from our discussion is how all this relates to the decline of the abstract values cohorts. These pieces come together in the third function of hard seed words as a language of characterization. Characterization is the nexus where the abstract values enter the picture because they represent language profoundly invested in describing, evaluating, and organizing character. By comparing the abstract values and hard seed fields as languages of characterization, we can see most clearly what's at stake in the shift from one to the other. The experience of social relation and the representation of character necessarily change as social space expands. Wordsworth captured the alienating effect of facing streams of strangers on the crowded city streets, but in the fully urban novels of Dickens we can see the effect this unfamiliarity and randomness have on the representation of people. Pip's introduction to London presents the city's streets and spaces as an encounter with unordered sensory details. People become just another one of these details. Pip sees a "quantity of people **standing** about, **smelling** strongly of spirits and beer," an undifferentiated mass that, alongside the noise of vehicles, simply reinforces the passage's overall feeling of sordidness. Even when people are individuated, like the proprietor, their characterization reveals a change. The horror of London seems to manifest for Pip in the proprietor's character, specifically in his attire: "(from his hat **down** to his boots and **up** again to his pocket-handkerchief inclusive) mildewed clothes, which had evidently not belonged to him originally, and which, I took it into my **head**, he had bought cheap of the executioner." Character here inheres almost exclusively in appearance. This mode of characterization works through surface and physical detail, fitting for a social space of strangers, random encounters, and sheer variety of people. With the breakdown of social legibility and human connection in the city and wider social spaces, one encounters people not just as strangers but as appearances, attire, anonymous bodies. Recall the behavior of one of the hard seed cohorts, body parts words (**Figure 6.19**). Its rise corresponds tightly with the shift to wider social spaces within novels. In the disorientation and unknowability of these communities, the attempt to place people within stable social schema comes up against surfaces of opaque physicality.

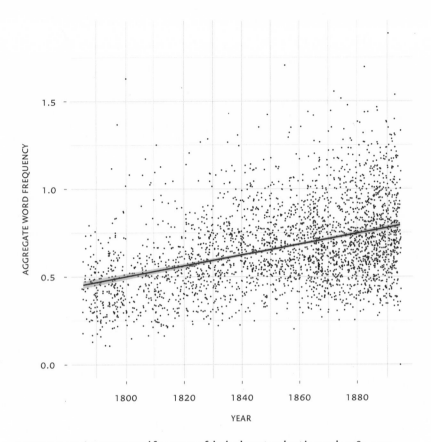

FIGURE 6.19 **Aggregate word frequency of the body parts cohort in novels, 1785–1900**

This comes through very clearly in another passage from *Great Expectations*, the first time Pip gets a good look at Mr. Wemmick. The introduction of a character is a highly saturated moment of characterization, so it's revealing to see the particular mode of description at work here. Again hard seed words are in bold, and note the prevalence of other concrete description words:

> Casting my **eyes** on Mr. Wemmick as we **went along**, to **see** what he was like in the light of day, I found him to be a **dry** man, rather short in stature, with a square **wooden face**, whose expression seemed to have been imperfectly chipped **out** with a dull-edged chisel. There were some marks in it that might have been **dimples**, if the material had been softer and the instrument finer, but which, as it was, were only dints. The chisel

had made **three** or **four** of these attempts at embellishment **over** his **nose**, but had given them **up** without an effort to smooth them **off**. I judged him to be a bachelor from the frayed condition of his linen, and he appeared to have sustained a good many bereavements; for, he wore at least **four** mourning rings, besides a brooch representing a lady and a weeping willow at a tomb with an urn on it. I noticed, too, that several rings and seals **hung** at his watch-chain, as if he were quite laden with remembrances of departed friends. He had glittering **eyes**—small, keen, and **black**—and **thin wide** mottled **lips**. He had had them, to the best of my belief, from **forty** to **fifty** years.

Two points jump out from this passage. First, the density of physical description. A lavish amount of attention is paid just to the topography of Wemmick's face, as well as to visual details such as the fraying of his linen and the number of mourning rings he wears. The hard seed words (which make up 11.4 percent of the passage) and other concrete nouns and adjectives are integral to this level of description. Second, notice how character emerges from this tableau of physical details. At no point does the passage directly state anything about Wemmick's character or personality. What we learn about Wemmick is implicit; it must be inferred from the physical details. This points to a general pattern where characters in the urban novel encounter strangers and must read them initially as bodies and appearances, and from there, may work to infer more about identity, character, and position. As inferences, these impressions are never entirely certain. Accordingly, Pip's language here is consistently couched in the subjective act of perception, interpretation, and inference: "I *found* him to be a dry man"; "whose expression *seemed*"; "I *judged* him to be"; "he *appeared*"; "I *noticed*"; "*as if* he *were*"; "to the best of *my belief.*" The tangible surfaces of body, attire, manner are evocative, revealing, even symbolic, but they aren't definitive.

To see the distinctiveness of this kind of characterization, let's compare Wemmick's description to a similar character introduction in *Pride and Prejudice*, one of the canonical novels in our corpus that is lowest in concentration of hard seed words (2.96 percent versus *Great Expectations*'s 7.17 percent) and highest in abstract values words (1.10 percent versus *Great Expectations*'s 0.44 percent). In the first sustained description of Mr. Collins, Austen draws heavily on the abstract values words and a much more direct presentation of character, which we can see in the choice of verbs (abstract values words are in bold):

> Mr. Collins *was* not a **sensible** man, and the deficiency of nature *had been* but little assisted by education or society; the greatest part of his life *having been* spent under the guidance of an illiterate and miserly father; and though he belonged to one of the universities, he had merely kept the necessary terms, without forming at it any useful acquaintance. The subjection in which his father had brought him up, *had given* him originally great **humility** of manner, but it *was* now a good deal counteracted by the self-conceit of a weak head, living in retirement, and the consequential feelings of early and unexpected prosperity. A fortunate chance had recommended him to Lady Catherine de Bourgh when the living of Hunsford was vacant; and the **respect** which he felt for her high rank, and his veneration for her as his patroness, mingling with a very good opinion of himself, of his authority as a clergyman, and his rights as a rector, *made* him altogether a mixture of **pride** and obsequiousness, self-importance and **humility**. (emphases added)

There are no physical details to speak of and they aren't necessary because there's no need for perception or inference. The narrator tells us directly about Mr. Collins's character and identity, what he is rather than what he appears or seems to be. The description places him in the social schema of the abstract values words, which make up 2.9 percent of the passage. Mr. Collins is insensible, self-conceited, obsequious, and self-important, and by the standards of this social world, the valuation of those qualities is absolutely clear. This is characterization not as perception and interpretation but definition.

The contrast between the two descriptions is extreme. From Collins's description to Wemmick's, there is a complete disappearance of abstract values words and an increase in the frequency of hard seed words of almost 600 percent. Setting the two side by side lets us see our data trends more tangibly on the page as a change in the very linguistic texture of these novels. But it also lets us see clearly that this is more than a change in word choice, it's a change in representation. Where characterization in *Pride and Prejudice* is definitive, direct, and evaluative, in *Great Expectations* it is ambiguous and inferential; not only are the character traits implicit behind surfaces of physical detail, but the valuation of those traits is at a further remove from clarity. The passage from *Great Expectations*, the canonical city novel richest in hard seed words, then exemplifies a mode of characterization that presumes no direct access to character, a mode characteristic of the less knowable community of urban social spaces. If these samples are representative,[28] a major part of what we are seeing in the hard seed trend is a shift in characterization away from explicit comment, judgment, and placement within a value system to a more indirect mode of presenting bodies, appearances, details. A shift from direct to indirect characterization. With the decline of the abstract values cohorts, we saw a dissolution of the stable social schema organizing relations as social spaces became wider and more complex. In the aftermath, we find a mode of characterization that reflects a mode of social relation made radically new through its sudden ubiquity: the everyday encounter with hundreds of strangers.

D. TRACING A RISE: CHARACTERIZING UNFAMILIAR SOCIAL WORLDS

We argued earlier that the hard seed fields' usage for setting revealed a change not just in *how* setting is rendered but *what* settings are rendered. As a consequence of the same underlying social transformations, characterization undergoes a similar process. We've established the change in *how* characters are represented but there remains the question of change in *what* kinds of characters are represented. The challenge presented by the characters in a wider, more complex social space is finding a language adequate for capturing these messy, conflicting, multitudinous social landscapes. Recall how the abstract values fields were revealed to be inadequate for doing this. The concrete language of the hard seed fields, however, can represent this greater range and openness of identity, position, and character. They can render ambiguity and variability very well. As we saw in the

---

28 A serious "if" for sure. As always in this kind of research there is more work that can and should be done. The decision to cut off a research project to write up its results is always to some extent arbitrary. The change in characterization is suggested by the trends we found, coupled with the spectrum's revelation of expanding social spaces and the corroborating topic modeling data; however, one of the major directions we have not yet had time to follow up is to take a rigorous and representative sampling of passages, read them, and code them to further test the arguments we are outlining here. This would be a time-consuming procedure, but a valuable one.

contrast between Wemmick's and Collins's descriptions, the language of materiality isn't explicitly valued, so it isn't organized into rigid categories and binaries like the axes of abstract values; correspondingly, it doesn't categorize its objects along these rigid axes. Instead, it sets out an enormous, almost infinite range of non-hierarchical nuances and differences. Rather than *moral* and *immoral*, we have *hard, rough, liquid, sharp, stiff, crooked,* and so on. If we keep in mind how physical detail can imply qualities, character, and identity, we can see how such language offers more range and specificity of human characteristics than a polarized, uniform field of social norms. The concrete fields then are a kind of language that can render a larger, more variegated character system, exactly what a novelist would need to express the character of more complex social spaces.

In thinking of character in wider social spaces, we should return to a range of the spectrum we've been neglecting in our discussion: the cluster of fantasy, adventure, science fiction, and children's novels at the extreme right. In many ways, the extra-societal spaces of these genres offer encounters with an even broader and wilder range of character types than the urban novel: cannibals, pirates, talking animals, princesses, goblins, citizens of future and past societies; the range of characters not contained by the stable social schema of the abstract values is nearly limitless. (It's pretty amusing, though, to imagine hordes of chaste cannibals, reserved goblins, and deferential pirates.) By attending to this extreme end of the spectrum, we see that the transformations we've been tracing do not end at the urban novel, important as it is in diagnosing some of the key changes; instead they place the urban novel within a larger pattern encompassing these other genres. Indeed, many of the arguments we've put forward are applicable to an even greater degree in these outlier genres. The abstract values fields would have little purchase in their exotic extra-societal settings. In "savage" adventure settings, the lack of social norms or laws is often a key source of conflict; in science fiction or fantasy settings, the protagonist is commonly dropped into entirely unfamiliar social worlds. The perceptual disorientation that the concrete field captures in urban novels is also at work in these unfamiliar adventure settings, which can be even more aggressively estranging than the modern city. The perspective of curiosity at entirely novel experiences and spaces in these genres would naturally lead to a heavy use of concrete language as these new settings are perceived and described.

Taking account of these other genre clusters on the spectrum is crucial. To theorize from our data, we have been emphasizing two paradigmatic social spaces in this discussion—tight rural spaces and wide urban spaces—but of course the spectrum is a spectrum, not a binary, and both the abstract values and hard seed trends are long shifts, not sudden transformations. The data shows a whole range in the use of these kinds of language, a range of linguistic positions that nevertheless follows a clear direction. This suggests a range of social spaces depicted in the novel even as the dominant movement is one of expansion. This spectrum of rural, urban, mixed, intermediary, and extra-societal novelistic spaces echoes the actual complexity of the transformations in British society.

CONCLUSION: FROM TELLING TO SHOWING

To conclude this discussion we should tease out one more macroscopic pattern that several threads laid out here have implied. The growing inadequacy of explicitly evaluative language, the change in characterization to an indirect mode of presenting concrete detail, the inversely related trends of the abstract values and hard seed cohorts—all of these point to an overarching shift in the novel's narration and style: a shift from telling to showing. Given the range of concrete description words in the hard seed cohort, many of which are not necessarily anthropocentric, we can see a broad change in the general mode of perceiving and representing people, objects, spaces, and actions in the novel. This change from abstract, evaluative language to concrete, non-evaluative language doesn't necessarily indicate the disappearance of evaluation. Given the patterns we've seen, it would be more accurate to say that the modes of evaluation and characterization changed, moving from explicit to implicit narration, from conspicuous commentary to the dramatization of abstractions, qualities, and values through physical detail. As we saw with characterization in the urban novel, though, this change is not a direct translation of categories of abstract values into ones of concrete detail. The change in mode is a change in quality, toward a finer-grained, more variegated and complex range of characteristics. Simultaneously, the indirectness of the mode, in which there is no clear one-to-one correspondence of concrete detail to abstract quality, suits the ambiguity and flux of widening and changing social spaces.

An attempt to sum up then: a pervasive expansion of social space in the 19th-century British novel in reaction to parallel changes in the actual social spaces of Britain; a concomitant concretization of novelistic language that constructs, reflects, and critically responds to this change in social experience; a spatialization of setting; a move from direct to indirect characterization; a fundamental shift in narration from telling to showing. A complex system of changes where, in varying degrees, each shift simultaneously drives and is driven by the others. In the end, the complexity of the range of mechanisms and forces we've been tracing cannot be separated from just how large these patterns are. Spanning nearly three thousand novels and encompassing about 5 percent of their language use, this data could have revealed little more than noise and random variation. But what emerges from the data is a system, a history of the novel with a definite shape. And that may be the most striking discovery of all.

2012

CHAPTER 7

Bankspeak

THE LANGUAGE OF WORLD BANK REPORTS

FRANCO MORETTI, DOMINIQUE PESTRE

What can quantitative linguistic analysis tell us about the operations and outlook of the international financial institutions? At first glance, the words most frequently used in the World Bank's Annual Reports give an impression of unbroken continuity. Seven are near the top at any given time: three nouns—*bank, loan/s, development*—and four adjectives: *fiscal, economic, financial, private*. This septet is joined by a handful of other nouns: *IBRD, countries, investment/s, interest, program/s, project/s, assistance*, and—though initially less frequent—*lending, growth, cost, debt, trade, prices*. There is also a second, more colorless set of adjectives—*other, new, such, net, first, more, general*—plus *agricultural*, partly replaced from the 1990s by *rural*.[1] The message is clear: the World Bank lends money for the purpose of stimulating development, notably in the rural South, and is therefore involved with loans, investments and debts. It works through programs and projects, and considers trade a key resource for economic growth. Being concerned with development, the Bank deals with all sorts

---

[1] Our corpus consists of the full text of the World Bank Annual Reports, 1946–2012, excluding the budgets and all financial tables. The word bank as used in the Reports generally refers to the World Bank. The International Bank for Reconstruction and Development (IBRD) was the original World Bank institution, established in 1944 at Bretton Woods; it is now subsumed within the World Bank Group, which includes an agency for private investment, an insurance agency, an arbitration forum, and the International Development Association, established in 1960 to offer concessional loans to the poorest countries. For an introduction to the history of the World Bank written from the inside, see Devesh Kapur, John P. Lewis, and Richard C. Webb, eds., *The World Bank: Its First Half Century* (Washington, DC: Brookings Institution Press, 1997); among the many critical histories, see Michael Goldman, *Imperial Nature: The World Bank and Struggles for Social Justice in the Age of Globalization* (New Haven, CT: Yale University Press, 2005).

of economic, financial and fiscal matters, and is in touch with private business. All quite simple, and perfectly straightforward.

And yet, behind this facade of uniformity, a major metamorphosis has taken place. Here is how the Bank's Report described the world in 1958:

> The Congo's present transport system is geared mainly to the export trade, and is based on river navigation and on railroads which lead from river ports into regions producing minerals and agricultural commodities. Most of the roads radiate short distances from cities, providing farm-to-market communications. In recent years road traffic has increased rapidly with the growth of the internal market and the improvement of farming methods.

And here is the Report from half a century later, in 2008:

> **Leveling the Playing Field on Global Issues**
>
> Countries in the region are emerging as key players on issues of global concern, and the Bank's role has been to support their efforts by partnering through innovative platforms for an enlightened dialogue and action on the ground, as well as by supporting South–South cooperation.

It's almost another language, in both semantics and grammar. The key discontinuity, as we shall see, falls mostly between the first three decades and the last two, the turn of the 1990s, when the style of the Reports becomes much more codified, self-referential, and detached from everyday language. It is this Bankspeak that will be the protagonist of the pages that follow.

1. SEMANTIC TRANSFORMATIONS

Nouns are at the center of World Bank Reports. During the first two decades, 1950–70, the most frequent among them can be grouped in two main clusters. The first, obviously enough, encompasses the economic activities of the Bank: *loan/s, development, power* (in the sense of electricity), *program, projects, investment, equipment, production, construction, plant*; further down the list are *companies, facilities, industry, machineries,* followed by a string of concrete terms like *port, road, steel, irrigation, kWh, river, highway, railway*—and then *timber, pulp, coal, iron, steam, steel, locomotives, diesel, freight, dams, bridges, cement, chemical, acres, hectares, drainage, crop, cattle, livestock.* All quite appropriate for a bank that offers loans and investments (the only explicitly financial terms in this long list) to promote a variety of infrastructural development projects.[2]

The second noun cluster is much smaller (just a dozen words), and describes how the Bank actually operates. Confronted with existing demands, its experts analyze *numbers*, but they also pay *visits*, realize *surveys*, and conduct *missions* in the field; the classic ingredients of a scientific approach to a complex situation, which requires the active presence of experts to collect and elaborate the data. Afterwards, the Bank proceeds to *advise* countries, *suggest* solutions, *assist* local governments, and *allocate* its loans. Rhetorically, investment programs are defined by the needs of the local economy, according to the basic idea that investment in infrastructure will lead to economic development and social well-being. At the end of every cycle, the Bank specifies what has been *lent, spent, paid,* and *sold,* and describes the equipment—*dams, factory, irrigation systems*—that has been put into operation. A clear link is established between empirical knowledge, money flows, and industrial constructions: knowledge is associated with physical presence in situ, and with calculations conducted in the Bank's headquarters; money flows involve the negotiation of loans and investments with individual states; and the construction of ports, energy plants, etc. is the result of the whole process. In this eminently temporal sequence, a strong sense of causality links expertise, loans, investments, and material realizations.

Apart from the Bank, three types of social actors appear in the texts during this period: *states* and *governments*; *companies, banks,* and *industry*; and *engineers, technicians,* and *experts.* This social ontology confirms the standard account of post-war reconstruction as industrial, Fordist, and Keynesian. The protagonists of economic growth are businessmen and bankers, working with industrial companies, economists, and engineers to implement projects within a national framework presided over by a state.

---

2 Adjectives are rare, in the solidly "material" universe of the Bank's early decades: aside from *fiscal, economic,* and *financial,* only *electric* and *hydroelectric* have a significant presence, later joined by *dairy,* which signals a concern with health, agriculture, and family life.

What has to be managed is *the economy*—"the self-contained structure or totality of relations of production, distribution and consumption of goods and services within a given geographical space," as Timothy Mitchell has put it—whose results are optimized by a "modern apparatus of calculation and government."[3] With the help of the Bank, governments adjust investments and financial parameters so as to *modernize* countries: that is to say, to *industrialize* them, beginning with basic material infrastructures. It's the legacy of Walt Whitman Rostow, author of *The Stages of Economic Growth: A Non-Communist Manifesto* (1960) and a key policy adviser to American administrations from Eisenhower to Johnson. Development proceeds in stages, and its "take-off" is triggered by the production of raw materials, the creation of infrastructures, and an agricultural sector oriented towards exports.

Let us pause briefly on a specific passage from 1969. It appears in the general introduction of the Report, in a section on agricultural loans, and its language is so simple, it seems almost featureless:

> Many developing countries need to transform their agriculture . . . the Bank Group continues to encourage these trends through its lending for general agricultural development, which totaled $72.2 million in the 1969 financial year. Diversification into new crops which provide a source of cash income, or improved production of existing ones, was encouraged by loans or credits to support traditional coffee production in Burundi at its normal level, palm oil development in Cameroon, Dahomey, the Ivory Coast and Papua, afforestation in Zambia, and mechanization of sorghum, sesame and cotton farming in the Sudan . . . A $13 million Bank loan to India will finance the production of seeds of new high-yielding varieties of foodgrains; at full development the project will produce enough seeds to plant seven million acres with the new varieties. This is the first loan the Bank has made for seed production.

Aside from the initial injunction that agriculture "needs" to change, the dominant note is one of factual precision: amounts, countries, materials, productive activities, objectives of the investments. Nouns are frequent and adjectives rare: things are being described, not advertised. Verbs

---

3 Timothy Mitchell, *Carbon Democracy: Political Power in the Age of Oil* (New York: Verso, 2011), 125, 123.

specify the type of action involved: *to encourage, provide, improve, support, diversify, produce, finance*. The present tense reports what is happening now (*the bank* continues *to encourage*); when a project has not yet been launched the tense shifts to the future (the credit *will finance* seed production), while the past accounts for what has been completed (diversification was *encouraged*, lending *totaled* $72.2 million). Clearly demarcating past accomplishments, current actions, necessary policies, and future projects, this temporal structure reinforces the sense of factuality of the early Reports.

A. TODAY'S KEYWORDS: FINANCE, MANAGEMENT, GOVERNANCE

Let's now shift to the most recent decades. Three new semantic clusters characterize the language of the Bank from the early 1990s on. The first—and most important—has to do with finance: here, alongside a few predictable adjectives (*financial, fiscal, economic*) and nouns (*loans, investment, growth, interest, lending, debt*), we find a landslide of *fair value, portfolio, derivative, accrual, guarantees, losses, accounting, assets*; a little further down the list, *equity, hedging, liquidity, liabilities, creditworthiness, default, swaps, clients, deficit, replenishment, repurchase, cash*. In terms of frequency and semantic density, this cluster can only be compared to the material infrastructures of the 1950s–60s; now, however, work in agriculture and industry has been replaced by an overwhelming predominance of financial activities. **Figure 7.1** is a good illustration of the Bank's new priorities.

The second cluster has to do with *management*—a noun that, in absolute terms, is the second most frequent of the last decade (lower than *loans*, but higher than *risk* and *investment*!). In the world of "management," *people* have *goals* and *agendas*; faced with *opportunities, challenges*, and *critical* situations, they elaborate *strategies*. To appreciate the novelty, let's recall that, in the 1950s–60s, *issues* were *studied* by experts who *surveyed* and conducted *missions*, published *reports, assisted, advised* and *suggested programs*. With the advent of *management*, the center of gravity shifts towards *focusing, strengthening* and *implementing*; one must *monitor, control, audit, rate* (**Figure 7.2**); *ensure* that everything is done properly while also helping *people* to *learn* from mistakes. The many tools at the manager's disposal (*indicators, instruments, knowledge, expertise, research*) enhance

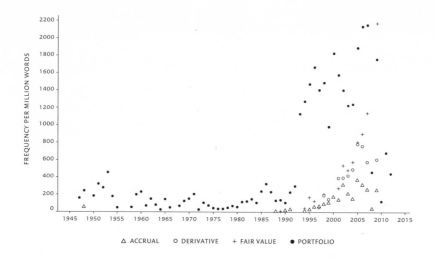

FREQUENCY PER MILLION WORDS

△ ACCRUAL   ○ DERIVATIVE   + FAIR VALUE   ● PORTFOLIO

FIGURE 7.1 **The rise of financial language, 1950–2010.** *Portfolio*, though present from the beginning in the text of the Reports, undergoes a vertiginous rise—a five- to ten-fold increase—in the mid-1990s, which is also the moment when the other terms become increasingly frequent.

effectiveness, efficiency, performance, competitiveness and—it goes without saying—promote *innovation*.

To better understand this "management discourse," as Boltanski and Chiapello have called it in *The New Spirit of Capitalism*, we decided to run a little experiment. We took two related expressions—"poverty" and "poverty reduction"—and followed their occurrences from 1990 to 2010, comparing their respective "collocates": that is to say, the words that tend to occur most often in their immediate proximity. Near *poverty*, the dominant note was one of straightforward economic realism: *bank* was the most frequent word; *million*, the second; and then *total, cost, population, incomes, services, problems, work, production, employment, resources, food, health, agriculture.* Which makes perfect sense, because these are indeed the terms that define the perimeter of poverty. What doesn't make sense, on the other hand, is that only four of them—*services, work, resources, health*—should reappear near *poverty reduction*. Poverty is the problem, poverty reduction the policy that should address it; they should have plenty of core terms in common. And instead, the most characteristic collocates of *poverty reduction* are not *cost, population, income*—let alone *production* or *employment*—but *strategies, programs, policies, focus, key, management,*

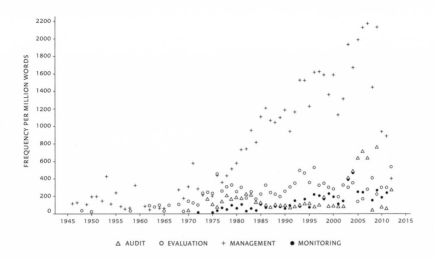

FIGURE 7.2 **Management discourse.** Though never absent from the Bank's vocabulary, management started its ascent in the late 1970s, when the debt question became central, and was subsequently associated with the drastic "structural adjustment" policies of the neoliberal offensive. But it's only in the 1990s–2000s that management discourse truly flourishes, hinting—at least in subliminal form—that the Bank's activities are being constantly evaluated and certified by the most advanced tools and the best experts, and that, as a consequence, its investments are the fruit of serious reflection, and their results are as good as they can possibly be.

report, goals, approach, projects, framework, priorities, papers. "Management discourse," in all its glory. Never mind *employment* and *income*: *focus, key, approach, framework*—*these* are the critical terms in reducing poverty. Policy turned into paperwork, with *goals* and *priorities* and *papers* inching their way through the department that—in the acronym-obsessed language of the Reports—is known as PREM: Poverty Reduction and Economic Management.

The third semantic cluster of the last two decades comprises *governance* and moral behavior.[4] *Governance*, first of all: this shibboleth of World Bank language first showed up in a crowded sentence of the 1990 Report—"the strength of managerial institutions and personnel and the quality of governance also determine how well reform policies are actually put into practice"—and then increased its presence to the point that it is

---

4 Dominique Pestre, ed., *Le gouvernement des technosciences: Gouverner le progrès et ses dégâts depuis 1945* (Paris: La Découverte, 2014).

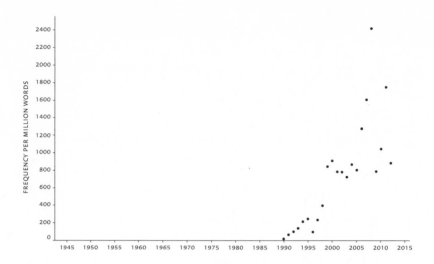

FIGURE 7.3 **Abracadabra.** In its irresistible rise, "governance" has been invariably associated with words of a positive, even euphoric nature: *good, reforms, assistance, growth, efforts, capacity, transparency, education, effective/ness, progress, stability, protection, health, access, implementation, human, new, sound, sustainable, strong, better, more,* and *most.* The same message is conveyed by verbs, which often appear in the progressive form, as if to identify the notion of governance with a tireless ongoing activity: *improve/ing/ed, strengthen/ing, support/ing, including, building, promoting, help/ing, restructuring.* The only black sheep in this uplifting list is—*corruption.* (When one of us consulted a World Bank employee on the meaning of "governance," the answer was: "It's the opposite of corruption.") Unlike *government,* in other words—which can be good, bad, even very bad—"governance" can only be good. It is hard to think of another term of political discourse with the same one-dimensional tilt.

now as frequent as "food," occurring ten times more often than "law" and a hundred times more than "politics" (**Figure 7.3**).[5]

Three adjectives have been shadowing *governance* in its irresistible progress: *global, environmental, civil.* They are complemented by *dialogue, stakeholders, collaboration, partnership, communities, indigenous*

---

5 When a word becomes so pandemically frequent, its uses multiply out of control, and before long no one knows what it means any longer. Here is the chief economic commentator of the *Financial Times,* Martin Wolf, writing about the Indian elections on May 21, 2014: "[Modi's] motto—'less government and more governance'—has caught the public mood. Yet it is not clear what this will mean in practice." And Robert Zoellick, himself a former president of the World Bank, writing on Chinese policy in the same newspaper: "The reforms will focus on economic governance and modernization. These terms may seem ambiguous to westerners . . ." (June 13, 2014). In a delightful twist of language, the term brandished by the World Bank to chastise developing economies is now used by those very economies as defensive camouflage against Western scrutiny.

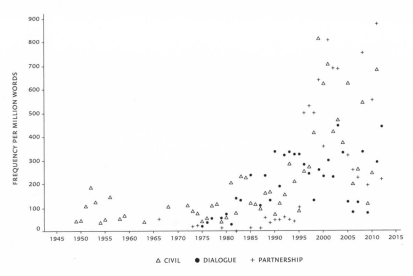

FIGURE 7.4 **The governance galaxy—i**

people, accountability—plus *climate, nature, natural, forest, pollution.*
Even *health* and *education* have ended up near the orbit of *governance*
(**Figures 7.4** and **7.5**).

Finally, the semantic cluster of *governance* includes a series of terms
that express a sense of compassion, generosity, rectitude or empathy with
the world's problems. Virtually absent in previous decades, these ethical
claims emerge in the mid-1980s, and become second nature by the early
1990s, when *responsible, responsibility, effort, commitment, involvement,
sharing, care* are suddenly everywhere.[6] Nor is the Bank blind to *fragile*
and *vulnerable* people, to *poverty* (revitalized in 1995 by the new Director
General James Wolfensohn), and to all that is *human.* This cluster also
includes *rights, law, justice,* and *(anti-)corruption.* People, behavior and
results are *outstanding, significant, relevant, consistent, strong, good, better.*
Enhancing and *promoting* what is *appropriate, equitable* and *sound*: this
is the Bank's credo. The overall effect is one of dedication and commitment; the Bank's sense of responsibility is as admirable as its efficiency
(**Figures 7.6** and **7.7**).

---

6 The expression "*fair* value"—where the ethically inflected adjective mitigates the businesslike realism of the noun—is particularly interesting in this respect.

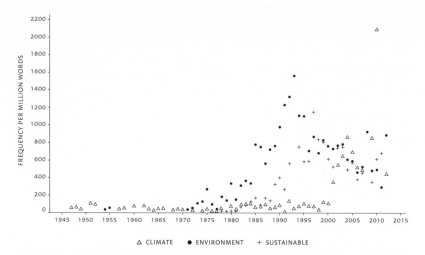

FIGURE 7.5 **The governance galaxy—ii.** *Civil* has been associated with various nouns over the years, but its rise in the 1980s is linked to the expressions *civil society* and *civil society organizations* (CSOs). *Dialogue*—mainly with CSOs and NGOs—grows from the mid-1970s to the mid-1990s; *partner/ship* emerges later, after the mid-1990s, when projects with other global organizations (WTO, IMF, UN, etc.) become increasingly frequent. All these waves indicate so many subtle shifts in the institutional meaning of *governance*. *Environment* first appears in the 1970s, and undergoes a meteoric rise in the 1980s. *Sustainable development* emerges a decade later (following the publication of the Brundtland Report in 1987), and its semantic tightrope-walking—that aims at superseding the crude antithesis between economic growth and the protection of the environment—makes it as important as *environment* after 1995. *Climate* (in the sense of climate change) becomes significant in the 2000s—largely absorbing references to *environment*—although the majority of its occurrences have actually to do with *business climate.*

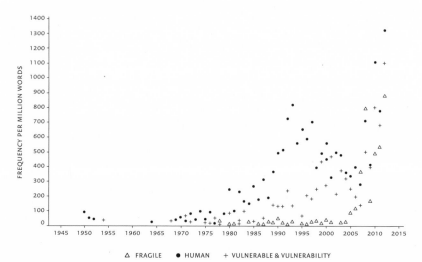

FIGURE 7.6 **The good bank**

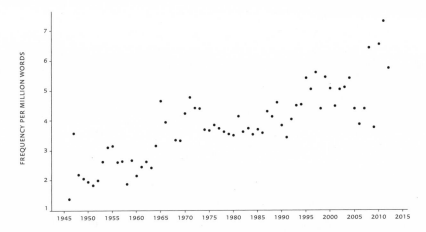

FIGURE 7.7 **The better bank.** The image charts the frequency of a small group of self-congratulating terms that include *outstanding, key, stronger, better, more, significant*, and *critical*.

Let us again pause on a specific passage to add some texture to our analysis. Here is the opening of the 2012 Report:

The World Bank is Committed to Achieving and Communicating Results.

In its ongoing dedication to overcoming poverty and creating opportunity for people in developing countries, the Bank is making progress both internally and in the field, and it continues to improve the way it serves its client countries.

A place full of "opportunities" that the poor may seize in order to change their condition: this is how the Bank sees the world. Within this scenario, its activity consists in establishing the legal and cultural framework necessary for a variety of initiatives to flourish; still investment in infrastructures, in a sense—except that they're no longer made of stone and steel. The Bank is *dedicated* and *committed*, thoughtful, invested in a better world. It is forward-looking, its dedication *ongoing*, constantly thinking about *improving* and *serving* the poor countries that are its . . . *clients*.

Clients? At first, the word is jarring: if *dedication* suggests a universe of moral justice, *client* refers to business, rational interests, and power relations. In deliberately linking them within a single sentence, though, the

Bank suggests that the two are no longer in opposition: nowadays, business is as attentive to *stakeholders* as to *shareholders*; like civil society and the Bank itself, it is socially and environmentally *responsible*, and engaged in *durable governance* made of multiple *partnerships*. Ethics is at the heart of the business world, and of its contractual relationships.

B. COMPLEXITY, HUMAN FACTORS, AND CRISIS: THE LATE 1960S AND THE 1970S

Having established the two contrasting paradigms of World Bank discourse, let us briefly sketch the process that led from the one to the other. A few adjustments aside, the intellectual framework that defined the Bank's operations in the '50s and '60s remained fundamentally in place up to the late 1970s: irrigation, chemical inputs, the Green Revolution, and the industrial–infrastructural synergy continue to be the key ingredients of economic take-off. But the belief in a linear approach is losing its force: as the 1960s come to a close, it becomes clear that, if building infrastructure is relatively simple, its reliable long-term operation is not: it requires specialists, qualified workers, and the regular supply of key products like electricity—none of which can be taken for granted in the countries of the South. To make things worse, international exchanges seem to respect neither the Bank's hopes, nor the theories of development à la Rostow. The prices of agricultural raw materials—crucial for the economies of the South—are far from stable and undergo major falls, from which recovery is difficult. The consequences of such instability can be dramatic: as prices drop, developing countries cannot afford to persevere on the virtuous path by which the export of raw materials finances the growth of infrastructure . . . and the repayment of foreign loans. Mindful of its investments, the Bank is worried.

The language of the Reports adapts to the changing environment; words like *commodities*, or *improvements*, raise the analysis to a higher level of abstraction than, say, *hydroelectric plants* and *cement*. And since leading the world by relying merely on material infrastructures no longer seems enough, other "factors" are taken into account: the market, of course, but especially the "human factor." On becoming the Bank's president in 1968, Robert McNamara places LBJ's "war on poverty" at the center of its strategy. It's the time of *small-scale farms* and *cooperatives* (faint echoes of decolonization and social unrest); of *farmers* (previously marginal to the Bank's policy); of *families* (and soon of *women*). *Education* is now seen as indispensable in maintaining progress, along with *school, primary, secondary, educational, training*. It's the time of the explosion of *towns* (and shantytowns); of rural emigration, and the deterioration of the *urban* (a ubiquitous adjective) way of life; whence a long list of new problems—*housing, drainage, sewers*.

In the second half of the 1970s, the oil crisis introduces new exogenous elements. Words like *debt, borrowed*, and *borrowing* become increasingly frequent, along with those that refer to a country's reliability (or lack thereof): *cost/s, exports, co-financing*. The discourse of *reform*—destined for unimaginable success—begins to take shape. And since debt is linked to the evolution of *prices*, these, too, become more visible in the Reports (in fact, it's amazing how *in*visible they had previously been). The crisis reveals the World Bank as, indeed, a bank—and one that finds it difficult to recover its loans: a fact that may seem obvious, but that, until then, had been largely muted.

In response to all this, the causal chain linking *loans* and *development*, investments and economic progress, is lengthened to include families and education, small farmers and sewers. This is hardly an unfeasible adjustment, and even the logic behind the debt continues to appear reasonably simple: there are loans, faltering exports, problematic reimbursements—the inter-connections are clear, comprehensible. But the world as seen through the World Bank Reports is becoming less linear than it used to be; socioeconomic dynamics are harder to disentangle, and there is a faint surprise in the face of events that aren't following the expected course. At times, the surprise seems genuine; if this were so (but is it possible?) it would speak volumes about the delusions of development in the post-war period. As the policy of infrastructural growth becomes partially destabilized, a sense of indecision and even openness emerges—in sharp contrast with the previous decades, when everything was self-evident and almost automatic. But the openness will not last; at the end of the 1970s, the autopilot will be reinserted—this time, en route to "structural adjustment."

C. DEBT AND THE LIBERAL OBSESSION: THE 1980S AND EARLY 1990S

The Reports of the 1980s are dominated by the debts of the South, and by the *structural adjustments* that are the keyword of the decade. The semantics of crisis is omnipresent—*deterioration, deficit, decline, indebted, issues, difficult*—and defines the parameters that must be met before granting any country a new loan: *balance of payments, current account, debt services*. The hope of *recovery*, for its part, is heard far less often. It's the "development philosophy" of the times: liberal recipes that will ensure the only thing that matters, the return to *growth*. This means *expanding trade, expanding the private sector*, raising *competitiveness*; the rules of economic activity must be redefined (making it freer), and the role of the state reduced. It's the moment of the *liberalization* of the *public sector*. People must learn to be *efficient* and *cost-effective*, care about *performance*, develop *incentives*. The Bank outlines the solutions, and demands that they be *implemented*, leaving little room for negotiation. *Restructuring* and *rescheduling* are the only way to reassure the creditors.

A few chronological details. In the years 1982–89, the main semantic cluster is still a melancholy one: *slowdown, stagnation, degradation, depreciation, devaluation, fall/fell, exacerbated, severe*. In the 1990s, there is a shift toward *private sector, privatization, privatized, financial sector, creditworthiness*, along with *market-oriented activities* and *institution building*, code words for the liberalization/privatization of public institutions. The lexicon of global finance has not yet emerged, although that of nature, the environment, and civil society is beginning to circulate. Meanwhile, *management* leaves its imprint on a series of verbs that express the harsh policies prescribed by the Bank: *to address, target, accelerate, support, restructure, implement, improve, strengthen, aim, achieve . . .*

Aside from individual words, it's the nature of the Bank's language that is changing: becoming more abstract, more distant from concrete social life; a technical code, detached from everyday communication and pared down to the economic factors crucial to the repayment of the debt. Solutions are disengaged from any specificity: they are the same for everybody, everywhere. Faced with the potentially devastating consequences of default, the Bank's chief objective is no longer development, but, more simply, the rescue of private lenders (Harpagon: "My casket! My casket!"). The banker must be saved before the client: doubts have disappeared, and the Bank's core beliefs are hammered home over and over again: the economy must be strengthened by making it leaner; the public sector must be restructured to create favorable conditions for private business and the market; the state must shrink and become more efficient. Such "solutions" transcend the need to respond to the debt crisis: they aim at social transformation through the return to an uncompromising liberalism.

2. GRAMMATICAL PATTERNS

So far, our findings have been rather straightforward: as the economic situation evolves, policy changes, and language too; yet the Bank itself remains the same. We will now shift our attention to aspects of language that change very little, and very slowly. A "bureaucratization" of the Bank's discourse, one could call it—except that it's more than that: it's a style that self-organizes around a few elements, then starts generating its own message. Let us try to explain, by returning to the two passages we quoted at the beginning of this essay. The one from 1958, on "the Congo's present transport system," was full of *rivers, farms, markets, railroads, ports, minerals, cities* . . . It couldn't have been clearer. The second passage, from 2008, was different. Here it is again:

> **Leveling the Playing Field on Global Issues**
>
> Countries in the region are emerging as key players on issues of global concern, and the Bank's role has been to support their efforts by partnering through innovative platforms for an enlightened dialogue and action on the ground, as well as by supporting South–South cooperation.

Issues, players, concern, efforts, platforms, dialogue, ground . . . "The whole tendency of modern prose is away from concreteness," wrote Orwell in "Politics and the English Language," and his words are as true today as they were in 1946. The Bank stresses the importance of what it's saying—*key, global, innovative, enlightened*—but its words are hopelessly opaque. What is it really trying to say—or to hide?

A. "A MASS OF LATIN WORDS FALLS UPON THE FACTS . . ."

Opacity is hard to understand, so we will break it down into smaller units, beginning with its movement "away from concreteness." In the passage from 2008, the terms *action* and *cooperation* belong to a class of words

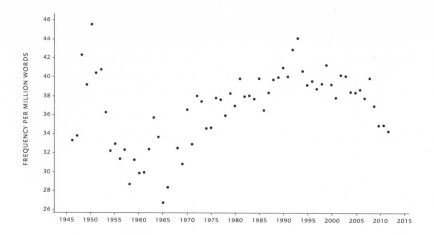

FIGURE 7.8 **Nominalizations**

usually known as "nominalizations," or "derived abstract nouns"; derived, in this case, from verbs: to "'act," to "cooperate."[7] In English, such terms are recognizable by their typical ending in -tion, -sion and -ment (implementation, extension, development . . .); so, we extracted from the Reports all the words with such an ending and hand-checked the top 600 (to eliminate "station," "cement," and the like). **Figure 7.8** presents the results. According to *Corpus Linguistics*, in academic prose the average frequency of nominalizations derived from verbs is 1.3 percent. In the World Bank Reports, the frequency is near 3 percent from the start, with a higher peak around 1950, and it keeps growing, slowly but steadily, plateauing at 4 percent between 1980 and 2005, and dropping slightly thereafter.

A class of words that is used two or three times more often than in comparable discourses.[8] Why? What do nominalizations do, that the Reports

---

7 On nominalizations, see Douglas Biber, Susan Conrad, and Randi Reppen, *Corpus Linguistics: Investigating Language Structure and Use* (Cambridge, UK: Cambridge University Press, 1998), 59–65; Douglas Biber, Stig Johansson, Geoffrey Leech, Susan Conrad, and Edward Finegan, *Longman Grammar of Spoken and Written English* (Harlow: Longman, 1999), 325ff.

8 This of course doesn't mean that *every* nominalization increases its frequency. In parallel with the semantic shifts described in the previous pages, many terms related to political processes [*legislation, representation*], inter-state diplomacy [*agreement, negotiation*], or forms of critical vigilance [*examination, investigation*] have become markedly less frequent over the years: *agreement* was the fifth most frequent nominalization in the early Reports, and is now the fifteenth; *legislation* has dropped from thirty-first to ninety-ninth, and so on. By contrast, other terms have enjoyed a lightning ascent: *management* was only the eighteenth most frequent nominalization at the beginning of the Bank's activity, and is now

should use them with such insistence? They take "actions and processes" and turn them into "abstract objects," runs a standard linguistic definition:[9] you don't support countries that are cooperating with each other; you support "South–South cooperation." An abstraction, where temporality is abolished. "The *provision* of social services . . . and country *assessments* and *action* plans which assist in the *formulation* of poverty *reduction* policies," writes the Report for 1990—and the five nominalizations create a sort of simultaneity among a series of actions that are in fact quite distinct from each other. Providing social services (action one) which will assist (two) in formulating policies (three) to reduce poverty (four): doing this will take a *very* long time. But in the language of the Report, all these steps have contracted into a single policy, which seems to come into being all at once. It's magic.

And then—the authors of *Corpus Linguistics* continue—in nominalizations, actions and processes are "separated from human participants":[10] cooperation, not states that cooperate with each other. "*Pollution*, soil *erosion*, land *degradation*, *deforestation* and *deterioration* of the urban *environment*," mourns another recent Report, and the absence of social actors is striking. All these ominous trends—and no one is responsible? *Prioritization* enters the Reports as debt crisis looms; meaning, quite simply, that not all creditors would be treated equally: some would be reimbursed right away, others later; some in full, and others not. Of course, the criteria according to which X would be treated differently from Y had been decided by someone. But *prioritization* concealed that. Why X and not Y? Because of prioritization. In front of the word, one can no longer see—one can no longer even imagine—a concrete subject engaged in a decision. "Rendition": an American secret agency kidnaps foreign citizens to hand them over to another secret service, in another country, that will torture them. In "rendition," it's all gone. It's magic.[11]

---

the second; *implementation, adjustment, evaluation, commitment,* and *assessment,* none of which were among the hundred most frequent nominalizations, are now in eighth, ninth, eleventh, thirteenth, and fourteenth place. See also **Figure 7.9**.

9 Biber et al., *Corpus Linguistics*, 61.

10 Biber et al., *Corpus Linguistics*, 61.

11 Black magic, in this case, consistent with the fact that "political speech and writing are largely the defence of the indefensible," as Orwell put it in his 1946 essay. Interestingly, Orwell himself had found nominalizations—"a mass of Latin words falls upon the facts like soft snow, blurring the outlines and covering up all details"—to be entwined with the phenomena he was describing: "Defenceless villages

This recurrent transmutation of social forces into abstractions turns the World Bank Reports into strangely metaphysical documents, whose protagonists are often not economic agents, but principles—and principles of so universal a nature, it's impossible to oppose them. Leveling the playing field on global issues: no one will ever object to these words (although, of course, no one will ever be able to say what they really mean, either). They are so general, these ideas, they're usually in the singular: development, governance, management, cooperation. It's the "singularization" that Reinhart Koselleck discovered in late 18th-century thought: "histories," which had "previously existed in the plural, as all sorts of histories which had occurred," becoming "history in general"; the "progresses" of the various technical and intellectual branches converging into a single "progress," and so on.[12]

For Koselleck, singularization was the result of the "growing complexity of economic, technological, social and political structures," which forced social theory to increase the "degree of generality" of its categories.[13] Which is true: singular abstract nouns allow us to synthesize and generalize, and are thus indispensable to the construction of knowledge. But World Bank Reports are not primarily about knowledge: they are about policy; and in policy, singularization suggests not a greater generality, but a stronger constraint. There is only one way to do things: one development path; one type of management; one form of cooperation. It's hard to believe, but the verb *to disagree* never appears in the Reports; *disagreement*, twice

---

are bombarded from the air," he writes, and "this is called *pacification*. Millions of farmers are robbed of their farms . . . this is called *rectification of frontiers*. People are imprisoned for years without trial, or shot in the back of the neck or sent to die of scurvy in Arctic lumber camps: this is called *elimination of unreliable elements*." ("Politics and the English Language," in *The Collected Essays, Journalism and Letters of George Orwell*, ed. Sonia Orwell and Ian Angus, vol. IV, *In Front of Your Nose* (Harmondsworth: Penguin, 1968), 166). The politico-military cast of Orwell's examples makes them of course quite unlike the typical World Bank nominalizations; unsurprisingly, "pacification," "rectification," and "elimination" are never used in the Reports. Our thanks to Dallas Liddle for pointing out this aspect of Orwell's essay.

12 Reinhart Koselleck, "On the Disposability of History," and "*Neuzeit*: Remarks on the Semantics of Modern Concepts of Movement," in *Futures Past: On the Semantics of Historical Time*, trans. Keith Tribe (Cambridge, MA: MIT Press, 1985), 200, 264.

13 It is of course far from irrelevant that "histories" became "history in general" in the specific context of late 18th-century Europe, which was increasingly imposing its rule over the other continents. In this respect, singularization created knowledge *and* hierarchies at once, subjecting the world system to a single European perspective.

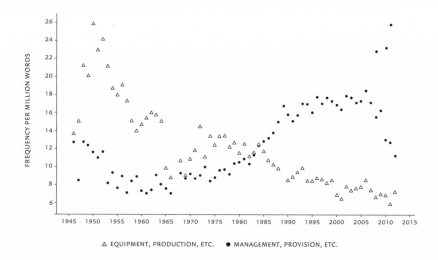

△ EQUIPMENT, PRODUCTION, ETC.   ● MANAGEMENT, PROVISION, ETC.

FIGURE 7.9 **Two policies, one grammar.** If one compares the twenty-five most frequent nomi-nalizations of the first and last decades of World Bank history, two very different political clusters emerge: the first group is defined by terms such as *equipment, production, construction, irrigation, operation, distribution, rehabilitation, completion, transmission;* the second, by *management, provision, statement, adjust-ment, evaluation, implementation, assessment, participation, corruption, option.* Only seven of the twenty-five terms are shared by the two groups—*development* being by far the most frequent in both cases. (The chart shows the frequency of the two groups once development has been removed.)

in seventy years.[14] It's the formula made famous by Margaret Thatcher: There Is No Alternative. And singularizations assert this, not with argu-ments, but with the unspoken "fact" of a recurrent grammatical pattern. World Bank policies change, as we have seen, but singularization does not: each new policy is the only possible one (**Figure 7.9**).[15]

The transition from semantic clusters to grammatical struc-tures—from the first to the second part of this essay—entails, so to speak, a certain loss of momentum: compared to the dramatic trajectories of **Figures 7.1–7.7**, with their five- or ten-fold increases, the mild incline of **Figure 7.8** is hardly impressive. But its slowness tells us something that

14 So hard to believe, that three separate people checked on four separate occasions—always with the same result. As for "agree" and "agreement," they appear 88 and 1,773 times respectively.

15 The fact that, in nominalizations, actions are entirely absorbed into the noun, increases the sense of a one-dimensional world. If one speaks of "managers," one can (at least in theory) imagine them act-ing in more than one way; if one speaks of "management," a specific form of activity is already inscribed in the term, and predetermined by it.

is just as important: behind all the changes, the first element of an institutional "style" had successfully crystallized. Nominalizations remained unusually frequent because they "worked" in so many interconnected ways: they hid the subject of decisions, eliminated alternatives, endowed the chosen policy with a halo of high principle and prompt realization. Their abstraction was the perfect echo of a capital that was itself becoming more and more deterritorialized; their impossible ugliness—"'prioritization': come on!—lent them a certain pedantic reliability; their ambiguity allowed for the endless small adjustments that keep the peace in the world order. And so, this mass of Latin words became a key ingredient of "'how one talks about policy." Specific semantic fields rise and fall with their referents; they are, one could almost say, the *histoire événementielle* of political language. Grammar is made of rules and repetition, and its politics is in step with longer cycles: structures, more than events. It defines, not *a* policy of the Bank, but the way in which *every* policy is put into words. It is the magic mirror in which the World Bank can gaze, and recognize itself as an institution.

B. AND . . . AND . . . AND . . .

We briefly discussed the collocates of *governance* in the caption to **Figure 7.3**, but we didn't mention that the biggest surprise came with the most frequent collocate of all: *and.* "And"? The most frequent word in English is "the": everybody knows that. So, what is "and" doing at the top of the list? Two passages from the 1999 Report may help to explain:

> promote corporate governance *and* competition policies *and* reform *and* privatize state-owned enterprises *and* labor market/social protection reform

> There is greater emphasis on quality, responsiveness, *and* partnerships; on knowledge-sharing *and* client orientation; *and* on poverty reduction

The first passage—a grammatico-political monstrosity—is a small present to our patient readers; the second, more guarded, is also more indicative of the rhetoric in question. Knowledge-sharing really has nothing to do with client orientation; poverty reduction, nothing to do with either. There is

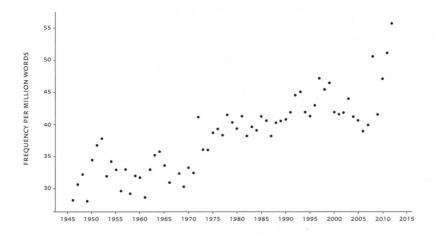

FIGURE 7.10 **World Bank parataxis.** Initially, the frequency of "and" in World Bank Reports was around 2.6 percent, which is also its average frequency in academic prose. Over the last sixty years, however, its presence has almost doubled (and it is even higher, close to 7 percent, in the proximity of "governance").

no reason they should appear together. But those "ands" connect them just the same, despite the total absence of logic, and their paratactical crudity becomes almost a justification: we have so many important things to do, we can't afford to be elegant; yes, we must take care of our clients (we are, remember, a bank); but we also care about knowledge and partnership and sharing and poverty!

"Bankspeak," we have written, echoing Orwell's famous neologism; but there is one crucial difference between the lexicographers of *1984* and the Bank's ghostwriters. Whereas the former were fascinated by annihilation ("It's a beautiful thing, the destruction of words . . . every year fewer and fewer words, and the range of consciousness always a little smaller"), the latter have a childish delight in multiplying words, and most particularly *nouns* (**Figures 7.11** and **7.12**). The frequency of nouns in academic prose is usually just below 30 percent; in World Bank Reports it has always been significantly higher, and has increased slowly and regularly over the years. It is the perfect rhetoric to bring the "world" inside the "bank": a "chaotic enumeration" of disparate realities—to quote an expression coined by Leo Spitzer—that suggests an endlessly expanding universe, encouraging a sense of admiration and wonder rather than critical understanding.

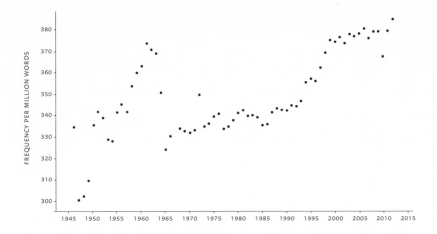

FIGURE 7.11 **Frequency of nouns in World Bank Reports.** The frequency of nouns in academic prose is usually just below 30 percent; in World Bank Reports it has always been significantly higher, and has increased slowly and regularly over the years.

The last passage we quoted—on "client orientation" and "poverty reduction"—is a good example of another tic of World Bank discourse: using a noun to modify another noun. Here are some examples of these "adjunct nouns," as they are usually called, from the 2012 Report:

> the Bank's *operations effectiveness*, including the quality and *results orientation* of its operations and *knowledge activities*, the performance of its lending portfolio, the mainstreaming of gender in its operational work, *client feedback*, and its use of *country systems*.

> Our agenda has included *gender equality, food security, climate change* and *biodiversity, infrastructure investment, disaster prevention, financial innovation*, and *inclusion*.

Adjunct nouns, the *Longman Grammar* explains, are a form of pre-modification: in "poverty reduction," for instance, "poverty" modifies "reduction" by coming before it (whereas in "the reduction of poverty" it does so by appearing after it, a case of post-modification). There is a difference: being "consistently more condensed than postmodifiers," the *Longman* authors explain, premodifiers are hence also "much less explicit in identifying the

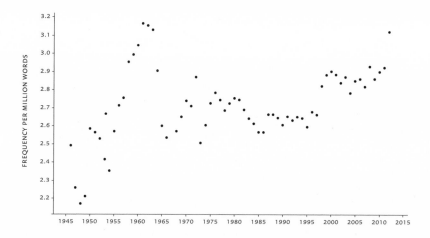

FIGURE 7.12 **Noun/verb ratio.** The ratio of nouns to verbs is a clue of whether an argument is mostly conducted by reference to stable entities (nouns) or to processes and events (verbs). That the language of the Reports inclines towards the former rather than the latter had already emerged in **Figure 7.8**, with its high frequency of abstract nouns derived from—and hence taking the place of—verbs; the noun/verb ratio, significantly higher than the 2.1:1 average of academic prose extends that initial finding.

meaning relationship."[16] More condensed, and less explicit: this is it. Condensed, first of all: this is a brisk rhetoric, succinct, even a little impatient; the language of those who have a lot to say and no time to waste. And then, there's the matter of explicitness. In the case of "the reduction of poverty," to keep using that example, if you know what the individual words mean, you also know what *the expression* means: the whole is just the sum of its parts. But "poverty reduction," like "disaster prevention," or "competition policies," is not just the sum of its parts; as we have seen, it is an expression in code—the code of "management discourse"—whose meaning has more to do with "approaches" and "frameworks" than with "employment" and "income." "Food security," writes the 2012 Report; and what exactly is that? It's the opposite of "food *in*security," first of all; which, in turn, is a UN neologism—half conceptual refinement, half bureaucratic euphemism—for what used to be called "hunger." If you don't know the new code, individual words are useless.[17]

---

16 Biber et al., *Longman Grammar of Spoken and Written English*, 588, 590.

17 And the point is, the World Bank wants to communicate in code. We mentioned above the experiment conducted on the collocates of "poverty" and "poverty reduction"; but the initial idea was slightly

Here, the process initiated with the advent of nominalizations (which have a clear elective affinity with adjunct nouns: "operations *effectiveness*," "results *orientation*," "disaster *prevention*" . . .) reaches its zenith: the "mass of Latin words" joins forces with the insider code of "management discourse," making social reality increasingly unrecognizable. But one question remains. How could such a tortuous form of expression become a leading discourse on the contemporary world?

C. FROM HERE TO ETERNITY

In their book *Laboratory Life*, Bruno Latour and Steve Woolgar wonder about the strange fate of scientific hypotheses: ideas that begin their existence as "contentious statements," besieged by all sorts of objections, yet at some point manage to "stabilize," and are accepted as "facts" pure and simple. How do they do that—how do the World Bank's contentious ideas become accepted as the "natural" horizon of all possible policies? The key move, write Latour and Woolgar, consists in "freeing" a statement from "all determinants of place and time, and all reference to its producers."[18] **Figures 7.13–7.14** show how decisively the World Bank has dealt with such "determinants."

The growing indifference to space and time is not just a matter of quantity. If one looks at the paragraphs in which the Reports are articulated, one detail leaps to the eye: their endings have completely changed. Here are some instances from 1955:

> A modern coffee-processing plant, financed by the Development
> Bank, was completed near Jimma, the center of an important coffee-
> producing area.

> Automatic telephone exchanges have been installed in Addis Ababa and
> Gondar, and manual exchanges in other towns.

---

different: we meant to compare "poverty reduction" and "the reduction of poverty," to see if there was any semantic difference between pre- and post-modification. However, we had to abandon our idea when it turned out that there were 1,198 occurrences of "poverty reduction," and only thirty-eight of "the reduction of poverty." Which of course is crazy, but at least makes perfectly clear that for the World Bank pre- and post-modification are not equivalent, and that its preference goes unabashedly to the more cryptic of the two constructions.

18 Bruno Latour and Steve Woolgar, *Laboratory Life: The Construction of Scientific Facts* (Princeton, NJ: Princeton University Press, 1986), 106, 105, 175.

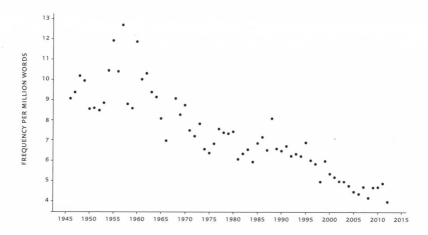

FIGURE 7.13 **Tempus fugit.** Between 1946 and 2008, the frequency of temporal adverbs ("now," "recently," "later," and so on) has dropped by more than 50 percent. As these adverbs are the simplest way to place events within a system of temporal coordinates, their disappearance suggests a drastic weakening of the sense of time in the Bank's Reports.

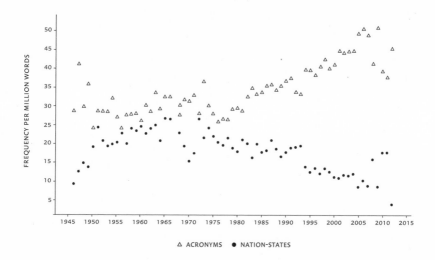

△ ACRONYMS   ● NATION-STATES

FIGURE 7.14 **Decline of the nation-state, rise of the acronym.** Mentions of nation-states rise in the 1950s, and plateau in the 1960s, with the recognition of many African states. In the late 1970s, after having run more or less parallel for a couple of decades, the frequencies of states and acronyms diverge dramatically, to the point that the latter are now four times as frequent as the former: a clear sign that the geopolitical actor where "determinants of place" are all-important is now being dwarfed by those trans-national entities—not just the UN, IMF, WTO, or FAO, but COSO [Committee Of Sponsoring Organizations], FASB [Financial Accounting Standards Board], PRSP [Poverty Reduction Strategy Papers], and so on ad libitum—where space seems to have been entirely transcended.

> This has encouraged investment in industries such as metals and
> chemicals which are large consumers of power, and has led Norway to
> develop more generating capacity per head than any other country.

Jimma, Addis Ababa, Gondar, Norway: in these sentences, a strong geographical specificity goes hand in hand with an equally strong sense of
time. The coffee-plant "was completed"; the telephone exchanges "have
been installed"; investment "has led." The focus is on *results*; the paragraph
comes to an end when the process comes to an end; the relevant grammatical category (the "aspect" of the verb's tense) is the "perfect," which
indicates that an action has been completed. This is true even in more
complex cases, like this one from 1948:

> The mission's conclusions *pointed out* that the factors which *had produced*
> a favorable foreign exchange position in the Philippines were *temporary*,
> and *stressed* the need to *conserve* foreign exchange, *restrict* inflationary local
> financing, *take* measures to *lessen* the impact of the *expected* reduction
> in dollar receipts, and *secure* technical aid *in the planning* of specific
> development projects.

Here, the initial sense of achievement ("pointed out," "had produced")
leads into the horizon of the present ("conserve," "restrict"), and then into
a many-layered future: the Philippines will have to "take measures" (soon)
"to lessen the impact" (later) of an "expected reduction in receipts" (somewhere in between those two futures). The temporality is complex, but its
dimensions are clear: the past is the realm of results; the present, of decisions; the future, of prospects and possibilities. In recent years, though,
this difference has been diluted. Here is a paragraph ending from 2003:

> IDA has been moving toward supporting these strategies through
> program lending.

Whatever program lending is, IDA has not actually done it; it "has been
moving," yes, but that's all; and not even moving towards doing, only toward
"*supporting*" doing. We've heard so many philippics on "accountability," in
recent years, we would expect a landslide of past tenses in the Bank's language; after all, accountability can only be assessed with reference to what

has been *done*. Instead, however, for the Reports the tenses of the past are no longer the right way to "conclude" a statement; in their place we find the blurred, slightly amorphous temporality of the progressive and the gerund (whose frequency has increased about 50 percent over the years). Some other recent examples:

> The Second Kecamatan Development Project is *benefiting* 25 to 30 million rural Indonesians by *giving* villagers tools for *developing* their own community. (2003)

> The Bank significantly accelerated its efforts to help client countries cope with climate change while *respecting* another aspect of its core mission: promoting economic development and poverty reduction by *helping* provide modern energy to *growing* economies. (2008)

The Bank has *accelerated*—but only its *efforts*; and all these efforts will do is—*help*; and all those helped will do is—*cope*; and the helping and coping will have to *respect* the *promoting* of the *helping* (again!) provided to *growing* economies. But there is no point in looking for the meaning of these passages in what they say: what really matters, here, is the proximity established between policy-making and the forms ending in -ing. It's the message of the countless headlines that frame the text of the Reports: "*Working* with the poorest countries," "*Providing* timely analysis," "*Sharing* knowledge," "*Improving* governance," "*Fostering* private sector and financial sector development," "*Boosting* growth and job creation," "*Bridging* the social gap," "*Strengthening* governance," "*Leveling* the playing field on global issues." All extremely uplifting—and just as unfocused: because the function of gerunds consists in leaving an action's completion undefined, thus depriving it of any definite contour. An infinitely expanding present emerges, where policies are always in progress, but also *only* in progress. Many promises, and very few facts. "If we want things to stay as they are, things will have to change," wrote Giuseppe di Lampedusa in *The Leopard*; and the same happens here. All change, and no achievement. All change, and no future.

2015

CHAPTER 8

Mapping London's Emotions

Ryan Heuser, Franco Moretti, Erik Steiner

A few years ago, a group of researchers from the Stanford Literary Lab decided to use topic modeling to extract geographical information from 19th-century novels. Though the study was eventually abandoned, it revealed that London-related topics had become significantly more frequent in the course of the century. When some of us were later asked to design a crowd-sourcing experiment, we decided to add a further dimension to those early findings, and see whether London place-names could become the cornerstone for an emotional geography of the city. In the *Atlas of the European Novel*, Franco Moretti had already worked on the geography of London.[1] But emotions have a more elusive reality than residences in Dickens or crimes in Conan Doyle, and only one of the *Atlas*'s hundred images—a map of foreign ideas in Russian novels—was somewhat comparable to the current project. To further complicate matters, when Moretti showed that image to Serge Bonin, the historical geographer who was advising him about the *Atlas*, Bonin was extremely critical: ideas like "materialism" or "equality" were not *ortgebunden*, as German geographers would say: they didn't have that intrinsic connection to a specific place that is the basis of every real map. And if ideas were not mappable, how could emotions be?

Then, we encountered a passage in Philip Fisher's *Vehement Passions*:

> Each citizen . . . has a specific cluster of dangers of which she is constantly or intermittently in fear. Each person will localize the general anticipatory

---

1 Franco Moretti, *Atlas of the European Novel* (New York: Verso, 1998).

fear in a personal geography of fear. . . . We now live in a new geography
of fear. . . . It is the passion of fear, above all, that isolates the element of
suddenness and the part it plays within the passions.[2]

Even more than the "geography of fear," it was Fisher's remark on the
"suddenness" of this emotion that we found illuminating. What is sudden
occurs at a specific moment in time, and hence also at a specific point
in space: it is definitely *ortgebunden*, to return to that notion. And if this
is so, then a geography of emotions—their actual distribution over a
map—becomes imaginable. A London of fear, joy, anger, hopefulness . . .

1. CORPUS, UNITS, PROGRAMS

In programming the study, we began by identifying all proper names in the
corpus via a Named Entity Recognition program, later removing from the
list those terms that had nothing to do with London, like foreign toponyms,
characters' names, and the like.[3] The results are shown in **Figures 8.2–8.3**.
The 382 London locations that had received at least ten mentions formed
the basis of our second corpus: about 15,000 passages that—in a version of
the keywords-in-context approach—included a specific place-name at the
center, plus the hundred words that preceded and followed it, as in the case
of "Regent Street" (see **Figure 8.1**). Taggers were then asked to read the 200-
word passage and identify the emotion that best characterized it.

FIGURE 8.1: **A London place-name and its narrative context.**

He would go through it, always armed, without a sign of shrinking. It had
to be done, and he would do it. At ten he walked down to the central
committee-room at Whitehall Place. He thought that he would face the
world better by walking than if he were taken in his own brougham. He

---

2 Philip Fisher, *The Vehement Passions*, 110, 117–8.

3 For the 18th century, our corpus included texts marked as fiction by the English Short Title Catalogue,
with additional texts coming from the Literary Lab's "Eighteenth-Century Fictional Marketplace" project; 19th-century texts came from the Chadwyck-Healey database, as well as from a collection released
on the Internet Archive by the University of Illinois; a handful of additional texts came from the Gutenberg project, Google Books, or Stanford library scans. We only used novels whose Optical Character
Recognition accuracy rate was above 90 percent.

gave orders that the carriage should be at the committee-room at eleven, and wait an hour for him if he was not there. He went along Bond Street and Piccadilly,

Regent Street

and through Pall Mall to Charing Cross, with the blandly triumphant smile of a man who had successfully entertained the great guest of the day. As he got near the club he met two or three men whom he knew, and bowed to them. They returned his bow graciously enough, but not one of them stopped to speak to him. Of one he knew that he would have stopped, had it not been for the rumour. Even after the man had passed on he was careful to show no displeasure on his face. He would take it all as it would come and still be the blandly triumphant Merchant Prince—as long as the police would allow him.

—Anthony Trollope, *The Way We Live Now*

At first, we were hoping to capture a wide spectrum of emotional attitudes; but the lack of agreement among the taggers—as well as among the English graduate students who offered to act as a control group—convinced us to reduce the options to the opposite extremes of fear and happiness.[4] As a further constraint, a passage would count as "frightening" or "happy" only if at least half of the taggers had identified it as such; and we re-ran all passages through a "sentiment analysis" program.[5] And, eventually, some patterns began to emerge. But before coming to them, we need to sketch out the main material transformations of 18th- and 19th-century London.

---

[4] The initial stages of the research are described in detail in Mark Algee-Hewitt, Ryan Heuser, Annalise Lockhart, Erik Steiner, and Van Tran, "Mapping the Emotions of London in Fiction, 1700–1900: A Crowdsourcing Experiment," in *Literary Mapping in the Digital Age*, ed. David Cooper, Chris Donaldson, and Patricia Murrieta-Flores (London: Routledge, 2016).

[5] Sentiment analysis is a text-mining technique that evaluates texts via a dictionary of terms organized around a "polarity" of negative and positive values. The process is a little more complicated than simply adding up the terms that belong to one or the other category, but, essentially, that is the basic mechanism. Clearly, everything hinges on the words that are included in the dictionary; the program we used, which was developed in the Stanford Linguistics department, has about 1,700 negative terms and 1,300 positive ones; since its training corpus is the *Wall Street Journal* (and similar sources), its understanding of emotions in 18th- and 19th-century texts is not impeccable.

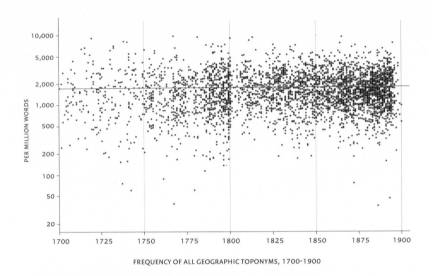

FREQUENCY OF ALL GEOGRAPHIC TOPONYMS, 1700-1900

FIGURE 8.2 **Geographic place names as a percentage of the words in our corpus**

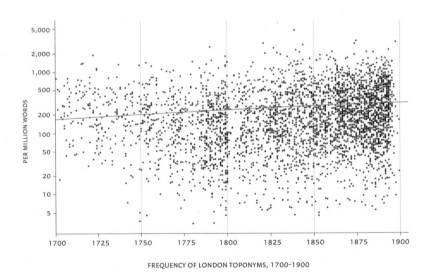

FREQUENCY OF LONDON TOPONYMS, 1700-1900

FIGURE 8.3 **London place names as a percentage of the words in our corpus, 1700–1900.**
These charts—in which each dot represents an individual novel—update and confirm the findings
from a few years ago, using a corpus of about 5,000 English novels published between 1700 and
1900: 304 for the period 1700–49, 1,079 for 1750–99, 1,290 for 1800–49, and 2,189 for 1850–99. The
values on the y-axis are logarithmic (to include texts that have as few as five or as many as 5,000 toponyms), and make the historical trend appear less dramatic than it actually was; in fact, the frequency of London toponyms almost doubled in a century—increasing from a median of 102 in 1780–1800
to one of 190 in 1880–1900—whereas that of geographical toponyms in general remained fundamentally flat.

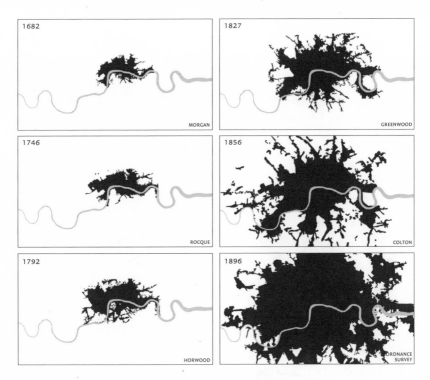

FIGURE 8.4 **The growth of London, 1682–1896.** Sources: Morgan, Rocque, Horwood, Green-wood, Colton, Ordnance Survey.

2. REAL LONDON, FICTIONAL LONDON

In the period covered by our study, London changed like never before. Its population grew from around 600,000 in 1700 to 1,000,000 in 1800 and then, more dramatically, to 4,500,000 (or 6,500,000, depending on the criteria) in 1900. The 19th century, when most of the demographic leap occurred, was also decisive in the redefinition of the space—and in fact the very shape—of the city. Our sequence of London maps in **Figure 8.4** clearly shows how, up to the first quarter of the 19th century, the fundamental urban axis ran horizontally from east to west on the north bank of the Thames, creating a strangely elongated rectangle.[6] It was only in Victo-

---

6 As often happens with such shapes, it became easy to see the city as dominated by a binary polarity, which in the case of London took the form of an opposition between West End and City (and, later, of

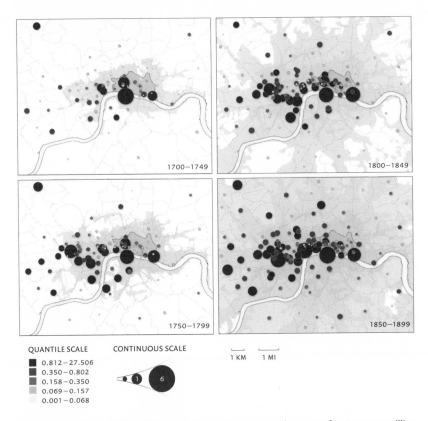

FIGURE 8.5 **The stability of fictional London, 1700–1900.** Place name frequency per million words. Sources: Morgan, Rocque, Horwood, Greenwood, Colton, Ordnance Survey.

rian times that London detached itself from the river, using major roads as so many tendrils to expand towards the north and south, and eventually transforming its initial shape into the circular pattern so typical of urban geography.

As 19th-century London had changed so much, and so quickly, we expected more or less the same from its fictional representation. But here, the only transformation occurred in the second half of the 18th

---

West and East End). Here is a narrative version of this state of affairs, from a conversation taking place in Mayfair:

> "I think I have heard you say that their uncle is an attorney in Meryton" "Yes; and they have another, who lives somewhere near Cheapside." "That is capital," added her sister, and they both laughed heartily.
> —Jane Austen, *Pride and Prejudice*

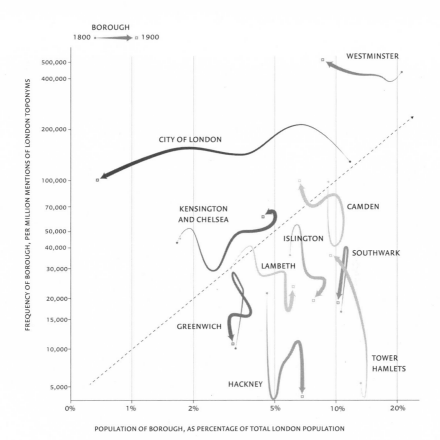

FIGURE 8.6 **London's real and fictional population, 1800–1900.** In this image, each borough is represented by a tapered line, which becomes thicker with each passing decade, so as to make the direction of the process immediately visible: in the case of Westminster and the City, for instance, fictional over-representation kept clearly increasing as the century advanced. (For the City, this has probably a lot to do with the fact that its residential population—as opposed to working commuters—shrank drastically during the 19th century.) Source: Historical Census Population from Greater London Authority (https://data.london.gov.uk/dataset/historic-census-population).

century, when the West End became as narratively populated as the City (**Figure 8.5**); afterwards, hardly anything changed. The number of geographical references kept increasing, yes, but they remained essentially localized in the City and in the West End: the rest of London—where most of the growth was actually taking place—never really mattered.

This drastic discrepancy between fact and fiction is synthesized in **Figure 8.6**, where the horizontal axis represents the population of the various boroughs, and the vertical one their presence in fiction. Along

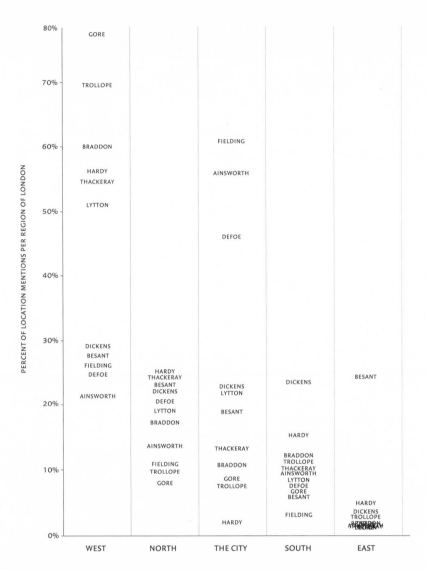

FIGURE 8.7 **"London" novelists?** Location mentions per region of London. This chart indicates in what area of London an author's geographical references are usually placed: the West End, for instance, scores almost 80 percent for silver-fork author Catherine Gore (with Trollope not far behind), while the City, being the oldest part of London, is inevitably the chosen domain of 18th-century writers (Fielding and Defoe), and of a master of Newgate fiction like W. H. Ainsworth. The only writer to pay consistent attention to the East End is Walter Besant (though his famous 1882 Stepney Green novel, *All Sorts and Conditions of Men*, had its protagonists involved in subplots in the West End). The chart also explains why Dickens is so often seen as the "real" London novelist: unlike others, he was equally interested in several parts of London (though not really in the East End), and his adoption of the multi-plot narrative structure allowed him to both pay attention to different areas, and turn this mosaic of little worlds into an organized whole.

the diagonal line, a borough's fictional presence corresponds exactly to its real population: it's the case of the City in the 1800s, Islington in the 1810s, Camden in the 1890s, and Kensington and Chelsea for much of the century. But the overall message of the chart lies in the clear, and in fact growing *divarication* between fiction and reality: with the dramatic over-representation of Westminster and the City on one side of the diagonal, and under-representation of Tower Hamlets, Southwark, and Hackney on the opposite one. Though we commonly speak of "London novels," then, this image reveals how partial the representation of the city actually was—and **Figure 8.7** further extends this line of inquiry by showing the favorite spaces of a few particularly well-known London novelists.

3. THE SEMANTICS OF SPACE

First finding of this research: in the course of the 19th century, real London changed radically—and fictional London hardly at all. In France, Zola's Paris was very different from Balzac's only thirty years earlier; in London, Sherlock Holmes's fin-de-siècle investigations still focused on the City and the West End, as they could have done a century earlier. Why? Where did this incredible stability come from? Probably, from two different sources. In the case of the City, the stability may be actually more apparent than real, as "the" City, though grammatically singular, had long consisted of a plurality of heterogeneous spaces. "The inhabitants of . . . Cheapside," Addison had written as early as 1712, are "removed from those of the Temple on the one hand and those of Smithfield on the other by several climates and degrees in their way of thinking and conversing." Several climates . . . in half a mile! And the same could be said of the Old Bailey and St. Paul's, the Bank and Newgate, the Pool of London (the city's main port, before the expansion of the Docks) and the hospital of St. Bart's (where Doctor John Watson will have his first encounter with Sherlock Holmes). Finance, long-distance trade, the law, local markets, incarceration, publishing, religion, medicine . . . The City's enduring fictional presence was fundamentally due to the fact that each of these worlds-within-a-world could turn into the fictional habitat of a different writer (or genre): gothic and historical fiction focused on the Tower, which lay just east of its wall (**Figures 8.8–8.9**); Newgate novels on the jail, and on the Old Bailey that was adjacent to it (**Figure 8.10**). Harriet

FIGURES 8.8—8.13: **The City and its novels.** In the course of the 19th century, English novelists used the City and its vicinity for a variety of different purposes, though a clear shift occurred from the earlier, sinister world of crime and punishment (**Figures 8.1–8.3**), to the more prosaic interactions of the modern professions (**Figures 8.4– 8.6**).

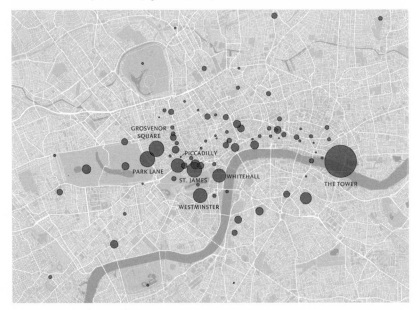

FIGURE 8.8 **Gothic Novel**

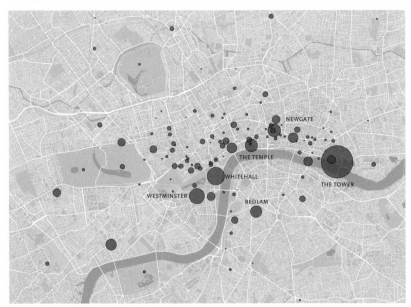

FIGURE 8.9 **Historical Novels**

RELATIVE EMPHASIS

LOW ◄   HIGH

NOTE: "Relative emphasis" is a measure of the proportional use of a specific toponym relative to all London toponyms used in that category or by that author. We use a uniform scale for all maps in order to give a general impression of the geographical focus of each.

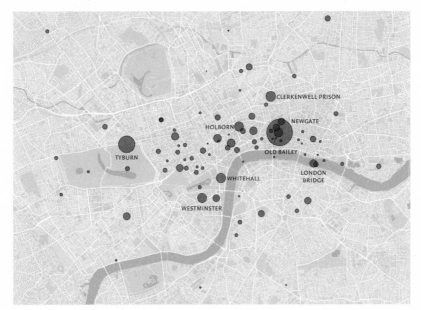

FIGURE 8.10 **Newgate Novels**

FIGURE 8.11 **Harriet Martineau**

FIGURE 8.12 **Charles Dickens**

FIGURE 8.13 **William Thackeray**

Martineau, a little atypically, focused on the economic hub around the Bank (**Figure 8.11**); while the interplay of publishing, the law, and finance became typical of the mid-Victorian generation of Dickens and Thackeray (**Figures 8.12–8.13**).

If the City's fictional presence is due to the heterogeneity of its components, that of the West End arises from the opposite mechanism: its being an extremely *homogeneous* space, where "the great Georgian estates remained (with their clones, such as Belgravia and Kensington) the chic places to live, shop, saunter and dine."[7] Eighteenth-century addresses that are still in fashion at the end of the industrial century: in other Western metropolises, where the new elites created their own enclaves in the Chaussée d'Antin, the Upper East Side or the Grunewald, this would be unthinkable. In London, though, the West End was never really challenged—only somewhat enlarged (north of Oxford Street, west of St. James, south of Hyde Park), to allow for the osmosis of the old and new ruling class. In an instance of what we could call the semantics of space, literary passages located in the West End acquired in the course of this process an unmistakable class flavor: a lexicon that combines the opulence of *square, park,* and *gardens,* the patrician ring of *earl* and *Edward,* and the sharp tone of mastery in *servants, ordered,* and *desired;* in a more indirect vein, we find the rituals of polite sociability (*acquaintance, conversation, visit, meeting, obliged, aunt,* and the inevitable *marriage*), where even adjectives and adverbs sound prudent and calculating (*hardly, grave, usual, particular, really*). Final touch, *her*: a sign of women's ambiguous centrality within this social space, at once dominant (*her,* not *him*) and dominated: not emerging as a (grammatical) subject, but as the object of other people's desires, plans and actions ("proceeded to inform *her,*" "after pacifying *her,*" "freely offered *her,*" "never forgave *her*"); or else, when *her* functions as a possessive determiner, as someone observed from the outside, with an ever-watchful attention that takes in, at times within a single sentence, material possessions ("*her* carriage," "*her* ladyship's dressing-table"), physical appearance ("*her* silk dress," "*her* veil"), behavior ("*her* loftiness of mien," "*her* playful manner"), and social relations "*her* selfish husband," "*her* friends," "*her* father's wealth").[8]

---

7 Roy Porter, *London: A Social History* (Cambridge, MA: Harvard University Press, 1995), 96.

8 The overrepresentation of *her* thus signals the affinity between the English upper class and the symbolic form of the marriage plot, in its various metamorphoses. With its plurality of genres, illustrated in

FIGURES 8.14–8.15: **The new/old geography of New Grub Street**

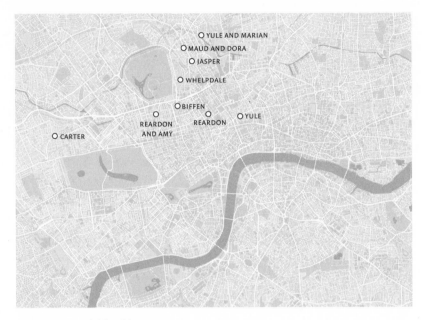

FIGURE 8.14 **Initial residences**

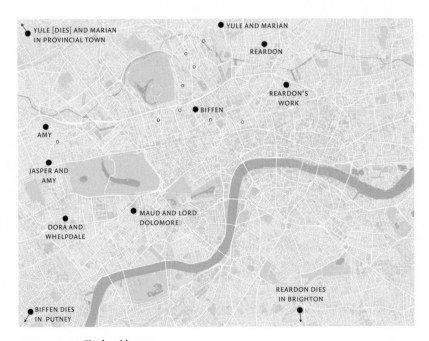

FIGURE 8.15 **Final residences**

The enduring force of attraction of the West End is still visible, at the end of the century, in Gissing's *New Grub Street* (1891). Focused on the new intellectual middle classes of North London, the initial geography of the novel stretches from the British Museum to Camden Town (**Figure 8.14**), thus remaining completely extraneous to the old east–west axis; as the story proceeds, however, this new geography disintegrates, as successful characters systematically relocate to West End addresses, whereas those who "fail" are scattered to the four winds: Biffen takes an interminable walk to commit suicide on Putney Hill; Reardon moves to Islington, works on the City Road, and dies in Brighton; Yule moves to, and then dies in an unspecified "provincial town," where Marian also ends up (**Figure 8.15**).

4. THE EMOTIONS OF LONDON?

London's historical expansion, and its fictional stability; the social mosaic of the City, and the homogeneity of the West End; *New Grub Street*, and the inflexibility of the old geography. And emotions? Where is the "geography of fear" promised in our opening section? **Figure 8.16** offers a first answer: the whiter the color (Harley Street, St. James Square, Hyde Park, Belgrave Square), the happier the passages occurring near that location; the darker the black—as at Newgate, Bedlam or the Pool of London—the more frightening the passages; while gray areas indicate those locations in which neither emotion is truly active.[9]

We will return to the association of the West End with happiness, and of (parts of) the City with fear. The most striking result of this map, though, was that so many passages turned out to be neither happy nor frightening. **Figure 8.17** highlights this fact by reorganizing the data, not

---

Figures 8.8– 8.13, the City's semantics are inevitably far less homogeneous: it includes terms that evoke threat (*death, crowd, dark*), indications of movement (*proceeded, against, front, through*), and snapshots of the urban transport system (*river, horse, train, boat*). Interestingly, both *England* and *king* are among the City's most distinctive words: possibly a sign of its acting as a symbol for the nation as a whole, in contrast to the exclusivity of *earl, park,* and *servants.*

9 The results were obtained by asking ten taggers whether a given passage was associated to fear or not, and a different group of ten whether it was associated to happiness or not; the passage would count as frightening or happy if at least five out of the ten taggers said so; otherwise, the passage would count as "neither."

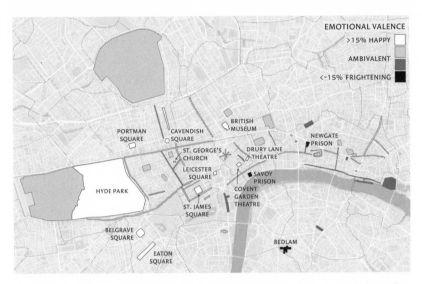

FIGURE 8.16 **The emotions of London, 1700–1900.** In this image, white is particularly prevalent in squares (the term that was also the most distinctive of the West End's lexicon), whereas passages where fear dominates are most often located in spaces of coercion and internment. Emotional valence is defined as the percentage of passage annotations per place indicating the passage associated happiness with its location, subtracted by the corresponding percentage for fear.

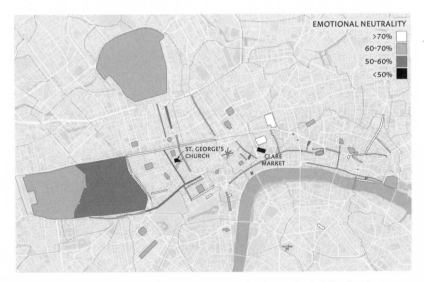

FIGURE 8.17 **Neutrality in London, 1700–1900.** Emotional neutrality is defined as the percentage of passage annotations per place indicating the passage associated neither happiness nor fear with its location.

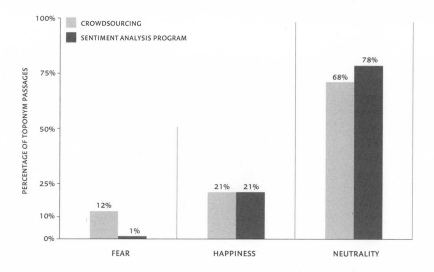

FIGURE 8.18 **Fear, happiness, neutrality**

in terms of fear *versus* happiness, but of "emotional neutrality" *versus* "emotional intensity": white indicates that emotions are absent; the two shades of gray, that they are weak; while only in the black areas is an emotional "signature" genuinely present. And the verdict is clear: ours was less a map of the emotions of London than *of their absence.* This emerged with equal clarity from both crowd-sourcing and sentiment analysis: though human taggers disagreed with our computer program about specific emotions—for the taggers, 21 percent of the passages were happy and 12 percent frightening, while the program, more intrepid, came up with 21 percent and 1 percent—they did agree that the large majority of passages was emotionally neutral: 67 percent according to crowd-sourcing, and 78 percent to sentiment analysis (**Figure 8.18**).

A map dominated by emotional neutrality. Did this mean that London novels avoided emotions? Not quite (though one does wonder what Paris novels would show). Remember: the passages on which our maps were based included the 200 words around a place-name—and place-names, as a rule, are part of the public realm. More than the emotions "of London," then, we had been measuring the emotions of London's public spaces: and if so, then the neutrality so conspicuous in **Figure 8.17** had perhaps less to do with the absence of emotions from novels, than with their silencing in the public dimension. To test this hypothesis, we took a

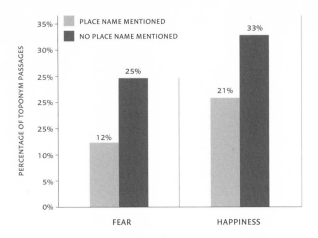

FIGURE 8.19 **Emotions in public, emotions in private**

a sample of 200-word passages *not* including place names, and asked the taggers to evaluate them. The histogram in **Figure 8.19** shows the results: if in the presence of place names, as we know from **Figure 8.18**, fear had emerged in 12 percent of the cases, and happiness in 21 percent, in their absence the frequency rose to 25 percent and 34 percent. Or in other words: when novels moved away from public geography, their emotional intensity dramatically increased.

Now, the muting of emotions in public had long been known to the sociology of bourgeois existence: from the "neutrality" of 19th-century male fashion,[10] to Georg Simmel's "blasé type"—who "experiences all things as being of an equally dull and grey hue"[11]—and the "unfocused interaction" of Erving Goffman's *Behavior in Public Places*. Our data clearly corroborated all this. But with a marked temporal discrepancy: Sennett's "neutrality"—as well as Holst Katsma's "neutralization" of novelistic loudness—had crystallized around the middle of the 19th century; Simmel's "grey hue" had emerged during the fin de siècle, and Goffman's "unfocused

---

10 "As numerous writers comment, [the clothing of the 1840s] was the beginning of a *style* of dressing in which neutrality—that is, not standing out from others—was the immediate statement." Richard Sennett, *The Fall of Public Man* (Cambridge, UK: Cambridge University Press, 1977), 161.

11 Georg Simmel, *The Philosophy of Money*, rev. ed. (London: Routledge, 1990), 256.

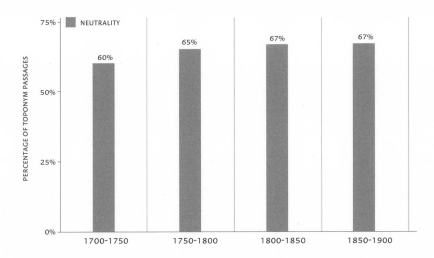

FIGURE 8.20 **The neutralization of emotions in public, 1700–1900.** Although this chart shows an increase in neutrality from 60 percent in the first half of the 18th century to 67 percent in the 19th, the transformation is much more modest than previous research would suggest.

interaction" even later. According to our findings, however, emotions in public had already been neutralized in the 18th century, and little seemed to have changed between 1700 and 1900 (**Figure 8.20**).

Interesting, when quantitative findings contradict previous research. Had we discovered in the eighteenth century a reason for the muting of emotions as strong as those associated with later periods, we would have trusted our results. *Not* having found anything of the sort, we still present them, but accompanied by a good dose of skepticism. In the next section, it will become clear why.

5. THE EMOTIONS OF LONDON

Figure 8.17 offered a synthetic overview of London's emotional temperature between 1700 and 1900; **Figure 8.21** breaks the data down into four distinct half centuries. In the first fifty years, the fear associated with Newgate, Tyburn, Bedlam, the Tower, and the Pool of London is clearly the dominant emotion in our corpus. In the following half century though, as the West End makes its appearance in the narrative geography of London, fear seems to undergo a significant decline (**Figure 8.22**).

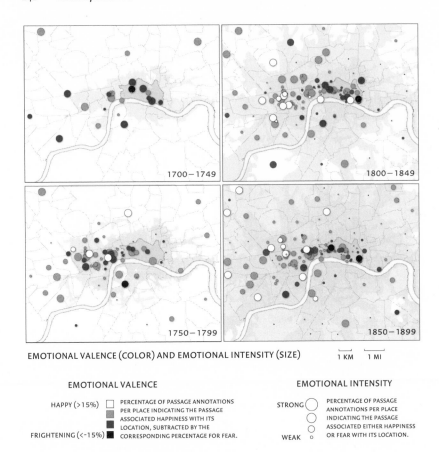

EMOTIONAL VALENCE (COLOR) AND EMOTIONAL INTENSITY (SIZE)   1 KM   1 MI

EMOTIONAL VALENCE

HAPPY (>15%) ☐   PERCENTAGE OF PASSAGE ANNOTATIONS
           ▦   PER PLACE INDICATING THE PASSAGE
                ASSOCIATED HAPPINESS WITH ITS
                LOCATION, SUBTRACTED BY THE
FRIGHTENING (<-15%) ■   CORRESPONDING PERCENTAGE FOR FEAR.

EMOTIONAL INTENSITY

STRONG ◯   PERCENTAGE OF PASSAGE
       ◯   ANNOTATIONS PER PLACE
       ◦   INDICATING THE PASSAGE
            ASSOCIATED EITHER HAPPINESS
WEAK   ·   OR FEAR WITH ITS LOCATION.

FIGURE 8.21 **The emotions of London, 1700–1900**

"Seems to"; because, if there is no doubt that "the overall reduction of fear," as Fisher puts it, has been "one of the central accomplishments of modern civilization," the key factors he singles out as causing the transformation—"night-time electrical lighting, insurance policies, police forces"—date to the middle (the police), or even the end of the 19th century (electricity and insurance): that is to say, a full hundred years later than the fall that appears in **Figure 8.22**. It's another discrepancy between quantitative and qualitative research; this time, though, we think we have found the reason. Here is the *incipit* of a forgotten Victorian novel, William North's *The Impostor* (1847):

> Midnight was at hand, as in a small ill-furnished room, above a low shop,
> in one of the dirtiest, narrowest, and most ancient looking lanes in the
> oriental moiety of the English metropolis, were seated two individuals

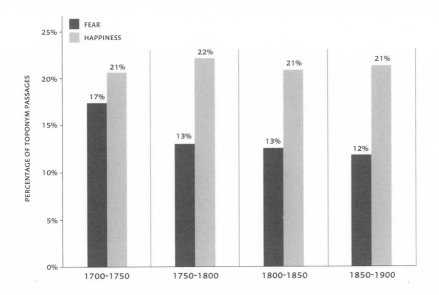

FIGURE 8.22 **The decline of fear, 1700–1900**

of the most opposite appearance conceivable. The one, an old man of
at least three score, exhibited a set of pinched up, calf-skin coloured
features in which dotage, stupidity, and cunning seemed to struggle for
the ascendancy.

"One of the dirtiest, narrowest, and most ancient looking lanes" . . . We
were measuring emotions in the proximity of London place-names—but
as this sentence proves, there can be plenty of alarming scenes that include
some form of localization, but without involving any place name at all (not
even "London"!) "A single lamp shed a sickly light on the linked and inter-
secting lanes (though lane is too lofty a word)" (Bulwer-Lytton, *Pelham*,
1828); "a maze of narrow lanes, choked up with dirt, pestiferous with nau-
seous odours, and swarming with a population . . ." (Reynolds, *The Mysteries of London*, 1845); "a bleak, dilapidated street" (Dickens, *Bleak House*,
1853). Lane, maze, street—court, row, alley, conduit, passage, byway . . . As
novelists increasingly turn to London as their fictional setting, geographical *reticence* emerges as a key ingredient of narrative fear—and one which
a Named Entity Recognition program inevitably misses: Dickens's "bleak
and dilapidated street" will not be counted as a street in the same way
as Oxford Street, and will therefore not appear in our maps and charts

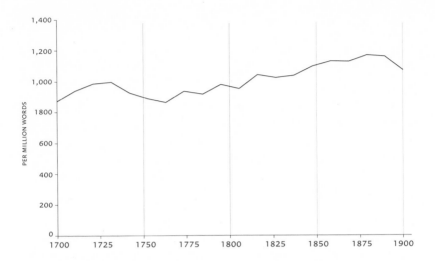

FIGURE 8.23 **"A maze of narrow lanes."** This chart shows the frequency per million words of
alley, alleyway, artery, back alley, back street, byway, conduit, dead end, drive, lane, passage, passageway, path,
place, row, thoroughfare, and *walk.* As can be seen, the presence of this group of terms increases regularly—from just over 800 to almost 1,200—between the mid-18th and the late 19th century. (The
list does not include *court,* which refers much more often to the British monarchy than to the London
equivalents of the Cour des Miracles.)

(**Figure 8.23**). And so, alongside the old threats associated with Saffron
Hill, St. Giles, Shoreditch, Smithfield, and Newgate, a new rhetoric of indi-
rection gives voice to the fact that, to quote Fisher one more time, "after
Hume and Adam Smith, the proxy for fear was *uncertainty.*" Newgate and
Bedlam are terrifying, but their nature is perfectly well-known; "a maze
of narrow lanes" evokes unfathomable horrors. "I looked round, but could
recognize nothing familiar in the narrow and filthy streets," writes the
narrator of *Pelham,* recalling his most frightening adventure: "even the
names of them were to me like an unknown language."

If the rhetoric of reticence contributed to the (apparent?) decline of
fear, the spatial clustering of happiness in the first half of the 19th century
is for its part the result of a perfectly explicit social geography. Here, as
the histogram in **Figure 8.22** showed, quantitative variation plays hardly
any role: in absolute terms, "total London happiness" (to use a Benthamite
expression) slightly contracts, compared·to the previous half century. But
it is now so concentrated in the West End that it almost isolates it from the
rest of London. And indeed, these were triumphal decades for the British

upper class: victorious on the European battlefield, unique in its world economic power, and implacable with workers at home. The erection of Regent Street (1817–23) was the monumental consecration of this state of affairs; "a boundary and complete separation," wrote its planner and architect, John Nash, "between the Streets and Squares occupied by the Nobility and the Gentry, and the narrow Streets and meaner Houses occupied by mechanics and the trading part of the community."

Perfect. Too perfect, perhaps? Is this convergence of wealth and "happiness" a product of 19th-century writers—or of 21st-century taggers? A sample of 200 passages tagged as happy—half of them taken from the entire period, and the other half from 1800–50—suggests that what was routinely recognized as "happiness" (more often by the "sentiment analysis" program trained on the *Wall Street Journal* than by human taggers, in fact) had indeed more to do with social well-being than with a specific type of emotion. This said, a comparison of the two sets of passages also showed that the 19th century had introduced some major changes in the affective tonality of such "well-being." The widespread "benevolence" of the previous century, for instance, with its strong inter-generational axis (from a parent, or an older mentor, to a child or ward), was replaced by the horizontal "affection" between young persons of the same age: lovers, of course, but also friends, siblings (especially sisters) and cousins. Even more dramatic was the contraction of the "pleasure" cluster, which used to range from the delight in scenery and people to the enjoyment of food, drink and loud (and vulgar) amusement. In the early 19th century, this pursuit of immediate satisfaction was both transmuted into a more sedate "worldliness," and spatially relocated: if "pleasure" could be found just about everywhere, "affection" and "worldliness" were now strictly concentrated in the West End. As has often been the case in history, the "refinement" of a ruling-class culture entailed its withdrawal into an exclusive enclave, where the semantics of space would coincide more and more with the semantics of class.

With the association of fear with a geography of the unknown, and of "happiness" with upper-class well-being, our research had reached a natural, if somewhat oblique, conclusion. And as the project was winding down, a long discussion with Matthew Wilkens—who had come to the Literary Lab to present his work on space in American literature—prompted us to a final, critical reexamination of the very idea of "narrative geography."

6. ON THE CONCEPT OF "NARRATIVE GEOGRAPHY"

So far, we have assumed that, when topographical indications appear in a novel, they always play more or less the same role. Our discussion with Wilkens made us reconsider this idea, and we decided to extract a sample of 200 passages to see how exactly place-names functioned within a story. Nearly half of the cases were perfectly straightforward: they indicated the setting of the ongoing action. Here are a few examples:

> And as soon as the stage in which he traveled reached **Westminster Bridge**, he got into an hackney-coach, and ordered it to be driven to the house of Mr Woodford.

> Shortly after they had gone away for the first time, one of the scouts came running in with the news that they had stopped before Lord Mansfield's house in **Bloomsbury Square**.

> Past Battersea Park, over Chelsea Bridge, then the weary stretch to Victoria Station, and the upward labour to **Charing Cross**. Five miles, at least, measured by pavement. But Virginia walked quickly . . .

> He was conducted first before the Privy Council, and afterwards to the Horse Guards, and then was taken by way of **Westminster Bridge**, and back over London Bridge—for the purpose of avoiding the main streets—to the Tower, under the strongest guard ever known to enter its gates with a single prisoner.

A character "taken by way of Westminster Bridge, and back over London Bridge": exactly the kind of direct information we had half-unconsciously expected to find. But this was not the whole story. In about one fourth of the cases, place names indicated, not the setting of the current action, but events that had occurred in the past (as in the first two passages below), or were expected to occur in the near future (third and fourth passage):

> They were married at **the Savoy**, and my grandfather dying very soon, Harry Barry, Esquire, took possession of his paternal property and supported our illustrious name with credit in London.

> Whereas a young boy, named Oliver Twist, absconded, or was enticed, on Thursday evening last, from his home at **Pentonville**, and has not since been heard of . . .

> "Though I should accompany you tomorrow, Madam," said she, "I shall have time sufficient for my walk to **Norwood**. The preparations for my journey cannot occupy an hour . . ."

> The letter of which he had spoken reached Monica's hands next morning. It was a very respectful invitation to accompany the writer on a drive in **Surrey**.

Around this basic asymmetry—present *versus* past/future—other differences crystallized. Current action was usually conveyed by an impersonal third-person narrator ("He was conducted first before the Privy Council"); references to past and future were more likely to occur in dialogue ("Though I should accompany you tomorrow"). The first group's most distinctive words had a clear spatial dominant: verbs of movement (*conducted, reached, followed, entered*), spatial nouns (*walls, churchyard, gate, window*), descriptive adjectives (*narrow, dark, melancholy, strong*), plus indications of social intercourse (*confidence, respect, invited, announced, attended*). In the second group, aside from dialogic markers (*speaking, replied, exclaimed*) and the contractions typical of colloquial style (*he's, can't, wouldn't*), we found a strong hypothetical register (*imagine, suppose, think, somewhere*), plus an odd financial fixation (*notes, bill/s, pounds, capital, trade, property*). And as if these differences weren't enough, a *third* group of place-names emerged, which had to do neither with the present, nor with the past or future of the story. Here are a few examples:

> "Look at the list of Directors. We've three members of Parliament, a baronet, and one or two City names that are as good—as good as the **Bank of England**. If that prospectus won't make a man confident."

> In the most careless, good-humoured way, he loses a few points; and still feels thirsty, and loses a few more points; and, like a man of spirit, increases his stakes, to be sure, and just by that walk down **Regent Street** is ruined for life.

Having concluded his observations upon the soup, Mr Osborne made
a few curt remarks respecting the fish, also of a savage and satirical
tendency, and cursed **Billingsgate** with an emphasis quite worthy of
the place.

We traced her to her new address; and we got a man from **Scotland Yard**,
who was certain to know her, if our own man's idea was the right one.
The man from Scotland Yard turned milliner's lad for the occasion, and
took her gown home.

Mrs Honeyman sternly gave warning to these idolaters. She would have
no Jesuits in her premises. She showed Hannah the picture in Howell's
Medulla of the martyrs burning at **Smithfield**: who said, "Lord bless you,
mum," and hoped it was a long time ago.

If the first two groups of passages had presented London as the space
of enigmatic private trajectories—"Whereas a young boy, named Oliver
Twist, absconded, or was enticed . . ."—this third group had a public and
almost *normative* ring: it implied that everyone knows (or should know)
what the Bank of England, Billingsgate and Scotland Yard stand for. Its
locations played no role in the narrative proper, but acted as so many sign-
posts in what we could call "the discourse of London": a small ideological
compendium of the British capital.

Three narrative geographies, then: the sharp, active foreground of
current events; the hazier, subjective background of the narrated world;
and the impersonal layer of a quasi-normative discourse (**Figure 8.24**).
The data are then rearranged in **Figure 8.25**, to show the elective affinities
between the three geographies and the social configuration of London.
Given that only 200 passages were examined, future research may significantly correct these initial figures, just as specific genres may show a
preference for one or the other of these spatio-temporal systems. It would
make sense, for instance, if adventure stories maximized the role of the
foreground, naturalist novels of the background, and essayistic writings of
"quasi-normative" toponyms.

As is often the case with our work at the Lab, the initial idea—quantifying and mapping novelistic emotions—turned out to be neither easy,
nor particularly satisfying: in the end, the map of the emotions of London

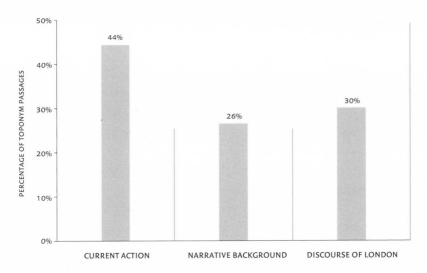

FIGURE 8.24 **Three narrative geographies**

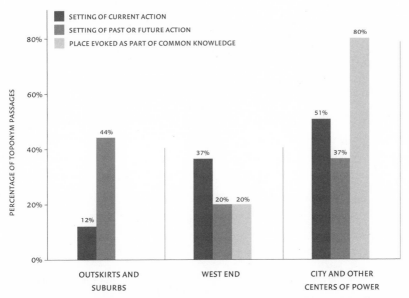

FIGURE 8.25 **Narrative geographies and urban structure.** Current action is typically associated with the West End (37 percent of the cases), and with the composite space of the City and other
centers of power (51 percent), while the outskirts of London appear in a mere 12 percent of the cases.
When we turn from foreground to background, however, the picture reverses itself: districts and villages around London are mentioned in 44 percent of the cases, while the presence of the West End
is halved (from 37 to 20 percent). Finally, the outskirts are completely absent from the "discourse of
London," 80 percent of which is divided into four main clusters: financial and political power (the
Bank of England, Westminster), trade (Cornhill, Smithfield, Billingsgate), the law (the Temple, Chan-
cery, Newgate), and history (Old London Bridge, Whitehall, Buckingham Palace).

was only partially accomplished. But in pursuing this objective, we found empirical evidence that supported existing theories about emotions in public; we showed how established narratological polarities (foreground/ background, story/discourse) preside, not only over the temporality of narrative, but over its geography as well; and we discovered a striking discrepancy between real and fictional geography, while also sketching the first lineaments for a future "semantics of space." Corroboration, improvement, and discovery: the three axes which have defined the variable relationship between quantitative literary research and existing scholarship. Corroboration, improvement, and discovery. Eventually, the day for theory-building will also come.

2016

PART

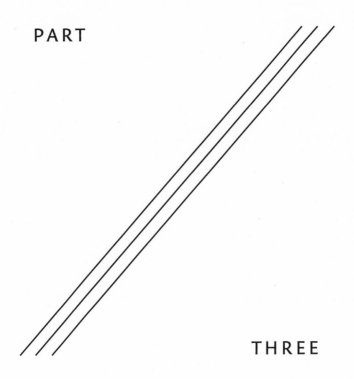

THREE

CHAPTER 9

Canon/Archive

LARGE-SCALE DYNAMICS IN THE LITERARY FIELD

Mark Algee-Hewitt, Sarah Allison, Marissa Gemma,
Ryan Heuser, Franco Moretti, Hannah Walser

1. SOCIOLOGICAL METRICS

A. DOWRY AND VEGETABLES

Of the novelties introduced by digitization in the study of literature, the size of the archive is probably the most dramatic: we used to work on a couple of hundred 19th-century novels, and now we can analyze thousands of them, tens of thousands, tomorrow hundreds of thousands. It's a moment of euphoria, for quantitative literary history: like having a telescope that makes you see entirely new galaxies. And it's a moment of truth: so, have the digital skies revealed anything that changes our knowledge of literature?

This is not a rhetorical question. In the famous 1958 essay in which he hailed "the advent of a quantitative history" that would "break with the traditional forms of nineteenth-century history," Fernand Braudel mentioned as its typical materials "demographic progression, the movement of wages, the variations in interest rates ... productivity ... money supply."[1] These were all quantifiable entities, clearly enough; but they were also *completely new objects* compared to the study of legislation, military campaigns, political cabinets, diplomacy, and so on. It was this *double* shift that changed the practice of history; not quantification alone. In our case, though, there is no shift in materials: we may end up studying two hundred

---

1 Fernand Braudel, "History and the Social Sciences: The *Longue Durée*," in *On History*, trans. Sarah Matthews (Chicago: University of Chicago Press, 1980), 29.

thousand novels instead of two hundred; but, they're all still novels. Where exactly is the novelty?

One hundred and ninety-nine thousand books that no one has ever studied—runs the typical answer—how could there *not* be novelties? It's a whole new dimension of literary history. "We know more about people exchanging goods for reasons of prestige than about the kinds of exchanges that go on every day," wrote André Leroi-Gourhan in *Gesture and Speech*, a few years after Braudel; "more about the circulation of dowry money than about selling vegetables."[2] Dowry and vegetables: perfect antithesis. Both are important, but for opposite reasons: dowry, because it happens once in a lifetime; vegetables, because we eat them every day. And at first sight, it seems like the perfect parallel for the 200 and the 200,000 novels. But as soon as we start looking deeper into the matter, complications arise. Take two historical novels published in the same year of 1814: Walter Scott's *Waverley*, and James Brewer's *Sir Ferdinand of England*. Intuitively, one would associate *Waverley* with the prestige of the dowry, and *Sir Ferdinand* with the humble role of chicory. In fact, though, Scott's novel was both a great formal breakthrough, and the book everybody was reading all over Europe: dowry and vegetables, rolled into one. But if that is the case, what difference can all the Sir Ferdinands of the digital archive make? We used to know nothing about them, and now we know something. Good. Does this knowledge also make a difference?[3]

---

2 André Leroi-Gourhan, *Gesture and Speech*, trans. Anna Bostock Berger (Cambridge, MA: MIT Press, 1993), 148.

3 It might not. James English has convincingly argued that a "a sample gathered on the principle that every individual work of new fiction must hold equal value in the analysis"—that is to say, a sample very similar to our "archive"—is actually not very "suitable for a sociology of literary production, where 'production' is understood to mean not merely (or even primarily) the production of certain kinds of texts by authors but the production of certain kinds of value by a social system, whose agents include readers, reviewers, editors and booksellers, professors and teachers, and all the many moving pieces of literature's institutional apparatus." (James English, "Now, Not Now: Counting Time in Contemporary Fiction Studies," *Modern Language Quarterly* 77, no. 3 (September 2016): 403.) The fact that, when the present chapter turned to the study of the archive, it ended up focusing almost exclusively on the "production of certain kinds of texts" seems clearly to corroborate English's thesis. On the other hand, in so far as a "social system" creates "value" not only by assigning it to certain authors or texts but also by denying it to others ("In matters of taste, more than anywhere else, all determination is negation; and tastes are perhaps first and foremost distastes": Pierre Bourdieu, *Distinction: A Social Critique of the Judgement of Taste*, trans. Richard Nice (Cambridge, MA: Harvard University Press, 1979), 56), readers and the rest of "literature's institutional apparatus" are present in our narrative—but always and only with a destructive role.

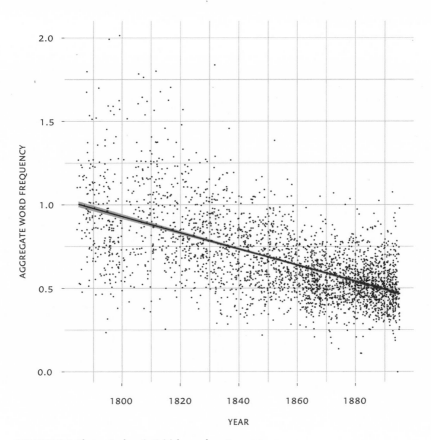

FIGURE 9.1 **Abstract values in British novels, 1785–1900**

Let us illustrate the problem with one of the findings from our own research: the decline of the semantic field of "abstract values"—words like *modesty, respect, virtue,* and so on—described in chapter 6 (**Figure 9.1**). Ryan Heuser and Long Le-Khac saw the width of the archive as a crucial aspect of their research. Had they studied the old, narrower canon instead, would their results have changed? **Figure 9.2** provides the answer: no. The canon precedes the archive by about fifteen to twenty years; but the historical trajectory is the same.

This does not mean that the new archive contains no new information; it means, however, that we must still learn to ask the right type of questions. But before doing so, something needs to be clarified. Canon and archive: what do we mean by these two words?

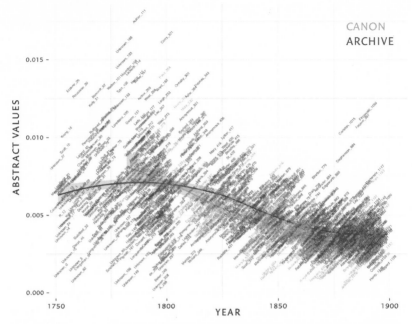

FIGURE 9.2 **Abstract values, canon, and archive in British novels, 1750–1900.** In this figure, the canon consists of the 250 novels originally included in the Chadwyck-Healey 19th-Century Fiction Collection.

B. BIAS IN THE ARCHIVE

Let's begin with three preliminary notions: the published, the archive, and the corpus. The first is simple: it's the totality of the books that have been published (the plays that have been acted, the poems that have been recited, and so on). This literature that has become "public" is the fundamental horizon of all quantitative work (though of course its borders are fuzzy, and may be expanded to include books written but kept in a drawer, or rejected by publishers, etc.). The archive is for its part that portion of published literature that has been preserved—in libraries and elsewhere—and that is now being increasingly digitized. The corpus, finally, is that portion of the archive that is selected, for one reason or another, in order to pursue a specific research project. The corpus is thus smaller than the archive, which is smaller than the published: like three Russian dolls, fitting neatly into one another. But with digital technology, the relationship between the three layers has changed: the corpus of a project can now easily be (almost) as large as the archive, while the archive is itself becoming—at least for modern times—(almost) as large as all of published literature. When we use the term "archive," what we have in mind is precisely this potential convergence of the three layers into one; into that "total history of litera-ture," to borrow an expression from the *Annales*, that used to be a mirage, and may soon be reality.

This, in theory. In practice, things are not so simple. Take the present project. Its initial corpus consisted of about four thousand English novels from 1750 to 1880; for the 18th century, they came from ECCO; for the 19th, from the Chadwyck-Healey Nineteenth-Century Fiction corpus and the Internet Archive of the University of Illinois.[4] By the old standards of liter-ary history, four thousand novels were a very large corpus; but its actual coverage turned out to be quite uneven. For the period 1770–1830, for instance, we had about one third of the titles listed in the Raven-Garside-Schöwerling bibliography; for the later 19th century, however, the percent-age was much lower, around 10 percent. The same for specific genres: we held 96 percent of Alison Adburgham's silver-fork bibliography, but only 77 percent of Catherine Gallagher's industrial novels, 53 percent of Anne H. Stevens's historical novels before Scott, and 35 percent of Federica Per-azzini's gothic bibliography.[5]

Clearly, these were slippery statistical grounds. Compared to the handful of texts usually considered canonical, our 190 gothic novels were a very large number, and it was tempting to identify them with the archive *tout court*; but were they truly representative of the "population" of the English gothic as a whole? Almost certainly not; simplifying somewhat, a sample is representative when it has been randomly chosen from a given population; but our 190 novels had definitely *not* been chosen that way. Ultimately, they all came from a few great libraries—and libraries don't

---

4 See https://archive.org/details/19thcennov. ECCO (Eighteenth Century Collections Online) is a two-part digital collection of 18th-century materials, based on the English Short Title Catalogue (ESTC), and sourced from a number of libraries in the US and UK; part II of ECCO is an update, consisting of texts or editions that were not available when the original ECCO was released.

5 Alison Adburgham, *Silver Fork Society: Fashionable Life and Literature from 1814 to 1840* (London: Constable, 1983); Catherine Gallagher, *The Industrial Reformation of English Fiction: Social Discourse and Narrative Form, 1832–1867* (Chicago: University of Chicago Press, 1985); Anne H. Stevens, *British Historical Fiction Before Scott* (Basingstoke: Palgrave Macmillan, 2010); Federica Perazzini, *Il Gotico @ Distanza* (Rome: Edizioni Nuova Cultura, 2013).

buy books in order to have representative samples; they want books they consider worth preserving. *Good* books; good, according to principles that are likely to be similar to those that lead to the formation of canons. Though our corpus was twenty times larger than the traditional canon, then, it was perfectly possible that its principle of selection *would make it resemble the canon much more than the archive as a whole.* That was the problem.[6]

We wanted our results to be reliable, hence we generated a random sample of the field to be studied: 507 novels tout court for the period 1750–1836, 82 gothic novels, and 85 historical novels before Scott.[7] All in all, 674 novels. In the digital age, this wouldn't take long.

We generated the sample at the end of the school year, in June 2014. Then we turned to our own database, where we found 35 of the 82 gothic novels, 35 of the 85 historical novels, and 145 of the 507 novels from the Raven-Garside bibliographies. In early July, we passed the list of the titles we had not found—roughly 460—to Glen Worthey and Rebecca Wingfield, at the Stanford Libraries, who promptly disentangled it into a few major bundles. Around 300 texts were held (in more or less equal parts) by HathiTrust and by Gale (through NCCO and ECCO II).[8] Another 30 were in collected works, in alternate editions, concealed by slightly different

---

6 To complicate matters further, different genres have different canon-to-archive ratios: whereas epistolary and silver-fork novels have relatively large archives and small canons, the opposite is true of the industrial novel and the bildungsroman, both of which attracted many major Victorian writers; while the two super-genres of gothic and historical novels lie somewhere in between the two extremes. On this—and much else—we need a lot more empirical evidence.

7 This last group was not a random sample: since Anne Stevens's bibliography included only eighty-five pre-Scott historical novels, we decided to look for all of them.

8 HathiTrust is a partnership of major research libraries, which serves as a repository for digital collections; these include volumes scanned as part of the Google project and the Internet Archive, as well as other smaller local projects. Gale's NCCO (Nineteenth Century Collections Online) is a digital collection of 19th-century materials, usually sourced from major collections, and ranging across disciplines (literature, science and technology, photography, etc.). Thus far, there are twelve parts to NCCO, one of which consists of the Corvey novel collection; unlike ECCO, NCCO is not based on a standard bibliography in the field, so it's hard to predict what is being added.

Gale is a large conglomerate of information and education services—run as a for-profit business—that sells content and services to libraries; it publishes both print works (reference and fiction) and electronic collections (ECCO, NCCO, and others). Its parent company is Cengage Learning, which defines itself as "a leading educational content, technology, and services company for the higher education and K–12, professional and library markets worldwide."

titles, in microfiche or microfilm collections, etc.; about 100 existed only
in print, and of 10 novels there were no known extant copies. In August,
requests were sent to Hathi and Gale—with both of which Stanford has
a long-standing financial agreement—for their 300 volumes. Of the 100
novels existing only in print, about half were held by the British Library, in
London, which a few months earlier had kindly offered the Literary Lab a
collection of 65,000 digitized volumes from its collections; unfortunately,
none of the books we were looking for was there. The special collections
at UCLA and Harvard, which held about 50 of the books, sent us a series
of estimates that ranged (depending, quite reasonably, on the conditions of
the original, and on photographic requirements which could be very labor-
intensive) from $1,000 to $20,000 per novel; finally, 6 novels were part of
larger collections held by ProQuest, and would have cost us—despite Pro-
Quest's very generous 50 percent discount—$147,000, or $25,000 per title.[9]

Remember: this was a search involving many excellent librarians in
London, Cambridge, Los Angeles, and of course at Stanford; a half dozen
researchers at the Literary Lab; plus people at Hathi, Gale, and so on. The
books we were looking for were only two centuries old; they had had print
runs of at least 750–1,000 copies, and in a part of the world that, at the time,
already possessed efficient libraries. The Literary Lab has some money
for research (though, make no mistake, not *that* kind of money). In other
words, one could hardly hope for better resources. And yet it took about
six months to receive from Hathi and Gale the set of texts that should have
allowed us to move from the initial 30 percent to around 70–80 percent
of the random sample:[10] a figure which would probably make many of our

---

9 To these figures one should add what the Stanford libraries have paid for ECCO, ECCO II, and NCCO
to begin with: with the usual generous discounts, something like $1 million for the three collections.
ProQuest is another for-profit education service whose products include the Historical Newspapers
series, Literature Online, Dissertation Abstracts, and others. Its parent company is Cambridge Information Group.

10 "*Should* have allowed," because receiving a text from these collections is not the same as being able
to work on it. Much of the data from Chadwyck-Healey and ECCO I used to be delivered on tape, in for-
mats requiring drives that are both hard to find and difficult to use; more "convenient" data deliveries
(such as network data transfer, or on external hard drive) have their own problems, ranging from the
vagaries of mail systems to bizarre firewall incompatibilities and odd documentary requirements of
usage agreements. (Most of Stanford libraries' licensing agreements, for instance, used to be quite
vague on the subject of text-mining, or sharing outside the Library preservation structures; over the
past five years libraries have explicitly insisted on the inclusion of text-mining rights in current licenses,
but previous agreements remain in a gray area.)

findings questionable, as the missing 20–30 percent would be, almost by definition, furthest from all conceivable forms of canonization.

Clearly, the idea that digitization has made everything available and cheap—let alone "free"—is a myth. As we became slowly aware of this fact, we decided to start working with a selection from the corpus we had: a database of 1,117 works, 263 from Chadwyck-Healey, and 854 from various archival sources. Initial results took us quickly in one direction; new findings added further momentum; and, by the time the (near-)random sample was (almost-)available, we were too involved in the work to restart from zero. We don't present this as an ideal model of research, and are aware that our results are weaker as a consequence of our decision. But collective work, especially when conducted in a sort of "interstitial" institutional space—as ours still is—has its own temporality: waiting months and months before research can begin would kill any project. Maybe in the future we will send out a scout, a year in advance, in search of the sample. Or maybe we will keep working with what we have, acknowledging the limits and flaws of our data. Dirty hands are better than empty.

C. FROM THE CANON TO THE LITERARY FIELD

If the selection of our archive was determined by historical library practices (which novels were on the shelves? which were easy to digitize?), that of our canon was a matter of critical judgment—though not our own. The first canon we turned to in this project was the Chadwyck-Healey

---

Finally, extracting data from an ocean of tape or hard drive, with insufficient or incorrect metadata and no database to assist, is a truly Byzantine process. The Libraries would search the ECCO database—for instance—using Gale's search interface, and citing its URL as that interface instructs. But for the Libraries to get a raw file to the Lab, they need to go through a couple of hard drives (or tapes) containing hundreds of thousands of directories named only with series of random numbers; the metadata "manifest" that Gale delivers with these raw files is contained in about ten Microsoft Word files formatted as if for print: two columns, authors in bold, very basic catalog data, a document ID, and ESTC ID, and a directory path. These documents are immense: ECCO II, Literature and Language module, Authors L–Z—which represents about one tenth of the ECCO II delivery—is a 2,750-page document. Second, the ID numbers included are *not* the ones that you see in the Gale interface; they are internal, invisible numbers. So, despite all the Lab's work in identifying ECCO sources using the database and noting the official Gale ID number, the Libraries have had to re-search each item by author or title in order to find the name of a file to copy: that Gale ID number is not included *at all* in the file manifest. "My lesson," concluded a research librarian who assisted through the whole process, "is this: even when we've found the file you need, we still haven't really *found* the file."

Nineteenth-Century Fiction Collection, designed by an editorial board of two, Danny Karlin and Tom Keymer.[11]

Compiled in the late 1990s, with new novels added subsequently, the marketing materials of the Nineteenth-Century Fiction Collection claim that it "represents the great achievements of the Victorian canon and reflects the landmarks of the period," while also covering "many neglected or little-known works, most of them out of print or difficult to find." From 1794, for example, the collection includes Ann Radcliffe's *Mysteries of Udolpho* and William Godwin's *Caleb Williams*, but also Jane Austen's *Lady Susan* (a very short novel probably written around then, but published posthumously in 1871), and Thomas Holcroft's radical *Adventures of Hugh Trevor*. The first two are obvious choices; the other two less so. It seems that selecting 250 texts makes room for lesser-known novels of critical or historical importance: not only the six major Austen novels, but also *Lady Susan*; not only Godwin, but also Holcroft. In so far as we understand a "canon" to signal a relatively small number of texts selected and consecrated for close study, Chadwyck-Healey—a major searchable collection immediately available to researchers today[12]—is not a bad proxy.

Still, a proxy it is; and we realized that relying on a single source was the wrong way to think about such a many-sided and elusive concept as that of the canon. In a 2015 Literary Lab pamphlet called "Between Canon and Corpus: Six Perspectives on 20th-Century Novels," Mark Algee-Hewitt and Mark McGurl had addressed a similar problem by presenting several lists of "best 20th-century novels" selected by very different groups, and then analyzing their varying degrees of proximity. We followed a different path, which led us from Chadwyck-Healey's short catalogue of books to two long lists of authors: those mentioned by the *Dictionary of National Biography*, and those listed as "primary subject author" for 20th-century academic articles indexed by the MLA Bibliography; in a lateral project, we also added the texts included in the Stanford PhD exam lists of the last thirty years. In doing so, we were neither looking for the "right" definition of the canon (which none of them was), nor hoping that the *DNB*, MLA,

---

11 Personal communication with Steven Hall confirmed that the editors were unconstrained in their choice of texts.

12 Provided, that is, that said researchers belong to an institution with the necessary resources. According to one university's ProQuest representative, in the entire world there are only "over 600" universities which subscribe to the Literature Online (LION) database.

and Stanford would agree with each other (which they didn't).[13] Rather, these different measurements were meant to replicate the multiple aspects of the idea of the canon: the fact that the national culture (*DNB*) defines it in one way, and international scholarship (MLA) in a somewhat different one; that it may be conceived of as a series of personalities (*DNB* and MLA), or as a collection of texts (PhD lists). The specific choices remained questionable—of course!—but the criteria that we had followed would be multiple, explicit, and measurable. That was the novelty.

Then, we realized that there were other features of the novelistic field that could enter the equation. In their bibliographies, Raven and Garside had for instance identified the novels that had been reprinted in the British Isles, or translated into French and German between 1770 and 1830; and one could envisage similar data for future research—from print runs to presence in circulating libraries and more. In these cases, too, the criteria would be multiple, explicit, and measurable; but with a major difference from the *DNB* and MLA. Reprints and translations measure the appeal of novels for a "general" audience, and through the institutions of the literary market; *DNB* and MLA focus on "specialized" readers, and institutions of higher education. One measures the "popularity" of novels; the other, their "prestige."[14]

---

13 Even leaving aside the representativeness of the Stanford PhD exams, the author-centered approach of the *DNB* and MLA places Scott's *Castle Dangerous*, or Thackeray's *Catherine*, on the same plane as *Waverley* and *Vanity Fair*, which cannot be right. But alternative criteria have similar flaws, or are impossibly time-consuming.

14 That popularity is measured on 19th-century data, and prestige is derived from 20th-century sources, is of course a problem. Twentieth-century studies have it better in this respect: in "Becoming Yourself: The Afterlife of Reception" (*Pamphlets of the Stanford Literary Lab* 3, 2011), for instance, Ed Finn charted the position of contemporary authors in the American literary field by using two categories—"consumption" and "conversation"—that belonged to the same chronological frame: "consumption" derived from Amazon.com "also bought" data, and "conversation" from contemporary reviews. Interestingly, "consumption" and "conversation" align rather well with our "popularity" and "prestige"; while the six "canons" discussed by Algee-Hewitt and McGurl also gravitate around market success on one side, and more "qualified" cultural selection on the other.

In an attempt to correct the discrepancy between 19th- and 20th-century data, follow-up studies may enlarge the prestige metrics by taking into account textbooks and anthologies for the school (as Martine Jey is doing for France), prizes (James English, *The Economy of Prestige: Prizes, Awards, and the Circulation of Cultural Value* (Cambridge, MA: Harvard University Press, 2005)), reviews from 18th- and 19th-century periodicals, or early collections of novels such as Barbauld's, Ballantyne's, and Bentley's. It is by no means certain, however, that collections and reviews should be seen as indicators of prestige, rather than as mere cogs in the developing novelistic market; in an interesting recent essay, Michael

Popularity and prestige. With this conceptual pair, our research found itself on the same terrain as Bourdieu's pathbreaking chart of the French literary field (**Figure 9.3**). By placing popularity data on the horizontal ("high/low economic profits") axis, and prestige ones along the vertical ("high/low consecration") one, we could provide a "British" version of Bourdieu's chart. For now, this covered only a single genre, and a handful of decades; but at this point, an empirical cartography of the literary field was no longer a daydream (**Figure 9.4**).

In **Figure 9.4**, all data are dwarfed by Walter Scott's incredible scores: only two novelists are slightly higher than him on the prestige axis (Goethe and Austen), and no one is even close in terms of popularity: the next author along that axis—Thomas Day, author of the Rousseauian best seller *The History of Sandford and Merton* (1789)—is seven standard deviations below Scott.[15] Once the out-of-scale results of "the author of *Waverley*" are removed from the picture, however, a tripartition of the British novel becomes clearly visible (**Figure 9.5**).

Let's begin with the group near the horizontal axis: writers with high popularity scores—five, eight, ten, thirteen standard deviations above the

---

Gamer has made a case for both possibilities, by presenting them as having canonical ambitions, while also competing in the commercial market. (See "A Select Collection: Barbauld, Scott, and the Rise of the (Reprinted) Novel," in *Recognizing the Romantic Novel: New Histories of British Fiction, 1780–1830*, ed. Jillian Heydt-Stevenson and Charlotte Sussman (Liverpool: Liverpool University Press, 2008), 155–191). William St Clair, for his part, has expressed unambiguous skepticism about the role of reviews ("In general . . . the influence of the reviews appears to have been greatly exaggerated both at the time and by subsequent writers. . . . I can discern no correlation between reviews, reputations, and sales"), and about the concept of novelistic prestige in the early 19th century: "As far as the prose fiction of the romantic period is concerned, there was no recognised contemporary canon. Indeed, the whole notion of a canon made little sense when most novels were published anonymously. One author dominated the age, 'the author of *Waverley*', not publicly acknowledged to be the famous poet Sir Walter Scott until the mid 1820s." See William St Clair, *The Reading Nation in the Romantic Period* (Cambridge, UK: Cambridge University Press, 2004), 189, 219–220.

On the other hand, the existence of a relationship between reviews and reputation has been recently—and convincingly—proposed by Ted Underwood and Jordan Sellers in "How Quickly Do Literary Standards Change?" (*figshare*, https://doi.org/10.6084/m9.figshare.1418394.v1). Underwood and Sellers study poetry instead of novels, and start their investigation in 1820, when St Clair's book and our own corpus more or less end; too much of a mismatch in object and time frame for a direct comparison. But we are slowly approaching the moment when evidence from independent studies may be successfully compared and integrated.

15 Since we are not measuring print runs, the chart actually understates Scott's popularity: whereas most contemporary novels had a first run of one thousand copies, the first three *Waverley* novels had opening runs of six thousand, eight thousand, and ten thousand respectively.

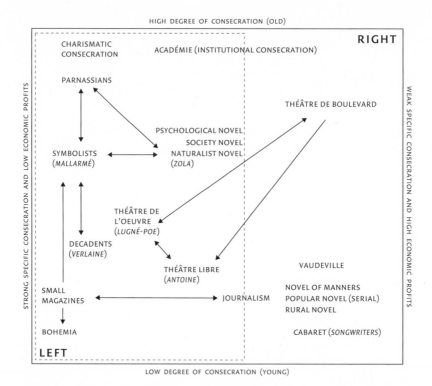

HIGH DEGREE OF CONSECRATION (OLD)

RIGHT

CHARISMATIC
CONSECRATION

ACADÉMIE (INSTITUTIONAL CONSECRATION)

PARNASSIANS

THÉÂTRE DE BOULEVARD

PSYCHOLOGICAL NOVEL
SOCIETY NOVEL

SYMBOLISTS
(MALLARMÉ)

NATURALIST NOVEL
(ZOLA)

THÉÂTRE DE
L'OEUVRE
(LUGNÉ-POE)

DECADENTS
(VERLAINE)

THÉÂTRE LIBRE
(ANTOINE)

VAUDEVILLE

SMALL
MAGAZINES

JOURNALISM

NOVEL OF MANNERS
POPULAR NOVEL (SERIAL)
RURAL NOVEL

BOHEMIA

CABARET (SONGWRITERS)

LEFT

STRONG SPECIFIC CONSECRATION AND LOW ECONOMIC PROFITS

WEAK SPECIFIC CONSECRATION AND HIGH ECONOMIC PROFITS

LOW DEGREE OF CONSECRATION (YOUNG)

FIGURE 9.3 **The French literary field at the end of the 19th century.** Bourdieu's diagram of the literary field, though wonderfully suggestive, offers no empirical evidence for the specific position of the various genres and movements. The absence of explicit and measurable criteria is probably the reason why—despite its elegance, and its wide influence—Bourdieu's chart has never become a genuine research tool, replicated and adapted by other scholars. The hard-to-believe regularity of the distribution, so unlike those of **Figures 9.4** and **9.5**, and of Bourdieu's own diagrams in *Distinction*, is itself probably a consequence of the speculative foundation of the diagram. Pierre Bourdieu, *The Rules of Art: Genesis and Structure of the Literary Field*, trans. Susan Emanuel (Stanford: Stanford University Press, 1996), 122.

average—but quite low on prestige; at most a couple of standard deviations, but often just one, or less. Here we find Henry Mackenzie's sentimental *Man of Feeling* and Day's educational best seller; the gothic cohort, with their frequent sentimental overtones (Radcliffe, Clara Reeve, Regina Maria Roche, Elizabeth Helme, Charles Maturin), Jacobin and anti-Jacobin novels (Charlotte Smith, Amelia Opie), national tales (Maria Edgeworth; Sydney Owenson, Lady Morgan), and the new hegemonic form of the historical novel (John Galt; Stéphanie Félicité, comtesse de Genlis; Horace Smith; Jane Porter; James Fenimore Cooper). We could call this the space of genre, in the sense of *all* genres: "the" novel unfolding as a family of distinct

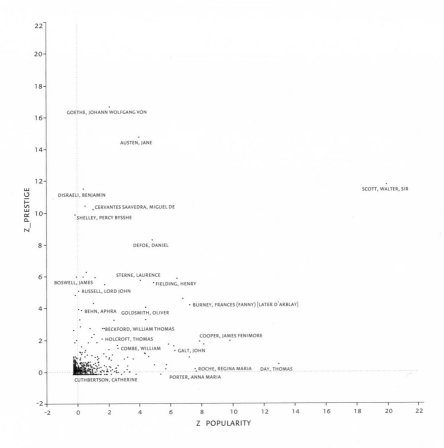

FIGURE 9.4 The British novelistic field, 1770–1830. Results for the popularity axis are based on the number of reprints (in the British Isles) and of translations (into French and German); for the prestige axis, they are based on the number of mentions as "primary subject author" in the MLA Bibliography, and on the length of *DNB* entries.

The position of writers is determined by the number of standard deviations above the mean of the field; John Galt, for instance, is 7.5 standard deviations above the mean on the popularity axis, and one above the mean on the prestige axis; at the opposite extreme, Percy Shelley is ten standard deviations above the mean in terms of prestige, but slightly below the field's mean in terms of popularity.

forms, whose easily recognizable conventions pave the way to market success. *Waverley*'s opening chapter, entirely devoted to generic allusions in titles, is the perfect symptom of this state of affairs.

Moving "up" from this region to the central part of the diagram takes us into very different territory. If one is ever justified in simply saying, "Here is the canon," this must be the case: Daniel Defoe, Samuel

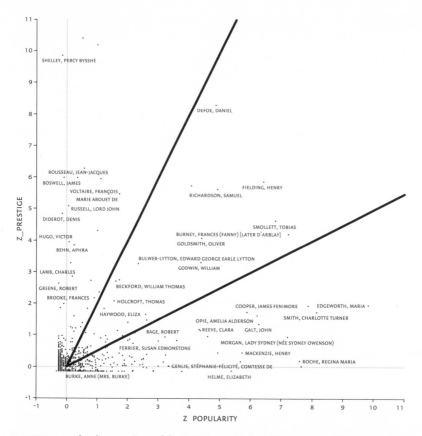

FIGURE 9.5 The three regions of the British novelistic field, 1770–1830. The three regions of this diagram express variable relationships between popularity and prestige. The area near the vertical axis has prestige scores at least twice as high as the scores for popularity; the area near the horizontal axis is its mirror image, with popularity at least twice as high as prestige; while in the central area the two sets of measurements tend to balance each other.

A study of popularity and prestige on a much larger time-scale is currently in progress at the Literary Lab, directed by J.D. Porter, with data collected both algorithmically and by a team of undergraduate researchers led by Micah Siegel.

Richardson, Henry Fielding, Laurence Sterne, Oliver Goldsmith, Tobias Smollett, Frances Burney, William Godwin ... All of them, clustered in a perfectly balanced space (four to seven standard deviations above the popularity mean, and three to eight above the prestige one), where the wide audience of formula fiction blends seamlessly with high cultural recognition. Looking at this central region makes you "see" the process of canonization as the combination of two simultaneous processes:

popularity slowly shrinking with the passing years along the horizontal axis—in that respect, most eighteenth-century giants are well below Roche, Porter, Charlotte Smith, and Opie—while prestige increases along the vertical one.[16] Though there is clearly more than one way of becoming a canonical writer,[17] the main lesson of this image is that the canon is not the "the economic world reversed" of Bourdieu's formula for the autonomous literary field; the canon—or at least *this* canon—is made of authors from whom commercial publishers are still expecting to make profits two or three generations after their initial success. And prestige, for its part, is not necessarily *in antithesis* to popularity; here, it seems rather to grow out of it, "distilling" economic returns into something more impalpable, but also more durable.[18]

Things are different in the "high-prestige" region of **Figure 9.5**, which is clearly dominated by foreign writers (Cervantes, Voltaire, Diderot, Rousseau, Goethe, Schiller, Hugo . . .), or by those British authors who, though they did write at least one novel, or even a few, can hardly be seen as "professional" novelists. Among them are the encyclopedic figure of Samuel Johnson, and the almost equally versatile Horace Walpole; poets like Percy Shelley (and, lower down, Thomas "Anacreon" Moore and James Hogg); the novelist-politician Benjamin Disraeli and the politician-politician Lord Russell (who published an improbable *Nun of Arouca* in 1822); essayists like James Boswell and Charles Lamb; at lower prestige levels, the, musician and playwright Charles Dibdin, the playwright and actress Charlotte Charke, the economist and travel writer Arthur Young.

---

16 In terms of shrinking popularity, Austen and her contemporaries would provide a perfect case study: as **Figure 9.4** shows, about twenty-five authors (one third of them from the 18th century) were more popular than Austen in the sixty years covered by the diagram. As 19th-century novelistic bibliographies become more reliable, we will know how many of them were still more popular than her a generation or two later (initial results from the 1830s and 1840s suggest: Scott, and no one else).

17 Scott's immediate fame *and* acclaim are different from Austen's significantly slower pace, or from the ambiguous status of authors long confined to specific niches because of their initial audience (Lewis Carroll) or genre (Radcliffe, Doyle). And then, of course, there is the nemesis of any general theory of the canon—*Moby-Dick*.

18 Although our findings are completely different from Bourdieu's idea of the French literary field, they don't necessarily falsify his thesis, as we are working only on novels (to the exclusion of poetry, drama, magazines, and so on), and on a different country and period. Truth be told, we need many empirical maps of literary fields (plural), from different cultures and epochs, for the "literary field" (singular) to become a solid historical concept.

Among the few novelists-novelists, politics plays an unusually strong role: aside from Russell and Disraeli, we encounter the bluestocking Sarah Scott (*Millenium Hall*), Mary Shelley, and Hannah More—whose *Coelebs in Search of a Wife*, legend has it, was the only novel Queen Victoria entirely approved of.

With the prestige/popularity diagrams, a first arc of our project had found its natural conclusion. Although, against our original intentions, we had ended up quite far from the archive,[19] our operationalization of the concept of the canon had been both surprising and satisfying: it had brought the notion down to earth, resolving it into the simpler elements of popularity and prestige—or, in plainer words: of the market and the school. Within these new coordinates, the canon remains as visible as ever, *but it loses its conceptual autonomy*, becoming the contingent outcome of the encounter between opposite forces. It is *these forces*, then, that deserve to be further investigated, if one wants to know more about the canon;[20] and future research might easily add print runs and presence in the circulating libraries to the popularity metrics, and excerpts from textbooks, or mentions in the nonfiction archive, to the prestige ones.[21] With each new addition, we will acquire a better sense of the composite nature of the

---

19 In **Figures 9.4–9.5**, which have as their cut-off point two or three standard deviations above the mean of the field, all authors in the high prestige and in the middle area, and about half of those in the high popularity area, can be considered canonical. As one descends "lower," the field's tripartition remains visible a little longer, then disappears. What happens *then* is a fascinating question—for another study.

20 Or more precisely: *if one wants to de-compose the concept of the canon into the two underlying elements of popularity and prestige*. Here, it's worth comparing the initial epistemological choice of this project with that of Algee-Hewitt and McGurl's "Between Canon and Corpus." The main difference is not that between texts ("Between Canon and Corpus") and authors ("Canon/Archive")—which could be easily ironed out—but between an analysis based on networks, and one based on a Cartesian diagrams. Networks are much better at investigating the relationships among *individual nodes* (the hyper-canonical cluster identified in Figure 3 of the study, the singular centrality of *Grapes of Wrath*, the disconnect between best sellers and the other groups), but *cannot connect the nodes to anything outside the network itself*. Cartesian diagrams, for their part, *embed the "outside" into their very axes* (like here popularity and prestige), but inevitably *loosen the relationships among individual data points* (in a diagram, there is no equivalent to network edges and clustering measures). Clearly, this is not a case of one strategy being "better" than the other, but of research projects that aim at investigating different properties of the system, and choose their means of analysis accordingly.

21 Needless to add, some of these measurements may be discontinuous and hard to come by (like print runs), while others (like textbooks) may start at a significantly later date. But if the notion of the literary field must help us understand different epochs and countries, having recourse to disparate his-

canon—and of its *historical* nature, too: the canon of 1770–1830 (and, we suspect, of the following seventy to eighty years) was the product of the happy age of the European bourgeoisie, when the imperatives of success and education could be seen as compatible with each other, as was appropriate for a ruling class which, for the first time in history, felt at home in the market as well as the school. To have made the dual nature of the 19th-century canon intuitively "visible"—such is the achievement of these initial sections.[22]

2. MORPHOLOGICAL FEATURES

A. MEASURING REDUNDANCY

Though different from Bourdieu's in many respects, the charts presented in the previous section shared his main methodological premise: they had a social rather than a literary foundation.[23] To make **Figure 9.5**, you don't need to open a single novel. As literary historians, however, we *wanted* to open the novels, and find out whether their social destiny—popular, prestigious, both, neither . . . —had any connection to their morphological features. So, while working at the diagrams of the literary field, we were also focusing on the internal composition of Chadwyck-Healey and of the sample from the larger archive. Here, the first step consisted in measuring the amount of redundancy and information present in the corpus. That readers prefer informative texts to redundant ones—thus keeping the former in print, while dooming the latter to extinction—is a widespread received idea, and we wanted to test it. Taking a cue from information

---

torical indexes will be inevitable; rather than hoping for a—chimerical—homogeneity of the sources, we should learn to make heterogeneous data conceptually comparable.

22 "Between Canon and Corpus" shows how much things have changed since then: in the 20th century, canon(s) are all characterized by a "systematic differentiation, if not contradiction, between artistic and commercial value." It is precisely this differentiation/contradiction that is absent from the "canonical" region of **Figure 9.5**.

23 "I propose that the problem of what is called canon formation," writes John Guillory, in a similar vein, "is best understood as a problem in the constitution and distribution of cultural capital, or more specifically, a problem of access to the means of literary production and consumption." (John Guillory, *Cultural Capital: The Problem of Literary Canon Formation* (Chicago: University of Chicago Press, 1995), ix.)

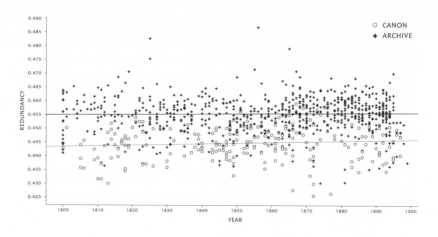

FIGURE 9.6 **Measuring redundancy, 1800–1900.** Crosses indicate archival novels, circles canonical ones.

theory, Mark Algee-Hewitt measured what is called "second order redundancy" (predictability at the level of individual words), using a modification of Claude Shannon's measure of information load that determines the information content of each text by assessing how predictable each word-to-word transition is, given the range of possible transitions. Since "of" is much more often followed by "the" than by "no," for instance, the word pair "of no" is far less predictable—hence more informative—than the bigram "of the."[24] **Figures 9.6** and **9.7** summarize Algee-Hewitt's investigation.

Figure 9.7 was particularly striking: that three-fourths of the Chadwyck-Healey collection would be less redundant than three-fourths of the archive was a *much* stronger separation than we had expected to find. And yet, we weren't completely happy. The clarity of the contrast had simply confirmed a received idea: forgotten authors used language in a redundant fashion; if they had remained unread, it was because they weren't really *worth* reading. And vice versa: we still enjoy reading Austen because she is a paragon of information, as the close-up of **Figure 9.8** makes perfectly clear.

---

24 Throughout this essay, we will use "redundancy" and "repetition" almost interchangeably, placing them in antithesis to "information" and "variety"; though this is a simplification, we don't think it affects the level at which we are working, nor the type of results we have found. On a similar note, the relationship between information and redundancy is often referred to as "entropy"; we have opted for different definitions in order to make the various aspects of this research as comparable as possible.

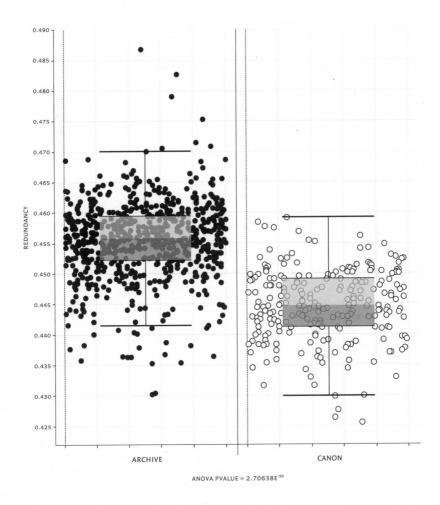

FIGURE 9.7 **Redundancy in the 19th century: a synthetic diagram.** This figure aggregates the data of **Figure 9.6** into the two sub-corpora of canon and archive. Each "box" includes the two central quartiles of the group, separated by a line that indicates the group's median value; the "whiskers" emerging from the box represent the two extreme quartiles, while outliers are indicated by individual dots.

Not exciting, corroborating a received idea.[25] And then, there was a second problem. Though Algee-Hewitt had operationalized the concept of redundancy, and produced striking quantitative findings, it wasn't clear

---

25 And it was already the second time: in **Figure 9.2**, the fact that the canon regularly preceded the archive by fifteen to twenty years seemed to "prove" that other received idea according to which great writers open the way, and the rest follow.

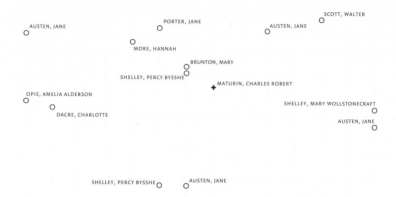

FIGURE 9.8 **Very low redundancy in the early 19th century.** A novel that never repeated a single word would have zero redundancy and 100 percent information—but this "information" would have no value, because it would rapidly become incomprehensible. Meaning always depends on a mix of repetition and novelty: that's why the scores in these figures oscillate in a rather narrow range. Differences *within* this range are however both consistent and significant, as is illustrated by this enlargement of the bottom left area of **Figure 9.6**.

how we could disaggregate the overall score and look at the results, determining which specific word pairs returned all the time—or never did so. We had successfully measured redundancy, but couldn't really *analyze* it: an unsettling departure from that interplay of quantitative measurement and qualitative interpretation that had been a constant of our work since the beginning. Here, statistical significance seemed impervious to critical meaningfulness: the "text" created by extracting the 100 most frequent bigrams from each novel in the corpus was a spreadsheet with over 100,000 cells: "reading" them was out of the question (**Figure 9.9**). A more technical approach—following the decay curve of the most frequent constructions—turned out to be equally inconclusive: very frequent bigrams ("there is," "I am," "to the") had very similar frequencies in all the texts, and variation occurred only in minute traces far down the curve. Plus, there were *so many* bigrams, in each novel, that their effects manifested themselves through an immense number of extremely small changes: in a relatively short text of 66,500 words, for instance, there were 66,499 bigrams, about 40,000 of which never repeated themselves. And whereas the number of shared words between two texts was substantial—at least 3–4,000—the shared bigrams were usually less than 1,000; too few for a solid comparative analysis.

of_the_1441	in_the_672	to_the_634	of_his_341	of_a_333	and_the_318	by_the_286	by_the_286
of_the_1148	in_the_578	to_the_521	of_his_309	of_a_308	the_master_294	with_the_237	with_the_237
of_the_266	in_the_99	to_the_95	on_the_86	of_his_69	by_the_66	from_the_58	from_the_58
of_the_942	in_the_404	to_the_365	of_his_245	to_be_197	and_the_179	on_the_171	on_the_171
of_the_1486	in_the_781	to_the_633	of_his_365	of_a_364	and_the_354	to_be_305	to_be_305
of_the_746	to_be_616	in_the_574	it_was_389	she_had_365	of_her_346	to_the_324	to_the_324
of_the_679	in_the_401	sir_ulick_348	to_the_330	to_be_298	he_had_292	of_his_239	of_his_239
of_the_702	in_the_494	of_her_440	to_the_404	to_be_387	lady_juliana_276	and_the_256	and_the_256
of_the_359	said_i_236	in_the_212	to_the_191	i_am_181	of_my_175	and_i_174	and_i_174
of_the_389	in_the_295	to_be_271	of_her_194	i_am_183	to_the_163	she_had_155	she_had_155
of_the_459	to_be_428	in_the_382	i_am_297	of_her_264	to_the_251	mr_darcy_233	mr_darcy_233
of_the_226	in_the_143	mr_glowry_84	and_the_71	of_a_69	to_the_63	on_the_56	on_the_56
of_the_161	in_the_91	to_be_85	to_the_52	i_am_40	of_a_40	for_the_38	for_the_38
of_the_342	to_the_246	the_marquis_215	in_the_214	of_his_212	and_the_164	to_his_125	to_his_125
of_the_245	to_the_196	in_the_184	mrs_villars_126	of_her_115	she_was_103	on_the_96	on_the_96
of_the_648	in_the_419	to_the_338	i_have_280	it_is_262	i_am_204	that_i_185	that_i_185
of_the_607	in_the_471	to_the_332	to_be_247	of_her_225	had_been_202	she_had_194	she_had_194
of_the_603	to_the_321	in_the_290	of_his_234	to_be_208	he_had_182	on_the_179	on_the_179
of_the_425	to_the_304	in_the_289	said_i_264	of_a_210	and_the_184	i_was_158	i_was_158
of_the_383	in_the_194	on_the_153	and_the_135	to_the_125	of_my_109	it_was_95	it_was_95
of_the_1627	in_the_1325	of_her_1315	to_the_1286	to_her_975	of_his_935	from_the_637	from_the_637
of_the_1004	in_the_626	to_the_573	he_had_441	he_was_389	to_be_364	she_had_351	she_had_351
of_the_751	in_the_452	to_the_412	he_had_399	she_had_350	to_be_298	she_was_283	she_was_283
of_the_4794	in_the_3327	to_the_2510	to_be_2195	of_her_2146	she_had_2072	of_a_1868	of_a_1868
of_the_1169	to_the_724	in_the_676	to_her_512	of_her_490	to_be_490	she_had_381	she_had_381
of_the_1681	to_the_703	in_the_653	said_the_525	and_the_403	of_a_349	it_is_331	it_is_331
of_the_1302	in_the_589	to_the_586	of_his_369	and_the_318	on_the_305	by_the_256	by_the_256
of_the_1632	in_the_688	to_the_649	the_earl_408	of_his_385	and_the_373	by_the_365	by_the_365
of_the_1465	to_the_555	in_the_525	said_the_379	of_his_358	and_the_300	of_a_270	of_a_270

FIGURE 9.9 **Reading bigrams: 0.00003 percent of the data.** A section of the spreadsheet used for the calculations behind **Figures 9.6–9.7**. Though the bigrams themselves are perfectly identified, it's nearly impossible to "interpret" what they mean other than in statistical fashion. In this respect, Walser and Algee-Hewitt observed, bigrams were comparable to Braudel's "demographic progressions" and "variations in interest rates": all phenomena that could not be perceived at the passage-by-passage level on which we typically conduct our readings.

We seemed to have created for ourselves a homegrown version of the uncertainty principle: the more precisely we measured redundancy, the harder it became to determine "where" it actually was. Redundancy operated at a scale that was all pervasive, and apparently decisive in shaping the destiny of books; but the whole process took place so far below the level of conscious reading as to be practically invisible. In the future, perhaps even

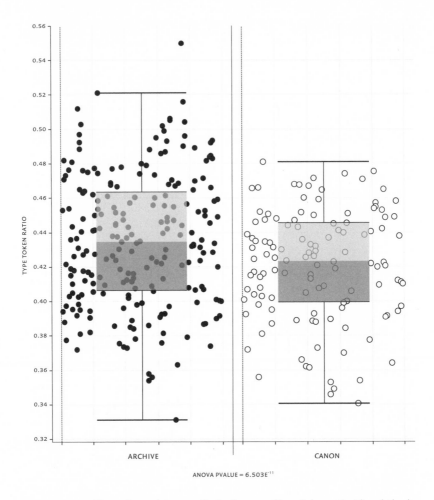

FIGURE 9.10. **Measuring variety: a synthetic diagram of type-token ratio.** Though the distinction between the two sub-corpora is here much less sharp than in **Figure 9.7**, the result is actually more dramatic: **9.7** had fully confirmed our expectations about canon and archive, whereas this chart completely contradicted them: the lexicon of the canon was not more varied than that of the archive, but significantly less so. (The procedure followed to determine type-token ratio is described in footnote 28, at the beginning of the next section).

the near future, such a problem might be addressed by experimental psychology; in the meantime, we turned to a standard linguistic measure of lexical variety known as type-token ratio.[26] The lower a text's redundancy,

---

26 This is how the *Longman Grammar of Spoken and Written English* defines type-token ratio: "The relationship between the number of different word forms, or types, and the number of running words, or tokens, is

we reasoned, the higher must its variety be: convex to concave. We would get an image that would be the exact reverse of **Figure 9.7**. So we did our calculations, and the result was **Figure 9.10**.

Placing **Figures 9.7** and **9.10** next to each other produced the following paradox: the canon was far less repetitive than the archive (hence much more varied) from the perspective of word pairs, and at the scale of the entire text; and less varied (hence more repetitive) from the perspective of single words, and at the scale of a thousand. In itself, the fact that different textual scales would behave differently was not a surprise: two previous chapters ("Style at the Scale of the Sentence" and "On Paragraphs") had focused exactly on that question. But in those cases, different scales had been associated *with completely different features*: sentences with style, paragraphs with themes, and so on. Here, the features measured were very closely related. How could results reverse themselves from two words to a thousand? And we mean that "how" literally, not as a cry of despair: concretely, what textual mechanism could transform the first result into the second?

Algee-Hewitt addressed the question by "translating" all words into parts of speech, thus reformulating redundancy via *categories* of bigrams rather than individual units; "clever little" and "first cruel," for instance, both became "adjective-adjective"; "a condition" and "the kitchen" became "determiner-noun," etc. Recalculating everything in terms of "grammatical redundancy" made it possible to identify which kinds of bigrams were most distinctive of the canon, and which of the archive **(Figures 9.11–9.12)**.[27]

---

called the type-token ratio (or TTR). Specifically TTR as a percentage = (types/tokens) × 100." See Biber et al., *Longman Grammar of Spoken and Written English*, 52–3.

The *Longman Grammar* follows the variations of type-token ratio across four registers (Conversation, Academic prose, Fiction, and News), and three sample lengths (100, 1,000, and 10,000 words). For 100-word segments the results are as follows: Conversation 63; Academic prose 70; Fiction 73; News 75. For 1,000-word segments: Conversation 30; Academic prose 40; Fiction 46; News 50. And for 10,000-word segments: Conversation 13; Academic prose 19; Fiction 22; News 28. Notice how the difference between the registers increases dramatically with the length of the segment: at 10,000 words, the type-token ratio of News is more than double that of Conversation, whereas it was only 16 percent higher at 100 words. We opted for 1,000-which seemed to be long enough to capture a good amount of variety, and short enough to allow direct analysis.

27 For this part of the work, Algee-Hewitt used the Stanford Parts-of-Speech Tagger; the abbreviations enclosed in parentheses (IN_NNP etc.) are however those used by the Treebank project of the University of Pennsylvania.

FIGURE 9.11 **Most distinctive grammatical bigrams: archive**

PREPOSITION—PROPER NOUN (IN _ NNP): to Shirley; in Ireland

ADJECTIVE-ADJECTIVE (JJ _ JJ): young happy; first cruel

NOUN-ADJECTIVE (NN _ JJ): child incapable; nomenclature peculiar

NOUN-NOUN (NN _ NN): iron will; evening sky

NOUN—PROPER NOUN (NN _ NNP): count Goldstein; uncle Gerard

NOUN—PLURAL NOUN (NN _ NNS): iron bars; autumn tints

PROPER NOUN—PREPOSITION (NNP _ IN): Alps of; Shelburne upon

PROPER NOUN—NOUN (NNP _ NN): Agnes' wedding; Manchester cotton

PROPER NOUN—PLURAL NOUN (NNP _ NNS): Cumberland coasts, Hector's lodgings

NOUN-PRONOUN (NN _ PRP): tail itself, driver himself.

FIGURE 9.12 **Most distinctive grammatical bigrams: canon**

CONJUNCTION-GERUND (CC _ VBG): and walking; and taking

DETERMINER-ADJECTIVE (DT _ JJ): the silly; an eventful

DETERMINER-NOUN (DT _ NN): a condition; the kitchen

DETERMINER—PLURAL NOUN (DT _ NNS): the environs; the travelers

PREPOSITION-DETERMINER (IN _ DT): at the; in a

ADJECTIVE—PLURAL NOUN (JJ _ NNS): folded arms; harsh features

NOUN-PREPOSITION (NN _ IN): account of; sense of

PLURAL NOUN—PREPOSITION (NNS _ IN): grains of; years of

POSSESSIVE PRONOUN—PLURAL NOUN (PRP$ _ NNS): their excursions; our girls

This time, the two sub-corpora were revealed to have very different centers of gravity: the archive was dominated by nouns, while the canon had a very large presence of function words (conjunctions, determiners, prepositions). The archive's delight in titles (count Goldstein, uncle Gerard), punctiliousness about places and people (in Ireland; to Shirley), and liberality with proper nouns in general (Hector's lodgings, Shelburne upon) finally gave us a clue to its high redundancy: "count Goldstein" and "Shelburne upon" may not appear very often in a novel—but when they do, the two words are likely to reoccur together, increasing the text's redundancy; and the same for constructions like the adjunct nouns "iron will" and "autumn tints." It wasn't an answer to all our questions, but it was a beginning. And then, in order to address the other side of the paradox, we turned back to type-token ratio.

B. "BUT I COULDN'T GO AWAY"

In the case of type-token ratio, the first thing that needed to be done was to come up with a mode of analysis appropriate to a corpus where most novels had not been reprinted for a century or two, making optical recognition difficult, and hence potentially invalidating all subsequent calculations. Ryan Heuser, who had first directed our attention to type-token ratio in the early phases of the project, found a way to measure it equally reliably across texts of very different quality.[28] Once the results were in, we started by looking at low type-token ratio, to see how its specific kind of repetitiveness compared to the redundancy calculated by Algee-Hewitt. We knew from **Figure 9.11** that low lexical variety would often correlate with canonical texts, and indeed the frequency of the Chadwyck-Healey collection, which amounted to around 20 percent of the corpus overall, rose to 50 percent among the five hundred segments with the lowest type-token ratio (whereas it was a mere 3.2 in the top five hundred). Among the fifty texts with the lowest scores, about half were from Chadwyck-Healey: several children's books (*Alice's Adventures in Wonderland, Through the Looking-Glass, The Water Babies, Black Beauty, Little Lord Fauntleroy, Island Nights' Entertainments* . . .), ten of Trollope's novels (*The Last Chronicle of Barset, Phineas Finn the Irish Member, Can You Forgive Her?, The Eustace Diamonds* . . .), plus two Irish novels (Edgeworth's

---

28 Heuser began by creating a very large dictionary of novelistic English—232,845 distinct words—and slicing all texts into segments of 1,000 "dictionary-words." (Actual segments would be anywhere from 1,000 to ~1,500 words long, depending on how many "non-dictionary" words—OCR errors, hapax legomena, etc.—they had.) Since the number of tokens was fixed at 1,000, dividing the number of types in each segment by 1,000 produced segment-based scores whose average gave us the type-token ratio for the text.

The function was written with two parameters: "slice_len" [the length of the segment (set at 1,000)] and "force_english" [whether to include words not in a very large English dictionary (set at False)]. The reasoning behind the "force English" parameter, which excluded all non-"English" words, was that, without it, the archive would have a higher type-token ratio simply by virtue of its bad OCR. Conversely, the concern with forcing English was that the same bad OCR would produce a lower type-token ratio: if the segment had to expand over ~1,500 "real" words in order to find 1,000 "English" ones, then it might privilege shorter, easier-to-spell-and-OCR words, which are also the most frequent in the language, thus driving type-token ratio downwards. In the event, these two undesirable outcomes seemed to balance each other out.

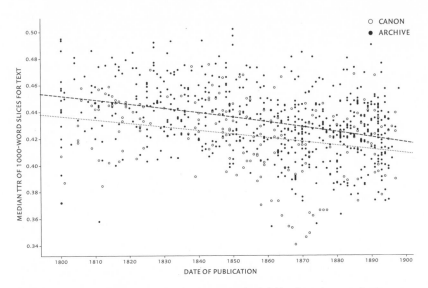

FIGURE 9.13 **Type-token ratio, 1800–1900.** The "pull" of children's stories towards a low type-token ratio is visible between 1860 and 1880; in general, though, the type-token ratios of both canon and archive remain rather stable across the nineteenth century.

Castle Rackrent and Samuel Ferguson's *Father Tom and the Pope*, with *The Absentee* not very far behind). In itself, this mix was not particularly representative of the canon (whatever one may mean with that term); more significant seemed to be the fact that Chadwyck-Healey's scores remained low across the century (**Figure 9.13**), and that the trend involved some of the greatest 19th-century stylists: all of Austen was below the corpus mean (with *Persuasion, Sense and Sensibility,* and *Mansfield Park* in the bottom 20 percent); all of Dickens was below the mean (with *Little Dorrit, A Tale of Two Cities, David Copperfield, Our Mutual Friend, Bleak House,* and *Great Expectations* in the bottom 20 percent); all of George Eliot was below the mean—and *Adam Bede* contained the passage with the lowest type-token ratio of the entire century.

Now, *Adam Bede* is a strange novel for that kind of result, because it contains Eliot's famous reflections on Dutch painting: a manifesto for aesthetic precision and variety, written with extraordinary precision and variety (**Figure 9.14**).

The first 100 words of this passage have a type-token ratio of 79: higher than anything, in any register, discussed by the *Longman Grammar*. And yet, later in the novel, Eliot's style runs to the opposite extreme (**Figure 9.15**).

FIGURE 9.14 **"This rare, precious quality of truthfulness"**

It is for this rare, precious quality of truthfulness that I delight in many Dutch paintings, which lofty-minded people despise. I find a source of delicious sympathy in these faithful pictures of a monotonous homely existence, which has been the fate of so many more among my fellow-mortals than a life of pomp or of absolute indigence, of tragic suffering or of world-stirring actions. I turn, without shrinking, from cloud-borne angels, from prophets, sibyls, and heroic warriors, to an old woman bending over her flower-pot, or eating her solitary dinner, while the noonday light, softened perhaps by a screen of leaves, falls on her mob-cap, and just touches the rim of her spinning-wheel, and her stone jug, and all those cheap common things which are the precious necessaries of life to her—or I turn to that village wedding, kept between four brown walls, where an awkward bridegroom opens the dance with a high-shouldered, broad-faced bride, while elderly and middle-aged friends look on, with very irregular noses and lips, and probably with quart-pots in their hands, but with an expression of unmistakable contentment and goodwill. "Foh!" says my idealistic friend, "what vulgar details!"

FIGURE 9.15 **The 19th century's most repetitive passage: Hetty's confession in *Adam Bede*.** The pound sign indicates that a word is being repeated within the given segment, while asterisks denote words that are not part of the "dictionary" used for the calculations. Some odd aspects of this and other passages are artifacts of the Stanford parser—which, for instance, considers negative contractions, such as "n't" at the end of "couldn't," as a separate word.

came all of a sudden, as I was lying in the bed, and it got stronger and# stronger# . . . I# longed so to go back again . . . I# could n't* bear being so# lonely, and# coming to# beg for want. And# it# gave me strength and# resolution to# get up and# dress myself. I# felt I# must do it# . . . I# did n't* know how . . . I# thought I#'d find a# pool, if I# could#, like that other, in# the# corner of# the# field, in# the# dark. And# when the# woman went out, I# felt# as# if# I# was# strong enough to# do# anything . . . I# thought# I# should get# rid of# all# my misery, and# go# back# home, and# never let'em know# why I# ran away. I# put on my# bonnet and# shawl, and# went# out# into the# dark# street, with the# baby under my# cloak; and# I# walked fast till I# got# into# a# street# a# good way off, and# there was# a# public, and# I# got# some warm stuff to# drink and# some# bread. And# I# walked# on# and# on#, and# I# hardly felt# the# ground I# trod on#; and# it# got# lighter, for# there# came# the# moon—O, Dinah, it# frightened me# when# it# first looked at me# out# o' the# clouds—it# never#

FIGURE 9.15 (CONTINUED)

looked# so# before; and# I# turned out# of# the# road into# the# fields, for# I# was# afraid o#' meeting anybody with# the# moon# shining on# me#. And# I# came# to# a# haystack, where I# thought# I# could# lie down and# keep myself# warm# all# night. There# was# a# place cut into# it#, where# I# could# make me# a# bed#; and# I# lay comfortable, and# the# baby# was# warm# against me#; and# I# must# have gone to# sleep for# a# good# while, for# when# I# woke it# was# morning, but not very light, and# the# baby# was# crying. And# I# saw a# wood a# little way# off#. . . I# thought# there#'d perhaps be a# ditch or a# pond there# . . . and# it# was# so# early I# thought# I# could# hide the# child there#, and# get# a# long way# off# before# folks was# up. And# then I# thought# I#'d go# home#——I#'d get# rides in# carts and# go# home#, and# tell'em I#'d been to# try and# see for# a# place#, and# could# n't* get# one. I# longed# so# for# it#, Dinah#——I# longed# so# to# be# safe at# home#. I# do# n't* know# how# I# felt# about the# baby#. I# seemed to# hate it#——it# was# like# a# heavy weight hanging round my# neck; and# yet its crying# went# through me#, and# I# dared n't* look at# its# little# hands and# face. But# I# went# on# to# the# wood#, and# I# walked# about#, but# there# was# no water" . . . Hetty shuddered. She was# silent for# some# moments, and# when# she# began again#, it# was# in# a# whisper. "I# came# to# a# place# where# there# was# lots of# chips and# turf, and# I# sat down# on# the# trunk of# a# tree to# think what I# should# do#. And# all# of# a# sudden# I# saw# a# hole under# the# nut-tree*, like# a# little# grave. And# it# darted into# me# like# lightning——I#'d lay# the# baby there#, and# cover it# with# the# grass and# the# chips#. I# could# n't* kill it# any other# way#. And# I#'d done it# in# came all of a sudden, as I was lying in the bed, and it got stronger and# stronger# . . . I# longed so to go back again . . . I# could n't* bear being so# lonely, and# coming to# beg for# want. And# it# gave me strength and# resolution to# get up and# dress myself. I# felt I# must do it# . . . I# did n't* know how . . . I# thought I#'d find a# pool, if I# could#, like that other, in# the# corner of# the# field, in# the# dark. And# when the# woman went out, I# felt# as# if# I# was# strong enough to# do# anything . . . I# thought# I# should get# rid of# all# my misery, and# go# back# home, and# never let'em know# why I# ran away. I# put on my# bonnet and# shawl, and# went# out# into the# dark# street, with the# baby under my# cloak; and# I# walked fast till I# got# into# a# street# a# good way off, and# there was# a# public, and# I# got# some warm stuff to# drink and# some# bread. And# I# walked# on# and# on#, and# I# hardly felt# the# ground I# trod on#; and# it# got# lighter, for# there# came# the# moon——O, Dinah, it# frightened me# when# it# first looked at me# out# o#' the# clouds——it# never# looked# so# before; and# I# turned out# of# the# road into# the# fields, for# I# was# afraid o#' meeting anybody with# the# moon# shining on# me#. And# I# came# to# a# haystack, where I# thought# I# could# lie down and# keep myself# warm# all# night. There# was# a# place cut into# it#, where# I# could# make me# a# bed#; and#

i# lay comfortable, and# the# baby# was# warm# against me#; and# I# must# have gone to# sleep for# a# good# while, for# when# I# woke it# was# morning, but not very light, and# the# baby# was# crying. And# I# saw a# wood a# little way# off#. . . I# thought# there#'d perhaps be a# ditch or a# pond there#. . . and# it# was# so# early I# thought# I# could# hide the# child there#, and# get# a# long way# off# before# folks was# up#. And# then I# thought# I#'d go# home#——I#'d get# rides in# carts and# go# home#, and# tell 'em I#'d been to# try and# see for# a# place#, and# could n't* get# one. I# longed# so# for# it#, Dinah#——I# longed# so# to# be# safe at# home#. I# do# n't* know# how# I# felt# about the# baby#. I# seemed to# hate it#——it# was# like# a# heavy weight hanging round my# neck; and# yet its crying# went# through me#, and# I# dared n't* look at# its# little# hands and# face. But# I# went# on# to# the# wood#, and# I# walked# about#, but# there# was# no water" . . . Hetty shuddered. She was# silent for# some# moments, and# when# she# began again#, it# was# in# a# whisper. "I# came# to# a# place# where# there# was# lots of# chips and# turf, and# I# sat down# on# the# trunk of# a# tree to# think what I# should# do#. And# all# of# a# sudden# I# saw# a# hole under# the# nut-tree*, like# a# little# grave. And# it# darted into# me# like# lightning——I#'d lay# the# baby# there#, and# cover it# with# the# grass and# the# chips#. I# could# n't* kill it# any other# way#. And# I#'d done it# in# a# minute; and#, O#, it# cried so#, Dinah#——I# could# n't* cover# it# quite up#——I# thought# perhaps somebody 'ud* come and# take care of# it#, and# then# it# would n't* die. And# I# made haste out# of# the# wood#, but# I# could# hear it# crying# all# the# while#; and# when# I# got# out# into# the# fields#, it# was# as# if# I# was# held fast#——I# could# n't* go# away#, for# all# I# wanted so# to# go#. And# I# sat# against# the# haystack# to# watch if# anybody# 'ud* come#: I# was# very# hungry, and# I#'d only a# bit of# bread# left; but# I# could# n't* go# away#. And# after ever such a# while#——hours and# hours#——the# man came#——him in# a# smock-frock*, and# he looked# at# me# so#, I# was# frightened#, and# I# made# haste# and# went# on#. I# thought# he# was# going to# the# wood#, and# would# perhaps# find# the# baby#. And# I# went# right on#, till# I# came# to# a# village, a# long# way# off# from the# wood#; and# I# was# very# sick, and# faint, and# hungry#. I# got# something to# eat there#, and# bought a# loaf. But# I# was# frightened# to# stay. I# heard the# baby# crying#, and# thought# the# other# folks# heard# it# too,——and# I# went# on#. But# I# was# so# tried, and# it# was# getting towards dark#. And# at# last, by the# roadside there# was# a# barn——ever# such a# way# off# any# house——like# the# barn# in# Abbot's Close; and# I# thought# I# could# go# in# there# and# hide# myself# among the# hay and# straw, and# nobody 'ud* be# likely to# come#. I# went# in#, and# it# was# half full o#' trusses of# straw#, and# there# was# some# hay#, too#. And# I# made# myself# a# bed#, ever# so# far behind, where# nobody# could# find# me#; and# I# was# so# tired and# weak, I# went# to# sleep#. . . . But# oh, the# baby#'s crying# kept waking me#; and# I# thought# that# man# as# looked# at# me# so# was# come# and# laying hold of# me#. But# I# must# have# slept a# long#

FIGURE 9.16 **"But I could hear it crying all the while"**

> And# I# made haste out# of# the# wood#, but# I# could# hear it# crying# all# the#
> while#; and# when# I# got# out# into# the# fields#, it# was# as# if# I# was# held
> fast#—I# could# n't* go# away#, for# all# I# wanted so# to# go#. And# I# sat#
> against# the# haystack# to# watch if# anybody# 'ud* come#: I# was# very# hungry,
> and# I#'d only a# bit of# bread# left; but# I# could# n't* go# away#.

Eliot's passage includes the central moment of Hetty's confession to Dinah: the recollection of having abandoned her child in the woods, and of waiting for "its" death (to use the pronoun she herself uses). But "waiting" is the wrong word (**Figure 9.16**).

Grammatically, the most arresting feature of these sentences is the flood of inflected verb forms with Hetty as their subject: I made haste . . . I could hear . . . I got out . . . I was held fast . . . I couldn't go away . . . I wanted . . . I sat . . . I was . . . I had . . . I couldn't . . . In narrative analysis, verb forms are usually seen as indices of "action"—and comprehensibly so. But here, in a grating dissonance between grammar and semantics, they stand for paralysis instead: Hetty desperately wants to "go away"—and can't. And just as she cannot leave the physical setting of the episode, she cannot relinquish the *words* that describe it. She cannot forget: that's where the repetition comes from. Better: she can neither forget, *nor really say what has happened.* In a textbook instance of the opposition between "repeating" and "working through," she keeps saying the same things over and over again, because she cannot bring herself to utter the one thing that really matters: the word "death" is *never* repeated, and only appears in an oblique, misleading construction at the end of the passage.[29]

Why repetition? Because a trauma has occurred, and repetition is a great way to express it in language: an imprisonment in one's own words whose enigmatic force explains why Eliot, despite her love for analytical details, could write the most repetitive passage of the entire century. And then, Hetty's confession also brings to light the fundamentally *oral* component of type-token ratio. Next to Eliot's page, the two segments with the

---

29 "But it was morning, for it kept getting lighter, and I turned back the way I'd come. I couldn't help it, Dinah; it was the baby's crying made me go—and yet I was frightened to death. I thought that man in the smock-frock 'ud see me and know I put the baby there." Notice how "death" is referred to Hetty instead of her child.

lowest lexical density are also confessions: of baby-changing in Edgeworth's *Ennui*,[30] and of love in Trollope's *Last Chronicle of Barset*.[31] In the same low range we find passages from children's stories (with their typically life-like narrators), Irish novels (which specialized in the imitation of speech), and countless instances of Trollope's petty-bourgeois stichomythia.[32] There are trial scenes (*The Ordeal of Richard Feverel*, *The Heart of Mid-Lothian*, William Scargill's *Tales of a Briefless Barrister*), ideological confrontations (*Marius the Epicurean*), an ecstatic vision of the "communism of happiness" (Mary Christie's *Lady Laura*),[33] and a great invective against money (Thomas Pemberton's *A Very Old Question*).[34] There are characters who talk too much because they are trying to be obliging (*Emma*), or because, like Van Helsing in *Dracula*, they need to rehearse the evidence over and over again. It could hardly be an accident, concluded Allison and Gemma, that our lowest ranked (and largely canonical) 1,000-word segments were in exactly the same range as conversation in the *Longman Grammar*: a mean of 30 in their case, and a range of 27–33 for our bottom five hundred segments.

We had turned to type-token ratio in the hope that it would lead us back to some kind of textual analysis—and we had not been disappointed: low

---

30 "I thought, how happy he would be if he had such a fine babby as you; dear; and you was a fine babby to be sure; and then I thought, how happy it would be for you, if you was in the place of the little lord: and then it came into my head, just like a shot, where would be the harm to change you?"

31 "You are so good and so true, and so excellent,—such a dear, dear, dear friend, that I will tell you everything, so that you may read my heart. I will tell you as I tell mamma,—you and her and no one else;—for you are the choice friend of my heart. I can not be your wife because of the love I bear for another man."

32 "Do you think that I am in earnest?" "Yes, I think you are in earnest." "And do you believe that I love you with all my heart and all my strength and all my soul?" "Oh, John!" "But do you?" "I think you love me." "Think!"

33 "All are not equally happy; all can not be equally happy. But there is a sort of communism possible in happiness. The unhappy have a claim upon the happy; the happy have a debt towards the unhappy." "But how can one share one's happiness with others? It seems to me impossible. It is what I have most wished to do, but I see no way in which it can be done." "In one sense certainly you can not share your happiness, and you can not give it away. It is essentially your own, a development of your being, a part of yourself that you may not alienate."

34 "Money!" she cried derisively. "Money! What is money to the trouble which has torn my heart ever since I have been married! What is money to those who thirst for love! I never wanted money; without money I was strong and happy; since I have had it I have been weak and miserable. Money broke down my poor father, and it was for money that Percy married, deceived, and has forsaken me. Thank God that the wretched money has gone!"

scores captured crucial aspects of narrative structure, signaling trauma, intensity, and orality. And high scores?

C. "EMBRASURES BRISTLING WITH WIDE-MOUTHED CANNON"

Figure 9.17 shows the ten novels with the highest type-token ratio in the corpus; **9.18** the top-scoring passage, from Edward Hawker's *Arthur Montague, or, An Only Son at Sea.*

If the privileged social position of the canon were always correlated with linguistic privilege—Dario Fo, 1997 Nobel prize for literature, once wrote a play entitled *The Worker Knows 300 Words, the Boss 1,000—That's Why He's the Boss*—then canonical authors should have a much more varied language than forgotten ones. In terms of the type of lexical abundance measured by type-token ratio, however, the opposite is true. "The whole language of aesthetics is contained in a fundamental refusal of the *facile*," writes Bourdieu: "'vulgar' works . . . arouse distaste and disgust by the methods of seduction."[35] Facile, Hawker's language? Seductive? If anything, the opposite. A dichotomy such as vulgar/refined will never explain the connection between the archive and high type-token ratio. We must look elsewhere.

As often in this research, we found an answer in corpus linguistics. This time, it was the concept of "register": the "communicative purposes and situational contexts" of messages described by Douglas Biber and Susan Conrad in *Register, Genre, and Style*.[36] In the study of register, the fundamental opposition runs between oral and written, and it is a well-established fact that the latter has in English a much higher type-token ratio than the former. If the archive has a greater lexical variety than the canon, then, the reason is that *the archive inclines toward the "written" register much more than the canon* (while the latter, as we have seen in the previous section, is much more at ease with "oral" conventions). It's not that archival novels with high type-token ratio have fewer oral passages (dialogue, speech, exclamations, etc.); Gemma's work in progress on colloquial discourse suggests that they may even have more; it's that

---

35 Bourdieu, *Distinction*, 486.

36 Douglas Biber and Susan Conrad, *Register, Genre, and Style* (Cambridge: Cambridge University Press, 2009), 2.

FIGURE 9.17 **High type-token ratio, or, the triumph of the archive**

Edward Duros, *Otterbourne; A Story of the English Marches*, 1832

Edward Hawker, *Arthur Montague, or, An Only Son at sea*, 1850

Emma Robinson, *The Armourer's Daughter: or, The Border Riders*, 1850

William Lennox, *Compton Audley; or, Hands Not Hearts*, 1841

Mary Anne Cursham, *Norman Abbey: A Tale of Sherwood Forest*, 1832

William Maginn, *Whitehall; or, The Days of George IV*, 1827

Thomas Surr, *The Mask of Fashion; A Plain Tale, with Anecdotes Foreign and Domestic*, 1807

James Grant, *The Scottish Cavalier: An Historical Romance*, 1850

Cecil Clarke, *Love's Loyalty*, 1890

Jane West, *Ringrove, or Old Fashioned Notions*, 1827

their "spoken" passages have a markedly "written" quality. Jane West's *Ringrove*, for instance, includes a lot of language typographically marked as "speech"—which however consists often of formal tirades that sound closer to a written disquisition than to an oral exchange.[37]

Linguistic conservatism is certainly one reason for the "written" quality of many archival works. A passage from William North's *The Impostor*—whose type-token ratio is near the top 1 percent of the corpus—expresses it well:

> There has of late years crept into our *belles lettres*, in addition to the *soi-disant* fashionable trash above mentioned, a violent predilection for low life, slang, and vulgarism of every kind. Dickens and Ainsworth led the way, and whole hosts became their followers. . . . Let us endeavor to reestablish pure classical taste.

Let us endeavor to reestablish . . . In their study of prestige and style, Ted Underwood and Jordan Sellers have found that many obscure books "at

---

37 Here is one, on Byron's misuse of his poetic gifts: "There is a deep condensation of thought, an appropriateness of diction, an elegance of sentiment, and an original glow of poetical imagery; ever happy in illustrating objects, or deepening impressions;—which so fascinate our fancy and bewilder our judgment, that we lose sight of the nature of the deeds he narrates, and the real character of the actors."

FIGURE 9.18 **The 19th century's least repetitive passage.** Arthur Hawker's landscape description has a type-token ratio of 60, well above the scores (46 for fiction and 50 for news) reported by the *Longman Grammar* for segments of equal length.

> then cut through some acres of refreshing greensward, studded with the oak, walnut, and hawthorn, ascended a knoll, skirted an expansive sheet of# water; afterwards entering an# avenue of# noble elms, always tenanted* by a# countless host of# cawing* rooks, whose clamorous conclaves* interrupted the# stillness that reigned around, and# whose# visits to adjacent cornfields* of# inviting aspect raised the# ire and# outcry of# the# yelling VOL. I. C urchins employed to# guard them from depredation. Emerging from# this arched vista, a# near view was obtained of# the# mansion, approached through# a# thick luxuriant shrubbery of# full-grown* evergreens. It was# a# straggling stone structure of# considerable size and# doubtful architecture, having on either side an# ornamental wing, surmounted by# glazed cupolas*, and# indented below with# niches containing statues and# vases alternate. The# front face of# the# building displayed a# row of# fine Corinthian pillars—their capitals screened by# wire-work* shields, to# defend them# from# the# injurious intrusions of# the# feathery tril*> e, who ever chirped* and# hovered about the# forbidden spots, coveting the# shelter denied them#. In the# vicinity of# the# house was# a# spacious flower-garden*, encompassed by# a# protecting plantation of# bay, holly, augustines*, arbutus, laburnum, yellow and# red Barbary, lilac, and# Guelder-rose*, ever# melodious with# the# shy, wary blackbird's whistle, the# sweet notes of# the# secreted thrush, and# the# varied carols of# their# fellow-choristers*, all conspiring to# give motion as well as# life to# their# leafy concealment. To# the# right, was# a# rich, park-like* prospect, sprinkled with# deer, grazing beneath clumps of# commingled oaks and# chestnuts or pulling acorns from# the# low, overhanging? branches of# some# solitary venerable stout-trinket* tree, whose# outspread limbs bent downwards to# the# earth from# whence their# life# was# drawn, as# if in# thankfulness for the# nourishment received. In# an# opposite direction stretched forth undulating woodland scenery, bordering on# an# open furzy down, which was# frequently occupied by# the# moveable* abodes* of# those houseless rovers—the# hardy, spoliating*, mendacious tribe, whose# forefathers Selim*, on#

the very bottom of [their model's] list . . . have some inspirational or hortatory purpose."[38] The same here: the "slang and vulgarisms" typical of oral registers offend "pure classical taste," and the cohort of **Figure 9.17** strike back, "elevating" the tone of discourse to the formal gravity of the written

---

38 Underwood and Sellers, "How Quickly Do Literary Standards Change?," 14.

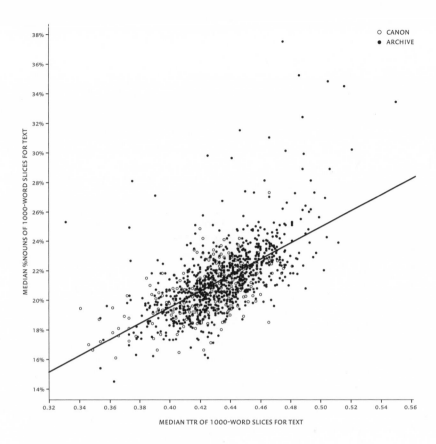

FIGURE 9.19 **Type-token ratio and nouns**

page: many nouns, many adjectives, and as few inflected verb forms as possible (**Figures 9.19, 9.20, 9.21**).[39]

---

39 The high frequency of nouns and adjectives takes us back to the "grammatical bigrams" discussed earlier in this chapter: the "adjective-adjective," "proper noun–noun," "noun-adjective" word pairs. By combining those results with what has emerged in this section, we can finally solve the paradox of texts with high redundancy at the level of bigrams, and high variety at that of type-token ratio. The "labeling" function of bigrams like "count Goldstein" and "uncle Gerard," or the cliché-like loquacity of "iron will" and "clever little," can easily repeat themselves in the course of the novel, thus raising redundancy as measured *at that scale*; but even a mediocre writer is unlikely to repeat "clever little" within a 1,000-word window, thus leaving type-token ratio quite high. And the opposite will happen with the "determiner-noun" or "preposition-determiner" bigrams that are typical of canonical texts: as "the" is the most frequent word in English, it will inevitably repeat itself dozens of times in a 1,000-word segment, thus lowering its lexical variety; but since the noun next to the article can easily vary, redundancy at the level of bigrams will remain relatively low.

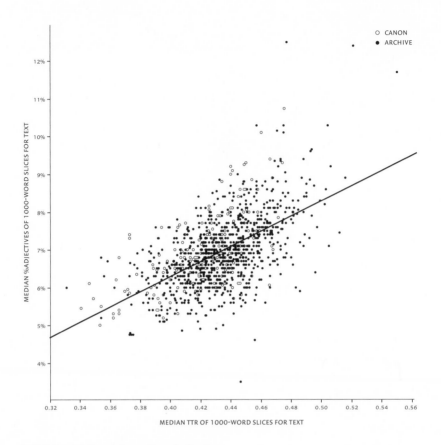

FIGURE 9.20 **Type-token ratio and adjectives**

So far, we have explained the affinity between high type-token ratio and the written register as the result of, loosely speaking, stylistic and ideological choices. But there is also a more neutral, "functional" reason for their correlation. In the findings of corpus linguistics, maximum lexical variety is consistently associated with news: a discourse which needs "an extremely high density of nominal elements," the *Longman Grammar* points out, in order to "refer to a diverse range of people, places, objects, events, etc."[40] There is a double source for lexical variety in news: the first is the necessary specificity internal to each distinct news item; the second, the utter discontinuity *between* one item and the next: as each article or correspondence begins, repetition is "reset" near zero, and type-token ratio can rise accordingly.

---

40 Biber et al., *Longman Grammar of Spoken and Written English*, 53–54.

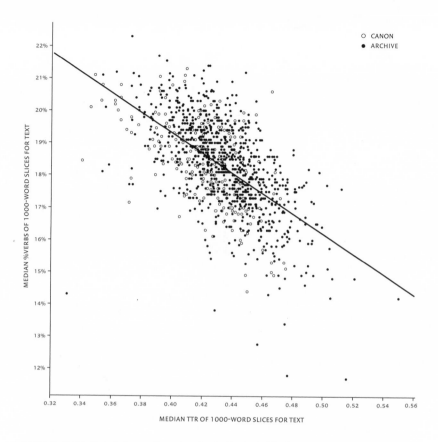

FIGURE 9.21 **Type-token ratio and verbs.** In Hawker's Gibraltar passage, in **Figure 9.18**, adjectives (and participles) are three times as frequent, and inflected verbs three to four times less frequent than the average in 19th-century fiction. By contrast, the *Adam Bede* passage in **Figure 9.16** contains only four nouns and one adjective—"hungry"—in seventy-five words.

This twofold logic returns in fictional texts with high type-token ratio: they include plenty of disparate materials, and further accentuate their diversity by using a plurality of generic forms. Jane West, six of whose novels are in the corpus's top 3 percent for type-token ratio, quotes poetry in seventeen of her twenty-four top-ranked segments; in the absence of poetry, she turns to elaborate metaphors ("expect a fearful tempest to arise, which will clear the tree of its unsound branches"), and even pastiche.[41] William North's

---

41 "First, Venus, queen of gentle devices! taught her prototype, lady Arabella, the use of feigned sighs, artificial tears, and studied faintings: while Esculapius descended from Olympus, and, assuming the

introduction to *The Impostor*—half literary criticism, half apologia—discusses a wide range of topics, and includes an excursus on . . . the wide range of topics he has decided to insert into his "romance."[42] Thomas Hope turns to political prophecy,[43] Lewis Wingfield to a half-parodic architectural digression,[44] Edward Duros to erudite antiquarianism,[45] Edward Hawker to naturalistic instruction . . .

But enough examples. It was time for some final reflections.

o o o

---

form of a smart physician, stepped out of an elegant chariot, and on viewing the patient, after three sagacious nods, whispered to the trembling aunt, that the young lady's disorder, being purely mental, was beyond the power of the healing art. Reduced to the dire alternative of resigning the fair sufferer to a husband or to the grave, the relenting lady Madelina did not long hesitate." (*A Tale of the Times*, 1799)

42 "By introducing literary criticism, satire of political and social evils, and popular illustrations of interesting facts in science, I have hoped to add to the interests of a romance, in which I trust no deficiency of adventure, plot, and carefully developed character will be found. But the day has gone by for mere fashionable novels. The age is utilitarian, and even novelists (the poets of present times) must conform to the mode."

43 "The time is at hand when all the tottering monuments of ignorance, credulity, and superstition, no longer protected by the foolish awe which they formerly inspired, shall strew the earth with their wrecks! Every where the young shoots of reason and liberty, starting from between the rents and crevices of the worn-out* fabrics of feudalism, are becoming too vigorous any longer to be checked: they soon will burst asunder the baseless edifices* of self-interest* and prejudice, which have so long impeded their growth. Religious inquisition, judicial torture, monastic seclusion, tyranny, oppression, fanaticism, and all the other relics of barbarism, are to be driven from the globe." (*Anastasius, or, Memoirs of a Greek*, 1819)

44 "a stately entrance hall in the most fashionable quarter of the metropolis, embellished with lofty Ionic columns of sham Sienna marble; in front of each a magnificent bust of sham bronze by Mr. Nollekins* on a pedestal of scagliola. From a heavily stuccoed* ceiling, wrought in the classic manner, depend six enormous lanterns in the Pagoda style, wreathed with gaping serpents. Along three sides there are rows of 'empire*' benches, covered with amber damask, on which are lolling a regiment of drowsy myrmidons in rich liveries*. Passing these glorious athletes, you enter an ante-room choked with chairs, sofas, settees*, whose florid gilding is heightened by scarlet cushions. Very beautiful." (*Abigel Rowe: A Chronicle of the Regency*, 1883)

45 "The shield, slung to his neck, bore no emblazonry, and his open bacinet and pennon-less* lance argued him neither to have undergone the colaphum, or knightly box on the ear(!); nor the osculum pacis, which more gently signified the chivalric brotherhood. He was, however, well mounted and perfectly armed. Judging from his simple habergeon, and a silver crescent which he bore, more in the way of cognizance than as his own device, he might be pronounced a superior retainer in the service of some great feudatory." (Edward Duros, *Otterbourne; A Story of the English Marches*, 1832)

3. LARGE-SCALE DYNAMICS IN THE LITERARY FIELD

It is not easy, "concluding" a project that had strayed so far from its original aim. We began with canon and archive as our objects of study, and with redundancy and type-token ratio as the means to investigate them; but then, the relationship between means and ends silently reversed itself: canon and archive moved to the periphery of our discussions, while redundancy and type-token ratio were increasingly occupying their center. There was nothing planned about this switch; for quite a while, we didn't even realize it had happened. But we were spending month after month wondering what bigrams actually "meant," and why on earth they managed to separate our texts as well as they did; later, once Allison and Gemma introduced the issue of oral and written registers, we spent even more time on type-token ratio, reading passages from unheard-of novels bristling with pound signs, asterisks, and words like "acclivities," "laburnum," and "commingling." Strange.

Why did we do that? Because we felt that working on type-token ratio would make us understand something about the "internal" forces—as distinct from the "external" ones discussed in section 1.c—that shaped the literary field. It was another slippage in our object of study: the supposed line of demarcation between canon and archive—the diagonal slash still visible in our title—lost much of its interest, reabsorbed within a much larger landscape. With all due sense of proportion, there was a similarity with Bourdieu's trajectory of forty years earlier: when, starting from a study of *Sentimental Education*, and of Flaubert's position within 19th-century French literature, he developed a general framework where Flaubert was still present, but only as one element among many. The same here: canon and archive were still "in" the picture, with their different markers; but now, the point of our diagrams consisted in throwing light on the literary field as a whole. A stylistic polarity exemplified by Eliot and Hawker no longer made us think of canon and archive, but of "oral" and "written" registers. The focus had shifted.

Still, a major difference persisted, between our work and Bourdieu's. For us, the sociology of the literary field *cannot rest on sociology alone*: it needs a strong morphological component. That's why redundancy and (especially) type-token ratio had become so important: their mix of the quantitative and the qualitative was perfect for the morpho-sociology of fiction that was our ultimate goal. Retrospectively, we must admit that the goal has remained out of reach—though it has moved a little closer. Out of reach, in the sense that, where the correlation between morphology and social fate was strongest—the case of redundancy—the elusive nature of the morphological unit of bigrams made a causal chain difficult to establish; whereas, by contrast, where the trait allowed for a rich and explicit analysis—the case of type-token ratio—the correlation was weaker, and became undisputable only for extreme cases. At the same time, two phenomena that had become visible near those extreme cases—the intensity of characters' voices near the lowest scores, and the topical miscellany of the narrator's prose at the opposite extreme—had opened a new line of inquiry, where the quantitative-qualitative continuum reemerged very clearly, and led straight to two key concepts of Bakhtin's theory of the novel: polyphony, and heteroglossia (the "other languages" of consolidated extraliterary discourses, like politics, aesthetics, geography, architecture, etc.). Usually, these two notions are seen as closely related (and Bakhtin himself seemed to think so); but as Walser pointed out in our final round of discussions, our findings revealed that *they were actually localized in opposite regions of the novelistic field*: polyphony tendentially associated with canonical texts, and heteroglossia with forgotten novels. The proximity between heteroglossia and failure was especially arresting. For Bakhtin, when the novel comes into contact with other discourses, it creatively transforms them, appropriating their strength and reinforcing its own centrality within the cultural system. It's as if, with heteroglossia, nothing could ever go wrong. But that's exactly what happened with our small army of forgotten authors: the encounter with other discourses had a paralyzing effect, producing lifeless duplicates of nonfictional prose in lieu of dialogic vitality. As far as survival within the British literary system was concerned, it was a very bad choice.

Heteroglossia as a potential pathology of novelistic structure, then? "There is no fact which is . . . pathological in itself," writes Georges Canguilhem in his masterpiece on 19th-century conceptions of "normality": "An anomaly or a mutation is not in itself pathological. These two express other possible norms of life."[46] If this thesis is right, what doomed Hawker

---

46 Georges Canguilhem, *The Normal and the Pathological* (trans. Carolyn R. Fawcett and Robert S. Cohen (New York: Zone Books, 1989 (1966), 144).

and North and Duros was less the choice of heteroglossia *in itself,* than the fact that it occurred in an age and country—in an ecosystem—*when the form of the novel was moving in the opposite direction*: tightening its internal narrative bolts, rather than looking for inspiration in external discourses (as was still happening in other countries). Even Dickens, for all his Parliamentarese, wrote novels with an outstanding measure of "orality." It was this specific historical conjuncture that made the "other languages" of heteroglossia bad for survival.

On this point, a longer historical view can be of help. Some time ago, the classicist Niklas Holzberg, wrote an essay whose key cognitive metaphor—"the Fringe"—has left a deep mark on the study of the ancient novel.[47] What Holzberg meant with his expression was that, around the extremely small cohort of Greek and Latin "novels proper," a much larger group of texts existed, where novelistic traits were mixed with elements from other discourses (historiography, travel reports, philosophy, political education, pornography . . .), thus expanding the scope of what the novel could do. In the twenty centuries that followed—as the novel "proper" increased its productivity, diversified its forms, and raised its status within the general culture—the role of the Fringe correspondingly contracted, and scholars of modern literature have hardly ever bothered with the idea. But in fact, the Fringe has never ceased to exist: the writers in **Figure 9.17** are its modern version, and their strange proliferation of topics is the typical sign of works situated on the border between the novel and other discourses. The real problem was that, in the meantime, the morphological function of the border—providing a favorable terrain for the encounter between the novel and other discourses—had become more uncertain. A century earlier, a novel engaging the nuances of spiritual autobiography, the mechanics of letter-writing, or the discontinuity of "sensation" could still grow into a masterpiece, and spawn a successful subgenre: *Pilgrim's Progress*, *Pamela*, *Tristram Shandy*, perhaps still even *Waverley*, had significant Fringe-like traits. But in the course of the 19th century—probably as a consequence of the division of intellectual labor, which increased the distance between fiction and the social sciences, making their languages less and less translatable into each other—the role of heteroglossia within the development

---

47 Niklas Holzberg "The Genre: Novels Proper and the Fringe," in *The Novel in the Ancient World*, ed. Gareth Schmeling (Boston-Leiden: Brill, 2003), 11–28.

of novelistic form became problematic. It was this that decided the fate of those forgotten writers.[48]

Whether this also answers our initial question—on the archive changing our knowledge of literature—is not for us to say. What we can say is that, as the work proceeded, we found ourselves devoting more and more time to *Ringrove*, *The Impostor*, and *Arthur Montague*; and that, in a few lucky moments, we felt that these books were raising questions that, say, *Adam Bede* never would. A *few* lucky moments: it isn't easy, keeping your focus on the archive. In part, it is the pull of well-known writers—the pull of what you already know—that draws you back to the beaten track. In part, it is the troubling nature of what forgotten authors force you to face: a vast wreck of ambitious ideals, very unlike the landscape literary historians are used to study. Learning to look at the wreck without arrogance—but also without pieties—is what the new digital archive is asking us to do; in the long run, it might be an even greater change than quantification itself.

2016

---

48 By the same token, from that moment on the masterpieces of heteroglossia—like *Moby-Dick*, or *Ulysses*—had to move increasingly away from the main axis of novelistic development, appealing less and less to nonacademic readers.

CONCLUSION

Patterns and Interpretation

Franco Moretti

1. ABSTRACTION

One thing for sure: digitization has completely changed the literary archive. People like me used to work on a few hundred 19th-century novels. Today, we work on thousands of them; tomorrow, hundreds of thousands. This has had a profound effect on literary history, but also on critical methodology. When we work on two hundred thousand novels instead of two hundred, we are not doing the same thing, one thousand times bigger; we are doing a different thing. The new scale changes our relationship to our object, and in fact it changes the object itself. "No one has ever seen the objects studied by contemporary historians," Krzysztof Pomian once wrote, "and no one *could* ever have seen them . . . because they have no equivalent within lived experience."[1] True. No one has a lived experience of demographic change, or of literacy rates, or of **Figure 10.1**—which the reader may remember from the chapter "Style at the Scale of the Sentence."

I will explain this chart in a minute. For now, let me just say that this is what literature has become in the new space of the literary lab. These are still novels, but prepared for analysis in a way that severs all connections with the lived experience of literature. Watching a play, listening to a poem, reading a novel—this is the concrete experience of literature. **Figure 10.1** is an abstraction. It takes certain novelistic elements, pulls them out of their context, and re-presents them in a completely different

---

1 Pomian, *L'Ordre du temps*, 31.

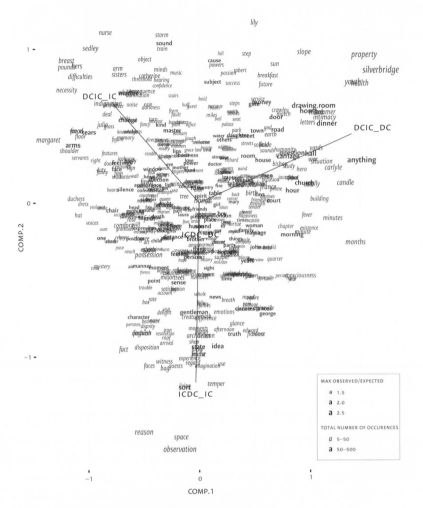

FIGURE 10.1 "Objects with no equivalent within lived experience"

combination. In this case, the presentation is based on principal component analysis, but it could have been a trend, a map, a tree of distances—or many other things. All of them, equally abstract. Alongside the explosion of the archive, then, and probably with deeper consequences, this is the great novelty of computational criticism: a redefinition of literature that foregrounds those traits that can be more easily abstracted, and hence programmed. Algorithms have changed *what* we study, and *how* we study it. Think of reading. For centuries, reading has been indispensable to the understanding of literature. In front of **Figure 10.1**, it is nothing. Nothing.

Just to be clear, it's not that we should stop reading books. Reading is one of life's greatest pleasures, it would be insane to give it up. What is at stake is not reading, it's *the continuity between reading and (a certain kind of) knowledge.* I read books, but when I work in the Literary Lab they're not the basis of my work. *Corpora* are; ideally, those two hundred thousand novels. Here, size is again crucial, because a corpus is not "just like a text, only more of it."[2] A text is a "communicative event," written by someone, in specific circumstances, to convey a specific meaning. No one writes corpora. They are not "communicative events"—they are not events at all, they are artificial abstract objects created by a researcher. A text is meant to address us, to "speak" to us. Corpora don't speak to us, which is to say, *they have no meaning in the usual sense of the word.*[3]

Now, meaning is not just one of the things literary critics study; it is *the* thing. Here lies the great challenge of computational criticism: thinking about literature, but removing meaning to the periphery of the picture. Of course this is also the great challenge *for* computational criticism. You discard meaning and replace it with—what? Dismembered in **Figure 10.1** is a sentence—"Yet when he arrived at Stone Court he could not see the change in Raffles without a shock"—which, when we encounter it in *Middlemarch*, triggers a chain of events that will turn a major character into an accomplice in someone's death. A very meaningful sentence. None of that remains visible in **Figure 10.1**. This is what we lose with a computational approach. What do we gain?

At a certain point in "Style at the Scale of the Sentence," we compared sentences in which the independent clause came first, and the dependent clause followed ("I opened the door, as soon as the bell rang": abbreviated to IC-DC), to those in which the order was reversed ("As soon as the bell rang, I opened the door": abbreviated to DC-IC). We were particularly interested in the latter type, because a sentence that begins with a dependent clause can't really stop there (As soon as the bell rang . . . what?). You have to go on, it's a very *narrative* arrangement, and we wanted to know whether it differed from the other type, not just in syntactical order, but in

---

2 Elena Tognini Bonelli, "Theoretical Overview of the Evolution of Corpus Linguistics," in *The Routledge Handbook of Corpus Linguistics,* ed. Anne O'Keeffe and Michael McCarthy (New York: Routledge, 2010), 19.

3 This "usual sense" is not a literary critic's idea of meaning; if anything, a strong link between meaning, context, and use is more typical of anthropologists like Clifford Geertz, or historians of political thought like Quentin Skinner and J. G. A. Pocock.

semantic content as well. So we broke the sentences down into four classes of clauses,[4] calculated their most distinctive words, and used principal component analysis to visualize the results. **Figure 10.1** is the conclusion of the process: the four clauses are the black vectors, and are surrounded by the nouns that most characterize them; the formatting of the words (bold or italic) indicates their raw frequency, their size their statistical distinctiveness, and good separation among the clauses suggests that syntax and semantics are indeed correlated. Good. And now?

2. PATTERNS

What we did—what most literary researchers would do, in these circumstances—was to look for signs of an unusual configuration. Luckily, in the upper right quadrant, around the dependent clause of the dependent-independent sequence, a cluster of related terms emerged: *drawing room, home, house, door hall, church, building, gate, town, road, street, palace, yards, slope,* and *park* (**Figure 10.2**). In the upper left quadrant, around the *in*dependent clause of the same type of sentence, there was a different, but equally consistent cluster: *feelings, jealousy, indignation, despair, admiration, fancy, interest, memory,* and *tears* (**Figure 10.3**). From what looked like chaos, a pattern had emerged (**Figure 10.4**). We remove meaning to the periphery of the investigation and replace it with what?, I asked a minute ago. With this—with patterns. From reading, to pattern recognition.

Great keyword of our times, pattern. What exactly does it mean? Certainly, not what it used to when it entered the English language. Derived from the French *patron*—master, owner, boss—"pattern" initially indicated, the OED tells us, "something shaped or designed to serve as a model from which a thing is to be made" (1324); "an example or model to be imitated" (c. 1450); "an example, an instance, esp. one taken as typical, representative, or eminent" (1555). In that period, pattern was a *normative* concept: people created patterns, and then imposed them onto the

---

4 Continuing the example, the four classes and their abbreviations are as follows: "*I opened the door,* as soon as the bell rang," independent clause of the IC-DC sequence, or ICDC_IC; "I opened the door, *as soon as the bell rang*," dependent clause of the IC-DC sequence, or ICDC_DC; "As soon as the bell rang, *I opened the door*," independent clause of the DC-IC sequence, or DCIC_IC; "*As soon as the bell rang,* I opened the door," dependent clause of the DC-IC sequence, or DCIC_DC.

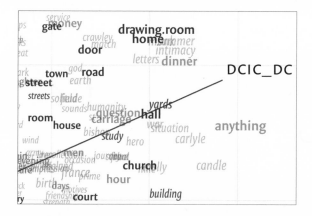

FIGURE 10.2 **Dependent clauses and their main semantic cluster**

FIGURE 10.3 **Independent clauses and their main semantic cluster**

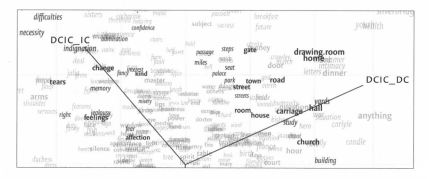

FIGURE 10.4 **A pattern emerges**

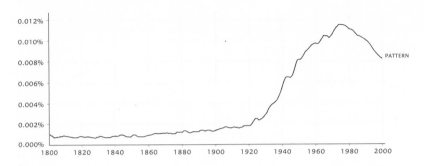

FIGURE 10.5 **"Pattern" in English, 1800–2000.** Source: Google Books Ngram Viewer, consulted on April 21, 2016.

world. Then, about a century ago, a 180-degree shift occurred. We no longer brought patterns into the world, but found them there. Patterns acquired an empirical, independent existence: "a regular and intelligible form or sequence discernible in certain actions or situations; esp. one on which the prediction of successive or future events may be based" (1883); "an arrangement or relationship of elements, esp. one which indicates or implies an underlying causative process other than chance" (1900).[5] It was at the moment these "objective" features emerged, incidentally, that the frequency of "pattern" suddenly increased (**Figure 10.5**).

A "relationship of elements"—like the one we had found between semantics and syntax in our study of the sentence. A "correlation," another great keyword of our times. A few years ago, the then-editor of *Wired* magazine, Chris Anderson, used this notion to declare "the scientific method obsolete":

> Scientists are trained to recognize that correlation is not causation, that. . . . you must understand the underlying mechanisms that connect the two. . . . But faced with massive data, this approach to science . . . is becoming obsolete. . . . Petabytes allow us to say: "Correlation is enough." . . . Correlation supersedes causation, and science can

---

5 In the new meaning of the term, the earlier subjective element hasn't quite disappeared, but it has shrunk to the merely subordinate function of "recognition." Subjectivity is still needed to extricate the pattern from its surroundings (to "discern" it, as in the 1883 entry), but it no longer imposes a model "onto" the world, as had been the case earlier.

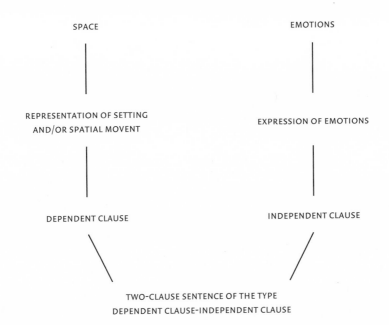

SPACE   EMOTIONS

REPRESENTATION OF SETTING   EXPRESSION OF EMOTIONS
AND/OR SPATIAL MOVENT

DEPENDENT CLAUSE   INDEPENDENT CLAUSE

TWO-CLAUSE SENTENCE OF THE TYPE
DEPENDENT CLAUSE-INDEPENDENT CLAUSE

FIGURE 10.6 **The form behind the pattern.** Here are a few instances of this abstract structure, all drawn from the corpus of "Style at the Scale of the Sentence": "When Peter perceived the village, he burst into a shout of joy" (Radcliffe); "When the day came round for my return to the scene of the deed of violence, my terrors reached their height" (Dickens); "When Deronda met Gwendolen and Grandcourt on the staircase, his mind was seriously preoccupied" (Eliot); "Yet when he arrived at Stone Court he could not see the change in Raffles without a shock" (Eliot).

advance even without coherent models, unified theories, or really any mechanistic explanation at all.[6]

This is a wonderful statement, because it expresses with absolute candor the ambivalence toward knowledge that is typical of our times. Correlations, yes. But no theories, no models, not even explanations! What is knowledge, without explanations? This expresses the same kind of anti-intellectualism as that generated by the Industrial Revolution two centuries ago, and for the same reason: knowledge is good—to make machines work. Period. "Useful knowledge," the Victorians called it; engineers, not

---

6 Chris Anderson, "The End of Theory: The Data Deluge Makes the Scientific Method Obsolete," *Wired*, June 27, 2008, https://www.wired.com/2008/06/pb-theory/.

scientists. The same in Silicon Valley today, this El Dorado of engineers where Anderson has now become a successful manufacturer of drones.

It's not that pattern recognition doesn't matter. It does—as a beginning. What *really* matters, though, are all those things Anderson had declared to be obsolete: finding the underlying mechanism, establishing causation, *explaining* why patterns are there in the first place, and what do they do. And this requires, as a first step, a further leap into abstraction. If the image in **Figure 10.1** seemed abstract, well, *it wasn't abstract enough*: we must take all the *home* and *door* and *road*, all the *tears* and *jealousy* and *fancy* of **Figures 10.3–10.4**, and reduce them to a purely *formal* relationship: space in dependent clauses—emotions in independent ones (**Figure 10.6**). From the chaos of data, through the emergence of patterns, to the clarity of form. Distillation. And it's not just a process of clarification: it's also the discovery of a *causal mechanism*. Form is the repeatable element of literature, as I wrote elsewhere, and *if there is a pattern in the data, it's because behind it there is a form which repeats itself over and over again*.[7] The pattern *is* this repetition. Spatial terms keep occurring in dependent clauses, emotional ones in independent ones, and eventually we notice what is going on; we see—we "recognize" the pattern. But what we see is just the shadow of the form in **Figure 10.6**. *Patterns are the shadows of forms upon data*. If you don't grasp the form, your hands are empty.

3. INTERPRETATION

The correlation between *home* and *road* and dependent clauses is—to use a word universally despised by contemporary criticism—a *fact*: meaning, that any investigation of these clauses would find the same quantities of homes and roads as we did.[8] That those words form a cluster, however, and that the cluster means space—these are not facts, but *interpretations*.

---

7 See "The Slaughterhouse of Literature," in Moretti, *Distant Reading*.

8 A fact because intersubjective, therefore, but also in the sense of *factum*—because the correlation we had found was not a "given," but the result of a series of operations: the identification of specific sentences, their division into clauses, the establishment of their most distinctive words, the decision to focus on nouns, the choice of a quantitative threshold for their analysis, their visualization via principal component analysis . . . Anyone repeating this series of steps would find the same values—but the steps themselves are dictated by a specific, and subjective, research interest.

Someone else may set *home* and *road* in opposition, as *inside* and *outside*. I cluster them together, as two versions of space. Here, subjective decisions clearly resume priority. Algorithms generate new facts, whose interpretation continues, however, to rely on a different hermeneutic tradition.

I began this essay by saying that computational criticism was replacing meaning with patterns; now, I am interpreting patterns on the basis of the meaning of words. But I don't think this is a contradiction. It's just that the term "meaning" can be used in (at least) two very different ways. In interpreting the pattern in **Figures 10.2–10.4**, I was referring to the "dictionary" meaning of words, which the founder of modern hermeneutics, Friedrich Schleiermacher, would usually indicate with the term *Bedeutung*; whereas earlier on, in discussing texts as communicative events, I was referring to meaning in a specific context, which Schleiermacher would usually call *Sinn*.[9] "Significance" may be a possible English translation of *Sinn*, leaving "meaning" for the more abstract dictionary use; *senso* and *significato* are used in Italian in a similar way, and comparable pairs exist in other languages. The point is not what words we use, but the awareness that our reflection on meaning may take two very different directions: dictionary meaning—or meaning-in-context; large aggregates—or the "given statement," as Schleiermacher put it, on the page where he defined "the rules of the art of interpretation."[10]

Schleiermacher's claim for this art is well-known, but it's so wonderfully shameless—and so challenging for what we are trying to do—that I want to repeat it: "The task [of interpretation] is to be formulated as follows: 'To understand the text at first as well as and then even better than its author.'"[11] This is, incidentally, the only justification for the existence of literary critics. Without us darkness would prevail, fortunately we are here, understanding literature better than its authors. But *why* do we understand better? Here lies Schleiermacher's stroke of genius. The reason is not our

---

9 "Some term what a word is thought to mean 'in and of itself' its meaning [*Bedeutung*] and what the word is thought to mean in a given context its 'sense' [*Sinn*]. Others argue that a word can have only a single meaning [*Bedeutung*] and not a sense [*Sinn*]; that a sentence regarded in isolation has a sense [*Sinn*], but not a purport [*Verstand*], for only a complete text has a purport." Friedrich Schleiermacher, *Hermeneutics: The Handwritten Manuscripts*, ed. Heinz Kimmerle, trans. James Duke and Jack Forstman (Missoula, MT: The Scholars Press, 1977), 117.

10 Schleirmacher, *Hermeneutics*, 111.

11 Schleirmacher, *Hermeneutics*, 112.

superior knowledge, but *our ignorance*: "we have no direct knowledge of what was in the author's mind," and so we're forced "to become aware of many things of which [the author] himself may have been unconscious." The author knows many things that, so to speak, he doesn't know he knows. An interpreter can only know them by making them explicit; that's what understanding a text "better than its author" means. And it's extremely elegant, but presents a big obstacle for quantitative and computational criticism. For Schleiermacher, the aim of this type of interpretation consists in understanding *individual texts in their "individuality,"*[12] and in relation to the "intention" (however defined) of the author. Of course corpora have neither individuality nor intentions. So?

Why is interpretation necessary in the first place? Because of the "many things" that an author "knows," but leaves implicit. And why does an author do that? Schleiermacher doesn't really say, but we can conjecture: because these things were learned *by doing*, not by explicit declarative knowledge. Know-how, more than know-that; practices and conventions which were widely shared in the author's world. *This* is what the interpreter must "become aware of": not hidden individual secrets, but habits that were socially ubiquitous, and that escaped attention, purloined-letter-like, precisely *because* of their visibility. What the interpreter recovers, in other words, is *the social within an individual oeuvre.*

Here, the ultimate aim of Schleiermacher's project and the means necessary to achieve it emerge as somewhat at odds with each other. The aim is the understanding of individual texts; the means, the making explicit of social practices. The latter are necessary to the hermeneutic enterprise, but in a purely instrumental way; in themselves, they are not interesting. On this, computational criticism clearly reverses the hierarchy. Conventions matter for us much more than any individual text. They matter *as such*, unlike what happens in the hermeneutic project. In another sense, though, our work can be seen as the perfect completion of hermeneutics, because the "abstract objects" computation produces—these objects no one experiences directly, but which we all somehow know how to take into account—are exactly what hermeneutics wants to raise to the level of consciousness. We could make Schleiermacher's motto our own: Quantitative

---

12 "Technical interpretation: The language and its determining power disappear and seem to be merely an organ of the person, in the service of his individuality" (161).

hermeneutics is the art of understanding conventions—forms, genres, styles, practices—better than their society ever did. It's not that we have invented the study of conventions: genre theory and stylistics have existed for a very long time. But our abstract objects are finally *the right objects of study* for this approach; better than their predecessors, anyway. They allow us to shift from "type thinking" to "population thinking," to use Ernst Mayr's concepts. What we've done is create the right laboratory environment for what had so far largely remained speculative theories.

4. FORM, HISTORY, EXPLANATION

More on this at the end. First, a quick step back to **Figure 10.6**. There is no logical relationship between space and emotions; so, why did they "click," and appear so frequently together? As always with form, the explanation is to be found in history. Around 1800, as nation building and early industrialization were violently reshaping European geography, novelists ceased to treat space as a mere "container" of the story—as a sort of "box" in which events unfolded on their own—and turned it into a force that actively *shaped* events: the "demonic" power of the *milieu*, as Auerbach put it in *Mimesis*. Social space had changed too much for literary space not to change as well. Likewise for emotions; around the same time, their expression on stage and on the written page was drawn towards that "rhetoric of excess," which, as Peter Brooks has shown in *The Melodramatic Imagination*, was a major symbolic consequence of the French Revolution.[13]

Why space and emotions? Because they had both been overheated by contemporary events, and combining them in the micro-unit of a two-clause sentence was a way to bring some unity into historical experience. This is what form *always* does. It selects some of the countless elements of the given world, recombines them, and creates a *model* of that world. Space has become so powerful, it generates events—and emotional intensity is a particularly significant event: this is what that sentence says. And it seems to have all originated with Gothic novels, where space and emotions were both sensational and inextricable: castles and terror, dungeons and

---

13 Peter Brooks, *The Melodramatic Imagination: Balzac, Henry James, Melodrama, and the Mode of Excess* (New Haven, CT: Yale University Press, 1976).

madness, caves and despair . . . Implausible. But, once the formal connection was in place, it could be endlessly refunctionalized—the repeatable element in literature—and adapted to the changing needs of the age. First came historical novels, where the space of internal peripheries provided an asylum for the grand passions banished from the modern world; later, it was the turn of the metropolises, and of their peculiar pathologies (Paris and ambition, London and eccentricity, Petersburg and radicalism, Madrid and folly); then the provinces, and the deadly dangers of modern boredom; while the great naturalistic cycles of the last quarter century endowed specific regions, like Verga's Sicily or Hardy's Wessex, with tragic significance. With each generation, the space-emotion complex was reinvented, joining a specific articulation of the nation-state to a different reaction to modern life. Chronotopes, saturated with feelings. No wonder writers kept returning to the structure of **Figure 10.6**.[14]

This was a crazily accelerated summary, of course. But I wanted to give an idea of how recognizing the form behind the pattern allows us to unify separate historical givens in a single explanation. If this essay began by moving away from the lived experience of literature towards abstraction, form has emerged as simultaneously *the apex* of the process, and the turning point that allows us to *reverse the direction*, and return from abstraction to literary history. Here, form functions very much like Max Weber's ideal-type: "a mental construct," he wrote in "'Objectivity' in Social Science and Social Policy," that "cannot be found empirically anywhere in reality" but that, once constructed, can be used "for *comparison with* and *measurement of* reality."[15] This is exactly how we should think of literary form: a mental construct which we will never find *as such* in individual works, but which we can use to "measure" their relationships. Form will *never* explain an individual text, and is the *only* thing that can explain a large series of data.

o o o

---

14 If this scenario is correct, the space-emotions complex should persist throughout the 19th century, while its specific semantic clusters should modify themselves every generation or so. Unfortunately, the corpus of the original study is not large enough to test this prediction, which remains therefore, for the time being, just a hypothesis.

15 Max Weber, "'Objectivity' in Social Science and Social Policy," in *The Methodology of the Social Sciences*, trans. Edward A. Shils and Henry A. Finch (Glencoe, IL: The Free Press, 1949), 90, 97.

5. NOISE

And yet, the return to "reality," to repeat Weber's term, may happen in more than one way. Let's ask ourselves: why do we look for patterns to begin with, and why are we happy when we find them? Because they reveal some kind of order, and we *want* to find order, especially when we are confronted with large masses of data. "It is not by chance," wrote a great precursor of computational criticism, Leo Spitzer, "that the 'philological circle' was discovered by a theologian, *who was wont to harmonize the discordant, to retrace the beauty of God in this world.*"[16] The beauty of God in the world—order in the strongest possible sense. The trouble is, there is no beauty of God in patterns. There can't be. From data through patterns to form, I said earlier, and that's exactly the problem: patterns lie halfway between two domains—the chaos of empirical data, and the clarity of conceptual form—that are too "discordant" to be truly "harmonized." Patterns somehow bridge the gulf between the empirical and the conceptual; they *make form visible within data*, and it's a small miracle. But, small: right in the middle of the spatial cluster of *town* and *road* and *door* you find . . . *god* (and a little lower there's a *bishop*; plus *sounds, questions, match, hero, letter,* etc.: **Figure 10.7**). The pattern is real, not perfect. Its borders are porous; its space, full of unharmonized discordance. What should we do with this discordance?

For the logic of research, discordance—disorder, noise, chaos, call it what you will—is fundamentally an obstacle that we must learn to ignore. In order to "see" the space-emotion pattern, we must somehow *not* see god, bishop, and company. They are there, we know they are there, but we don't look at them. We have put on blinders, to use Weber's great metaphor in "Science as a Vocation." Once we have seen the pattern, we can take off the blinders, and then, it's impossible not to notice how *small* the region of order actually is. Form is everywhere encircled by noise: a maelstrom of semantic options that have kept whirling around, without ever crystallizing into stable structures. Failed conventions. Failed styles. Noise. Now: what if we took this noise *as itself an object of knowledge?* Not an obstacle to interpretation, but its aim. What would interpretation become—what would a *hermeneutics of noise* be like? This is the ultimate challenge of

---

16 Spitzer, "Linguistics and Literary History," in *Representative Essays*, 32 (emphasis mine).

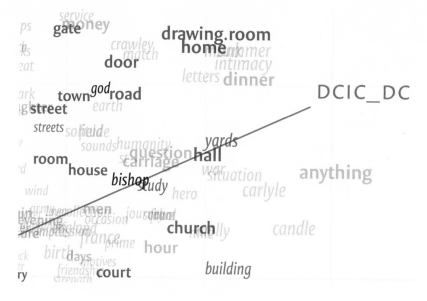

FIGURE 10.7 **Patterns are real, but never perfect**

digitization to literary theory. Traditional interpretation, once it had removed noise from the horizon of research, could legitimately keep it out of the picture forever. The alliance of algorithms and archive puts noise in front of our eyes again, and again, and again. "The times have been," muses Macbeth at the sight of Banquo's ghost, "That, when the brains were out, the man would die, / And there an end; but now they rise again." Computation takes all the Banquos who have been slaughtered in the process of literary selection, and brings them back to life. Speaking to these ghosts will be our task.

2017

WORKS CITED

Adburgham, Alison. *Silver Fork Society: Fashionable Life and Literature from 1814 to 1840*. London: Constable, 1983.

Algee-Hewitt, Mark, and Mark McGurl. "Between Canon and Corpus: Six Perspectives on 20th-Century Novels." *Pamphlets of the Stanford Literary Lab Pamphlet* 8. January 2015. https://litlab.stanford.edu/LiteraryLabPamphlet8. pdf.

Algee-Hewitt, Mark, Ryan Heuser, Annalise Lockhart, Erik Steiner, and Van Tran. "Mapping the Emotions of London in Fiction, 1700–1900: A Crowd-sourcing Experiment." In *Literary Mapping in the Digital Age*, edited by David Cooper, Christopher Donaldson, and Patricia Murrieta-Flores, 25–46. London: Routledge, 2016.

Allison, Sarah. "Discerning Syntax: George Eliot's Relative Clauses." *ELH* 81, no. 4 (Winter 2014): 1275–97.

Anderson, Chris. "The End of Theory: The Data Deluge Makes the Scientific Method Obsolete." *Wired*. June 27, 2008. https://www.wired.com/2008/06/pb-theory/.

Auerbach, Erich. *Mimesis*. Translated by Willard R. Trask. Princeton, NJ: Princeton University Press, 1974.

———. *Travaux du séminaire de philologie romane*. Istanbul: Devlet Basimevi, 1937.

Alt, Mick. *Exploring Hyperspace: A Non-Mathematical Explanation of Multivariate Analysis*. New York: McGraw-Hill, 1990.

Bain, Alexander. *English Composition and Rhetoric: A Manual*. London: Longmans, Green, and Co., 1866.

Bakhtin, Mikhail. *The Dialogic Imagination*. Translated by Caryl Emerson and Michael Holquist. Austin, TX: University of Texas Press, 1981.

Banfield, Ann. *Unspeakable Sentences*. Boston: Routledge & Kegan Paul, 1982.

Barthes, Roland. *Image-Music-Text*. Translated by Stephen Heath. New York: Hill and Wang, 1977.

Barthes, Roland. *Writing Degree Zero*. Translated by Annette Lavers and Colin Smith. New York: Hill and Wang, 1967.

Benveniste, Émile. *Problems in General Linguistics*. Translated by Mary Elizabeth Meek. Coral Gables, FL: University of Miami Press, 1971.

Biber, Douglas, Stig Johansson, Geoffrey Leech, Susan Conrad, and Edward Finegan. *Longman Grammar of Spoken and Written English*. Harlow: Longman, 1999.

Biber, Douglas, and Susan Conrad. *Register, Genre, and Style*. Cambridge, UK: Cambridge University Press, 2009.

Biber, Douglas, Susan Conrad, and Randi Reppen. *Corpus Linguistics: Investigating Language Structure and Use.* Cambridge, UK: Cambridge University Press, 1998.

Blei, David M. "Topic Modeling and Digital Humanities." *Journal of Digital Humanities* 2, no. 1 (Winter 2012).

Blei, David M., Andrew Y. Ng, and Michael I. Jordan. "Latent Dirichlet Allocation." *Journal of Machine Learning Research* 3 (July 2002–March 2003): 993–1022.

Bourdieu, Pierre. *Distinction: A Social Critique of the Judgement of Taste.* Translated by Richard Nice. Cambridge, MA: Harvard University Press, 1984.

———. *Outline of a Theory of Practice.* Translated by Richard Nice. Cambridge, UK: Cambridge University Press, 1977.

———. *The Rules of Art: Genesis and Structure of the Literary Field.* Translated by Susan Emanuel. Stanford: Stanford University Press, 1996.

Boyle, Robert. "A Proemial Essay, wherein, with some Considerations touching Experimental Essays in general, Is interwoven such an Introduction to all those written by the Author, as is necessary to be perused for the better understanding of them." In *The Works of the Honourable Robert Boyle*, edited by Thomas Birch, 299–318. 2nd ed. London: J. and F. Rivington, 1772.

Braudel, Fernand. *On History.* Translated by Sarah Matthews. Chicago: University of Chicago Press, 1980.

Bremond, Claude. "Concept and Theme." In *The Return of Thematic Criticism*, edited by Werner Sollors, 46–59. Cambridge, MA: Harvard University Press, 1993.

Bremond, Claude, Joshua Landy, and Thomas Pavel, eds. *Thematics: New Approaches.* Albany, NY: State University of New York Press, 1995.

Bridgman, P. W. *The Logic of Modern Physics.* New York: Macmillan, 1927.

Brooks, Peter. *The Melodramatic Imagination: Balzac, Henry James, Melodrama, and the Mode of Excess.* New Haven, CT: Yale University Press, 1976.

Canguilhem, Georges. *The Normal and the Pathological.* Translated by Carolyn R. Fawcett and Robert S. Cohen. New York: Zone Books, 1989.

Cavalli-Sforza, L. Luca, Paolo Menozzi, and Alberto Piazza. *The History and Geography of Human Genes.* Princeton, NJ: Princeton University Press, 1994.

Christensen, Francis. "A Generative Rhetoric of the Paragraph." *College Composition and Communication* 16, no. 3 (October 1965): 144–56.

Cohen, Dan. "Searching for the Victorians." *Dan Cohen's Digital Humanities Blog.* October 4, 2010. http://www.dancohen.org/2010/10/04/searching-for-the-victorians/.

Crystal, David. *A Dictionary of Linguistics and Phonetics.* 5th ed. Oxford: Wiley-Blackwell, 2003.

Dames, Nicholas. "Wave-Theories and Affective Physiologies." *Victorian Studies* 46, no. 2 (Winter 2004): 206–16.

———. *Physiology of the Novel: Reading, Neural Science, and the Form of Victorian Fiction*. Oxford: Oxford University Press, 2007.

Denniston, J. D. *The Greek Particles*. 2nd ed. Revised by K. J. Dover. Oxford: Oxford University Press, 1950.

English, James. *The Economy of Prestige: Prizes, Awards, and the Circulation of Cultural Value*. Cambridge, MA: Harvard University Press, 2005.

———. "Now, Not Now: Counting Time in Contemporary Fiction Studies." *Modern Language Quarterly* 77, no. 3 (September 2016): 395–418.

Finn, Ed. "Becoming Yourself: The Afterlife of Reception." *Pamphlets of the Stanford Literary Lab Pamphlet* 3. September 2011. https://litlab.stanford.edu/LiteraryLabPamphlet3.pdf.

Fisher, Philip. *The Vehement Passions*. Princeton, NJ: Princeton University Press, 2002.

Frank, Joseph. *Dostoevsky, The Miraculous Years, 1865–1871*. Princeton, NJ: Princeton University Press, 1995.

Gallagher, Catherine. *The Industrial Reformation of English Fiction: Social Discourse and Narrative Form, 1832–1867*. Chicago: University of Chicago Press, 1985.

Gamer, Michael. "A Select Collection: Barbauld, Scott, and the Rise of the (Reprinted) Novel." In *Recognizing the Romantic Novel: New Histories of British Fiction, 1780–1830*, edited by Jillian Heydt-Stevenson and Charlotte Sussman, 155–191. Liverpool: Liverpool University Press, 2008.

Gemma, Marissa. "Exceedingly Correct: Stylistic Polemics in Nineteenth-Century American Literature." PhD diss., Stanford University, 2012.

Ginzburg, Carlo. *Clues, Myths, and the Historical Method*. Translated by John and Anne C. Tedeschi. Baltimore: Johns Hopkins University Press, 1989.

Goldman, Michael. *Imperial Nature: The World Bank and Struggles for Social Justice in the Age of Globalization*. New Haven, CT: Yale University Press, 2005.

Gross, Adolf. *Die Stichomythie in der griechischen Tragödie und Komödie, ihre Anwendung und ihr Ursprung*. Berlin: Weidmann, 1905.

Guillory, John. *Cultural Capital: The Problem of Literary Canon Formation*. Chicago: University of Chicago Press, 1995.

Hancock, John Leonard. *Studies in Stichomythia*. Chicago: University of Chicago Press, 1917.

Hands, D. Wade. "On Operationalisms and Economics." *Journal of Economic Issues* 38, no. 4 (December 2004): 953–68.

Hegel, G. W. F. *Aesthetics: Lectures on Fine Art*. Vol. 1. Translated by T. M. Knox. Oxford: Clarendon Press, 1975.

Holzberg, Niklas. "The Genre: Novels Proper and the Fringe." In *The Novel in the Ancient World*, edited by Gareth Schmeling, 11–28. Boston-Leiden: Brill, 2003.

Hope, Jonathan, and Michael Witmore. "The Hundredth Psalm to the Tune of 'Greensleeves': Digital Approaches to Shakespeare's Language of Genre." "New Media Approaches to Shakespeare," ed. Katherine Rowe, special issue, *Shakespeare Quarterly* 61, no. 3 (Fall 2010): 357–90.

———. "Shakespeare by the Numbers: On the Linguistic Texture of the Late Plays." In *Early Modern Tragicomedy*, edited by Subha Mukherji and Raphael Lyne, 133–53. London: Boydell and Brewer, 2007.

———. "The Very Large Textual Object: A Prosthetic Reading of Shakespeare." Special issue, *Early Modern Literary Studies* 9, no. 3 (January 2004): 1–36.

Huddleston, Rodney, and George K. Pullum. *The Cambridge Grammar of the English Language*. Cambridge, UK: Cambridge University Press, 2002.

Jockers, Matthew. *Macroanalysis: Digital Methods and Literary History*. Urbana, IL: University of Illinois Press, 2013.

Johnson, Steven. *Where Good Ideas Come From: The Natural History of Innovation*. New York: Riverhead, 2010.

Kapur, Devesh, John P. Lewis, and Richard C. Webb, eds. *The World Bank: Its First Half Century*. Washington, DC: Brookings Institution Press, 1997.

Kaufer, David, Suguru Ishizaki, Brian Butler, and Jeff Collins. *The Power of Words: Unveiling the Speaker and Writer's Hidden Craft*. Mahwah, NJ: Lawrence Erlbaum Associates, 2004.

Kay, Christian, Jane Roberts, Michael Samuels, and Irené Wotherspoon, eds. *Historical Thesaurus of the Oxford English Dictionary*. Oxford: Oxford University Press, 2009.

Keefe, Rosanna, and Peter Smith. *Vagueness: A Reader*. Cambridge, MA: MIT Press, 1997.

Koselleck, Reinhart. *Futures Past: On the Semantics of Historical Time*. Translated by Keith Tribe. Cambridge, MA: MIT Press, 1985.

Koyré, Alexandre. *Études d'histoire de la pensée philosophique*. Paris: Armand Colin, 1961.

Kuhn, Thomas. *The Essential Tension: Selected Studies in Scientific Tradition and Change*. Chicago: University of Chicago Press, 1977.

Lambert, Mark. *Dickens and the Suspended Quotation*. New Haven, CT: Yale University Press, 1981.

Latour, Bruno, and Steve Woolgar. *Laboratory Life: The Construction of Scientific Facts*. Princeton, NJ: Princeton University Press, 1986.

Leroi-Gourhan, André. *Gesture and Speech*. Translated by Anna Bostock Berger. Cambridge, MA: MIT Press, 1993.

Lewis, Edwin Herbert. *The History of the English Paragraph*. Chicago: University of Chicago Press, 1894.

Longacre, R. E. "The Paragraph as a Grammatical Unit." In *Discourse and Syntax*, edited by Talmy Givón, *Syntax and Semantics* 12, 115–34. New York: Academic Press, 1979.

Liu, Alan. "Where Is Cultural Criticism in the Digital Humanities?" In *Debates in the Digital Humanities*, edited by Matthew K. Gold, 490–509. Minneapolis: University of Minnesota Press, 2012.

Michel, Jean-Baptiste, et al. "Quantitative Analysis of Culture Using Millions of Digitized Books." *Science* 331, no. 6014 (January 14, 2011): 176–82.

Mitchell, Timothy. *Carbon Democracy: Political Power in the Age of Oil.* New York: Verso, 2011.

Moretti, Franco. *Atlas of the European Novel.* New York: Verso, 1998.

——. *The Bourgeois.* New York: Verso, 2013.

——. *Distant Reading.* New York: Verso, 2013.

——. *Graphs, Maps, Trees.* New York: Verso, 2005.

——. "Network Theory, Plot Analysis." *New Left Review* 68 (March–April 2011): 80–102.

——. *The Novel: History, Geography, Culture.* Princeton, NJ: Princeton University Press, 2006.

Orwell, George. "Politics and the English Language." In *The Collected Essays, Journalism and Letters of George Orwell*, edited by Sonia Orwell and Ian Angus, 156–70. Vol. 4, *In Front of Your Nose, 1945-1950*. Harmondsworth: Penguin, 1968.

Pascal, Roy. *The Dual Voice: Free Indirect Speech and Its Functioning in the Nineteenth-Century European Novel.* Manchester: Manchester University Press, 1977.

Perazzini, Federica. *Il Gotico @ Distanza.* Rome: Edizioni Nuova Cultura, 2013.

Pestre, Dominque, ed. *Le gouvernement des technosciences: Gouverner le progrès et ses dégâts depuis 1945.* Paris: La Découverte, 2014.

Pomian, Krzysztof. *L'Ordre du temps.* Paris: Gallimard, 1984.

Popper, Karl. *The Logic of Scientific Discovery.* New York: Harper & Row, 1965.

Porter, Roy. *London: A Social History.* Cambridge, MA: Harvard University Press, 1995.

Propp, Vladimir. *Morphology of the Folktale.* Translated by Laurence Scott. Austin, TX: University of the Texas Press, 1968.

Randel, Don. *The Harvard Concise Dictionary of Music and Musicians.* Cambridge, MA: Harvard University Press, 1999.

Rimmon-Kenan, Shlomith. "What is Theme and How Do We Get at It?" In Bremond et al., *Thematics*, 9–19.

Rodgers, Jr., Paul C. "A Discourse-Centered Rhetoric of the Paragraph." *College Composition and Communication* 17, no. 1 (February 1966): 2–11.

——. "Alexander Bain and the Rise of the Organic Paragraph." *Quarterly Journal of Speech* 51, no. 4 (December 1965): 399–408.

Sack, Graham Alexander. "Simulating Plot: Towards a Generative Model of Narrative Structure." Papers from the AAAI Fall Symposium, 2011.

Scarry, Elaine. *Dreaming by the Book*. Princeton, NJ: Princeton University Press, 2001.

Schleiermacher, Friedrich. *Hermeneutics: The Handwritten Manuscripts*, edited by Heinz Kimmerle. Translated by James Duke and Jack Forstman. Missoula, MT: The Scholars Press, 1977.

Schmidt, Benjamin M. "Words Alone: Dismantling Topic Models in the Humanities." *Journal of Digital Humanities* 2, no. 1 (Winter 2012).

Segre, Cesare. "From Motif to Function and Back Again." In Bremond et al., *Thematics*, 21–32.

Sennett, Richard. *The Fall of Public Man*. Cambridge, UK: Cambridge University Press, 1977.

Shapin, Steven, and Simon Schaffer. *Leviathan and the Air-Pump: Hobbes, Boyle, and the Experimental Life*. Princeton, NJ: Princeton University Press, 1985.

Shklovsky, Viktor. *Theory of Prose*. Translated by Benjamin Sher. Elmwood Park, IL: Dalkey Archive Press, 1990.

Simmel, Georg. *On Individual and Social Forms: Selected Writings*. Chicago: University of Chicago Press, 1971.

———. *The Philosophy of Money*. Rev. ed. London: Routledge, 1990.

Spitzer, Leo. *Representative Essays*. Stanford: Stanford University Press, 1988.

St Clair, William. *The Reading Nation in the Romantic Period*. Cambridge, UK: Cambridge University Press, 2004.

Stevens, Anne H. *British Historical Fiction Before Scott*. Basingstoke: Palgrave Macmillan, 2010.

Tognini Bonelli, Elena. "Theoretical Overview of the Evolution of Corpus Linguistics." In *The Routledge Handbook of Corpus Linguistics*, edited by Anne O'Keeffe and Michael McCarthy, 14–27. New York: Routledge, 2010.

Tomashevsky, Boris. "Thematics." In *Russian Formalist Criticism: Four Essays*, 61–98. Translated by Lee T. Lemon and Marion J. Reis. Lincoln, NE: University of Nebraska Press, 1965.

Underwood, Ted, and Jordan Sellers. "How Quickly Do Literary Standards Change?" *figshare*. https://doi.org/10.6084/m9.figshare.1418394.v1.

Watt, Ian. "The First Paragraph of The Ambassadors: An Explication." In *Twentieth Century Interpretations of The Ambassadors*, edited by A. E. Stone, Jr., 75–87. Englewood Cliffs, NJ: Prentice-Hall, 1969.

Weber, Max. *The Methodology of the Social Sciences*. Translated by Edward A. Shils and Henry A. Finch. Glencoe, IL: The Free Press, 1949.

Weinrich, Harald. *Tempus*. Stuttgart: W. Kohlhammer, 1964.

Williams, Raymond. *The Country and the City*. Oxford: Oxford University Press, 1973.

Wolf, Martin. "India's election remakes our world." *Financial Times*. May 21, 2014.

Woloch, Alex. *The One vs. the Many: Minor Characters and the Space of the Protagonist in the Novel*. Princeton, NJ: Princeton University Press, 2003.

Zoellick, Robert. "The aim of Xi's reforms is to preserve party control." *Financial Times*. June 13, 2014.